From the Jaws of Victory

Charles Fair

Simon and Schuster
New York

Contents

INTRODUCTION: The Uses of the Past   11

CHAPTER I: Crassus—The Nemesis of Success   27

CHAPTER II: Medieval Warfare: The Twilight of Common Sense   45

CHAPTER III: The Brave vs. the Effectual   63

CHAPTER IV: Goodbye, Knighthood; Hello, World Conquest   101

CHAPTER V: The Tiny Lion and the Enormous Mouse   139

CHAPTER VI: "Whose Blood Have I Shed?"   179

CHAPTER VII: State of the Union 1861-62   203

CHAPTER VIII: From the Jaws of Victory   235

CHAPTER IX: The German Century   289

PART 1: Bismarck and France   289

PART 2: The Kaiser and Europe   307

PART 3: Hitler and the World   341

CHAPTER X: Johnson vs. the Eastern Intellectuals   351

Notes   405

Bibliography   413

Index   417

From the Jaws
of Victory

The Uses of the Past

This is a book about war—more specifically about the consequences of stupidity in high place. It is obvious that the topic
has a certain timeliness. It is also clear that in military matters
(as in statecraft) the Hero Theory of failure is inadequate.
Throughout history there have been few men so strategically
placed and so overpowering in their authority that they were
able, as it were, single-handedly, to bring on a general disaster.
Even in the most rigid dictatorships, such solo performances involve more in the way of public support and approval than those
who provided them may later be willing to admit. The commander who loses a Trafalgar, a Stalingrad, a Dien Bien Phu, is
apt to have had far more behind him than his own idiosyncratic
weaknesses. He *stands* for something, as do the bad statesmen
who are his collaborators and the betrayed common folk who
give so much in the service of both. All, in effect, stand for the
same thing—for errors in outlook so widespread and so little questioned, so diverse and subtle in their consequences, that one
hardly knows where to begin an analysis of them. Yet without
such analysis, no great reverse is really understandable. The outcome of the three battles I have mentioned was not *just* a matter
of the three commanders being up against three better ones, any
more than American embarrassment in Vietnam was *just* a matter of Westmoreland fighting a war unsuited to the country, or of
Johnson pursuing a policy unsuited to the age.

When it comes to historic blunders, to failure on a truly grand scale, the problem of tracing causes and assigning responsibility is immense, not merely because the defects of intellect and character of a whole people may be involved but because, in defeat, the first concern of those officially responsible is always to shift the blame onto others and to prove their own conduct to have been above reproach, if not wasted in its brilliance (which it sometimes is). The more obvious our failure in Vietnam became, the more we heard it was not due to military incompetence or the stupidity of the State Department. Far from it; we were being sabotaged by dissidents at home. Our generals were being "held back," presumably by those too cowardly to sanction the use of bacterial warfare or tactical nuclear weapons.

The management of the French navy in the eighteenth century affords many an example of these same principles in action. Respect for reason and the intense cultivation of intellect are a prominent part of French tradition. French lucidity is a byword —among the French, of course, but in other countries as well. To be lucid means, among other things, to have one's head full of clearly reasoned theories about how to do this and that. From the War of 1870, the French learned that the attack possesses an inherent advantage. Thus by 1914 they had abandoned all faith in fortifications of the type which enabled the Belgians, at Liége, to inflict such appalling casualties on the Germans during the first few days of the war. By World War II the authorities of St. Cyr, with the concurrence of England's Liddell Hart, had again come to see that the defense is all—modern firepower having made the attack prohibitive. They were therefore ready for the Germans with the Maginot Line.

In the eighteenth century the French navy, according to Mahan,[1] operated on the theory that the main objective was not destruction of the enemy's fleets; it was the furtherance of "ulterior operations"—usually the landing of troops at some vital point, maintenance of their stores, etc. The French also fully understood the principle of division of one's own forces—a principle not unrelated to middle-class habits of thrift. While one of their better admirals, Suffren, was outmaneuvering the Englishman Hughes off the coasts of southeast India and Ceylon in the 1780s, the naval authorities at home sent him supplies and reinforcements in such small convoys that most of the latter ended up as English

Robertson and Law as well. At that stage in the war (December-February, 1863-64) the Confederacy could hardly afford the time out from duty and the loss of morale* which these proceedings cost, but Longstreet was too high in rank and had, until then, been too successful to be ignored.

Because every major battle and quite a few minor ones bring such floods of recrimination and disingenuous reporting in their train, it is sometimes difficult to sort out what really happened, beyond the fact that A won and B was defeated. And sometimes there remains considerable argument even about that. Did McClellan win at Malvern Hill or didn't he? If you read Douglas Southall Freeman,† you might suppose that he did, but most standard textbook historians leave the opposite impression and some don't bother even to mention that engagement.‡ One sign that the Federals *did* win is that right after Malvern Hill the Confederate General Magruder was widely blamed for various tactical mishaps, accused of drinking on the job, and transferred to the West—though not before making a detour to Richmond, where he presented a massive written report in his own defense, much of it so misleading as to be worthless. The same can probably be said of many of the accusations made against him in the first place; and of the reports which he and D. H. Hill sent in directly after the battle, while McClellan was withdrawing to Harrison's Landing. Both Confederate generals maintained that the amounts of baggage left behind by McClellan's men suggested that the South had won a great victory after all. These verbal efforts may not have been without result. Today, at the distance of a century, few besides professional historians seem to

* "After Law left East Tennessee with his resignation in his pocket Longstreet began to hear strange tales about the fine Alabama regiments in Law's command. It was reported . . . that certain officers . . . were circulating a petition . . . for transfer to their native state."[4]

† In the climactic action of the day, D. H. Hill's troops charged the very strong federal position. "It was not war; it was mass murder. As in every action of the campaign, the men in the ranks did all they could to make good the blunders and delays of their leaders; but this time they were sent to achieve the impossible."[5]

‡ For instance, W. E. Woodward, in his *A New American History*, doesn't. But since he gives the whole Peninsular Campaign only four paragraphs, and since that campaign was mostly not in McClellan's favor, the omission is understandable.

be aware that McClellan won *any* battle in the Peninsular Campaign.

Likewise the recent battle of Dak To in Vietnam may soon appear in our history books as the Pentagon reported it—or in what might be called the Hill-Magruder version. As the North Vietnamese slipped away from their fortified hilltop, having badly cut up two of our battalions and achieved their strategic aim of forcing a transfer of American forces from the south to the Central Highlands, our high command announced a great victory, explaining the absence of enemy dead on Hill 875 by the supposition that they had been carted off during the retreat.*

It might be apropos to note here that such claims are disingenuous in a special sense. I believe that most military men today accept Clausewitz' first principle as axiomatic. The primary objective in war is to destroy the enemy's army or his fleet or both, and any operation which is merely an indirect means to that end must be treated accordingly. Hence occupation of territory, destruction of enemy industry, and the wholesale slaughter of his civilians, while perhaps helpful, are not *the* objective. Of the three, the conquest of territory is apt to be the most unrewarding; and if not accompanied by a corresponding attrition of the enemy's armed forces, may become a calamity, as Napoleon and Hitler learned in Russia. Therefore, if a general announces a major victory, and gives as his main evidence the seizure of a piece of ground, beware. He is trying to cover up a real reverse, or is supplying a pseudo-triumph in response to political pressure from · home, or else he doesn't know the fundamentals of his profession and should be relieved at once. In some cases, including the one just mentioned, all three statements may apply.†

Quite naturally, the least gifted commanders are usually the most political. One sometimes gets the impression that the mod-

* The enemy objective, according to a report in *The New York Times*, was disclosed in documents found on a dead North Vietnamese officer which quite accurately forecast the outcome of the action. The passage above was written before the Tet offensive, when it became clear that battles like Dak To had set us up for Giap's later attacks by maneuvering our troops into positions where they would be least effective when the real shooting started.

† In fairness, however, one should point out that D. H. Hill was evidently an able field commander. And Westmoreland *was* relieved; if not at once, eventually.

ern staff system was created to provide berths for them. In World War II, Generals Keitel in Germany and Cavallero in Italy seem to have been of this type. However screened they may be from real events and however diluted their authority, such officers can still be quite troublesome.

On May 12, 1942, Count Ciano recorded in his diary: "Cavallero outlines our program for carrying on the war in the Mediterranean. At the end of the month Rommel will attack Libya with the aim of defeating the English . . . Then all forces will be concentrated for an attack on Malta . . . It will take place in July or August at the latest . . . Cavallero does not conceal the fact that he hopes to derive a great deal of personal glory from this operation. . . ."[6]

And on May 13: "Colonel Casero does not share Cavallero's easy enthusiasm for the attack on Malta. Malta's anti-aircraft defense is still very efficient, and their naval defense is entirely intact. The interior of the island is one solid nest of machine guns. The landing of paratroops would be very difficult . . . The same must be said for landings by sea . . . Only two days of aerial attacks by us was enough to make their defense more stubborn. In these . . . we, as well as the Germans, have lost many feathers. Even Fougier considers an eventual landing operation with much anxiety . . . The supporters of the undertaking are Kesselring and Cavallero, *the latter going through his usual tricks to put the responsibility on the shoulders of others.*"[6] (Italics added.) Malta of course was never taken.

A tendency to rationalization does not in itself make for outstandingly bad generalship. (If it did, good generals would be even scarcer than they are.) Sometimes all that is needed is one serious defect.* In war, as elsewhere, history has turned up quite a number of such men—the Fatal Flaw type, the good strategist who is a poor tactician, or vice versa; the able corps commander who loses his poise and common sense when given an army ("Fighting Joe" Hooker at Chancellorsville); the brave and seasoned officer who cannot see the value of some powerful new weapon or tactic (Crassus vs. the Parthian archers;† the American High Command vs. the late General Billy Mitchell); the

---

* I.e., in an otherwise satisfactory repertoire of real skills.
† See Chapter I.

"logical" commander who acts with such circumspection that even his best-fought battles turn out disappointingly.

This last is the general who waits too long to commit his reserves; whom the unexpected always upsets; who can never make the most of his good luck from an ingrained fear of bad; who, given a bird in the hand, accepts it and superstitiously looks no further; whose mania for security makes him prodigious in preparation and therefore more formidable than he knows on the field. In contrast to his public manner, Lord Montgomery is reputed to have been a general of this type. McClellan seems definitely to have been one, though he was perhaps relieved too soon, and has therefore been underrated.

Admiral Suffren exemplifies the opposite extreme. Whereas McClellan was all caution and forethought, Suffren, though never grossly unprepared, had a tendency, once he had sighted the enemy, to fling himself helter-skelter into action. In doing so he often fell short of the results which his immense energy and intelligence should have earned him. In the Franco-British war of the 1780s he was probably the only top-ranking French naval officer to understand and systematically ignore the home-office doctrine of the "ulterior operation." In his view *the* operation was to sink the enemy and thereby gain control of the seas. Unfortunately, to accomplish that requires not only a fine strategic sense and fighting ardor, which he had, but also a well-drilled, tactically reliable squadron, which he did not have. But for the straggling of his ships, his surprise attack on Johnstone in the Cape Verde Islands might have been an overwhelming success. It was not, nor were his subsequent actions against Hughes off the coast of India in 1782-83. In every move short of the very last ones leading into battle, Suffren clearly outclassed his opponent. Lacking reinforcements from home and a base of his own in India or Ceylon, he refitted his squadron as he went, and succeeded not only in maintaining the offensive against Hughes but also in capturing the important port of Trincomalee in Ceylon.

What he could not do, apparently, was pull his force together in a tactical sense. No sooner had he closed with the enemy than all his plans would go awry. Ships lost their place in line; orders were misinterpreted; a move made by one vessel would suddenly and senselessly be imitated by all the others. On one occasion the lead ships in Suffren's line turned into the wind in order to present their broadsides to the English. Immediately all ships in the line astern did likewise, despite the fact that most of them were too far off to join in the action and having lost headway were likely to remain so. At a stroke, the maneuver Suffren had been trying to make was canceled by the idiocy or perversity of his captains and his effective fleet strength became a fraction of what it should have been. An English admiral would doubtless have set-tled the matter by court-martial shortly afterwards; but French naval discipline was too poor and officer arrogance too intense to make such action possible to Suffren.

In a later battle, his flagship fired a single gun, signaling, as was the custom then, that an order given earlier had not been carried out. The shot was mistaken for an order to open fire, which the whole squadron promptly did, at too long a range to have any possible effect, most of their broadsides simply falling into the open sea. It is no wonder that during his months in India Suf-fren's patience wore thin, particularly as he also had "the mortifi-cation of learning that now one and now another of the small detachments sent to his relief were captured or driven back to France before they were clear of European waters."[7]

I have brought up Suffren's case at the outset partly because he is not a true failure, and so doesn't belong in the company of those whose histories follow, but mainly to illustrate a principle. Just as some failures are that through too perfectly representing their era and their tradition, some geniuses are driven to near-failure and madness through having been born at the wrong time or into the wrong nation, or both. Had Suffren and Hughes each commanded the other's squadron, the outcome would almost cer-tainly have been different. The crucial fact, for Suffren, was that he happened to come of a people who, despite their generally acknowledged intelligence and their extensive coastlines, seem to have no great gift for the sea. Perhaps it is not "logical" enough for them. Even more than life on land, seafaring is full of disagree-able surprises. For centuries both the law and man's control of purely physical events have been weakest on the ocean; and this extreme fluidity of circumstances must surely have repelled the orderly and somewhat theory-ridden Gallic mind.

In reading about their naval operations in the 1780s and the

later Napoleonic era (or even up through World War II) one
gets the impression that the French have never rid themselves
of a certain uneasiness on the water. With the huge allied squadrons of Napoleon's time, they mostly rode up and down doing
nothing. The history of the French navy from its beginnings under Saint Louis (1226-70) is one of almost chronic vacillation,
some rulers promoting the national seapower, others letting it
fall into decay. France began as primarily a Mediterranean naval
power, with fleets of galleys based upon Aigues Mortes, and later
Narbonne and Marseille. Philip IV (le Bel; reigning 1285-1314)
began operations on the Channel in rivalry with Edward I of
England. He did not, however, build ships suited to those more
treacherous waters, but, with the help of two Genoese, established a *clos des galées* (galley yard) at Rouen. Though logical
in a constricted sense,*[1] his decision to set up a Mediterranean
fleet in North Atlantic waters may have helped to insure the English that maritime superiority over the French which they have
enjoyed almost from that day to this.

While the majority of naval officers, in both France and England, came from the nobility, and while the recruiting practices
and treatment of ordinary seamen were deplorable in both countries down to the end of the eighteenth century, the French seem
to have had far more difficulty making their navies work. A part
of their trouble may have had to do with what Suffren called
"'the trading temper, independent and insubordinate, [which]
is absolutely opposed to the military spirit.'"[8] Whereas the English are usually regarded as the more mercantile of the two
nations, that view may have derived more from England's *effectiveness* in trade than from a clear understanding of English
habits of mind. The fact that the French have been, by comparison, poor colonists, and were late to industrialize (if indeed they
can be called a first-rank industrial power even now), does not
imply a greater indifference on their part to material advantage.
Far from it. Their very anxiety for the goods of this world, the
perquisites of glory, may have cost them much which the less
feverish English acquired with ease. Besides a fondness for
money and *la gloire*, many Frenchmen (as Queen Victoria re-

---

* For instance, in the sense of being the most convenient and cheapest
course.

marked of Louis Philippe) appear to have a love of intrigue for
its own sake. They are drawn, as it were, to the aesthetics of
duplicity, deriving from plots and subterfuges the kind of satisfaction which, one imagines, a master engraver feels upon coun-
terfeiting his first banknote, or a watchmaker on having designed
what he believes to be the perfect time bomb. It was apparently
this peculiarity which led to the strange conduct of Marshal Bazaine in the War of 1870 (see Chapter IX). It may also have
figured since in the tendency of French generals or politicians
to get rid of just those high-ranking officers who might have
saved them from defeat. On the eve of World War I, General
Michel, the chief of staff, who had accurately forecast what the
Germans would do, was in effect fired. In Indochina, after World
War II, General Revers, one of the few who understood the hopelessness of the policies his government was trying to enforce, was
framed by his opponents so as to appear a traitor, and relieved
of his duties.

The same peculiarities of temperament produced a nobility in
France incapable of yielding to circumstance and therefore, perhaps, amenable only to the violence by which it was finally destroyed.* These were the men whom Suffren was called upon to
mold into a disciplined, smoothly working corps of officers, and
the task understandably proved too much for him. Although he
too resorted after the fact to wholesale denunciation of his subordinates, we have the word of his adversary Hughes that much
that he complained of was real enough.

Suffren died in 1788, officially of a heart attack (he was quite
overweight). Years later, however, his body servant told a M. Jal,
historian of the French navy, that he had been killed by Prince
de Mirepoix in a duel. "The cause of the encounter, according to
the servant, was that Suffren had refused, in very strong language, to use his influence to [restore] to the navy . . . two of
the prince's relatives who had been dismissed for misconduct."[9]

It is only fitting that the system, which cheated this brave and

* And for centuries before that, the French Second Estate, while it cast
up a few such splendid soldiers as Henry of Navarre, was also quite rich in
commanders of the caliber of Philip VI, his successor John (captured by the
English at Poitiers), and Charles the Bold of Burgundy, whose inability to
solve the Problem of the Pike cost him his life (see Chapter III).

able man of victories he should have won, ended by costing him his life as well. Considered in historical perspective, his career perhaps illustrates the thesis that failure is not necessarily an individual matter or confined to specific enterprises, but may, as it were, be built into the traditions of a nation, often taking quite grandiose forms and victimizing the capable and the incapable alike.

Certainly most people today would consider that description to apply to modern Germany. In World War I the Germans had few generals who were downright awful, and in World War II they had many who were excellent. In both cases Germany lost because of bad generalship of a higher order. It was generalship of the same order which caused us, in the 1960s, to invade Vietnam with half a million men, and with hardly more result than might have been achieved by setting down the same force in Antarctica. (I am assuming, perhaps prematurely, that Vietnam will not after all escalate into a nuclear war between Russia and the United States.)

There is of course nothing new about this phenomenon. Philip II of Spain (see Chapter V) exemplified it on an almost global scale. His was, and still is, the supreme form of the art, as it combines consistent disastrous losses on the battlefield with a maximum of economic and moral damage at home. Today we talk constantly about the brutalizing effects of war, but, at least in America (which is still new to the game), we do not really believe in them. That is, we believe other, less prosperous, less shielded nations may become brutalized, may even revert to a primitive authoritarianism, as a result of war; but not us. In the more innocent past, people did not think in these terms at all. What we call brutalization they regarded as simply that minimum of manliness without which the realm could not survive. Today not only nuclear weapons but such "conventional" arms as napalm and the cluster bomb put the whole question of manliness in another light. Nations which are equally powerful and have citizens of nearly the same virile ferocity are no longer made secure by this combination of instruments and virtues; on the contrary, the more these are perfected the greater the chance that in war both contenders will be all but obliterated. No sooner was the nuclear age upon us than the most active minds in both camps saw the danger; and seeing it became fearful; and out of fear, armed their respective nations to the teeth; which brought us, quite logically, to where we now stand—at a point at which one more round of bad generalship, à la Philip, or even one bumbling overanxious field commander, can precipitate the world's last battle.

One of the chief differences between ourselves and the ancients lies not (unfortunately) in human nature, but rather in the proliferation of our skills, and our institutions, and therefore in the number of niches in which the incompetent can now install themselves as persons of consequence. The principle involved—a variant of Parkinson's Law—is that in any organization the opportunities for misplacement of personnel (or anything else) go up as the square of the complexity. In the upper ranks of the military this principle has done much to offset the advantages conferred by high technology and a university education, for it has meant that once modern armies grew large enough, a bad commander might prolong his professional life almost indefinitely through a combination of politicking and concealment of results. I have been told of one American general who, having arranged for the delivery of millions of dollars worth of heavy equipment to an Arctic base (where it was useless), allowed it to be covered over and lost under the snow. He filed his report on the matter under "top secret," trusting to the discretion of his fellow officers to keep it there. (Bar a rumor or two, they have evidently done so.) Still others owe their longevity in office to the good will of their opposite numbers in politics—corrupt premiers, allegedly drunken congressmen who control powerful committees, Presidents with more regional or class loyalties than sense.

Historically, needless to say, all this is old stuff. Whenever possible bad generals have usually enlisted the aid of strong patrons, and being politically less dangerous than more capable colleagues, have often been preferred over them. But the profession has changed in certain ways. In olden times a general who had not learned his trade stood a good chance of being killed as well as defeated. Instead of improving the species, however, this Darwinian mechanism has had the unexpected result of causing topranking officers to be among the safest of minorities in modern war—safer often than the civilians in big cities back home. A

corollary is that battles have tended to become bloodier and
more protracted roughly in proportion as those who directed
them ceased to be in the vicinity. And instead of death or dishonor, a losing commander nowadays has mainly to fear a bad
press.

Out of this fact has arisen a new military language which
speaks of strategic withdrawals, removals to prepared positions,
regrouping of forces, and exaggerated enemy claims of success.
Most recently the trend has been toward pure numbers—kill ra-
tios, estimates of the foe's declining manpower and plant capacity, the usual meaning of which is: "He can't go on much
longer—not with such fearful losses as these." If he *does* go on,
then of course there are more strategic withdrawals, regroupings,
etc. Chiang Kai-shek was a great master of this style of warfare.
For years, as he retired before the Japanese and then the Communists, his communiqués beamed with a puzzling optimism. He
seemed to conceive of campaigning as a sort of seven-day bicycle
race. "Unleashed," he simply disappeared over the horizon. Generations of Russian generals, from Peter the Great to Kutuzov,
and even Marshal Timoshenko (see Chapters VI, VII, and X)
had done the same with ultimately good results, but they had had
a vast, sparsely populated continent behind them. In a land as
crowded as China, it was just too difficult perhaps to maintain the
necessary momentum.

Any general worth his salt today has no need to go to the
lengths poor De Grasse did to clear himself. Good publicity techniques added to the sheer scope of modern field operations tend
to conceal his mistakes almost as he makes them. Everyone who
has served in the armed forces knows the magnitude these snafus
can reach, often with no one at home ever being the wiser. I have
given what may be an instance of one in Chapter IX—the strange
disposition of Russian forces on the Russo-German frontier on the
day in 1941 when Plan Barbarossa went into effect. It was reported to me by a German officer who was serving on that front
at the time; but although later Russian accounts admitted that
a great deal was wrong with their management of the war during
the first weeks of the German invasion, I have never seen this
particular blunder mentioned. In fact I have never seen it mentioned in *any* written account—almost as though the loyalty of

the high brass to their own transcended nationality, forbidding
them to disclose the worst *gaffes* of even an enemy colleague to
the people out front.

In many cases, however, tactful suppression of the facts may
not be necessary. Because of the immensity of modern battles, it
is next to impossible to follow what goes on in them; a year or
two or five later, when the official reports begin to appear, almost
everything but the outcome may become blurred, and sometimes
even that remains in doubt. World War I was the first great struggle of this kind. One can no longer write the old-fashioned battle
set pieces about most of it. The clarity and brevity of battle itself
were gone. Tolstoy would have been hard put to make anything out of Loos or the Marne. The best modern battle pano-
ramas suffer from being rather vague and schematic, or from a
chaos of detail out of which little emerges but an impression of
tremendous plans gone hopelessly off the rails.

It was in the bloody confusion of 1914-18 that the bad general
finally came into his own—sitting miles beyond danger, surrounded by aides and telephones, ordering thousands upon thousands, finally millions, of common soldiers to their deaths, and
betweenwhiles giving out brave statements for the press or dic-
tating heartening reports to the home office. After centuries of
the most frightful risk he was at last in the catbird seat. So long
as the nation's factories could crank out more matériel and the
recruiters or the draft kept on supplying him with replacements,
he was defeat-proof. And if the generals opposing him were
equally stupid (which in that war they mostly were), the final
result depended simply on the relative strength of the contending
factory systems and on the numbers of men available to the two
sides, *and no one at all, in either G.H.Q., was to blame for anything.* It was an achievement unique in military history, a sort
of pinnacle—indeed, a great mountain of dead, higher than any
ever heaped up before, upon which its creators could sit in perfect security, respected by all who survived. Sir Douglas Haig,
Foch, Pétain, Hindenburg, Pershing, went home as saviors of
their countries. The Germans would say of course that they had
really won—we had simply had more resources, while their own
war effort had been stabbed in the back by Jews and radicals (a
view in which political generals like Ludendorff naturally helped

the home folk along). But for the military at least it was a Caucus Race—all had won and all should have prizes.

Alas, things were never to be the same again. The *Panzers* and the *Blitzkrieg* came, and then the Bomb, and the equilibrium of 1914-18 was all upset. In the mid-1960s we believed we had solved the problem with the *Bulldozerkrieg.* The technique here consists not in defeating the enemy in open battle (which has proved rather difficult) but in putting down a curtain of high explosives across his entire country—nationwide drumfire. Any general intelligent enough to master this concept (and sufficiently rich in resources to act on it) has only to pick up a phone and call in the right experts, and *voilà!* Vietnam will not bow to our President and his team of "advisers"? Wipe her out. Mr. Johnson will assist, as a sort of World War I general himself, in a bunker 12,500 miles behind the lines, picking his bombing targets like a man doing the daily crossword.* This is the method now; it *has* to work, particularly with hard-hitting P.R. and good kill-ratio figures, however arrived at. Such is the ancient art as we find it today. What will it be tomorrow? With the Bomb that is difficult to say.

But let us first see what it was.

* It is not yet clear whether Mr. Johnson's successor has taken as keen a personal interest in the prosecution of the war.

prizes and Suffren was left to go it with what he had. At about the same time, De Grasse in the Caribbean, with a view to protecting an imminent French landing on Jamaica, elected to retire before the fleets of Rodney and Hood. During the retreat a freak in the weather left nine of Hood's ships open to attack by fifteen of the French. The attack was not made. Far from causing an uproar at home, De Grasse's conduct on this occasion was judged quite sound. Here is the opinion handed down at his court-martial: "The decision to persist in engaging with only a part of our fleet may be considered as an act of prudence . . . dictated by the ulterior projects of the campaign."[2] That decision resulted in his total defeat.

After his capture by the English in 1782, De Grasse spent years trying to clear himself, using what were, for his time, pioneering methods of self-vindication.* Our own Civil War, so modern in many respects, was outstanding in this sort of expertise. Not only had techniques of rationalization improved since De Grasse's day; we also had, in the earlier years of the war, a number of exceptionally bad generals. Being a democratic nation we have always been acutely sensitive to the public-relations aspect of our actions. In a sense, everyone in this country is up for re-election all the time. Not a few generals in our Civil War ran for office afterwards, winning governorships or seats in Congress (and one, of course, a Presidency). The list includes men like Ben ("Beast") Butler and Ambrose Burnside, whose careers in the field needed prodigies of rephrasing to be even mentionable in later life. They seem to have handled the problem with case. History has found them ludicrous but their constituents clearly thought the world of them.

Even generals who seldom had to resort to buckpassing did so quite readily when circumstances required it. General Longstreet, after his failure to dislodge Burnside from Knoxville, "decided the fault was not his but that of his senior division commander," McLaws.[4] He filed formal charges against that officer, and against

---

* As soon as he was safely aboard the English flagship he began writing denunciations of his subordinates, who, he said, had disobeyed orders, deserted him, etc. While in London, where he lived as an honored guest, sometimes making appearances on his balcony before admiring crowds, he expanded his operations, writing a series of pamphlets in his own defense, which he had printed and distributed throughout Europe.[3]

CHAPTER I

Crassus—The Nemesis of Success

Marcus Licinius Crassus was a commander, politician, and financial virtuoso whose weaknesses, though grave, were anything but idiosyncratic. He was, in several senses, the all-American Roman of his day. De Tocqueville remarked that "in democracies men are never stationary; a thousand chances waft them to and fro . . . Their life is always the sport of unforeseen . . . circumstances. Thus they are often obliged to do things which they have imperfectly learned, to say things which they imperfectly understand, and to devote themselves to work for which they are unprepared by long apprenticeship."[1]

That, exactly, was Crassus' situation. The Rome in which he grew up was a disintegrating republic in which men were not merely wafted but hurled to and fro, many thousands being killed in the process. On the whole he met the challenge of his age with phenomenal success. It was just that circumstances, added to his intense natural competitiveness, drove him to undertake too much. At that time military campaigning afforded one of the shorter routes to political eminence, and Crassus quite naturally took it. In whatever he did, he seems to have shown great drive and tenacity, to have had that combination of expansive optimism and devotion to his own purposes which, in America, is supposed to be unbeatable. In his case it very nearly was. His only major reverse was his last, and there was something quite American even in that. Like the tycoons of the 1920s, some of whom were later indicted or jumped from window ledges, Crassus went out big. Win, lose, or draw, he was Somebody. History took note of him.

The Rome in which he grew up was disintegrating, partly, or perhaps chiefly, as the result of a succession of victorious wars overseas. By 100 B.C. (when he was fifteen) the small farmers and landholders of old Republican times were gone. What with the years away from home which military service had cost them, and the advantage always enjoyed by big-city finance over the independent producer, they had long since forfeited their lands and their very existence as a class, disappearing into the mass of urban poor while the farms they had once owned were consolidated into huge estates and thereafter worked by slaves.

The Roman world of this era was one dominated by an increasingly unbridled realism. The latter showed itself not merely in the Romans' popular entertainments and their expansionism abroad but, most critically, in their politics. Just before Crassus was born, two attempts at a New Deal, under the Gracchi, had been bloodily suppressed. And with that, it appears, the attitude of both major parties—the oligarchs or effective patriciate, represented by the Senate, and the *proletarii*, represented by the Popular Assembly—hardened to the point that neither would stop at anything. The result, in Crassus' lifetime, was civil war, which first went in favor of the proletarians under Marius and Cinna, and finally of the oligarchs under Sulla. In savagery these wars had no parallel in the earlier history of the Republic, and with them the last remnants of Roman character seem to have been destroyed. Roughly from the victory of Sulla (in 82 B.C.) on, the Republic was dead, in the sense that the principles of decent forbearance, compromise, and regard for law upon which its existence had depended no longer commanded respect. Men increasingly failed to honor those obligations of class and country which common sense should have told them were important to their own survival, let alone to the continuance of a tolerable or reasonably civilized society. Life became a Darwinian struggle for personal eminence, in which one's only loyalty was to the success of a leader for as long as it might last. As a leader, one's only loyalty was to oneself. Incapable of the strain of such "realism,"

especially as its fruits were mostly denied them, large numbers
of the commonalty retreated into a violent, almost demented religiousness.* At higher social levels no class or institution could
any longer enlist that dedication to ideals (as opposed to facts)
which might have enabled it to withstand the brilliant adventurers who in the end made the nation their private property.
The Republic was not destroyed by its egoists; it became their
natural prey. In the vacuum of a general animalism, they were
simply the most capably animal—or as we would say, the most
"adaptive."

At the start of the revolutionary epoch—in the days of the
Gracchi—the issue had been clear enough. Unless certain concessions were made to the deprived majority, the electoral process
would presently become meaningless, and the Republic itself
would fail. Whether or not the form of the state was changed, the
apathy and moral shapelessness of most of its citizens would
guarantee the return of a primitive *Realpolitik*. In fact, of course,
that is what occurred. Even as the rapacity of those in power
increased, the ordinary voter, far from seeing the franchise as his
last recourse, either ceased to use it at all or put it up for sale.
Meanwhile the growth of Roman power abroad continued in the
same paradoxical way that America's is now doing—without the
majority at home either clearly consenting to those distant enterprises or really understanding them.

It was in this tumultuous age that Crassus arose. He came of
the Equestrian Order, which was roughly equivalent to the industrial peerage of England or the American upper middle class. His
name derives from the same Latin root as our word "crass" (*crassus* meaning "dense, thick, fat"). He seems, from the first, to have
had a keen sense not only of the odds—he allied himself with
Sulla against the popular party—but also of the innumerable ways
in which the national disaster could be turned to private account.
After hiding out awhile in Spain to escape Cinna, he is reported
to have gotten together a small force and begun his military
career with the sack of the Roman town of Malaca (Málaga).
With some of his campaign expenses thus paid in advance, he
proceeded to North Africa, where he briefly joined with Metellus;

* For instance, the cult of Bellona, whose priests (Mommsen said) "in
their festal processions shed their own blood as a sacrifice."[2]

and thence to Italy, where he became one of Sulla's commanders
—according to Plutarch a fairly good one. During this period he
grew immensely rich, chiefly, it appears, by buying up at a discount the property of various citizens proscribed by his leader.
In the same period he seems to have come into rivalry with the
young Pompey, whom Sulla rated very high among his field officers.

". . . In these times . . . though Pompey was the younger man
and . . . descended of a father that was disesteemed by the
citizens . . . yet . . . he shone out and was proved so great that
Sulla always used, when he came in, to stand up and uncover his
head, an honor which he seldom showed to older men and his
own equals . . . This fired and stung Crassus though, indeed, he
could not with any fairness claim to be preferred; for he both
wanted experience and his two innate vices, sordidness and avarice, tarnished all the lustre of his actions."[3]

This jealousy of Pompey—which oddly enough never extended
to Caesar*—was to be the undoing of Crassus. Plutarch makes
much of Crassus' greed, but in his fervor as a moralist may have
misunderstood his man. There can be no doubt that Crassus had
an eye for a deal, but if avarice was really his ruling passion, it is
hard to explain why he continued in politics and military campaigning long after he had become probably the richest man in
Rome. Why didn't he retire, like Sulla, or simply continue, as a
civilian, making money? The answer, I think, may be that Crassus
was not a financial type as such nor merely greedy. He seems
rather to have been the competitor *par excellence*, a sort of Darwinian primitive unmoved by any ideal or abstract standard of
excellence. In forcing his way to the top, he used the likeliest
means which presented themselves, of which money was one. In

* More accurately, Crassus was not *as* jealous of Caesar. During the Triumvirate which he shared with Caesar and Pompey, he seems to have played
one off against the other. On one occasion he underwrote Caesar to the extent of twenty million sesterces, when the latter's creditors had seized his
equipage as he was about to set out on another campaign. The object was
probably less to accommodate Caesar than to preserve a balance of power
against Pompey. Crassus would evidently take considerable risks to turn a
sesterce. Despite the fact that tampering with a Vestal Virgin was a grave
offense, he became attentive to one who "stood possessed of a beautiful
property in the suburbs." A scandal ensued, but he was finally acquitted,
"his avarice so to say serving to clear him of the crime."[4]

such a man the dominant passion is apt to be, not avarice, but a mortal hatred of his most serious rivals. That he seems to have had, in particular for Pompey. And while he is usually ranked as low member of the first Triumvirate, he was in a sense the most versatile, being not only a fair commander but clearly foremost in money matters.

Crassus' greatest success as a general and also, as it turned out, the critical point in his character development, was his campaign against Spartacus. The Spartacan revolt, which began in 73 B.C., nearly a decade after the close of the civil wars, turned overnight from a minor disturbance into a national calamity. It started when a handful of gladiators, armed with cooks' chopping knives and spits, fought their way out of Capua and seized some wagon-loads of arms on the highroad. Before long they had fought several successful pitched battles and had grown to an army of 90,000 men.* In 73 B.C. Spartacus soundly defeated the praetor Varinius at Lucania, and moving northward the following year did the same to every Roman commander sent against him. "The slaves naturally showed no more mercy to their captives than was shown to themselves by their masters; they crucified their prisoners and some . . . compelled them to slaughter each other in gladiatorial combat."7 Spartacus' plan was apparently to fight his way out of the peninsula and then disband his men, permitting them to return to their homelands.

He was well along toward succeeding when the Senate, in some alarm (and possibly at the prompting of certain privately interested parties), gave Crassus the command against him. In their first engagement two legions, under Crassus' lieutenant Mummius, were repulsed with great loss.† Sensing the gravity of the situation, Crassus severely punished all concerned, requiring soldiers who had abandoned gear on the field to replace it at their own expense and decimating, "before the eyes of the whole army," approximately a cohort (600 men) of those who had led in the rout.8

His next move was to maneuver Spartacus out onto the peninsula of Rhegium, where he bottled him up by causing a ditch to

* According to Grant.5 Mommsen sets their number at 40,000 in 73 B.C.6
† Mummius had apparently disobeyed orders and sought an engagement instead of merely reconnoitering.

be dug across the isthmus "three hundred furlongs long, fifteen feet broad and as much in depth, and above it a wonderfully high and strong wall."* Spartacus broke out of this trap, "taking the opportunity of a snowy stormy night" and extricating a third of his army over bridges of boughs and earth. However, his troops, sensing a turn in their fortunes and never under the best of control, became mutinous. During these disorders Crassus surprised a detachment of Spartacans encamped by Lake Lucania, falling upon them in force and inflicting severe casualties. Although Spartacus himself arrived in time to prevent this small victory from turning into a massacre, Crassus now had the measure of his opponent and apparently felt that decisive victory was within his reach. "He began to repent that he had previously written to the Senate to call Lucullus out of Thrace and Pompey out of Spain; so that he did all he could to finish the war before they came."[9]

In a surprise attack which miscarried at the last minute he nonetheless managed to kill 12,300 of the enemy and force Spartacus to retreat into the mountains, where the latter beat off and routed a pursuing force under two of Crassus' officers. According to Plutarch, this proved to be the slave leader's undoing because his men, now elated and overconfident, forced him into seeking a decisive engagement with Crassus—"the very thing which Crassus was eager for." So Spartacus marched back into Lucania and fought a pitched battle in which his army was destroyed and "he himself . . . surrounded by the enemy and bravely defending himself was cut in pieces."[10]

Unfortunately for Crassus, the alert Pompey, responding to his earlier call, had arrived to take part in mopping-up operations; and that fact, coupled with his recent more glamorous military successes in Spain, enabled Pompey to claim most of the credit for suppressing the slave rebellion. He was honored with a triumph in the capital, while Crassus had to settle for a mere ovation (and lost still more face, Plutarch says, for having done so). It is quite possible that this turn of events ruined Crassus by inflaming still further ambitions he should never have entertained in the first place. For in an age which was coming to respect force, and therefore generalship, before all else, he had the ex-

* A furlong is one-eighth of a mile, or 220 yards. The ditch was therefore 37½ miles long, a figure perhaps slightly exaggerated.

treme bad luck to have, as his companions in power, the two best
military brains of the day. Thus for all his triumphs in other fields,
he remained balked in this one. The absolute top of the peck-
ing order—supremacy over all others in everything—was denied
him. He was moreover getting on in years, well into that period in
which the characters of many seem to set, often into rather
strange shapes—the once chatty and affable becoming monsters
of garrulity; the once spirited, cantankerous; the once mildly
opinionated, implacable dogmatists. Plutarch reports a change of
this kind in Crassus, who, "adding to his old disease of covet-
ousness a new passion after trophies and triumphs, emulous of
Caesar's exploits, not content to be beneath him in these points
though above him in all others, could not be at rest. . . ."11

Crassus' chance came after he and Pompey had frustrated, by
violence, a last attempt at a consular election; and after the
Triumvirs, having secured their own consulships by proclamation,
had parceled up the Roman world among themselves. Caesar, to
the distress of future schoolboys, already held Gaul. Pompey drew
Spain and Crassus Syria. In the Middle East, Roman influence
then (and subsequently under most of the emperors except Trajan), reached only as far as the Euphrates. Beyond, in Mesopotamia and Persia, lay the feudal kingdom of the Parthians. Besides being a tricky and elusive foe, the Parthians had for some
time taken turns with Rome in making a "client" state of Armenia. They were thus not only beyond Roman power but powerful
enough themselves to be a perennial threat and a nuisance. Crassus decided that he would settle the Parthian question; nor did
the politics of the day require any Tonkin Gulf incident to permit
him to do so. He was at this time about sixty, and "so transported . . . that it was manifest he thought he had never had
such good luck befall him as now, so that he had much to do to
contain himself before company . . . but amongst his private
friends he let fall many vain and childish words which were un-
worthy of his age and contrary to his usual character, for he had
been little given to boasting hitherto."12

Once the idea of suppressing the Parthians had taken hold of
him, it led on, as though already a *fait accompli*, to still grander
projects. ". . . Being strangely puffed up . . . he would not limit
his fortune . . . but . . . proposed to . . . pass as far as Bactria

and India and the utmost ocean"[13] (which the reader will recall was what Alexander did). His expedition began badly enough. Accustomed as the Romans were to war, the sheer arbitrariness of this one, which Crassus himself had perhaps made all too plain, aroused some public resistance.* Ateius, a tribune of the people, attempted to block his departure, and he was obliged— with what feelings one can imagine—to ask Pompey to come to his aid. The latter did so, appearing "with a pleasing counte- nance, and so [mollifying] the people that they let Crassus pass quietly." Ateius thereupon had one of his officers forcibly detain Crassus, but as the other tribunes were not agreed on the matter, he was released, Ateius cursing him "with dreadful imprecations, calling upon . . . several strange and horrible deities."[14] These curses were felt to be so powerful that both the utterer and the object of them were as good as doomed. As one of the last of the older sort of Roman—which is to say a public-spirited citizen and man of conscience—Ateius risked his neck in more ways than one to stop Crassus in what he and some others regarded as an immoral folly. But too much power had already passed into the hands of the new men, the Total Realists; or (what amounts to the same thing) too few of the older sort were left to constitute an effective check on them. From that standpoint, Crassus' going was but an episode in the now inevitable "expansionism" of the dying Republic.

Following the contretemps with Ateius, Crassus proceeded to the port of Brundisium, where he was in such haste to set sail that he would not wait for a storm to pass, and so began his voyage by losing a number of ships. The Roman commander in Syria at the time of his arrival was a man named Gabinius, who had been campaigning with some success against the Parthians and who, after time out for a police action in Egypt, was about to resume operations. Crassus relieved him, and during the summer of 54 B.C. prepared his own offensive. His reconnaissance convinced him that instead of taking the roundabout route through Armenia he should advance directly across the Mesopotamian desert, counting on the support (as Mommsen says) of the "numerous Greek and

---

* I.e., a Tonkin Gulf incident might have helped, though none was for- mally required.

half-Greek towns"[15] of the region which had long been under
Parthian control.

He seems, at this stage in his operations, to have made several
important mistakes. The most important, in Plutarch's view, was
his failure to free Babylon and Seleucia to the south, "cities that
were ever at enmity with the Parthians." Instead "he spent his
time in Syria more like an usurer . . . computing the revenue of
the cities, wasting many days in weighing by scale . . . the
treasure that was in the temple of Heirapolis, issuing requisitions
for levies of soldiers upon particular towns and kingdoms, and
then . . . withdrawing them on payment of sums of money"[16]—
an illustration of the ancient truth that old habits, especially in
the old, are not easily broken. In fairness, however, it should be
said that the taking of those two cities might, in view of their
location, have cost more than they were really worth as bases to
the rear.

More serious was Crassus' evident failure to acquaint himself
with his enemy. He had at least two sources of information—
Gabinius, the commander who had been waging war on them,
and Roman soldiers from Mesopotamian garrisons who "brought
word that the danger was worth consideration, urging their own
eyewitness of the numbers of the enemy, and the manner of their
fighting when they assaulted their towns." The Parthians concentrated on cavalry, using mounted archers and (as shock
troops) mounted lancers. "By flight it was impossible to escape
them, and as impossible to overtake them when they fled, and
they had a new and strange sort of dart, as swift as sight, for
they pierced whatever they met with."[17] Plutarch is here refer-
ring, probably, to the laminated horn bow, which was "made of
several plates, like the springs of a carriage. . . . This short composite bow was quite old in human experience. It was the bow
of Odysseus; the Assyrians had it in modified form. It went out
in Greece [because of the damp climate and the shortage of horn]
but . . . survived as the Mongol bow. It was quite short, very
stiff to pull, with a flat trajectory, a remarkable range and a great
noise."[18]

By thus combining exceptional firepower and mobility, the
Parthians had developed a hit-and-run *Panzer* type of warfare
which was quite modern in concept. What they seem to have

lacked was the infantry and the staying power for stand-up combat, with the result that in their continual struggles with the Romans they won few decisive victories but fought many skirmishes and rear-guard actions which their skill with the bow made costly to the enemy. They were, in a sense, a guerrilla force like the modern Vietcong. Crassus' problem, like General Westmoreland's, was somehow to pin them down—to trap them into fighting on terrain in which their peculiar advantages would be nullified. There is no sign that he understood what the situation called for. He seems to have believed that a search-and-destroy operation carried out by conventional Roman methods would do the trick.

His next mistake was to refuse the advice of King Artabazes of Armenia, who came to his aid with six thousand troops and "urged Crassus to invade Parthia by way of Armenia, for not only would he be able there to supply his army with abundant provisions, but his passage would be more secure in the mountains and hills with which the whole country was covered, making it almost impassable to horse . . . Crassus returned him but cold thanks."[19] If true, this report strongly implies that Crassus had little grasp of the tactical difficulties he would presently be facing on the sandy plains of Mesopotamia.

His final and, as it proved, decisive mistake he made on the field. Having taken his army out of winter quarters in 53 B.C., he proceeded to Zeugma on the Euphrates, and crossed to the east bank. As on earlier occasions in the expedition, there were ominous mishaps.* Crassus' force consisted of seven legions (approximately 42,000 men†) supported by four thousand cavalry and an equal number of light infantry. At this point his aide Cassius advised him either to make for a fortified (Roman) town from which he could safely reconnoiter, or else to proceed along the river bank toward Seleucia, thus keeping his right flank covered and guaranteeing a line of supply by water. Crassus did

---

* As described by Plutarch, some of these were like the "omens" which preceded Crécy—happenings which inspired an eerie feeling in the troops, already perhaps half-aware of the defects of their commander and what these portended.

† The legion came, in Marius' time, to consist of ten cohorts of 600 men each, but figures given by ancient historians suggest that legions, like modern divisions, were often not up to strength.

neither. Instead he gave ear to a local Arab chief, Ariamnes, who reported that only a token force of Parthians, under Surena (or Surenas), opposed him, while the Parthian king, Hyrodes, was hanging back, undecided as to whether to risk a real war with the Romans. The Arab urged that Crassus pursue Surena and come to grips with him with all speed, before the king should change his mind and commit his main forces.

Perhaps inflamed with the idea of defeating his enemy in detail, and entirely indifferent to the difficulty of forcing a battle in open country on an army much more mobile than his own, Crassus took the Arab's advice. The latter thereupon offered to act as his guide, and "drew him from the river into vast plains, by a way that was at first pleasant and easy but afterwards very troublesome by reason of the depth of the sand."[20] After the Roman army had gone some distance into the desert, a messenger arrived from Artabazes in Armenia, saying that he had been attacked by Hyrodes and would therefore be unable to send the additional help he had promised Crassus. He suggested that Crassus turn back and join forces with him against Hyrodes, and repeated his earlier advice about avoiding an encounter in the open with the Parthians. Crassus replied with his usual tactlessness, declining to join forces and adding that he would "revenge himself" later on the Armenian for his treachery in withholding help at the last minute. Having thus cost himself an ally, Crassus now lost his guide and false friend as well. The Arab took himself off, on the pretext of going to stir up discord among the enemy, and the Roman army, numbering close to 50,000 men, was left, in effect, stranded in the Mesopotamian desert somewhere east of the Euphrates, not far from the river Belias* and the fortified town of Carrhae (Haran).

Shortly afterwards, as the army was moving east toward the Belias, some scouts returned with the report that the rest of their party had been killed and that "the enemy was at hand in full force and resolved to give . . . battle."[22] Crassus seems to have been thunderstruck, organizing and reorganizing his battle order

* This is the river Plutarch calls the Balissus. It is given under the shorter name in *Ginn's Classical Atlas*.[21] It flows in a north-south direction, roughly from Edessa to Nicephorium on the Euphrates, some eighty miles to the south.

in a series of rapid changes; after which he marched on to the river, where his parched troops refreshed themselves. Here something of his old headlong aggressiveness evidently returned. At the prompting of his son, Publius Crassus, but against the advice of others, he decided to seek an engagement at once, had his men eat in ranks, and pressed on at quick march. When the Parthian army first came into view, it appeared to be no very great force. Their leader, Surena, "had hid his main force behind the first ranks, and ordered them to hide the glittering of their armor with coats and skins."[23] He had also made certain other preparations— one being to dispense entirely with infantry for this engagement, the other to back up his ten thousand mounted archers with a thousand supply camels. The first move increased his already great advantage in mobility over the Romans, while the second gave him a reserve of firepower equivalent, by one estimate, to a gain over the usual of one hundredfold.[24] It is quite possible that the latter move in particular upset Crassus' calculations. Like other Roman commanders before him in the eastern theater, he seems to have counted on withstanding a concentrated but necessarily short-lived barrage from the enemy's archers, after which he could expect to ignore them and close with the main body in the conventional manner. It was not Surena's intention that the battle should go that way; nor did it. Like every good commander, he had taken the initiative away from his opponent almost from the first—misleading Crassus as to his plans and numbers, maneuvering the Romans onto the battleground most advantageous to himself, anticipating their conduct of the action, and finally, just before he struck, making skillful use of psychological shock tactics.

Having first let the enemy see an apparently small, unarmored cavalry detachment, he quickly deployed his forces in full battle array, at the same time ordering them to sound the drums.* "Immediately all the field rung with a hideous noise . . . When they

* "For the Parthians do not encourage themselves to war with cornets and trumpets, but with a kind of kettle-drum, which they strike all at once in various quarters. With these they make a dead hollow noise, like the bellowing of beasts, mixed with sounds resembling thunder . . . [They have], it would seem, very correctly observed that of all our senses, hearing most confounds . . . us, and that the feelings excited through it most quickly disturb and most entirely overpower the understanding."[25]

had sufficiently terrified the Romans . . . they threw off the
covering of their armor, and shone like lightning in their breastplates and helmets of polished Margianian steel, and with their
horses covered with brass and steel trappings."[26]

The Romans meantime formed into a square. The Parthian
mounted lancers made an attempt to break their line, but seeing
its depth and the firmness with which the dense infantry formations stood, they pretended "to break their order and disperse,"
and instead encircled the Romans "before they were aware of
it."[27] They now released a terrible rain of arrows on Crassus'
troops, driving back his skirmishers and causing startling casualties in the main body, by virtue of the "strength and force of their
darts which . . . passed through every kind of covering, hard
and soft alike. The Parthians, now placing themselves at [a dis-
tance], began to shoot from all sides, not aiming at any particular
mark for indeed the order of the Romans was so close they could
not miss if they would. . . ." When the Romans tried to improve
their position by counterattacking, the Parthians, being mounted,
easily drew out of reach, firing as they went—an art in which,
Plutarch says, only the Scythians were their superiors; "and it is
indeed a cunning practice, for while they thus fight to make their
escape, they avoid the dishonor of a flight." A more modern
writer would see in this simply a superior tactic, the sort of thing
armored formations do when forced to retire.

As the archery barrage continued, Crassus, "seeing no end to
it," ordered his son Publius to mount a more determined counterattack. The latter, taking a force of thirteen hundred horse, five
hundred archers, and eight cohorts (4800 men) of heavy infantry,
set out to charge the Parthians, who fled before them. Encouraged
by their flight, Publius detached his cavalry to press on after
them, he himself following with his foot soldiers. The object of
the Parthian withdrawal was soon clear enough, for when the
Romans under Publius had gone a sufficient distance from the
main body, the enemy suddenly reappeared in force; but instead
of attacking frontally they rode round and round the legionaries,
raising "such a cloud of dust that the Romans could neither see
nor speak to one another, and being driven in upon one another
in one close body, were . . . hit and killed, dying not by a quick
and easy death . . . for writhing upon the darts in their bodies,

they broke them in their wounds, and when they would by force pluck out the barbed points . . . they tore and tortured themselves . . . When Publius exhorted them to charge, they showed him their hands nailed to their shields and their feet stuck to the ground. . . . He charged in himself boldly, however, with his horse,"[28] and though having the worst of it in some ways, did better in others. His mounted Gauls carried lances too light to be effective against the heavily armored Parthians, so they switched to the tactic of seizing the enemy's heavier lance and wrestling him to the ground, where his armor made him next to helpless. Alternatively, the Gauls leaped from their horses and disemboweled the enemy's mounts, unseating riders and causing general confusion.

But the Romans were greatly outnumbered and had already sustained losses too severe to have a hope of winning. With the remnant of his force, Publius retreated to a nearby hill and there, after refusing the suggestion of two Greek friends that he try to escape with them to Carrhae, he fought on to the end, ordering his armorbearer to run him through after an arrow wound in his arm had critically incapacitated him. Two of his aides likewise took their own lives, and all but 500 out of a force of approximately 6500 died fighting.

With this disaster the battle of Carrhae was really over, although Crassus was not yet aware of the fact. Indeed, having learned that Publius was in pursuit of the enemy and seeing fewer troops confronting him than before, he thought the action had turned in his favor. This illusion was strengthened by the circumstance that the first messengers Publius sent back, asking for reinforcements, were intercepted. When some finally got through with news of Publius' now desperate position, Crassus was apparently taken aback, and vacillated. By the time he began to move it was too late. For what he now saw was the entire enemy force converging upon him once again. As this host advanced, a Parthian trooper riding in the forefront displayed the head of Publius on his lance for all the legionaries to see. Crassus himself rallied bravely but the morale of his men was broken. Having no recourse they fought on, listlessly and with great losses, until nightfall.

During the night they managed a disorderly retreat to the

fortified town of Carrhae, a move made terrible by the cries of
the wounded left behind, some four thousand of whom the Parthians slaughtered the next morning. Crassus' problem was now,
of course, to extricate himself from a siege. He first seems to have
entertained the incredible hope that the Armenians would come
to his rescue. He next repeated an earlier and crucial mistake; he
hired a guide—this time a spy named Andromachus—to lead him
from Carrhae by night. Apparently it was agreed that what was
left of the Roman expeditionary force should break up and go its
way under various commanders, some of whom did in fact escape.
But Surena was determined that Crassus should not elude him.
To that end he had Andromachus lead Crassus into yet another
trap. This time, however, his attack was not decisive. Crassus'
pathetically small force managed to rally and defend their general. Surena, deciding to trade on Crassus' credulity once more,
persuaded him by various means that he meant to sign an honorable peace, and lured him with a small party of officers and
men into the Parthian camp. There a brawl developed in which
Crassus was killed. Except for some picturesque details, that was
the end of the matter. Of an army of about 50,000, 40 percent
were said to have been killed and an additional 20 percent taken
prisoner.

Surena, who was reported to wear make-up and to travel with
"a whole Parthian Sybaris in his many wagons full of concubines,"
was rewarded by a grateful monarch by being put to death—"out
of mere envy" so Plutarch says—a piece of heartless stupidity
which was its own reward, since the Parthians were never to
produce another general capable of inflicting such defeats on the
Romans. On the other hand, Rome rarely produced generals as
bad as Crassus, though when it did, they were terrible (witness
poor Varus, whose legions the Germans exterminated in the Teutoburger Wald in 9 A.D.).

Carrhae was a severe blow to Roman military prestige. As a
reverse it outdid Dien Bien Phu in being far speedier and more
complete. To their credit, however, it must be said of the Romans
that they knew a morass when they saw it and seldom thereafter
ventured into this one. In that Crassus was less prudent and
might, had he lived, have gone interminably on with his enterprise, he was more in the spirit of our age than in that of his own.

As a statesman he forecast those of today, who, having adopted nonsensical policies, refuse under any circumstances (including total failure) to give them up. As a commander he anticipates the military counterpart of those statesmen: the type of general who hopes by sheer technical and numerical superiority to bludgeon his way to victory. Such a commander counts heavily upon "energy of will"*—which is to say less upon intelligence than upon pure resolve backed by the knowledge that however stupid one may be and however able the enemy, one still has the upper hand in resources. One goes forth simply as the representative of the better ant hill. Crassus' difficulty was that Rome was not *that* much better than Parthia; and lacking modern transport, machine guns, and napalm, it simply could not afford Crassus, who paid what some might consider a fair price for the suffering and disaster he brought upon others. It is one seldom exacted from twentieth-century generals or heads of state, whose powers of inflicting death have become so incredibly greater. (Oddly enough, it was we in America who moved to reinstate that ancient form of justice, in the Nuremberg trials of a few decades ago.)

Although certainly legalistic in civil life, the Romans never appear to have bothered their heads over this particular problem. As practical men they understood that in war the burden of costs and punishments is almost automatically borne by the loser.† And since you may one day be the loser yourself, it is hardly good sense to put into the hands of some future conqueror a legal instrument which will sanction, and thereby perhaps aggravate, outrages he is likely to commit against you in any case.

Notwithstanding the Wilsonian position we have tried to adopt in regard to criminal responsibility among belligerents, we have abandoned the still more elementary form of justice which cost Crassus his life. Nowadays the very worst of commanders is apt to be safe both on the field and in his later career, the usual method in civilized nations being not to cashier or execute generals for their more ghastly mistakes, but to promote them to still

* The phrase—which certainly applied to Crassus—is General Westmoreland's (see Chapter X).

† Until quite recently it was customary to enslave or massacre defeated armies. Insurrectionists might receive any punishment the victor was ingenious enough to devise. After Spartacus' defeat, the Appian Way from Capua to Rome was lined with crosses to which were nailed his surviving followers.

higher posts where they can do less harm.* However, this curious solution to the problem of military incompetence was still centuries off. In the meantime, through the remainder of the classical age, and in Europe roughly from Clovis' day to the battle of Waterloo, the older system prevailed—though less and less so, of course, as time went on. Even at its height, in the Christian Middle Ages, when leaders like Robert of Artois or Charles the Bold might die with their men in some spectacular reverse, the effect of such hazards on generalship was not striking. In fact generalship was probably never worse, which supports the view of those who regard capital punishment as a poor deterrent.

* It is almost unheard-of for a modern general to be so bad as to be captured in battle, and the few who are are generally spared the indignities visited on common prisoners. To torture a general to obtain information would be thought quite barbarous.

CHAPTER II

Medieval Warfare: The Twilight of Common Sense

The Roman army of Crassus' period was a "modern" one—had been at least since the time of Scipio Africanus (c. 200 B.C.) and continued to be for some centuries afterwards. The defining characteristics of a modern army are roughly that it is based upon infantry, controlled by a central command, flexible in maneuver as the result of exhaustive drill, and backed by a well-organized system of supply and replacement. The Romans in addition understood the principle of combining missile and shock. Besides archers, or the Balearic slingers of Caesar's Gallic Wars, they used a type of short-range field artillery, the ballista and the catapult, to soften up the enemy for attack, not only during sieges—for which these engines were probably designed in the first place— but later in direct combat. At the siege of Dyrrhachium, preceding the battle of Pharsalus (48 B.C.), in which Caesar liquidated his surviving co-ruler Pompey, an incident occurred which showed the power of these machines. A detachment of Caesar's troops had seized a hill and set about fortifying it when Pompey's artillery opened up on them with such effect that they were forced to withdraw.* According to J. F. C. Fuller, the legion "at

---

* It was, for example, Prussian drill which enabled Frederick the Great's infantry to reload and fire faster than any other army of the day (five volleys a minute, with muzzle-loading flintlocks) and to combine this fire attack with more forward movement than other troops of the period were able to do. His

some time after Caesar's day . . . possessed an artillery train of sixty carrobalistae (ballista wagons) and ten catapults, the equivalent of sixty field guns and ten howitzers."[*1]

Given this kind of military machine, it is probable that many Roman commanders (like their modern equivalents) could be quite devoid of resourcefulness or finesse and still do tolerably well, even brilliantly, as career men. In later days, however, as the empire passed through the long twilight of the Antonine Age[†] into its final centuries, the Roman army slowly lost internal organization and coherence until, in the reign of Justinian, it was no more than a conglomerate of feudal mercenaries, scraped together as the need arose, and kept in being chiefly by the hope of plunder. In this, and in its lack of the disciplined heavy infantry of former times, it resembled many of the armies of medieval Europe. Indeed, the battle of Taginae, fought in Italy during Justinian's reign (in 552 A.D.) between his eunuch general Narses and the Gothic King Totila, remarkably anticipates Crécy, which occurred nearly eight hundred years later, in 1346.[‡] Both Narses, the Roman (actually Byzantine) commander, and Edward III of England faced opponents whose chief arm was cavalry and whose chief tactic was "shock" or direct frontal assault. Both commanders chose a defensive strategy and, lacking infantry, made shift to create some by dismounting a portion of

---

most famous victory, Leuthen (1757), depended upon his "oblique order" attack, which enabled him to bring his full firepower to bear on the Austrian left.

[*] There seems to be some confusion in terminology here, the Eleventh Edition of the Britannica listing the catapult as the smaller of the two engines. It describes the catapult as a forerunner of the medieval crossbow, weighing about 85 pounds and capable of shooting a "three-span" (26-inch, one-half-pound arrow) to an effective range of 400 yards. The ballista was much larger, throwing stones or logs, and intended more for battering down walls than killing personnel directly.

[†] The Age of the Antonines ended in 180 A.D. with the death of Marcus Aurelius, whose unattractive son Commodus initiated the era of brutal confusion which followed.

[‡] Even to the numbers reportedly involved, though these estimates vary and probably should not be taken very seriously. It is clear that Edward III had about 8000 men in the field and was heavily outnumbered by the French. The size of the force opposing Narses is unclear, but his own was evidently far smaller than those used during the Principate—for instance, by Trajan—and would probably have been no match for an equal number of legionaries of that earlier period.

their cavalry. These foot troops were protected by lines of archers raked forward so as to flank the attacking enemy with their fire. "Ten thousand Heruli and Lombards, of approved valor and doubtful faith, were placed in the center,"[2] these apparently being spearmen, on foot, arranged in phalanx. According to Gibbon, each wing amounted to about 8000 men of whom half were archers. ". . . The right was guarded by the cavalry of the Huns, the left was covered by fifteen hundred chosen horse, destined, according to the emergencies of action, to sustain the retreat of their friends or to encompass the flank of the enemy. From his proper station at the head of the right wing, the eunuch rode along the line, expressing by his voice and countenance the assurance of victory. . . ."[2]

Except for a limited engagement in which Narses and his men watched fifty of their archers, in a forward position, repel three attacks by Gothic horsemen, nothing happened for a while. "At the distance of only two bow-shots, the armies spent the morning in dreadful suspense"—the reason being that Totila was awaiting 2000 reinforcements. By Fuller's account the Gothic commander had placed his cavalry in the front rank and his infantry and archers to the rear, the latter being under orders not to shoot. The reasons for this order and this disposition of troops remain obscure. Indeed, the remarkable point about both the Gothic commander and his later equivalent at Crécy (Philip VI of France) is that neither seems to have paid the slightest attention to the very strong position taken up by the enemy. In Totila's case, this fact is all the stranger since he had had, in the years just before, considerable experience in clearing the peninsula of the armies of the Eastern Empire. And against another great commander of the day, Belisarius, he had shown much foresight and engineering skill in blocking off the Tiber (to no purpose, as it turned out; although Belisarius, having broken these defenses, was also denied victory by the poor quality of his own troops).

At Taginae, while waiting for the enemy to attack, Narses had his men eat their midday meal standing in ranks. Totila passed the time by appearing between the lines in armor "enchased with gold" and giving both sides a curious display. ". . . He cast his lance into the air, caught it with the right hand, shifted it to the left, threw himself backward, recovered his seat, and managed a fiery steed in all the paces and evolutions of the equestrian school."[3] That done, he changed into battle dress and ordered his cavalry forward, as Gibbon puts it, "between the horns of a crescent," where they "were saluted from either side by the volleys of four thousand archers. . . . The Gothic cavalry was astonished and disorganized, pressed and broken." It had also, in charging, left its infantry support far behind, and being so closely engaged, probably could not have hoped for, or gotten, much help from its own archers. When at last the Gothic horse bolted, the foot troops to their rear were too disordered to open ranks and let them through. The fleeing horsemen rode down their comrades-in-arms, thus completing Narses' victory for him. It only remained to mop up—which in those days, if not most of the time since, meant killing everyone within reach. Six thousand Goths fell on the field itself and thousands more in the pursuit. Totila, wounded by a lance, was carried to a village a few miles away, where he died. His defeat, and that of Teias, his successor, the following year, ended the Gothic kingdom;* while Totila's earlier siege and conquest of Rome, and their sequels, likewise brought an end to the Roman Senate, a class and institution which with varying fortunes had endured for thirteen centuries. In these rather negative ways Taginae was decisive, marking the close of a struggle which effectually liquidated both contestants. (The Byzantines never developed a secure hold on Italy, and soon ceased to be either Roman or Greek themselves.)

One may deplore Totila's conduct of Taginae, but it is puzzling, since in the past he had shown himself to be fairly capable. Perhaps he was simply a victim of his own origins (as were most American Indian leaders in their wars against the whites). The Italian Goths of the sixth century were still barbarians, part of the successive waves of invasion which had transformed Roman

---

* It had never in fact amounted to much. As one writer put it, "The Goths always remained a conquering army; according to the German custom, they took possession of one third of vanquished territory, but while forbidding the Romans to bear arms, left their local administration intact. . . . The Kingdom founded by [Theodoric] had no solid basis."[4] However, like Theodoric before him, Totila seems to have been a man of some decency. In victory he was more merciful than many commanders of the day, including his last opponent; and he is said to have taken stern disciplinary measures to discourage his men from rape. By comparison with his Merovingian contemporaries across the Alps, he was a man of high civilization.

into Frankish Europe. Taginae was approximately contemporaneous with the ramshackle kingdom then being constructed in France and hither Germany by Clovis' sons Theuderich, Chlodomer, Childebert, and Clotaire.*

An interesting feature of the period was that the Germanic invaders and the later Romans seemed for a time to reach approximately the same level of civilization though getting there from opposite directions. Even as the tribes on the imperial periphery acquired by imitation some of the ideas and customs of the people they were soon to swallow up, the Romans themselves were sinking to a state in some ways worse than that of their primitive contemporaries. The change had begun long ago, in the "modern" era of the Revolution and the Triumvirs. But after the death of Marcus Aurelius toward the end of the second century A.D., "social decay"—meaning essentially a nonfunctioning realism—reached the proportions of a mortal disease. Nothing was any longer safe from plain force or the animal shortsightedness of the men who exercised it. As the struggle for power at the center grew more unbridled, administration of the provinces was increasingly left to the local military, who increasingly neglected it for the more rewarding business of looting their own citizens.†

* The Merovingians, in fact, tried to annex the peninsula and one of their commanders, Buccelin, was defeated by Narses at Casilinum in 554. Unlike the Goths, who relied on mailed cavalry as their chief arm, the Franks of the northwest still fought on foot, though with much better weapons than of old. These included a strong oval shield with a center boss; the angon, a barbed javelin; and the fearsome *francisca*, named in their memory—a single-bladed battle ax balanced for accurate throwing. After a missile attack with these instruments, they fell to with long sword or the shorter (18-inch) *scramasax* meant for stabbing at close quarters. "Such was the equipment of the armies which Theudebert Buccelin and Lothair(e) led down into Italy in the middle of the sixth century," Oman writes.[5] At Casilinum, Narses used the same battle order he had used against Totila. The Franks attacked frontally "in one deep column," were flanked on both sides, and suffered "the same fate which had befallen the army of Crassus. Hardly a man of Buccelin's followers escaped from the field." Even at Tours (732) the Franks seem to have used the infantry square, cavalry only coming to be the main arm in Charlemagne's time. The persistence of infantry in England cost Harold the battle of Hastings. For some centuries thereafter, foot troops were regarded on the Continent as "residue," and misused accordingly.

† For instance, see MacMullen: "From the end of the Severan dynasty down to the end of the empire itself, probably no one took for granted the tranquility that had smiled upon the Antonine reigns . . . Here the soldier was quite at home and showed no mercy in the use of force." The local

Defense of the frontier became problematical and finally impossible. Except for that of Darwinian self-promotion (which like vanity is everyone's birthright), principles ceased to have any hold over men. The result, over centuries, was that Rome became first an empire, then a vacuum, and at last a wreck.

The visible state having finally collapsed, the barbarians who rushed into the ruins found little enough there to help them. Whereas the Italian Goths had managed for a while by allowing what remained of the Roman civil service to run things for them, the conquerors of Roman Gaul appear not to have done so, possibly because there was too little to work with. For want of any model on which to reshape themselves and their institutions, they continued for hundreds of years in a state of such disorder that by the tenth century Christian civilization seemed about to fail altogether. The empires, so called, of the Merovingians, in the sixth century, and of Charlemagne, at the end of the eighth, had barely survived their founding by thirty years. "Decentralization" and serfdom were universal; literacy, law, and thought all but extinguished; currency and manufactures scarce and next to impossible to maintain. The majority of men probably lived much as they had done in neolithic times—briefly and wretchedly, in terror of the unknown and (still more) of one another. Europe consisted of a patchwork of barnyard despotisms, the administration of a local baron apparently being a somewhat more violent form of the misrule practiced in late Roman times by the provincial garrison chiefs and "captains of the village." War of various sorts, from the killing affray to the raid or pitched battle, became the condition of the state—or more properly, of the estate, since the feudal system was essentially a matter of personal ownership of land and the people who happened to go with it. The latter consisted of defenseless commoners (i.e., those who had failed to become lords) who either bound themselves over to serve at arms under the *patrocinium* or who held their fields and dwellings under an arrangement aptly known as the *precarium* tenure.

commanders begin to impose their own taxes and frighten off civilian tax collectors. "Small wonder that a notorious influence peddler makes a point of dining every day with the resident commander" . . . thus showing "contempt for the older municipal authority, the senate, . . . supported by the imperial laws—'empty silhouettes . . . from which one expects nothing,'"[6] etc., etc.

These institutions, which had sprung up in later Roman days, reappeared in modified form in European feudalism, having in both cases the same *raison d'être*. Stripped of the protection afforded by law or by the internal constraints which correspond to it and are known as decency, men gave themselves back into slavery in the hope at least of survival; and having done so were lucky to find their side of the bargain honored. In war, by which the most "fit" continued with the unending business of eliminating one another, the protectees or subject population might expect to share modestly in their protector's good fortune, but quite fully in his reverses.

Seen against this background Totila appears as a tragic naïf, one among thousands of now-forgotten chieftains of marauders who flourished for a time at the expense of a dying countryside, and were themselves finally cut down. Not a bad man nor a truly bad commander, he was simply engulfed by his times.

Though Totila's disaster could scarcely have been improved upon, the French débâcle at Crécy was fully as serious and can fairly be said to have shown an even more obdurate stupidity on the part of the defeated. Philip VI of France, the loser in that engagement, was quite another phenomenon, a man far from his barbaric origins. By his day, the Church had risen to become a great secular power under Innocent III (reigned 1198-1216), and therewith, despite its increasing persecution of the heterodox, a powerful instrument for the spread of learning, or at least of simple literacy. In the same period, the feudal system—which one writer describes as "anything but systematic. It was confusion roughly organized"[7]—began to be threatened by the monarchy, or secular centralism, on the one hand, and by the rise of the towns, or a more or less independent world of business, on the other. Philip Augustus of France (1165-1223) is said to have been the first French king to "take the Bourgeoisie into partnership." He "surrounded himself with clerks and legists of more or less humble origin, who gave him counsel and acted as his agents,"[8] granted monopolies and other privileges to merchants, and by his decisive victory at Bouvines (1214), over a coalition of rebel vassals and Rhenish German princes, established the boundaries of France and the power of the kingship with a clarity till then unprecedented. His successor next but one was Louis IX (reigned 1226-

70), who combined an unfortunate zest for crusading and a somewhat bloodthirsty piety* with a most remarkable enlightenment and morality in his administration of affairs at home. Finally, at the end of the century, came the diabolical Philip le Bel (reigned 1285-1314), who further consolidated the power of the throne by the murder and plunder of the Templars, the looting of Jews and Lombard bankers, and the *reductio ad absurdum* of the papacy in the person of Clement V, whom he not only maneuvered into office but moved to Avignon, as it were for safekeeping. His successor next but one† was Philip V (the Tall), who, though not blameless, was on the whole an intelligent ruler. He tried to reform and centralize the currency (the estates blocked him in this encroachment on their feudal prerogatives). He also granted towns the right to arm in their own defense, abolished garrisons except on the national frontier, and surrounded himself with Provençal poets, whose works he emulated. He died in some disrepute, suspected of extortion.

After the short reign of Charles IV (the Fair; 1322-28), Philip VI came to the throne in 1328. It is clear that at his accession he enjoyed advantages of position and historical perspective such as poor Totila could scarcely have imagined, let alone have created for himself out of the chaos of that earlier time. From a military standpoint, the defect of Philip's position was that he ruled a people among whom feudalism, although declining, was by no means dead. For feudalism reduces to the paradox that the dominant class, the barons, while dedicated to war, never seem to become very good at it. The evolution of weapons and battle tactics, of larger policies of conquest or consolidation, is in such eras almost biologically slow; and in some feudal societies may come to a halt for centuries (*vide* preindustrial Japan).

It is only logical to ask why this should be so—why men whose success, not to say survival, depends upon force should have such difficulty improving in the use of it. The answer, I suspect, is to

---

* Saint Louis, the true type of the religious crusader, once said that a layman ought to argue with a blasphemer only by "running his sword into the blasphemer's bowels as far as it would go."⁹

† Louis X (the Quarreler) reigned for a short while in between (November, 1314, to June, 1316), and from need of money offered the serfs in his domains the chance to buy their freedom. The move apparently met with little response. He seems to have been not quarrelsome but dim.

be found in the conservatism of instinct. It seems to be typical of our instincts or innate inclinations that they direct us with great energy toward certain actions (such as killing one another). However, the repertoire of our instinctive aims is small—to survive, to win the girl, to beat down our enemies, perhaps to be admired—and the force with which we are inwardly driven to attain them is often such as to discourage clear thinking. While passion may inspire eloquence, the approach of a fight is more apt to evoke shouts and threatening displays, usually followed by actions which are no less primitive (and sometimes no more effectual).

In the beginning, the success of the medieval noble presumably depended upon his individual prowess—that is, his ability to make subordinates of those nearly, but not quite, as ferocious as himself. The conservatism of instinct then very naturally prompted this class to make personal prowess a permanent item of faith. Courage, fitness, skill with weapons, an awesome fieriness or fighting *élan*, became staples of the aristocratic character, and were vividly exemplified in crusaders such as Godfrey of Bouillon and Raynald of Chatillon.* "The feudal organization of society made every person of gentle [*sic*] blood a fighting man, but it cannot be said that it made him a soldier." Of the fact that "discipline or tactical skill may be as important to an army as mere courage, he had no conception. Assembled with difficulty, insubordinate, unable to maneuver, ready to melt away from its standard the moment that its short period of service was over, a feudal force presented an assemblage of unsoldierlike qualities such as have seldom been known to coexist."[10]

The odd fact is that the same warrior-nobles who would fling themselves pell-mell into hopeless frontal assaults evidently gave much thought to improvement of the defensive. The English longbow and the later Swiss system of the long pike excepted, almost the only improvements in the *métier* of war between Hastings and the mid-fifteenth century were in the design of armor and fortifications. The crusaders, whose logistics and tactical notions were

* Raynald's depredations, from the great fortress of Krak (Kerak), upon the Red Sea trade and the caravans moving between Damascus and Egypt helped to precipitate the disastrous battle of Hattin, in 1187, and the subsequent downfall of the Latin Kingdom.

notoriously primitive, left castles in the Holy Land which were masterpieces of military engineering.*

Perhaps by the same logic, some of the most crushing defeats of the Middle Ages were inflicted by armies on the defensive. One of these defeats was the battle of Courtrai, fought in Flanders in 1302 between the allied burghers of Bruges, Ypres and Courtrai, and the French army under Count Robert of Artois. In that the burghers fought on foot, with only a few hired cross-bowmen as auxiliaries, it was the first true infantry engagement since Hastings. And in its outcome it prophesied the not-distant day when solid foot troops and cannon would put an end to the supremacy of cavalry, and to the system of feudal levies† which for centuries had reduced tactical control to a minimum and infantry to the status of "residue."

* Exposure of European engineers to Byzantine examples during the Crusades evidently gave castle building great impetus and certain standard principles of design. These included the "concentric castle" with one or more lines of inner defense, the use of projecting towers to flank the walls, and the substitution of curved for squared corners to reduce the effectiveness of battering rams. How rapidly the construction of castles, in contrast to the other arts of war, improved can be seen by comparing the crude log-palisade fortifications of the Normans, as described by John, Bishop of Terouanne, toward the end of the eleventh century, with the splendid outlines of the Krak des Chevaliers in the Holy Land or Richard Cœur de Lion's Château Gaillard, built in 1197. John's account begins: "The rich and noble of that region, being much given to feuds and bloodshed, fortify themselves . . . and by these strongholds subdue their equals and oppress their inferiors. . . ."[11] The destruction of feudalism could not, indeed, be completed until it had become possible to reduce castles by cannon fire in the fifteenth and sixteenth centuries, and the fact seems to be that this last innovation was not directly in the hands of the nobility. "The possessors of cannon were usually private individuals of the middle classes, from whom the prince hired the *matériel* and the technical workmen"[9]—this despite the fact that cannon had apparently been used at Crécy and played a major part in protecting Ziska's *Wagenburgs* or horse-drawn convoys during the Hussite Wars of the early fifteenth century.

† It is interesting that the French, long after mercenary armies organized on modern lines into infantry, cavalry and artillery had come to prevail on the Continent, retained remnants of the feudal system, in the shape of large private contingents. Maintained, for instance, by the houses of Guise, Cossé-Brissac, and Condé, these persisted into the sixteenth, and in one case as late as the mid-seventeenth century. Belief in fighting *élan* as the essence of tactics—a belief especially pronounced in the French medieval commanders—revived in that country as recently as 1900-10, and seems to have contributed at least as much as did the stolid incapacity of the British to the Allies' staggering losses in World War I.

The battle was a by-product of Philip le Bel's struggle with the formidable Edward I of England, during which Flanders came under French control through the defeat of the Counts of Bar and Flanders in 1297. Because the Flemish weaving industry depended upon raw wool from England, Philip's success was a heavy blow to the Flemish towns. Moreover, the latter had been among the earliest to become powerful *vis-à-vis* the local baronage, and had long shown a disposition toward intransigence and abrupt action. This they took, in May of 1302, massacring the French garrison at Bruges. A French force under Count Robert was sent to recoup the situation, and came face to face with the improvised Flemish army near Courtrai two months later. One writer describes the Flemings as armed with spears, cleavers, and flails, but their major weapon seems to have been the *godendag*. "Probably only a burgher could have thought of such a practical fighting tool; for the clublike staff served well to knock a knight out of the saddle, and the stout spike at the end proved horribly useful for dispatching a prone man in armor."[12] The burghers took up a strong position, protected by streams on either side and marshy ground in front. By one account, they also tied themselves together as the ancient Gauls had done when going into battle.

Robert of Artois first sent in his foot troops and crossbowmen against them. Although these were apparently having some success in driving in the Flemish center, he soon ordered them aside in favor of the cavalry, perhaps wishing to reserve the glory of victory to proper warriors and members of his own order. Without waiting for the field to be cleared, the French knights charged over the "residue," lost all formation in doing so, and were soon floundering into streams and boggy places where their horses lost headway and their heavy fighting gear left them next to helpless. The burghers thereupon counterattacked with fearful effect. Disregarding the upper-class custom of taking captives for ransom, they slaughtered the French knights to a man, Robert included— his foot soldiers having in the meantime fled, under the impression that they were being ridden down from the rear by hostile cavalry (as in a sense they were). After the battle some seven hundred pairs of golden spurs were collected from the field and hung in a nearby abbey church to commemorate the occasion. To paraphrase Mahan,* a military operation (at least from the French standpoint) could scarcely have been worse carried out.

Again the question arises as to how men who make a profession of warfare can, when the moment of decision arrives for them, be so totally, almost insanely, stupid. It surely required no great intelligence for a trained horseman—as Robert of Artois very likely was—to see that a cavalry charge over the ground at Courtrai was certain to fail. Why then did he order one, and so impatiently as to reduce its tiny chances of success even further? Perhaps his eyesight was bad—in which case he need only have consulted aides who could see better and had perhaps reconnoitered the terrain. Possibly he had too thoroughly fortified himself with wine.† Even had he done so, however, his failure could probably not have been attributed to any such simple cause —any more than Grant's defects as a general could be said to have grown out of his drinking.

Gross military errors such as Robert made, and the crusaders made before him, may rather have been ingrained in the civilization of the time, originating in a certain ideal of the manly, a doctrinaire ruthlessness and overconfidence which seem to be characteristic of the aristocracies we call feudal, but are to some extent a feature of all aristocracies.‡ In turn this concentration

---

* Who was speaking of a battle of Suffren's, bungled by that admiral's subordinates.

† This raises a question to which I have been unable to find any clear answers, namely, how much medieval warriors may have shored up their courage with drink. Montross mentions that the Mongols were known for their drunkenness,[13] but Mongol tactics, on the other hand, were the best of the thirteenth century. Froissart, in his account of the Battle of the Thirty (see Chapter IV), says that during the time out in that engagement some of the combatants drank wine, but that may have been as much a matter of heat and thirst as of faltering morale.

‡ In his analysis of conspicuous leisure and conspicuous consumption, Veblen showed quite clearly that some of the basic principles of primitive aristocracy survived in the nineteenth-century world of business—which is to say in classes whose power is at one remove from that of direct force.[14] The English "squirearchy," or society of the counties, which to an extent still exists, has preserved certain similar values—such as a respect for good horsemanship, heartiness, pluck, etc., together with a bluff distrust of intellect and bookishness. Although the medieval nobility became in time somewhat more receptive to poetry and the arts than their modern counterparts seem to be, the line of descent from one to the other is still quite clear. By the late nineteenth century many eminent businessmen had become sufficiently interested in acquiring a noble ancestry to make the faking of coats of arms a thriving

upon primal virtues and as it were personal display or panache, at the expense of the larger, more objective view needed to grasp and manage a complex event such as a battle—this peculiar ego-istic narrowness, even among men often elaborately educated, illustrates the principle I mentioned a few pages ago. The price of the life of instinct—of accepting adaptation, almost uncon-sciously, as *the* way—seems to be a kind of self-centered inertia in thought and a rigidity in social custom which exactly mirror the limitations of instinct itself. Thus while one might logically have expected the barons of early Christian Europe to settle down promptly and change their ways so as to favor a more or-derly, cooperative, statesmanlike management of their spoils, they did nothing of the kind but remained, instead, prisoners for centuries of the primitive "values" which had made them top dogs to begin with.

The basic "value" in this scheme is bravery, and, of course, strength, both of body and of personality. One strives for valor, for excellence in combat, above all for a commanding or over-powering presence. As a young nobleman one studies not strategy or tactics so much as *fighting;* one goes not to military college but to the tiltyard. And one of the lessons learned there is that, given two opponents of about the same strength and skill, the deciding factor is often emotional—a matter, again, of *presence*, of a cer-tain animal confidence which readily blazes up into fury. In physi-ological fact, most of us have these reserves of *élan* or maniacal energy, and intense fear or rage can indeed release them. Their value in the common soldier is obvious, a considerable part of "shock" being psychological, a matter of suddenly, at the critical moment, battering down the enemy's morale. (Hence battle cries, bagpipes, and the like, which help to rouse the attackers to frenzy and, perhaps equally, to daunt the attacked. Witness also Surena's dramatic opening of the engagement with Crassus, in which he had his cavalry suddenly deploy in strength, drop the cloaks which hid their polished steel armor, and send

enterprise. Oddly enough, the construction of lineages to order seems par-ticularly to have been a vogue in America, notwithstanding the dogma ac-cording to which ours is the branch of western civilization most thoroughly disencumbered of the social *idées fixes* of the past.

up a great noise of drums and shouting.*) It is precisely the emotional training which young nobles, the future leaders of retinues or of whole armies, received as a result of the stress laid upon individual prowess which may later have made them unfit for command. For the value of fighting ardor is that it releases and gives violent impetus to physical actions already well learned, its drawback being that it all but suspends thought at the same time. Unless he is losing, a commander has little need of his own fighting skills, but every reason for keeping a clear head. One can only suppose that Totila and Robert of Artois were ignorant of this principle or had, so to speak, been trained out of it. Totila's display of virtuosity before Taginae was perhaps intended to put him in the properly overweening state of mind to inspire and lead a shattering attack. Similarly, at Courtrai, the progress of Robert's infantry was perhaps too slow for his already inflamed nature to tolerate. The crucial effect of shock, he may have felt, was being lost, frittered away in foot-by-foot advances, and must be regained at once, details of terrain be damned.

In short, the man who learns fighting rather than warfare is apt to regard battles as little more than mass collisions, and that is the way most medieval commanders fought them—head-on, with the greatest possible bravery, honor vindicated beyond praise, and not a grain of regard for the most obvious difficulties lying ahead. Questions of liaison, of maneuver, of maintaining lines of supply, of tactical combinations, were simply beyond them. It was as though to think clearly about such things, to allow oneself to be daunted by the practical, to consider alternatives once a fight had fairly begun, were the traits of a coward. Reflection and calculation were best left to the priest and burgher classes; in a nobleman leading an army they appear to have been thought out of place. The curious thing is that these same noble-

* Still another example is the Swiss infantry of the later Middle Ages. Exceedingly steady and well drilled, they carried eighteen-foot pikes, those of the second, third, and fourth ranks projecting with those of the first to form a dense array or hedge. Men in the ranks to the rear of these formed a reserve and carried their pikes at the vertical. In their swift advance, the Swiss squares of pikemen presented the appearance of a "forest of spears," and it was their habit, apparently, to preserve a terrible silence until the moment of closing. Beginning in the fourteenth century and reaching an apogee between 1475 and the first quarter of the sixteenth, the Swiss were the terror of European battlefields, and not because of fighting efficiency alone, their stolidity under attack being equaled only by their bloodthirstiness when victorious.

men often showed a most remarkable skill in intrigue, perhaps because, being concerned with the political and so not directly controlled by the warrior's primitive code, their mental processes in that case enjoyed far freer play. That is to say, they eluded to a considerable extent the narrowing or near-paralysis which certain branches of instinct, particularly those directly concerned in survival or self-aggrandizement, seem often to impose on men's thinking. Intrigue, to be sure, usually aims at achieving the same ends, but it has the advantage of working from a distance, in the chill privacy of meditation, or in small groups gathered not to fight but to scheme. It is not until the same cold, unhindered mental processes are brought to bear upon the conduct of battles proper that war achieves that virtuosity in destruction, that global frightfulness we have managed to give it today.

In the Middle Ages the nearest approach to this ideal was made, not by any European, but by the Mongols, a violently unattractive people who fought, it appears, solely for plunder and the joy of massacring the unarmed or defeated. By the time they had overrun the eastern reaches of the Moslem world and begun to burst through into Russia and Hungary they had, evidently with the help of captive Chinese experts, evolved a highly modern system of tactics based upon tightly controlled and disciplined cavalry units. These, armed with bow, lance, or scimitar, were used by their commanders with the greatest skill, in a kind of fluid *Panzer* warfare. The pincer movement and rapid flanking attack, the use of overwhelming firepower in the shape of mounted archers, and the "firestorm" type of assault on fixed positions were staples of their technique. Before them, the Islamic hordes and the feudal levies of Hungary, Poland, and Russia (which still fought on foot with spears and axes in the old Frankish style, and sought shelter in highly combustible log fortresses) went down to swift fearful defeats. The Mongols anticipated the Nazis also in their use of subornation and "nerve warfare," sending out an advance guard of spies and secret agents whose mission was to gather intelligence, seek out usable traitors, and spread terrifying rumors. Roger Bacon, in the middle of the thirteenth century, regarded them as the army of Antichrist, and they lived up to his assessment by being the most effective, gratuitous, and indefatigable exterminators of human life ever to appear on earth until just recently. Moreover, there is evidence to suggest that their policy of annihilation, like that of the Nazis, grew not out of bloodlust alone, but was a matter of cold intention, methodically put into practice—i.e., a policy. It was perhaps fortunate for the rest of Europe—even though Mongol tactics were better suited to open plains than to irregular wooded country or mountains—that a dynastic problem at home caused the Mongols to withdraw before the end of the century. One imagines they might have made short work of the burghers of Bruges, not to speak of the French knights.

The Mongols' phenomenal skill might be thought to argue against the thesis I have developed here. In fact, however, they seem in the beginning to have been undisciplined raiders like the Huns or the Parthians. But under Jenghiz Khan they managed to break into China, and there acquired a full complement of "Chinese officers . . . mechanics . . . artificers . . . engineers and . . . scholars of war."[15] As members of a civilization grown old and cold-hearted in its knowledge of the world, the Chinese evidently provided the organizational "know-how" and the nihilistic refinements I have been describing, the Mongol tribesmen serving simply as a *Lumpenproletariat* whose rewards were the intermittent gratification of three basic lusts—to rape, to plunder, and to kill. The Mongol troops were not in fact noted for their bravery but fought rather like jackals, wounding and wearing down their prey. Their leaders appear to have had few notions of personal honor or bravery but were simply planners in the uninhibited modern style,* working out "final solutions" for one great city after another. They had the enormous advantage which every great civilization, in its decline, seems for a while to confer, namely a total absence of any higher belief or moral standard which might prevent the accumulated skills of the mind from being turned simply and totally to the service of instinct. Caesar and Pompey would have understood the Great Khan; Edward III, the victor of Crécy, would not.†

* Even to anticipating the Nazis and Stalinist Russians (e.g., during the Finnish War) in their use of captives as hostages or living shields.

† Not that Edward was a model of military restraint. His treatment of Scots, for example, was exceedingly brutal. Nevertheless, chivalric ideas had some hold on him, since he allowed himself to be dissuaded from executing the six burghers of Calais by the pleas of his queen and Sir Walter de Manny.

Whereas the Mongols, like the Nazis, were highly systematic but had no real objective beyond the immediate and obvious ones, their contemporaries in medieval Europe often had little system, at least in military matters, but highly complicated objectives.‡ The result was a great deal of poorly managed, indecisive fighting, and the maintenance of a warlike aristocracy in a state of vigorous, if inept, readiness for centuries together.

With the exception of Edward I of England, and the Bohemian military geniuses of the Hussite Wars (Ziska; Prokop the Great), little real progress seems to have been made in the art of warfare from Hastings to about the mid-fifteenth century. In a sense it was precisely because warfare, or more properly combat, was *treated* as an art that it failed for so long to mature into the science of lethal advantage-taking we have since made it. It was then, in this *mise-en-scène*—enveloped, so to speak, in a meshwork of complex and stupid custom; as splendid, as motionless, as full of poetic appeal to minds of more distant ages as the great tapestries—that the battle of Crécy was fought, and very badly too.

‡ *Vide* the Crusades, or the intricate relations between the Crown and the estates in England (e.g., from the time of William Rufus). See also the reigns of Philip Augustus of France and Frederick II of Sicily.

CHAPTER III

The Brave vs. the Effectual

In comparison, say, to the Hundred Years' War, those of our own day are far more complex in technique but if anything cruder in their objectives. Part of the reason, perhaps, is that the internationalism of the medieval ruling class* has no parallel in our world, and if revived would probably be regarded with the keenest suspicion.† The issue now is simply My Tribe against Your Tribe (Communist bloc vs. capitalist bloc; or on a smaller scale, Russia vs. China, Israel vs. the U.A.R., and so on). Circa 1900 it was: Would the old Big Powers accept a new Big Power as their equal without a fight? Would the new Big Power in fact try to improve its status by any other means (or settle for equality if victorious)? The answer in all cases was no, and the result, two world wars.

Once, however, it has been decided to settle these bald questions by the usual recourse, the difficulties multiply beyond imagining. For while the aims of total war are of biological simplicity, its conduct is intricate in the extreme, requiring the mobilization of a nation's most unlikely resources, as well as a massive outpouring of its more obvious ones. Besides taxing its people nearly to bankruptcy, a modern state at war must persuade its scientists and intellectuals to contribute to the general effort—which it

---

* Including, of course, the higher clergy, whose diplomatic language was Latin.

† Almost the only form of internationalism in the West today is financial, and it *is* regarded with the keenest suspicion, sometimes justifiably.

usually has no great difficulty doing, thanks to the prestige and pay involved. An immense variety of machines and organizations must then be put together with all speed, supply and transport arrangements for millions of men made almost overnight, and armadas dispatched in time to prevent those of the enemy from reaching one's own borders first. In the field, most twentieth-century armies show a tactical cohesion which is all the more remarkable in view of the huge numbers engaged and the uproar of battle itself.* To use a current term, our military operations are far more "sophisticated," though not necessarily any more rewarding in outcome, than those of our ancestors.

In the fourteenth century the conduct of war proper was often simple to the point of idiocy, but the same cannot be said of the intentions apparently underlying it. In some cases it almost seems that the combatants lost track of their various supposed objectives and continued to fight for the sheer love of it—a failing many historians think they detect in Edward III. The Hundred Years' War, which began in his reign, was on the whole very poorly waged. Its greatest victories (Crécy, Poitiers, Agincourt) were without issue. Neither side ever appears to have consolidated its gains or hewn to a clear line of policy. And although the French finally gained their point, it took them from 1339 to 1453 to do so, and might have taken much longer had it not been for the outbreak of a dynastic civil war (the Wars of the Roses) in England.

The supposed prime cause of the Hundred Years' War was of course the survival, in France, of English possessions dating from the time of William the Conqueror, and more particularly of Henry II (1133-89), whose queen was Eleanor of Aquitaine.† The precipitating events seem chiefly to have involved the vanity and as it were reflex rivalry of kings, and the economic interdependence of England and Flanders—so that one suspects that even without the issue of the English presence in Guienne and

---

* In decibels alone, a modern battle such as Stalingrad must eclipse even those of a hundred years ago—for example, the famous cannonade which preceded Pickett's charge at Gettysburg. By contrast, the clangor and shouting of medieval engagements must not have amounted to much.

† Sometimes called Eleanor of Guienne, Guienne being a subdivision of Aquitaine. Control of Guienne became an important issue from the reign of Edward I onward.

Gascony, a contest between the two countries might still have occurred. Though the peasant and burgher classes—the burghers of Flanders in particular—suffered heavily as result of it, the war was not in a modern sense total. There were numerous respites; the armies engaged were small, temporary, and slow-moving, and their depredations limited accordingly. And throughout, the royal houses of the two countries continued to intermarry. For example, a few years after Henry V had won Agincourt (in 1415) he took the hand of Catherine, the daughter of France's Charles VI. Similarly, more than a century before, Edward I of England, having been provoked into a declaration of war by Philip le Bel, did a *volte-face* and clinched the peace for a time by marrying Philip's sister Margaret. In the Hundred Years' War, French territory conquered by the English simply underwent a change in tax collectors and was by modern standards wretchedly administered.* For the rulers of nations continually at odds to be continually making relatives of their enemies through marriage is a practice to our minds somewhat odd—much as if, in World War II, Mussolini had concluded a separate peace and as a binder given his daughter Edda to wed Randolph Churchill. If such marriages were intended to guarantee a lasting entente, they seldom did so. If anything, the reverse; they simply bred further intrigue and bewildering new alignments among the powerful. A good example occurred in the reign of Edward II (1284-1327), who—probably under some duress, as he appears to have been devoted to young men—took Isabella, daughter of Philip le Bel, as his queen. Edward was a capricious and incapable ruler, who temporarily undid his father's work in Scotland by losing the battle of Bannockburn to Robert Bruce in 1314, and whose troubles at home evidently came in part from an inclination to promote the fortunes of his male favorites, to the great irritation of existing magnates of the realm. He seems also to have neg-

---

* For example, in the Breton War Edward III was obliged to "farm out" areas to his commanders for ready cash; and they in turn sublet these to anyone who could handle the job and meet their price. When the English candidate for the dukedom, John of Montfort, finally won, he did not ally himself with England as we should have expected. He did homage to the French King Charles V, Brittany was returned to the kingdom, and that was that. What advantage all the earlier bloodshed and expense brought to the English is hard to say—perhaps merely Edward III's satisfaction at having had his way in a matter of feudal succession.

lected Isabella; and she, after a sojourn in France, where she acquired a lover, Roger Mortimer, returned with the object of dethroning and liquidating her husband. That accomplished—by methods which would have been the admiration of her cold-blooded father*—she became a champion of her son, Edward III, in respect of his claims upon the throne of France. I.e., she, daughter of a French king, now undertook to make France an English dominion. To the upper-class mind of that period there was apparently nothing disloyal or otherwise strange in such a proceeding; one simply used one's position in whatever way offered, to extend one's power in any likely direction. The resulting system of statecraft is sometimes thought to have been far superior to our own but in fact differed from modern governments chiefly in being less efficient. Its aims were no better; it simply lacked the means to carry them out.

Both tactically and politically the Hundred Years' War may be said to have begun in the thirteenth century, during the reign of Edward I (1272-1307). His early campaigns to subdue Wales, in the 1270s and 1280s, apparently established the longbow as a major weapon of the English.† In the 1290s, Philip le Bel began encroaching upon English power in Gascony, precipitating a war between the two countries which lasted formally from 1294 to 1303, as well as a series of internal crises which were to occupy Edward for the rest of his days. Just as he was about to sail for France from Portsmouth, in 1294, the Welsh rose in revolt, forcing him to turn back and subdue them once again. With his usual deadly acumen, Philip then created another diversion by allying himself with the Scots (a move as it were made legal by the betrothal of the Scottish heir apparent to the daughter of Charles

---

* Edward II was first exposed to all sorts of hardship in the hope that he would sicken and die. That failing, he was reportedly murdered by having a red-hot poker thrust up his rectum. Strange stories persisted that he in fact was not murdered but escaped abroad, dying as an obscure commoner in Italy.

† Some authors think the longbow was adopted from the Welsh, who had used a powerful elm bow since as early as 1150. From Hastings to the reign of Henry III, the old short bow, drawn to the breast, not to the ear, and the crossbow, or arbalest, had predominated in England. Edward I used the longbow with great effect in Wales, but such is the inertia of custom that as late as 1281, in the payroll for the garrison of Rhuddlan castle, longbowmen are rated at 2d per day, crossbowmen at 4d.[1]

of Valois, who had recently invaded Gascony on Philip's behalf). Years of war between England and Scotland followed. It was in this multiple emergency that Edward in 1295 summoned what later came to be known as the Model Parliament.* "What touches all" said his writ of summons "should be approved of all, and it is also clear that common dangers should be met by measures agreed upon in common." Thus with the longbow, which admitted the common freeholder or yeoman to the ranks of organized fighting men,† and with the use of a general assembly to obtain assent in royal policy, Edward and the English were already drawing away from the rest of feudal Europe.‡

In the course of putting his military projects on this relatively firm footing, Edward ran into financial difficulties of the kind which were to cause his grandson, Edward III, so much trouble. Wool and leather for export were seized by the king's sheriffs, to be released only on payment of the "maletolt" (a duty raised sixfold over the usual 6s 8d the sack). Property taxes were imposed upon all above a certain minimum worth. And in 1294 a tax amounting to 50 percent of revenues was asked of the Church, touching off a long dispute which was in the end to maneuver

---

* Which, strictly, it was not. For one thing, the Parliament of 1275 was quite like it. For another the parliaments of that day were still similar in principle to the French, or to the assemblies of the great age of Spanish constitutionalism. That is, they were "a combination of several separate communes or estates, deliberating apart from each other and often returning different answers to the king's demands."[2] A basic difference between the English Parliament and its foreign equivalents was that its third estate included not only townsmen but representatives from the countryside.

† "[European] infantry, in the twelfth and thirteenth centuries, was absolutely insignificant: foot soldiers accompanied the army for no better purpose than to perform the menial duties of the camp [for tips?] or to assist in . . . sieges . . . Occasionally they were employed as light troops to open the battle by their ineffective demonstrations. There was, however, no really important part for them to play. Indeed their lords were sometimes affronted if they presumed to delay too long the opening of the cavalry charges, and ended the skirmishing by riding into and over their wretched followers."[3] In the fifteenth century Charles VII of France attempted to create a militia of Free Archers, but the peasant population seems to have responded with understandable apathy, and many militiamen, who had joined for tax remissions, were portly and overage.

‡ In his land laws affecting the feudal barony and further grants of land to the Church, and in his writ confining ecclesiastical courts to Church business, he also did much, as one writer puts it, "to eliminate feudalism from political life."[4]

Edward into the position of John, the signer of the Magna Carta. Apparently the basic difficulty was that the nation could not readily support even necessary defensive wars, so that when the first enthusiasm for the king's projects wore off, the liberty and consideration he had granted the estates came back to plague him in the shape of disagreements or threats of open rebellion. Even Edward's barons balked at the prospect of conducting a campaign in Gascony—no doubt on the ground of expense.

The net result was that he was forced to suspend war with France (protecting his position by his expedient marriage) and ended his days fighting the intractable Scots. His victory over Wallace at Falkirk in 1298 might be taken as one of the opening engagements of the Hundred Years' War, partly because of the Scottish involvement with France and partly on account of Edward's tactical use of the longbow, which anticipated Crécy.

At Falkirk, and indeed habitually, the Scots fought on foot, using dense masses of spearmen in a formation called the *schiltron*. In this they anticipated the Swiss pikemen of the fourteenth and fifteenth centuries, evidently understanding the great difficulty which such close formation presents to horsemen, especially unorganized horsemen, accustomed to making blind headlong rushes. Wallace drew up his force behind a swamp, dividing it into four main groups or *schiltrons*, with light troops (including archers, using the short bow) filling the intervals between. He also had a cavalry reserve—probably not a substantial one, since the Scottish knighthood seems not to have amounted to much either in quality or in numbers. Edward advanced with his forces in three divisions, or "battles," with archers in the intervening spaces. The leading "battle," commanded by the Earl Marshal, made the expected—in medieval warfare, almost the obligatory—move of charging the enemy's center. His cavalry, bogging down on the swampy ground, were severely harassed by the Scottish archers, who fired into their disordered ranks at close range. The second "battle," led by a fighting prelate, the Bishop of Durham, declined to compound this mistake, but instead tried to take Wallace in flank, at which point the Scottish cavalry fled. The bishop's men evidently dispersed the archers and other light Scottish troops, but the heavier *schiltrons* were able to stand off their attack with great loss to the English. It was Edward's "battle," encircling the marsh, which decided the outcome.

With a force of archers and cavalry, he drew close to the Scots' main body. As the latter's archers had been driven off, the English could shoot into the masses of infantry at will. Edward directed and concentrated their fire so as literally to cut holes in the enemy's ranks, whereupon his cavalry rode in among the lines of pikemen and cut them to pieces. For its combination of missile and shock skillfully used to break down a type of infantry formation particularly formidable to horse, Falkirk might have served as a model for later feudal commanders in their wars against the Swiss. Of course it did not, as the several calamities of Charles the Bold* of Burgundy (to name only one) clearly show.

It is ironic that the Swiss themselves, although masters of maneuver with the dense phalanx of pikemen, became, like the ancient Macedonians, the victims of gross overconfidence and stereotypy. Their success on the battlefield, in the course of nearly two centuries, depended in part simply on the inability of their opponents to think out any solution to the problem they presented. In part it may also have depended on their fearsome reputation, which they continued to maintain when fighting not for freedom but for money. Given the opportunity, as they often were, they slaughtered the entire enemy force, wounded, surrendered and all; and possibly from an awareness of the mercy likely to be shown them in return, they fought, when cornered, to the last pikeman and halberdier (as at St. Jacob-en-Birs in 1444, when 1000 Swiss died fighting 15,000 French, under the Dauphin, at a cost to the enemy of double their own number—a victory so expensive that Louis abandoned the campaign).

The fact which seems strange in retrospect is that during the

---

* His descriptive title, Charles le Téméraire, is sometimes translated "the Rash," probably depending upon the translator's familiarity with his campaigns. In his last defeat by the Swiss, at Nancy, on a bitter winter's day in January 1477, he was left dead on the battlefield, "his head cleft to the chin by a single blow from a halberd."[5] As bad generals go, he seems in a minor way to have been outstanding, and like many in those days, paid the supreme price of his incompetence. An imaginative picture of him in Guizot's History of France shows him in full armor, with his helmet off and his hand on his broadsword, staring keenly into the distance. He was noted for the splendor of his court and of the raiment in which he himself appeared on state occasions.[6]

centuries when the longbow, pike, and arquebus were gradually destroying feudal battle capacity and therewith feudalism itself, the hereditary magnates who might have prolonged their power by adopting the new weapons and tactics largely failed to do so. Cannon, for instance, whose use developed very slowly despite the obvious possibilities of the field gun, continued to remain in the hands of private owners who hired them out.* The explanation, already suggested, may be that the code of primal virtues of the old Frankish warrior caste had set so hard in Europe that it resisted any change so long as it continued to work at all. To say that archery on the English model did not develop in France because a class comparable to the yeomen did not exist there is correct but inadequate. Archery throve in England because it was in several senses encouraged from above. As for the French, it simply did not suit the temper of that arrogant aristocracy to set about arming or paying any consistent attention to the lower orders. Indeed, for centuries European nobles and clergy alike inclined to look with suspicion upon the efforts of other classes, in particular the lowest, to better themselves. (Guizot cites Guibert of Nogent, a chronicler of the miseries of Laon in the twelfth century, who described a sermon given by the Archbishop of Rheims to the townspeople "touching those execrable institutions of communes, whereby we see serfs, contrary to all right and justice, withdrawing themselves by force from the lawful authority of their masters."[7])

With a few exceptions, such as the unappreciated Philip the Tall, it seems never to have occurred to the French nobility that an opposite policy might, by favoring the wealth and military efficiency of the realm, redound to their advantage, more espe-

---

* There is evidence that the Germans used guns in the siege of Cividale, in Italy, in 1331. Edward III had a few gunners, some of whom evidently fought at Crécy, though these may have used primitive hand guns. The invincible Ziska, of the Hussite Wars (1419-24), built an army and a tactical system on wagon trains or laagers armed with long-barreled two-pounders and a few ribaudequins, or many-barreled machine guns. Notwithstanding Ziska's great successes and, much later, Henry of Navarre's skillful use of a few fieldpieces to decide battles, it was not really until the time of Gustavus Adolphus, in the seventeenth century, that field artillery appeared—although "carts with gonnes" did figure in the battles of the sixteenth. Roger Bacon's advice (in the mid-thirteenth) to moisten gunpowder to facilitate mixing was ignored for centuries, with many ill effects in the field.

cially since they themselves were few in number, unfitted for business, and not even very skilled in warfare. The more usual course in raising the crown's revenues was that followed by Philip le Bel. On the same principle of systematic improvidence, foot troops in Europe remained "residue" and archers, hired crossbowmen. From the beginning of the chartered towns, the habit of the nobility to live by looting their own commoners was a cause of great trouble and unnecessary slaughter,* with the decision (as in the case of Courtrai) occasionally going to the commoners.

In this atmosphere it is hardly surprising that little in the way of a self-respecting yeomanry grew up in France. And in being the disorganized rabble they evidently were, whether as foot soldiers or rioting burghers, the commonalty were only acting the part in which their betters had cast them. In Europe the days of organized rabble were yet to come. Meantime, the existing order was such as to minimize military efficiency in time of war, and to place a maximum of obstacles (including merciless taxation and the social stigma attaching to toil or money-making) in the way of necessary production at all times. As a system for guaran-

---

* How desperate this struggle was can be seen from a fascinating account in Guizot's *History of France* of the attempt of the burghers of Laon to obtain a charter from Louis the Fat, at the beginning of the twelfth century. By paying off the local bishop and the nobility, as well as the king himself, they arranged for certain freedoms and rights to self-government. But as the money was paid in a lump sum instead of annually, it was soon exhausted, and at that point the magnates concerned, the bishop in particular, began to have second thoughts about what they had done and "meditated reducing to the old condition the serfs emancipated from the yoke." Shortly afterward Louis revoked the charter. The townsmen retired stunned into their houses and, after an interval of silence, emerged as an enraged mob. They fired the grandees' mansions, murdered the bishop, and then, in their dread of royal vengeance, deserted Laon entirely to seek the protection of a ferocious local baron, one Thomas de Marle. Hearing this news, peasants flocked in from the countryside, looted the buildings lately vacated, and fought and killed each other for possession of the spoils. Louis overtook Thomas and killed the bishop's murderers by hanging, but then apparently persuaded the magnates of Laon to be a little less high-handed with their townspeople.[8] Laon eventually recovered and received a more lasting charter, but the French aristocracy were to go on repeating such atrocities for centuries, notably in Laon once again in 1177. In Germany, nobles and ecclesiastics deplored the tendency of serfs to escape into the anonymity of the towns. It is from the period of the medieval communes that the German expression *"Stadtluft macht frei"* ("City air makes men free") is said to date.

teeing disasters on the battlefield, with or without the help of outstandingly bad leaders, this one was next to perfect. In that respect it was almost the reverse of the later Swiss, whose pike formations were so well drilled that they won often, if not usually, without distinguished leadership—through a combination of instinct, good petty officers, and desperately stupid opponents.

The two monarchs—Edward III of England and Philip VI of France—under whom the Hundred Years' War began were far from evenly matched. Edward appears to have inherited many, though not all, of the considerable abilities of his grandfather, Edward I. Philip, for his part, showed little of the flinty astuteness of his late uncle, Philip le Bel, although he was capable on occasion of a similar savagery. As a commander he had some glimmerings of strategic sense (as, for instance, in his attempt to prevent Edward from fording the Somme, before Crécy), but his control of his troops was poor and he was without tactics. In all his undertakings he evidently lacked consistent energy or constancy of purpose. His financial policy included imposition of the violently unpopular *gabelle* or salt tax, and periodic debasements of the currency. And although the States-General had required their consent to the levying of special taxes, he evidently exacted large provincial subsidies without it. He is said to have been much under the thumb of his wife, "the masculine queen" Jeanne of Burgundy.

Edward III exhibited, one might say, a more restrained kind of foolishness. While much given, as Philip was, to tourneys and the like, and to knightly enterprises overseas which cost more money than the Crown, in that day, could readily exact (or the realm readily afford), he nonetheless went about making his demands more sensibly, respecting the principle of parliamentary assent which his grandfather before him had helped to establish as a permanent feature of English life. His sense of political strategy was keen, although accompanied, some say, by a certain slipperiness which led him to make many promises not later honored. On the field he was a brave and tenacious commander and one who sometimes acted according to the ideals of chivalry. His chief defect was as a (military) strategist—as though, once engaged in war, he was so carried away by the delight of it that he lost sight of its larger objectives and, unless an enemy was squarely in front of him, wandered about the countryside with his army, not quite certain what to do next, except of course for the usual looting and burning. Most of his campaigns seem to have had this rambling air, which turns out to have been prophetic of England's future as a continental power. Part of the difficulty was simply, perhaps, that no feudal kingdom was up to the task of conquering and invading another, especially one anywhere near its equal in power and extent. Armies were too small, enlistments too short, fortifications too effective, national resources too limited, barons too unreliable, and all political alignments too fluid. Edward was also, one suspects, too much a man of his time to consider this problem from a sufficient distance; he lacked originality, though even with it he might not have accomplished much more than he did. His advantages as a leader were considerable, and not least of these was the English military system of the day. He contributed only a little to it himself, but saw to its proper maintenance and in battle used it with exemplary skill.

The two kings came to power within two years of one another, Philip VI in 1328, by baronial election, and Edward III in 1330, by a Hamletlike coup, in which he and a band of followers entered Nottingham Castle by night, through an underground passage, and seized his mother's lover, Roger Mortimer. Shortly afterwards, following condemnatory proceedings in the House of Lords, Mortimer was executed at Tyburn and Edward, having been warden of the kingdom for four years, became king in fact.* He was then nineteen years old, to Philip's thirty-seven.

Very early in his reign Philip became uneasy about Edward's intentions as a pretender to the throne of France and ordered him to do homage. After first appearing in person and raising certain objections, Edward sent letters patent, in 1331, making the full acknowledgments asked, and there the matter might have rested but for a situation which had sprung up in the meantime. This last was dramatized by an event which occurred on the day of Philip's coronation. Louis of Nevers, when announced by the

---

* Since the dethroning of Edward II, Isabella and Mortimer had been the *de facto* rulers of England, and it apparently began to be a question as to when they would step down. Having thus summarily cut the roots of his mother's power and curtailed her private pleasures, Edward III thereafter observed the chivalric decencies toward her, allowing her to keep her dower and live out her life unmolested. (She died in obscurity, in 1358.)

king's heralds as the Count of Flanders, refused to acknowledge this designation of himself on the ground that the country of Flanders was his only in name. Not to be outdone, the new king promised that as his first royal act he would restore Louis' countship and make the French presence felt in Flanders as it had not been since before the days of Courtrai. And despite the objections of some of his advisers, who pointed out that it was a bad time of year (no doubt recalling the outcome of earlier French cavalry battles fought in wet weather in the Lowlands), Philip set off at once with a large army. He came face to face with the Flemish at Cassel, a hilltop fortress town in which they had installed themselves under the command of one Nicholas Zannequin, a rich burgher of Furnes. For a time nothing happened. Philip's men did the usual burning and plundering in the environs,* and then all sat down to wait. At about 3:00 P.M. on August 24, 1328, as the king lay asleep ("after a carousal," Guizot says), and disarmed knights played chess, or talked and wandered about among the tents, the king's confessor suddenly shouted an alarm. The Flemish had stolen down from their hilltop and were attacking in three groups around the perimeter of the camp. One story has it that Zannequin himself was standing over Philip with his mace raised, ready to smash in the king's skull, when a party of French knights rushed up and forestalled him. However that may be, the luck of Courtrai was not with the Flemings this time. The French somehow rallied, beat off the attack, and then—probably through a combination of better weapons and superior numbers —got the upper hand. No doubt aware of the fate which awaited them with Louis of Nevers returned as their count and recent adversary, the sixteen thousand burghers stood their ground and "were left there dead and slain in three heaps, without budging from the spot where the battle had begun."

Although this dismal victory was not much to boast about,

---

* On a tower, the Flemings had flown a flag showing a cock and the inscription:

"When the cock hereon shall crow
The foundling king shall herein go"

"The foundling king" was a reference to the fact that Philip was in some sense not legitimate, not being in the direct Capetian line. It is reported to have caused him great annoyance, which he vented on the surrounding countryside, then and later.

Philip is said to have done so, and quite properly too, inasmuch as he never won another.*

Having put Cassel to the torch, Philip (according to Froissart) made the following speech to Louis of Nevers: "Count, I have worked for you at my own and my barons' expense; I give you back your land recovered and in peace; so take care that justice be kept up in it and that I have not, through your fault, to return. . . ."[9]

Louis at once began the systematic punishment of Flanders, suspending or drastically limiting the privileges of the great towns, destroying the fortifications of Bruges, Ypres and Courtrai, and forcing the burghers of Bruges to come to his castle of Mâle and beg forgiveness of him on their knees. "He chastised, despoiled, proscribed and inflicted atrocious punishments" says Guizot, adding, "Neither the king of France nor the count of Flanders seemed to remember that the Flemish communes had at their door a natural and powerful ally who could not do without them any more than they could do without him. . . . It was from England that they chiefly imported their wool, the primary staple of their handiwork."[10] The Flemish issue, which was perhaps the crucial one in the next decade, reduced essentially to the rights of looting versus the rights of trade—in effect, to differences in the form taken by self-interest which have distinguished the French from the English more or less ever since.

In the nine years after Cassel, a variety of events converged on the same end, producing at last a crisis wholly beyond control. French infiltration of Guienne continued until in 1337 Philip declared it forfeited to the French crown. Like his late uncle, Philip le Bel, he elected to meddle in Scottish affairs by sheltering David Bruce, a contender for the throne of Scotland, and preparing an expedition in his behalf (in 1336). By one account, Louis of Nevers, at Philip's instance, had all Englishmen in Flanders arrested and thrown into prison, to which Edward III replied by suspending the export of wool to that country, thereby reducing the great towns, Ghent in particular, to nearly instant destitu-

---

* In 1332 he took the cross; and it was perhaps fortunate for him that trouble with England precluded his crusade (one of whose aims was political: to involve the English in a distant campaign), since had he led it, it is quite possible that he would not have come back.

tion.[11] (According to another version, Edward acted first, the cessation of the wool trade being followed by the arrest of Englishmen in Flanders, and of Flemings in England.[12])

In this same period a renegade French nobleman, Robert of Artois, fled to England and is said to have incited Edward to assert his claim to the throne of France, which he presently did, at the Nottingham Parliament of 1336, and later in a letter to the pope. These seem, however, to have been in the nature of threatening countermoves, since Edward had already, with some demurrers, given up his claim; and later on never reasserted it, as he might have done, for instance, after Sluys or Crécy. He busied himself raising money and buying allies in Germany (most of whom dropped him when his credit became shaky in 1341). The Flemings had meanwhile found a leader in Jacob (or James) van Artevelde, formed a coalition of towns, forced Louis of Nevers to flee, and sued for a new trade agreement with England, which Edward was prompt to grant. English arms were at this time in a promising state, partly as the result of an act of 1334 which had greatly clarified the terms of military service.*

However, except for the destruction of the French garrison on the Isle of Cadsand, off the coast of Flanders, in 1338, the English did quite poorly at first. When Benedict XII suspended the proposed crusade (at the end of 1335), Philip had transferred the fleet assembled for that adventure from Marseille to the Channel Ports. French and Genoese galleys now began a succession of raids on English coast towns, burning Portsmouth, Portsea, and Southampton, visiting slaughter and destruction on the Channel Islands, the Isle of Wight, Dover, Rye, Sandwich, and Winchel-

---

* ". . . The barons and knights had to respond to the summons of the king, who took them into his pay or allowed them to buy themselves off; secondly, the king made a levy among the freemen with arms, 'the strongest, most adept, most skillful in shooting with the bow or handling the lance, most inured to fatigue.' Thus was created a redoubtable body of infantry. . . . A regular military education was envisaged. The knightly sports, so different from real warfare, were forbidden and replaced by contests with bows and arrows." By contrast, the French in the same period could count neither on the military service theoretically owed the Crown by the nobility, nor on levies of a standing militia. "An army could only be raised by special musters, with promises of high pay and large rewards to nobles . . . and to Genoese or German adventurers. The assembling, equipping, and provisioning of this mixed horde gave rise to abuses and to trickery. Further, the equipment of the nobility was both clumsy and ridiculous. . . ."[13]

sea. These excesses, like the almost reflex devastation wreaked on
the French countryside by Edward's armies shortly afterwards,
may have been a mistake. A principle one can infer from the wars
of our own day is that if sheer terror and wantonness are not
pushed far enough, they are apt to recoil on their perpetrators. By
butchering instead of making allies of the Ukrainian separatists,
and by miscalculating their own powers of total destruction in the
Battle of Britain, the Germans prepared their own defeat in
World War II. It is reported that after Johnson and Westmoreland ordered wholesale bombing of North Vietnam, infiltration
from the north steadily increased, resulting finally in the Tet offensive of 1968. In the same way, Philip's naval raids may have
set up a climate of emergency in England which made it all the
easier for Edward to raise the men and money he needed for a
counteroffensive. The French interception of wool ships such as
the *Christopher* and the *Edward* may seem to have been more
practical but in reality was not, as it served to increase the distress
of their Flemish dependency and so strengthened van Artevelde
and the anti-French party (whom Philip and Count Louis had
belatedly been trying to buy off with tax concessions and other
favors).

Edward's first move was not by sea; it took the form of a brief,
meandering campaign in the Lowlands, which ended with a refused engagement at Buironfosse, in October of 1339. There, as at
Halidon Hill in Scotland six years before, Edward chose to fight
on the defensive, partly no doubt because of his inferior numbers
and partly because, in any case, his archers could less easily be
ridden down when fighting from a prepared position, defended
by hedges of pointed stakes. Philip for his part broke the medieval code of invariable direct assault, not, it seems, from any tactical consideration but because his horoscope—cast by his cousin,
King Robert of Naples, "a mighty necromancer and full of . . .
wisdom,"[14]—forecast defeat.* Edward came home £300,000 in

* A slightly hysterical atmosphere seems to have prevailed in the French
army on this occasion. A hare, dashing out of the grass and among the front
ranks, caused a commotion, so that those to the rear thought the battle had
begun. As was the custom on the eve of combat, a number of knights were
created on the spot, those at Buironfosse coming to be called Knights of the
Hare.

debt, the English meanwhile having lost the stronghold of La
Penne, far to the south in Guienne (January, 1339).

In 1340, Edward assumed the arms of France, quartered with
those of England—this at the prompting of van Artevelde, whose
position as his Flemish ally was thus in some sense legalized, and
of Robert of Artois, who hoped Edward's ambition might be the
agency of his own triumphant return to France. To seal off Flanders, the French now began massing ships on the coast of Zeeland,
near Sluys.* The fleet reportedly came to about one hundred
forty large vessels, with perhaps two dozen smaller auxiliaries
and a complement in all of 35,000 men. It was apparently divided
into three squadrons. Two were French, under the command of
Admiral Hugh Quiéret and of Nicholas Béhuchet, the king's
treasurer. The third consisted of some twenty-four hired Genoese
galleys led by a sailor of fortune named Barbavera (or Barbanero).

Edward evidently had no difficulty convincing his subjects of
the magnitude of the emergency which this new move represented. Armed with a huge parliamentary subsidy, he set about
collecting a fleet approximately equal in numbers to that of the
French, together with a body of archers and men-at-arms. At last,
on Thursday, June 22, 1340, he set sail aboard the cog *Thomas*.†
The event was almost festive, the fleet including some auxiliaries
which carried three hundred men-at-arms and a party of damsels
who were to join the queen, Philippa, then in Ghent.

On the following day the English sighted the enemy in the harbor of Sluys, the French ships anchored in such dense array that,
in Froissart's phrase, their masts formed "verily a forest."[15] Edward divided his force in three, with his heaviest ships in the van
and a reserve (including the damsels and their guard) apparently

---

* Whose harbor silted up centuries ago, but which was then a seaport.
Cadsand, then a nearby island, is now part of the mainland.

† A cog was a blunt-ended sailing ship of a type then much used. The
French fleet seems mainly to have consisted of galleys of the medieval Mediterranean type, each with a single bank of oars with several rowers to the
oar. They also had some captured English cogs in their battle line, including
the *Edward* and the *Christopher*. The English fleet evidently consisted chiefly
of sail, and besides archers carried catapults and a few primitive cannon.
The masts of the ships of both fleets were equipped with "top castles" from
which men shot arrows or quarrels or simply threw down heavy objects,
mainly stones.

held astern and to windward of the two engaged squadrons. For every two of his ships loaded with longbowmen, there was a third carrying men-at-arms.

The French likewise put their heaviest vessels, including four captured cogs, in their van; and to make their line more difficult to break, are said to have chained their ships together. Their missile defense consisted chiefly of Genoese crossbowmen, and of men in the top castles armed with stones. Both sides (as the custom was then, and continued to be till after the battle of Lepanto in the sixteenth century) prepared to fight what was in fact a land battle launched from floating platforms. Nonetheless, seamanship is of some consequence in such engagements, in that the better disposed and more mobile force can commit itself as it chooses. Edward held this advantage by remaining upwind and seaward of his opponents. He also had clear superiority in missile power. So long as his ships carrying archers took care not to close too promptly with the enemy, his firepower could not be injured by direct attack. The two main French squadrons obliged him by making no effort to maneuver, but instead taking a fixed position close inshore, huddled together as if to form a marine fortress. Barbavera appears to have been horrified at this decision. "Sirs," said he, to Admiral Quiéret and the treasurer Béhuchet (who, as Froissart spitefully remarks, "knew more about arithmetic than seafights"), "here is the king of England with all his ships bearing down upon us. If ye will follow my advice . . . ye will draw out into the open sea." Béhuchet rebuffed him, at which the Genoese detached himself from their service, saying, "Sirs, if ye will not be pleased to believe me I have no mind to work my own ruin, and I will get me gone with my galleys out of this hole."[16]

Authorities differ as to when the battle began. Guizot says at six in the morning of Saturday, June 24, 1340.[17] Fuller cites an English chronicler of the period who set the time at "after midday," and adds the reasonable hypothesis that Edward, seeing the immobility of his enemy, felt free to attack when he liked. By waiting till afternoon he is supposed to have gained the advantage of a fair wind and tide, and of the sun at his back. "To the sound of trumpets, nakers [kettledrums], viols, tabors, and other instruments, Sir Robert Morley . . . sailed straight for the French

van,"[17] and as the two lines collided the English archers released
great sheets of arrows which swept the men-at-arms from the
French decks much the way Edward I's archers had cut swaths
through the massed Scottish pikemen at Falkirk, forty-two years
before. The slaughter was fearful but by no means one-sided. The
French fought with great stubbornness, their men-at-arms standing up to the terrible fire poured upon them, and their missile
arm apparently having some success.* But they and their
Genoese arblasters were no match for longbowmen firing on them
at close range, many no doubt from ships still too far off to board
and too well handled to be drawn to close quarters. On the decks
of some of their own ships not a man was left alive, and the sea
around was dyed with their blood. Barbavera with his twenty-
four galleys had meanwhile made good his escape, though not
before fighting a rear-guard action in which Edward himself was
wounded in the thigh and an English ship lost by capture. By
Guizot's account, although the English were getting the best of
the main engagement, it was the arrival of a huge Flemish fleet
of two hundred sail which decided the day.[18] When "the French
heard echoing about them the horns of the Flemish mariners,
sounding to quarters,"† they must have known for a certainty
they were lost. Panic swept the second and third ranks of their
line, resulting in a rush for the boats and more capsizing and
deaths by drowning. The English meanwhile methodically en-

* Almost the entire personnel of one English ship was reportedly stoned to
death.

† Cited from Froissart. Fuller's account, based on other chroniclers, has it
that Flemish "boats"—presumably miscellaneous harbor craft—put out late in
the battle and attacked the French from the rear.[12] This seems the more
likely version. If the Flemish had had as large a fleet as Froissart says, Edward, never unmindful of odds, would quite probably have waited for it to
join him. On the other hand, if the Flemings did attack from small boats, as
Fuller reports, they would naturally have done so late in the day when the
enemy was clearly in difficulties. Such a move would have been entirely in
keeping with their somewhat ambivalent and fluid foreign policy, which kept
them dealing with the French even during the period of their closest alliance
with England. In fact, the towns were never pro-English *en bloc,* and this
seems in part to have been due to class rivalry and the tendency of the richer
merchants to identify themselves with the nobility. The merchants evidently
comprised much of the pro-French faction—the *leliaerts,* or party of the lily.
Sohier of Courtrai, van Artevelde's father-in-law, was one of these; he made
the mistake of changing sides and then falling into the hands of Count Louis,
who beheaded him.

larged their advantage, taking the enemy ship by ship until the
last resistance had been fought down. The French lost their
whole fleet of one hundred sixty-six vessels and, by one (probably exaggerated) estimate, thirty thousand men. Guizot reports
that Quiéret surrendered but was killed anyway;[19] Fuller describes him as falling "in a fair fight."[20] Guizot has the Flemish
hanging poor Béhuchet from his own yardarm in revenge for the
French investment of Cadsand; Fuller reports him executed in
the same way, but by the English, for the burning of Portsmouth.
By Guizot's account, Queen Philippa came "the very next day" to
join her husband, who was confined to his ship with his wound.
Fuller reports that Edward spent "several days of high carousal"
aboard the *Thomas,* with "trumpets blowing and tambours beat-
ing," after which he celebrated high mass on shore with the help
of three hundred imported priests, only then riding on to see his
queen and their newborn son, John of Gaunt (Ghent).

Whatever the details may have been, certain essentials are
clear. French naval power, not four years established on the
Channel, had been obliterated there at a single blow. The English were free not only to trade with Flanders but to invest that
country against the French, or even to push the war into northern France. From the modern standpoint the logical thing would
have been for the English to act with all speed in mounting a
land offensive, so as not to lose the psychological advantage
gained by their great victory. But for all his tactical ability and
his taste for battle, Edward had little strategic sense or feeling
for timing. He understood an engagement but not a war, sometimes not even two engagements in a row. He was a defensive
commander in the most thorough sense, propelled into action not
spontaneously, by his own designs, but under the pressure of extreme emergencies of the kind which precipitated Sluys. The
very fact that he had dealt with that one so handily may have left
him at a loss for further plans. Philip, on the other hand, seems to
have understood war, having engineered this one with some skill,
but he entirely lacked the ability to plan or win a battle, his one
victory, Cassel, being chiefly the result of a miscalculation on the
part of his enemies.

Consequently, while Sluys, as Fuller remarks, gave the English
command of the Channel for some decades (and so led up to

Crécy and Poitiers), its immediate result, for Edward, was a second anticlimactic campaign, ending with the suspended siege of Tournai and the truce of Esplechin (September 25, 1340). On balance, the French came out rather better than they had a right to expect, having in the meantime enlarged their control of Gascony while their Scots allies recaptured Perth. Edward returned to England in an ugly mood, convinced that he had failed through the fault of others. Parliament, he maintained, had not voted him sufficient funds. He denounced one of his former ministers, Archbishop John Stratford, in a letter to the pope ("I believe he wished me to be betrayed and killed. . . ."²¹). A crisis similar to that between Becket and Henry II sprang up. (Stratford, however, survived it, if not politically at least bodily.) And Edward in his turn was put under some pressure to grant Parliament rights of audit and of the nomination of chief ministers, and to give up his "household" system of administration in favor of one relying on "hereditary counsellors of the Crown . . . the peerage."²² Partly, no doubt, for these domestic reasons the war with France was called off for some years, although Edward indirectly continued it by supporting John of Montfort in the Breton War, waged against Charles of Blois, Philip VI's nephew and Philip's preferred claimant to the dukedom of Brittany.

In 1345, van Artevelde, whose popularity had declined and whose cause suffered from England's inaction, was assassinated shortly after a last meeting with Edward at Sluys. In the same year the Earl of Derby was having some success in the south of France recovering territories which the French had occupied. Philip replied by sending an army which, under the Duke of Normandy, laid siege to the castle of Aiguillon, on the Garonne (April, 1346). The siege was raised when news came that Edward had invaded the north of France. This might seem to have been a clever diversionary move, intended to relieve the pressure on Derby and protect English gains in Aquitaine. But according to one account Edward *meant* to sail for the south of France and was only prevented from doing so by unfavorable winds. "He then announced that he would go where the wind wanted him to," and on July 11, 1346, landed at La Hogue in Normandy.*²³

---

* However, again authorities disagree. In contrast to the author cited, Fuller reports that Edward was already en route to Gascony when a Norman

Excellent in detail, as always, he brought with him an army much smaller than that of the French—probably between 10,000 and 12,000 men—but far better paid and organized. It was not, as Fuller points out, the usual assemblage of feudal levies, but a picked force recruited by Commissions of Array, which systematically exacted direct service or substitutes, or the payment of scutage, from landlords and others of the propertied classes according to their means. Archers, as mentioned, were drawn from the yeomanry. The composition of this army was approximately 3700 archers;* 3500 Welsh troops, half spearmen and half archers; 2700 hobelers (mounted infantry, either spearmen or archers, originally used to operate with heavy cavalry on raids into Scotland); 1150 men-at-arms (full-armored mounted men of the fighting nobility); and a complement of supernumeraries possibly including a few cannoneers.[25]

Having landed where he did either by a freak of weather or by last-minute choice, Edward proceeded at once to the sack of Caen, with the intention of transferring the booty to his ships on the Orne. The fleet, however, disobeyed orders and sailed for home, leaving him for the moment stranded in the land he had come to conquer and balked in this first small move to defray campaign expenses. Abandoning his spoils, he marched, with no obvious plan, up the Seine toward Paris, pillaging and laying waste the countryside en route with the same thoroughness he

in his party convinced him that Normandy would be a better place to land because it was rich and fertile and poorly defended. Edward thereupon "changed his mind" and headed for St. Vaast-la-Hogue on the Cotentin peninsula.[24] Neither version speaks well for Edward's consistency of strategic purpose.

* The bows they used were about five feet long, made of yew, ash, elm, or wych-hazel (a variety of elm), and shooting a three-foot (clothyard) shaft to a range of around 250 yards. They were said to be able (presumably at intermediate ranges) to pierce two coats of mail. At Abergavenny in Wales, in 1182, an archer reportedly shot an arrow through an oak door four inches thick, the head standing out a hand's breadth on the far side. It is quite possible that at close range an arrow from a longbow could penetrate most or all of the layers of a knight's "coat of plates," so that it did not require a lucky hit or careful aiming for weak spots for an archer to bring down a man-at-arms.

The crossbow was much older, having come into general use in Europe in the tenth century. (It was condemned by the Lateran Council of 1139, without effect.) In its heavier versions it probably had more shocking power, but in most other respects is thought to have been inferior to the longbow.

habitually showed in Scotland.* Philip permitted him to cross the Seine unopposed at Poissy (August 16, 1346) while he himself withdrew to St. Denis. After reaching Grisy, Edward decided for some reason to turn northward. It is difficult to imagine what the object of his operations up to this point may have been. If to harass and disconcert the enemy, it must have been clear that no strategic purpose would be served by this course. Once his raid was over, the war in the south would resume; French incitement of the Scots would continue as before. Perhaps the advance on Paris was meant as a demonstration warning of what might happen if Philip persisted in vexing his English rival. As a tactic, this one could hardly have succeeded because of its air of anticlimax; nor would it have been worth the trouble, particularly in view of Edward's constant difficulties with expense. Whatever his intentions were, they will never be known, since he was a man of action who, like many, seldom troubled to explain himself. From his history as a whole, however, one gets the impression that he rarely had long-range plans but rather lived from crisis to crisis like a man in a melee, alert and skillful so long as a fight was on, but immediately at a loss when it let up.

From Grisy he made forced marches to Airaines, near the Somme, with Philip and a French force perhaps half again the size of his own in pursuit. There his reconnaissance disclosed no way of passing the Somme. He moved on to Abbeville and thence to Acheux, while Philip's troops massed at Amiens not far behind. The invasion which had so far gained the English neither plunder nor victories was turning into a flight to avoid entrapment. On August 23, at Acheux, Edward offered a reward to anyone who could point out an unguarded ford across the river. A local villager, Gobin Agache, responded, and on midnight of the same day, with the villager as a guide, the English army set out for the ford of Blanque Taque (or Blanche-Tache), which was passable

---

* "In 1336 . . . Edward III equipped a numerous army, devastated the Lowlands and a great part of the Highlands, and destroyed everything he could find, as far as Inverness. . . . And in 1355 . . . in a still more barbarous inroad [he] burnt every church, every village and every town he approached."[26] Similar disasters were visited upon Scotland by English invaders during the reigns of Richard II (in 1385) and Henry V (in 1400), and the hunger and desperation of the country became such that, according to Buckle, well documented cases of cannibalism occurred.[26]

only at low tide. Philip evidently learned of this ford himself, for
he sent a force under a Norman baron, Godemar du Fay, to cut
Edward off. Edward arrived in time to catch the tide, fought his
way through du Fay's detachment, and gained the farther bank;
and so for the moment the English were safe, although at the
cost of large quantities of provisions abandoned in Airaines.*

It was at this juncture that Edward, having been spared an
action on the enemy's terms, apparently decided to invite one on
his own. He had in fact little choice, since the French were fast
closing in on him. His best move was to use the time granted him
by their delay at the Somme to select a position which would
permit him to deploy his army on a narrow front, thereby mini-
mizing his inferiority in numbers and allowing him to use his
superior firepower to maximum effect. He found the position he
sought at Crécy-en-Ponthieu, some five leagues from Abbeville.
He disposed his army on a low rise, with the village of Crécy and
a small stream, the Maye, on his right, and the village of Wadicourt at the extreme left. He divided his forces into the customary
three "battles." Two formed his front line, the right battle being
under command of Edward the Black Prince (the Prince of
Wales, then a youth of sixteen) and the left under joint command
of the Earls of Northampton and Arundel. These were composed
of dismounted men-at-arms, whose horses, together with the
army's baggage wagons, had been assembled in an enclosed park
to the rear. Edward himself commanded the third battle, which
was held in reserve along with a complement of archers and
Welsh spearmen. Between the two front-line battles was a formation of archers dug in *en herse*—that is, in a v-shaped salient, both
sides of which were protected from direct cavalry assault by
hedges of steel-pointed stakes, the archers themselves standing
in shallow firing pits. On the far right a second formation of archers was dug in in the same way, their line raking forward so as to
enable them to shoot into the flank of cavalry attacking the right
battle. To protect this end of the line further Edward had a series
of ditches dug. The right battle was also protected by *trous-de-*

---

* While du Fay was hastening to Blanque Taque, Philip's main force entered Airaines, where they found "a great store of provisions, meat ready
spitted, bread and pastry in the ovens, wines in barrel, and many tables
which the English had left ready set and laid out."[27]

loup.* The missile cover on the left was approximately the same, except that the line of archers was nearly parallel to the battle of heavy infantry, the object of this disposition being perhaps to extend the front so as to discourage a flanking movement at that end. By this time in the campaign Edward's numbers seem to have dropped to about 8500 men, as compared to perhaps 13,000 on the French side.† His army was facing southeast, in the direction in which he expected Philip to advance from Abbeville. These moves were evidently completed and the English in position in full battle array by the morning of Saturday, August 26, 1346.

On the same morning the French set out as Edward had foreseen, and soon learned of his whereabouts. But by the time they were approaching Crécy it was already so late in the afternoon, and Philip's army was so strung out along the line of march, that he decided to halt for the night and attack the next morning. He appears to have issued orders to that effect; but his nobles, by that time no doubt in a fever to do great feats of arms and batter down the foe by sheer might and frenzy, would not heed him. At least some would not, which created considerable confusion, since (by Froissart's account) those to the fore stopped as commanded, while the irreconcilables (or simply the uninformed) continued to push on from the rear. While this development perhaps served to concentrate Philip's forces for him, it also destroyed whatever internal order they may have had, by running all ranks together. The situation was further complicated by the fact that swarms of excited citizens had now begun to appear along the way, or in it, brandishing swords and shouting "Death! Death!" ("And," adds Froissart, "not a soul did they see," except of course their own sovereign and his floundering troops.) In the last stages of his advance, Philip was seemingly swept on to Crécy by the overwhelming force of others' excitement, like a man on a runaway horse. It was in this way that the two armies finally

---

* *Trous-de-loup*, according to the Concise Oxford Dictionary, are "small conical pits with a stake in the center of each, as a defense against cavalry."

† Estimates by historians vary enormously. I have used the most conservative on the ground that to support and manage even such small forces as these must have seriously strained the resources of medieval nations and the military skill of their leaders.

came face to face some time late in the afternoon of August 26, 1346.

On the English side, there was no stir. Hours before, Edward, mounted on a little palfrey and carrying a white baton, had passed before the troops with his marshals, inspecting the dispositions that had been made and encouraging his men "with so bright a smile and so joyous a mien," says Froissart, that all were greatly heartened. They had then eaten a meal in ranks, "drunk one draught," and sat quietly waiting "with their head-pieces and their bows in front of them, resting themselves in order to be more fresh and cool when the enemy should come."[28]

Opposite them, across the Vallée des Clercs, there now appeared, in no particular order, the pick of French chivalry—knights by the thousands with blazoned shields and surcoats* and splendidly caparisoned horses, together with a sizable body of Genoese crossbowmen and the usual rabble of ill-armed villeins and supernumeraries of the camp. Both sides must have presented a brilliant appearance, the French in spite of their disorder, the English in part because of their dense, businesslike array and the air of silent steadfastness with which the archers and men-at-arms now stood to their posts. (Modern battles, though often less bloody, entirely lack this sort of grandeur, being fought by dirt-encrusted men and vehicles to an unending brutal din of explosives and usually in seas of mud or surrounded by the most depressing kinds of industrial wreckage. It is no wonder our poets do not celebrate them as the medieval poets, on occasion, celebrated theirs.)

Accompanying Philip with their retinues were some of the greatest nobles of the day, among them John of Luxembourg, the

---

* The armor of that time, though not so massive and elaborate as it was to become in the fifteenth century, was still highly developed. It typically included the rounded or pointed basinet and the attached aventail or mail covering for the cheeks, neck, and shoulders; plated gauntlets; sabatons for the feet; the haubergeon, or mail body coat; the aketon, or quilted undergarment; and the gambeson, often made of silk, embroidered with coats of arms, and worn as a surcoat; the coat-of-plates, made of cloth or leather with plates stitched on, and worn between the surcoat and hauberk; a plate defense for chin and neck called a gorget, or bevor; plate defenses for the arms, viz., the vambrace, rerebrace, couter, and spaudler; demigreaves or schynbalds for the lower leg; poleyns for the knee; and lastly the great helm worn over the basinet or its near relative the cervellière.[29]

blind King of Bohemia; his son Charles, King of the Romans; James III, King of Majorca; Charles, Count of Alençon (Philip's brother); Louis of Blois (his nephew); Louis of Nevers, Count of Flanders (his protégé); Rudolf, the Duke of Lorraine; and John of Hainault (who was related by marriage to both Philip and Edward, and had settled his troublesome problem in loyalties by being Edward's ally when the war was fought in Flanders and Philip's when it was fought in France). The total number of men-at-arms on the French side, by more conservative estimates, was about 8000, as compared to 1000 to 1500 on the English side. One report places the French strength in crossbowmen at 6000, a second at 15,000, both of which seem excessive. Another report says simply that there were "thousands" of Genoese.[30] The crossbow itself was certainly a formidable weapon, which in the Crusades had done good service against the mounted horse archers of the Turks and Egyptians. To judge from the figures given for the ballista (see note [*], page 46), its range must have been nearly that of the longbow; it could be sighted like a firearm and threw a heavy dart, or quarrel. Its chief defects were that in comparison to the longbow it was clumsy to handle, and as it had to be cranked up rather than simply drawn, it could be fired only about one-fifth as often.

Such were the two armies which faced each other in the late-afternoon sunshine, Edward with it at his back, Philip and his men facing into it. It is doubtful whether Philip's original division of his force into three battles survived his march. Partly perhaps to gain time and partly to counter the enemy's missile power with his own, Philip ordered the Genoese forward into the Vallée des Clercs at the foot of the slope on which the English were waiting. The crossbowmen appear to have hung back, being "sore tired with going a-foot that day more than six leagues and fully armed;"[31] and their reluctance stirred Charles of Alençon to an ominous burst of wrath. A brief thundershower thereupon occurred, accompanied by a flight of ravens which hovered in the air over the French, "making a loud noise." When the rain had stopped the sun came out more brightly than ever. The Genoese at last began their advance.

As they crossed the valley, they raised a loud shout "so as to strike dismay; but the English kept quite quiet and showed no sign of it."[32] At the third shout the Genoese opened fire. "The English archers then advanced one step forward, and shot their arrows with such force and quickness that it seemed as if it snowed. When the Genoese felt these arrows, which pierced their arms, heads, and through their armor, some of them cut the strings of their cross-bows, others flung them to the ground and turned about and retreated, quite discomfited."[33] "Between them and the main body of the French," the chronicler continues, "was a great hedge of men-at-arms watching the proceedings. When the king of France saw his bowmen thus in disorder, he shouted to the men-at-arms, 'Up now and slay all this scum for it blocks our way.'"[34] A wild melee ensued, the French cavalrymen rushing forward to hack down their own mercenaries, while the English poured arrows on all alike. Wounded horses went plunging in among the fleeing Genoese, adding to their casualties and to the general disorder. The first wave of French knights was already falling, dead or wounded or simply unhorsed, before the battle had properly begun.

Recovering from this débâcle, the tired French* organized a second attack, this time directed against the enemy. To reach Edward's main line of dismounted men-at-arms, they had now to enter a double funnel consisting of his salients of archers dug in behind their hedges of stakes. They were exposed to fire at close range from both sides and, because of the shortness of the English front, were obliged to send in their cavalry in waves, each one more obstructed than the last by the debris of those that had gone before.† At the start of the fight, Edward's position had one adverse, and possibly unexpected, consequence. It acted, particularly on the right, before the Prince of Wales' battle, to drive the enemy into a tight wedge-shaped formation which then tended to carry by its own momentum right up to the English line. The first waves of French thus "coasted the archers,"[35] their horses shying from the bowmen into compact masses which struck Edward's battle with such force as nearly to drive it in. The prince sent to his father for reinforcements; and after a speech about

* They had been on the road from Abbeville all day, and the battle according to Froissart, began at vespers, i.e., about 6:00 P.M.
† Fuller mentions that apparently no effort was made to clear away the dead and wounded between charges.[35]

letting the lad win his spurs, Edward dispatched the Bishop of Durham and thirty knights—a modest enough force—to his aid. The emergency, however, was soon past. For as the French pressed their attack, "the bowmen let fly among them at large, and . . . every arrow told on horse or man, piercing head, or arm, or leg among the riders and sending the horses mad. . . . Some stood stock still . . . others rushed sideways [or] began backing in spite of their masters . . . some were rearing and tossing their heads at the arrows, and others . . . threw themselves down. So the knights in the first French battle fell, almost without seeing the men who slew them."[36] As the field became littered with fallen knights and their mounts, it was perhaps no longer possible for those who came after to "coast the archers" or to keep any formation at all during the charge. We hear no more of the Prince of Wales being in difficulties.

For their part, the French, summoning those reserves of valor which in their long history they have seldom been found to lack, and have not infrequently needed, flung themselves into a series of increasingly ragged and bloody assaults. In the pauses between, Welshmen with long knives appeared between the lines and killed many as they lay in their armor,* either wounded or merly fallen and half-stunned. Hearing how the battle was going, blind King John of Bohemia called his liegemen about him, saying, " 'I pray you and require you to lead me . . . to the front . . . that I may strike a blow with my sword; it shall not be said I came hither to do naught.' . . . To acquit themselves of their duty and that they might not lose him in the throng, they tied themselves all together by the reins of their horses and set the king their lord right in front. . . . And the king went so far forward that he struck a good blow, yea three and four. . . . And they served him so well . . . and charged so well forward upon the English that all fell there and were found the next day on the spot round their lord."[37]

Long after poor King John had fallen, the onset continued. The French made, in all, some fifteen charges, the last evidently after dark, before they broke off the battle. Edward made no further

* At which Edward, when he learned of it, became quite angry, since many of those killed might have brought sizable ransoms, making up in part for the lost booty of Caen.

move, but prudently kept his men in position through the night, easily repulsing a contingent from Beauvais and Rouen which appeared the next morning, not yet having learned of Philip's defeat. The French losses included one king (John), one duke (the Duke of Lorraine), ten counts (including Louis of Flanders), 1542 knights and esquires, and common soldiers in the thousands. Other estimates run much larger than these, and probably none is trustworthy. Philip himself suffered a neck wound from an arrow, lost a horse, and finally withdrew to the castle of Broye, on the advice of John Hainault, who said, "I see no remedy here. It will soon be late; and then you would be as likely to ride upon your enemies as amongst your friends, and so be lost."[38] In that one respect Philip did better than his successor, King John II, who at the battle of Poitiers, ten years later, not only lost to the Black Prince but was captured by him, spending more than three years as an honored guest and triumphal object of the English.

By an equally unreliable estimate, Edward's losses at Crécy were fifty to eighty men. This startling victory did what Sluys failed to do; it established the reputation of English arms on the continent for some while to come. Indeed, along with Poitiers and Agincourt it is one of the few battles which anyone today, however ignorant of the history of the Middle Ages, is likely to have heard of. Sluys, on the other hand, though certainly more decisive in its results (since it gave back control of the Channel to the English), as well as being one of the bloodiest and most crushing naval defeats England ever inflicted on her enemies, seems to have made little impression then and is scarcely remembered now.*

What is more puzzling, at least to minds of this century, is that Philip learned so little from it. True, he did not take part in the battle,† but he must certainly have had reports from survivors, and in view of the staggering losses he sustained, one would have expected him to inquire carefully into the reasons for them. He

---

* For instance, Guizot's history does not even mention it.
† He reportedly learned of the defeat from his court fool, who said, "The English are cowards." When asked what that meant, he replied: "Because they lacked the courage to leap into the sea at Écluse [Sluys] as the French and Normans did."[39] One wonders if this joke was typical of the professional humor of the day, and what may have been the fate of its author.

did nothing of the kind, apparently. And at Crécy, although he was forced into an action by the enthusiasm of his own troops, it is striking that, once committed, neither he nor they showed the slightest sign that they understood the difficulties which faced them. The English position, from all accounts, was quite plain to see. The French merely declined to study it. In men whose pre-occupation was warfare, and who were far from being the bar-barians which Totila and his army were, this indifference to the simplest matters of terrain and tactics—to perils which were made obvious to all, from the outset—is surely astonishing. Primal ex-citement simply overcame them, it would appear, the battle from the French side proceeding as a vast tic, without plan or order or regard for loss. Those who led it did so essentially as herders crying on their beasts. Both the concept and, evidently, the gift of the *coup d'œil* were still centuries away, except for rare com-manders such as Edward III. But that faculty, along with a con-siderable skill in preparing and handling his forces, was almost his whole repertoire. Indeed, after Crécy, having declined to pur-sue Philip (quite understandably, since his small army, depend-ent as it was on archers, could not hope to overtake a mounted force, however ill organized), he made the one clearly farsighted move of his career. He laid siege to Calais (on September 4, 1346) and almost a year later took it. His success was assured by his control of all approaches to the port. Thanks to Sluys, it could not be relieved by sea, and he had seemingly so discon-certed Philip at Crécy that for six months the French made no move against him by land. In the meantime Philip's Scottish ally King David was defeated and captured at Neville's Cross (Oc-tober 17, 1346). The French king's plans, so well conceived and ill executed, were in ruins. For more than two hundred years Calais remained in English hands, serving as a counterthreat to invasion from the mainland and as a sort of clearing house through which (originally by Edward's order) English goods passed on their way to the Continent. Not only was Calais his strategic masterpiece; it was his only one, the single solid result of his campaigns—if not, as Fuller remarks, "the sole [English] gain of the whole of the Hundred Years' War."[40]

It is not correct to suppose that the French learned nothing from their disaster at Crécy. At Poitiers (in 1356) and again at

Agincourt (1415) they imitated Edward's methods to the extent of dismounting their cavalrymen and attacking in part on foot. Writing of King John's plan of attack against the Black Prince at Poitiers, Oman says: ". . . It was absolutely insane to form the whole French army into a gigantic wedge—where corps after corps was massed behind the first and narrowest line—and to dash it against the strongest point of the English front. That, however, was the plan which the king determined to adopt." The Black Prince's army was arrayed "on a plateau protected by a hedge along which English archers were posted. Through a gap in the hedge John thrust his vanguard, a chosen body of 300 horsemen, while the rest of his forces, three great masses of dismounted cavalry, followed close behind."[41] The result was another catastrophe. After the English archers had cut down numbers of the French vanguard by focusing all their fire on the single point of King John's attack, the Black Prince counterattacked at the same point with the main body of his men-at-arms, while sending a small force to create a diversion on the French left flank. This combination of surprise and shock proved too much for King John's army, most of which took flight. The king, finding himself surrounded by the enemy and about to be captured, reportedly cried out, "To whom shall I yield me? Where is my cousin, the Prince of Wales?" That same evening the Prince's marshals "entered [his] pavilion . . . and made him a present of the king of France."[42]

At Agincourt, fifty-nine years later, Henry V had with him an even smaller force than Edward III had had at Crécy—about 5000 archers and 1000 men-at arms. Like Edward he chose a strong defensive position with a front, according to Oman, of no more than 1200 yards, well protected by woods on either flank and in front by sodden plowed ground. His three battles were drawn up into a line, with archers in the intervals between. (He seems to have had too few men to hold any in reserve.) The French, under nominal command of the Constable of France, formed into three much larger groups, one behind the other, each composed chiefly of dismounted men-at-arms. Small numbers of crossbowmen were stationed behind each group, where (like Totila's archers, centuries before) they served no obvious purpose. Small French cavalry squadrons led the attack and were for the most part shot down en route or as they got to point-blank range. These were followed by rank upon rank of heavily armored men* trudging through the muck under a fearful rain of arrows. By bravery and sheer press of numbers, some managed to reach the English line and a desperate fight at close quarters began. "The decisive moment came when King Henry ordered his archers to put aside their bows and fall to with ax and sword. Exhausted by the combat and their long struggle through the mud, the French men-at-arms were no match for their lighter-armed opponents. Helplessly they stood while the agile yeomen 'beat upon their armor with mallets, as though they were smiths hammering upon anvils.' "[43] The first line of French troops at last fell back upon the second, throwing it into confusion as it tried to advance to the attack. The third, seeing the fate of the first two, "melted away." Agincourt was over.

Perhaps the chief lesson of these two sad engagements is that it is far worse for military leaders to draw the wrong conclusions from mistakes of the past than to draw none at all. Since the founding of great academies such as West Point,† the detailed management of war has improved somewhat but the failure rate among generals remains high. As many battles seem to have been lost in recent times through adherence to some crackbrained theory as ever were in Edward's day by reliance upon sheer ardor. We simply prepare our mistakes better and execute them on a grander scale. Since the Second Empire, for instance, each generation of French military savants has looked back over the work of its predecessors, decided they were wrong, and reversed its own position accordingly—in almost every case with lamentable results. When Hitler set out to subdue the world he was resolved not to repeat the error of the kaiser's generals. Whereas they had sunk their armies in hopeless position warfare, he would keep his perpetually on the move—a plan which succeeded splendidly so long as the enemy country was small in area and feebly defended. American theorists, applying a variant of the same idea,

---

* Much more heavily armored, in all probability, than those who had fought at Crécy.

† At the suggestion of George Washington. The fort (which Benedict Arnold had meant to turn over to the British) was occupied in 1781 by a "corps of Invalids," who evidently served as the Point's first instructors.

apparently concluded that a tiny colonial nation like Vietnam could not stand up six months under firepower as overwhelming as ours. Heaven only knows what surefire schemes of conquest the academicians of nuclear warfare have in store for us.

At least in the Middle Ages, men were spared some of the worst consequences of military miscalculation by the fact that no nation, victorious or defeated, could long support a struggle. A few weeks of campaigning in Flanders were sufficient to cause Edward serious financial embarrassment at home, and a good portion of his time seems to have been spent in drumming up funds to maintain what we would scarcely call an army. (At Crécy his whole force was less than an American Civil War division, which Sherman put at 9000-10,000 men.) Least of all could a medieval general afford years of defeat, since he depended on the booty which victory was likely to bring him. In modern war there is not much immediate booty, mostly just wreckage, both human and inanimate, which the conqueror is obliged to clean up and which the people at home resign themselves to paying for as part of the cost of success. In Vietnam we have been put in the odd position of having to foot the bills of victory without actually winning it. Bad as he may have been as a strategist, Edward III would not have understood this concept of warfare at all. Despite the far more modest cost of battle in the fourteenth century, no country could then afford the luxury of this sort of failure, and even some successes came too high, it being partly for this reason that the Hundred Years' War was so often interrupted by truces.

Philip VI, while perhaps not *the* worst commander of the Middle Ages, was still a fair representative of the type.* His misfortune was to have been not only stupider than Edward but heir to a far less practical fighting apparatus. Neither man had much originality, both representing the ideals of their people and their age almost to a fault. It is worth adding that the military system worked out by Edward I and used with such skill by his grand-

---

* Fortunately for France, not all of her kings or their field officers were as inept; for instance, Charles V (who succeeded John II) and his constable du Guesclin were not. Despite the terrible ravages of the Plague in France during the 1360s they made considerable headway against the English, partly by improved tactics, partly by adopting a fabian strategy of harassment and evasion.

son was little if at all improved by their successors. It seems almost to have been a freak of military insight, without issue because imperfectly understood by those who inherited it. (The practice of using systematic combinations of arms was still centuries off, although in the fifteenth and sixteenth centuries a number of experiments along that line were made, some of which are described later on.) The example of Falkirk was never applied—was perhaps quite forgotten—by the time the Swiss *schiltrons* had become the terror of battlefields in the fifteenth century. In England itself, after Edward III, there were no further innovations in the tactical use of archery; if anything, the contrary.* The longbow as a major weapon had a remarkably short history, roughly from Falkirk (1298) to the Wars of the Roses in the mid-fifteenth century.

As for Edward, one may say that, like other famous and successful commanders, he was fortunate in his opponents. How much was his success due to deliberate exploitation of their *idées fixes* and how much the result, simply, of acting according to his own? Although it is clear that at Crécy he behaved as though convinced that the French would fling themselves upon him as they did, we still have no explicit evidence as to his thoughts on that occasion. He may equally well have been fighting by rote, trusting to the precedent of Halidon Hill. His position was not in fact as strong as Philip's tactics made it look. According to the maps usually given, his front was about a mile long. Since his archers were concentrated in salients and about a third of his force held in reserve, his main line was evidently rather thin.† Moreover, having dismounted these men, he was at a great dis-

---

* According to one authority, archers, once "the cadre of the English tactical system," were by du Guesclin's time "diminished in numbers, prestige and importance." In the fifteenth century, during the brief heyday of the Maid of Orleans, "the knights and the nobles of France and the mercenary captains and men-at-arms as well, *rode down* the stationary masses of the English, lances and bowmen alike."[44]

† Out of a total of 8500 men, one-third of them archers, perhaps 6000 were committed. Of these, around 4000 were dismounted cavalry, one-quarter being men-at-arms, and three-quarters hobelers and other more lightly armed troops. Granted that this force took up about two-thirds of the front (the other third being occupied by archers), Edward had a little better than one man per foot of front, or enough for two ranks at slightly less than two feet of front per man.

advantage in mobility. A more sensible commander than Philip VI, having tried a feint or frontal demonstration, might have concluded that a head-on assault was out of the question and instead executed a flanking movement during the night, preferably around Edward's left, based on Wadicourt. Such a movement might have had some chance of success, since, unless skillfully anticipated, it would have brought the whole of the French cavalry to bear upon Edward's mounted reserve and his dismounted left battle, while leaving approximately two-thirds of his archers unable to act except at the cost of leaving their prepared positions and so exposing themselves to being ridden down.

To give Edward the benefit of the doubt, it is probable that he understood his enemy well enough to know how safe he was from surprises of this sort. The question remains, however, as to how effective he might have been against a force as well organized as his own or a commander as skilled in avoiding poor odds as Constable du Guesclin. Unfortunately for these speculations, by the time du Guesclin and his king, Charles V, had become the principals on the French side, Edward was declining into lascivious old age.* According to Guizot, a year after the death of the Black Prince (in June, 1377) "died his father, Edward III, a king who had been able, glorious and fortunate for nearly half a century, but had fallen towards the end . . . into contempt with his people and into forgetfulness on the continent of Europe, where nothing was heard about him beyond whispers of an indolent old man's indulgent weaknesses to please a covetous mistress."[45]

---

* His queen, Philippa of Hainaut (or Hainault) died in 1369. Besides bearing Edward a total of twelve children, she seems to have been an active and on the whole benign co-ruler. She established a colony of Flemish weavers at Norwich, promoted coal mining at Tynedale, apparently acted as pro tem commander in rallying the English against the Scottish invasion of 1346, saved the citizens of Calais by interceding for them with Edward at the close of the siege, and retained Froissart as her secretary from 1361 to 1366. Her chaplain, Robert of Eglesfield, founded Queen's College, Oxford. Alice Perrers, her successor, became Edward's mistress in 1366, evidently after a term as lady in waiting to the Queen. She was remarkable chiefly for a tendency to meddle in and corrupt the law in favor of her friends or paying acquaintances, exerting so great an influence that Parliament, in 1376, passed an act forbidding women to practice in the law courts. She was twice banished and allowed to return, and spent her declining years in lawsuits, almost, it would seem, out of habit.

One hears, today, that the notion of national character is out of date, if not suspect as being covertly racist. I am told too that in the formal study of history, battles are no longer considered very important, being (like almost everything else) an outgrowth either of existing economics or sheer chance. In the light of these ideas it is all the more remarkable, perhaps, that certain major differences between France and England, in their domestic policies and styles of fighting, seem to have remained constant during several centuries, and through a long succession of political and economic changes which (according to modern historical theories) should have transformed the national character of both peoples almost beyond recognition. I hasten to add that if such constancy in national character is a fact, the genetic (racial) contribution to it may be trivial in comparison to that of the tradition.

However all that may be, it is interesting that the same habits of mind which made the French army a bad one at Crécy in 1346 were still operative and led to much the same result on the Plains of Abraham at Quebec, over four centuries later. In that year (1759) the English under Brigadier General James Wolfe had sailed up the St. Lawrence with the object of dislodging the French from Quebec and thereby from the whole of Canada. Wolfe's army consisted of about 7500 men, including 800 officers and noncoms. The French, under the Marquis de Montcalm, mustered at Quebec "five regular battalions, the Militia and 1,000 Redskins . . . a total of between 10,000 and 14,000 armed men." Fuller adds, "All males from 10 to 60 years of age were enrolled by companies in the Provincial Militia, which was little more than an armed rabble."[46] (Compare this with Oman's description of foot troops on the Continent during the Middle Ages; and with the accompanying brief account of Charles VII's attempt to create a militia of Free Archers in fifteenth-century France.)

Besides having a rag-tag army, Montcalm was on bad terms with his co-commander, Governor General Vaudreuil, and hampered in his own operations not only by divided command but by the corruption and inefficiency with which the colony as a whole was run. Fuller quotes him as saying, " 'Everybody appears to be in a hurry to make his fortune before the colony is lost; which event many perhaps desire as an impenetrable veil over their conduct.'" Fuller adds that "the head brigand was François Bigot, Intendant of Canada, who pillaged the government, settlers, and Indians."[47] Those not in on the take suffered from understandably low morale and may have been less disposed to fend off the English than their superiors would have wished. Nevertheless, when the time came they fought with their usual almost fatalistic bravery.

While he clearly made some tactical mistakes, Montcalm was by no means an easy opponent, and for three months balked all of Wolfe's attempts to breach his position. His crucial mistake, as we all know from our schooldays, was in assuming that the English would not attempt to scale the heights along the St. Lawrence to the south and west of the city—and that of course was what Wolfe finally did, in an amphibious operation begun at two in the morning. Surprised by the enemy in force on the Plains of Abraham, Montcalm took the offensive. He did so reportedly because he had only two days' supplies in Quebec and realized that the English, given even one more day to entrench, could bring up heavy guns and devastate the city.

"By about nine o'clock of September 12, 1759, Montcalm's line of battle—formed some six hundred yards from his enemy—began to advance, covered by skirmishers. As they darted forward among the bushes Wolfe ordered his men to lie down and threw out his skirmishers."[48] The forces engaged were about equal in numbers, possibly slightly larger on the English side—on the order of 4000 to 5000 men each. By ten o'clock contact was complete and the French at two hundred paces opened their fire attack, the English standing to meet it. The French line at once became disordered due to the fact that the Canadian militiamen threw themselves down between volleys to reload. However, "The French redressed their line and again moved forward cheering, while the English stood silent like a wall." (As at Crécy, when the Genoese advanced shouting "to strike dismay; but the English kept quite quiet and showed no sign of it.") Wolfe had trained his men "not to halloo or cry out upon any account whatever"[49] until ordered into a bayonet charge. He also taught that cool, deliberate fire was more effective than fast, frenzied shooting: before Quebec, he ordered his men to withhold their volleys until the French came within twenty yards. In fact, the French fire was apparently so punishing that Wolfe, himself already wounded in the wrist, ordered his own men forward and opened at forty yards. The result again recalls Crécy: " 'With one deafening crash . . . the most perfect volley ever fired on battlefield burst forth as if from a single monstrous weapon, from end to end of the British line,' and a dense cloud of smoke drifted over the field. Under its cover the English reloaded, stepped forward and fired again, and continued to do so for six to eight minutes."[50] ("The English archers then advanced one step forward, and shot their arrows with such force and quickness that it seemed as if it snowed."*) Except for the pursuit, the battle of Quebec was over. Both generals were killed, Wolfe by a second musket ball which hit him in the groin. English casualties in dead and wounded amounted to about 15 percent. The French losses are unknown. The battle which in effect decided the question of the French presence on this continent was itself decided in just under fifteen minutes.

* This passage is from Froissart's account of Crécy.

CHAPTER IV

Goodbye, Knighthood;
Hello, World Conquest

Although Christianity produced little change in the rigid instinctive code which medieval fighting men no doubt owed to their neolithic forebears, it perhaps had *some* effect, and not on the conduct of war only. The ideals of chivalry and of courtly love might never have come into being without it, and indeed in pre-Christian Europe there was little enough to suggest their imminence. They represent an attempt to transmute lust (or in modern terms, sex) into a passion more poetic and less self-regarding than it ordinarily is; and to bring some element of gentlemanliness or decent restraint into the ancient business of fighting down one's rivals.

The fact is, however, that the chivalric code, so far as it worked at all, was a class phenomenon. It did not apply to those who were simply a lord's creatures, the peasants and common foot troops, or "residue," of the realm. To the medieval warrior-noble almost the whole world outside his own order was "residue" and he treated its members accordingly.* Even clerics were on occasion quite roughly handled by their temporal superiors. Moreover, to the degree that Christianity brought learning and cultivation chiefly into the upper orders it may, by exaggerating the dissimilarity of the classes, have worsened relations between

* Witness the habit of victors, in the Middle Ages, of murdering the foot soldiers of the enemy, simply to prevent them from turning to brigandage.

them. Whereas the Frankish chief of old had been an illiterate roughneck much like his followers, a twelfth-century noble such as Thibaut of Champagne (who covered the walls of his château with poetry and left us estimable samples of his art on paper) must have found his serfs, with their rags and primitive speech, scarcely human. (The Victorians developed a similar view, for instance of the poor mill hands of the New England and Midlands towns. In either era it of course had the advantage of making gross injustice appear to be a matter of natural law.) It is apparent from the accounts of the battles of Courtrai and Crécy that this attitude on the part of the French nobility—if I have judged it correctly—had an extremely bad effect on the military methods of the day. Between the fondness of knights for "feats of arms" and their contempt for their own auxiliaries (whom they simply left to their own devices on the field or cut down when they became a nuisance, and who were seldom properly armed or trained to begin with), most medieval armies could hardly be said to have been organized at all. Chivalric ideals may if anything have contributed to this state of affairs, since they tended to confine a man's nobler feelings to his fellow nobles, thereby eliminating what little may have remained of the democracy or general comradeship of early Frankish times.

The point is that while religious in origin, the notion of chivalry was quickly turned to practical account, providing a code according to which members of the ruling class showed their peers more consideration than they had done in the past (and their inferiors possibly less). To do so was only sense. Having risen in the first place through an aptitude for fighting, the medieval nobility then found themselves at the mercy of their own primal virtues. As late as the eleventh century their continual struggles with one another kept Europe on the edge of barbarism. If only to have more use and enjoyment of their power, they needed some new system of constraints, some ideal or polity, to keep their belligerence within reasonable limits. Chivalry or the concept of gentlemanliness did to some degree serve that purpose. A gentleman no longer sent his retainers to ambush a rival by night;* he challenged him to a fair contest, man to man.

---

* Nonetheless, this unpleasant custom persisted for centuries. The dueling code, as Trevelyan points out, developed as a substitute for the "killing af-

Whereas common soldiers might be massacred after a battle, a knight was held for ransom (which was a way not only of conserving the decencies but of making them yield a cash return). Of course there were numerous breaches of the code. A potentially dangerous claimant to the throne, or a noble suspected (like Oliver de Clisson) of loyalty to an alien monarch, was by definition a traitor, and normally dealt with in the old summary way.* Nevertheless, the chivalric idea had some influence on men's behavior, producing episodes on the battlefield which strike us today as slightly insane.

In 1351, for instance, during the Breton War, a French knight, Sir Robert de Beaumanoir, left his Castle Josselin and presented himself and his forces before Ploermel, then held by the English under "a captain called Brandebourg" (Froissart's spelling;[2] the name may have been Bemborough). "'Brandebourg,' said Robert, 'have ye within there never a man-at-arms or two or three who would fain cross swords with other three for love of their ladies?'" After demurring at the numbers suggested, Brandebourg replied: "'I will tell you what we will do, if it please you. You shall take twenty or thirty of your comrades and I shall take as many of ours. We will go out into a goodly field where none can hinder or vex us, and there will we do so much that men shall speak thereof in time to come in hall and palace and highway. . . .' 'By my faith,' said Beaumanoir, 'tis bravely said and I agree; be ye thirty and we will be thirty too.'" The two groups of thirty met shortly thereafter on a suitable field, "parleyed" with one another, and then "fell back and made all their fellows go far away from the place." At last "one of them made a sign and forthwith they set on and fought stoutly all in a heap, and they aided one another handsomely." The first round of this contest (which seems to have been fought on foot) went to the English, the score, at the half, being four French dead to two English.

"They rested by common accord . . . and there were some who

fray," a form of bushwhacking practiced in England as late as the Wars of the Roses or the period of the Paston letters (1422-1509).[1] And dueling, of course, was abused by bullies who baited inferior swordsmen into fighting them, the challenged having the choice of probable death or the loss of his "honor"—which is to say the respect of his peers.

* De Clisson was one of a dozen or so nobles put to death by Philip VI for their alleged involvement with the English.

drank wine which was brought to them in bottles. They re-
buckled on their armor which had gone undone, and dressed
their wounds. . . . Then the battle recommenced as stoutly as
before and lasted a long while. They had short swords of Bordeaux, tough and sharp, and boar-spears and daggers, and some
had axes, and therewith they dealt one another marvellously
great [blows], and some seized one another by the arms
a-struggling, and they struck one another and spared not. At last
the English had the worst of it; Brandebourg, their captain, was
slain, with eight of his comrades; and the rest yielded themselves
prisoners . . . Sir Robert, and his comrades who remained alive
. . . carried them off to Castle Josselin . . . and then admitted
them to ransom when they all were cured, for there was none
that was not grievously wounded, French as well as English. I
saw afterwards," Froissart continues, "sitting at the table of King
Charles [V] of France, a Breton knight who had been in it . . .
and he had a face so carved and cut that he showed full well
how good a fight had been fought. The matter was talked of in
many places; and some set it down as a very poor, and others
as a very swaggering, business." The Battle of the Thirty, for
centuries commemorated by a "simple stone" set up beside the
road from Ploermel to Josselin, received a full-sized monument
in 1811, and survives in the more detailed histories of the period
as a sort of military curiosity. It apparently served no practical
purpose; we do not hear that Ploermel was surrendered in consequence of it. The very fact that it received so much attention
argues that on the battlefield such regard for principles of fair
play was distinctly exceptional.

In another incident of the time, during Edward's abortive campaign of 1339, a party of English knights rode into a French town
where John, Duke of Normandy (later John II), was bivouacked.
Their object was to kidnap him, but finding that too difficult, they
took some French knights prisoner instead. While making their
way out of the town, however, they stirred up an alarm. Realizing they could not hope to escape with their prisoners, they released them on the latter's word of honor that they would present
themselves to the English in Brabant. The French knights are
said to have done so and, in due course, been ransomed.[3]

In 1363, after John II had returned to France from his English captivity, he learned that one of his sons, the Duke of Anjou, whom the English held as a hostage pending the execution of the treaty of Bretigny, had escaped. John, in other matters, including family ones, capable of great ruthlessness, was said in this case to have been quite upset. His son had been guilty of a breach of faith. "If good faith," Guizot has him saying, "were banished from the world, it ought to find asylum in the hearts of kings."[4] He then announced his intention to return to England in his son's stead. His councilors at Amiens, who heard him, quite naturally protested, but he maintained that he would be in no danger since "he had found in his brother, the king of England, in the queen, and in his nephews their children, so much loyalty, honor and courtesy. . . ."[4] (One chronicler of the time, William of Nangis, adds: "Some persons said that the king was minded to go to England to amuse himself."[4]) Whatever his motives, he went, dying the following year, evidently of natural causes, "at the Savoy hotel in London."*

These episodes have faint equivalents in, for instance, the combats between the famous "aces" and fighter-plane squadrons of World War I, and in the magnanimous German sea raider of the same war, Count von Luckner, who is supposed to have sunk none of his victims without warning and to have treated the survivors more as guests than as prisoners aboard his own ship.† But the grim functionalism which has overtaken warfare since the fourteenth century, and which has been a major feature of war in most periods, does not favor this sporting approach. What

---

* Nor was this sort of conduct confined to the nobility of Europe. Almost two hundred years earlier, in the Holy Land, Saladin, losing patience with Raynald of Chatillon, who had been harassing Moslem traders from his great stronghold of Krak, suddenly appeared before the place and laid siege to it. Inside, a royal marriage was going on. A message, together with a bit of bridal cake, was sent to the Saracen commander, who thereupon "gave strict orders . . . that the nuptial tower of the bride and bridegroom should be scrupulously respected by his archers and artillery."[5] (The artillery referred to was of course not cannon but catapults and the like.) Saladin discontinued the siege shortly afterwards. He never took the fortress, but did not need to, as five years later he all but obliterated the crusaders in a pitched battle at Hattin (1187).

† When I was a boy in boarding school in New England, Count von Luckner came to give us a talk about his war experiences. He was a jovial man, very keen on fitness, who ended his presentation by tearing a Manhattan telephone book in two.

there was of true chivalry in the Middle Ages largely disappeared with the rise of the Swiss pikemen, the Landsknechts, and the larger mixed armies of the fifteenth and sixteenth centuries. Even in Edward III's day, it was a rare and somewhat fragile phenomenon, always in danger of being swept away in the emotional excesses of battle.

Edward the Black Prince,* who at sixteen had commanded a front-line "battle" at Crécy and later defeated John II at Poitiers, subsequently married Joan, "the fair maid of Kent" (a love match fortunately approved by his father), and set up his court in Bordeaux as the English ruler of Aquitaine. Though he ended by taxing his subjects rather heavily, he had some administrative skill, suppressing the "free companies" (essentially unemployed soldiery) which were then ravaging other parts of France unchecked, and favoring the towns over the local landed gentry. Unfortunately, he went campaigning in Spain, where he defeated du Guesclin and caught a disease (possibly malaria) which was soon to kill him. Upon his return the Aquitanian nobles rose in revolt and the Hundred Years' War was on again. When Limoges surrendered to the enemy, the Prince seems to have taken it as a personal affront. So ill he had to direct operations from a litter, he laid siege to the place, mined its walls, and forced an entry. "A horrible butchery [followed], for no quarter was given, neither age nor sex spared. The women and children threw themselves in vain on their knees before the prince to beg their lives. He looked grimly on while they were slaughtered before his eyes until several thousand . . . had been cut down. . . . The bishop, on whom the chief guilt of the treason lay, was seized in his palace. The prince swore that he would have his head, and only refrained . . . at the entreaty of Pope Urban . . . [The] captains, John de Villemur, Roger de Beaufort and Hugh de la Roche, drew up their men, with banners unfurled, before an old wall. There they stood, at bay, defending themselves with desperate valor, till nearly all were struck down. The prince

---

* He was known to his contemporaries as Edward of Woodstock. His more romantic surname seems to trace back only to the sixteenth century and to refer to his supposed habit of wearing black armor. Guizot remarks bitterly that at the siege of Limoges he truly became the Black Prince. At age seven (in 1337) he was made Duke of Cornwall, the first duke ever named in England.

watched . . . from his litter, and spared the gallant commanders who were engaged in hot combat with the Duke of Lancaster and the Earls of Pembroke and Cambridge, in recognition of their bravery."[6]

That done, Edward fired the town. Even at the peak of his ferocity, however, he apparently could not bring himself to exterminate those of the highest ranks, but contented himself by killing numbers of their subjects, most of whom were doubtless without complicity in the French régime but simply the creatures of whatever government happened to be in control at the moment.* This policy of punishing the mass for the man, of deflecting anger from enemies of one's own class to their underlings or the general populace, who are often mere bystanders, seems to be a basic principle in warfare. It was perhaps never more so than in feudal times, when class divisions were most absolute† and when the common citizenry had least to say in affairs of state. The same principle, however, is in use today—witness the mass bombings of London and of German cities in World War II or of North Vietnam in the mid-1960s. Unlike our ancestors, we have an elaborate rationale for such actions.‡ They are aimed at "enemy installations," or are a form of "psychological warfare"— essentially an extension of Clausewitzian principles to include not merely the enemy's armed forces but everyone on the other side.* As Tinbergen and others have pointed out, man is one of

* However, some historians report that sentiment in Aquitaine was then running in favor of France, so Edward's suspicions, if not his methods, were perhaps justified.

† So that killing a man's serfs and townspeople, who were almost by definition of another and greatly inferior race, was hardly to be distinguished from destroying his physical property.

‡ On the positive side, captured generals are rarely subjected to the indignities or outrages suffered by common prisoners. Moreover, some generals have expressed an aversion to killing their opposite numbers. In Poland, Charles XII happened to be encamped across a river from his adversary, Augustus, who daily promenaded on the far bank. One of Charles's soldiers thought he could pick the Polish king off, but Charles forbade it, threatening to hang the man if he did so.

* C. P. Snow's memoir on the Lindemann-Tizard struggle makes it plain that in advocating mass bombing Lindemann was probably intent upon punishment of the Germans. American bombing raids in North Vietnam were routinely described in press releases as being aimed at bridges, factories, etc., but American observers on the spot reported seeing small villages obliterated and noted the high percentage of CBUs (cluster bomb units) used, for in-

the few mammals singularly lacking in any innate mechanism which deters him from destroying his own kind.[7] What the ethologists have failed to notice is that one mechanism—namely, regard for an opponent's social status—does act to limit our ferocity,* and not always for reasons as obvious as the fear of reprisals.

One form which this limitation took in the Middle Ages—when both nobles and clergy spent much time fighting—was a principle according to which, as an aristocrat, one granted one's equals something like a fair fight. While often overridden by political considerations it was still perhaps a principle of some consequence, leading to "feats of arms" such as, for example, John Seton's before Noyon.

While his son was engaged in the destruction of Limoges, Edward III dispatched a force of 6000, including a company of Scottish warriors, to Calais. Under command of Robert Knolles, they marched across the north of France into Champagne, ravaging and levying "blackmail" on the smaller towns.[5] At Noyon, a Scot, John Seton, "signalised his bravado by a singular feat. Spurring his horse and followed by a single page, he dashed right up to the palisade . . . jumped over the barrier sword in hand and rushed at a dozen French cavaliers standing near. 'Gentlemen,' he cried, 'since you will not come out, I have come in. . . . Conquer me if you can.' Thereupon he laid about him . . . —one against a dozen—the townspeople standing by in great admiration while he stretched a couple of his assailants on the ground. Anon his page approached the palisade and shouted, 'My lord it is time to stop, for ours are going.' With two or three . . . strokes to part with, the . . . Scot vaulted back and mounted his horse. 'Adieu, adieu, gentlemen, many thanks,' cried he, galloping away amid the applause of both cavaliers and citizens."[8]

However much such episodes may have been improved upon in the retelling, it seems probable that some did occur and in-

---

stance, against Hanoi. The cluster bomb is a device for scattering phosphorus-covered shrapnel over large areas. It is useless against "installations" but highly effective in inflicting a horrible death on people.

* The fact that the Nazi leaders were, by other nations' standards, such a low-class lot may have made it all the easier to execute them. By contrast Hirohito, a "legitimate" ruler of the medieval type, was permitted to survive in decent seclusion, much the way John II lived on in England after Poitiers.

volved (as Guizot said of the Battle of the Thirty) a curious mixture of motives—not merely biological ones, but also some impulse toward purity in the manly virtues, some not altogether animal pride in being able to hold oneself together and adhere to certain ideals of conduct even in the face of death. The Knights Templar, whom Philip le Bel arrested, imprisoned, and accused of fearful crimes, evidently in order to rob them of their great wealth, mostly confessed under torture to such offenses as denying God and spitting on (or "near") the Cross.[9] But many later retracted and died bravely at the stake,* one of the last and most dramatic cases being that of Jacques de Molay, the grand master of the order. Brought before the king, the papal representative, and the public at Notre Dame in Paris (1314) he was expected to repeat his earlier confessions and in return be granted life imprisonment. He did not, but announced to the multitude that he and his order were innocent. He and the others with him were burned at once.† The fortitude of these men under the horrible injustices inflicted upon them suggests that close connection between chivalric and Christian ideals which the knightly orders were in fact supposed to represent. Their behavior was certainly not, by present standards, realistic, and many today might regard it as demented.

Modern historians have suggested that in encounters of the time the attack was often made head-on because that was the more "honorable" course, in contrast to feinting, moving by the flank, and so on. We probably do not have enough evidence to decide whether that was ever or often the case, but during Edward's siege of Calais, in 1347, an incident occurred which suggests that some such notion was at least in the air.

Quite late in the siege, when John de Vienne and his fellow townsmen had been reduced to near-starvation, Philip appeared before Calais with an army, apparently intending to relieve them. Edward, however, had so skillfully entrenched himself (and Philip had become so wary of his enemy), that the French king

* The fate prescribed by the Inquisition for those who denied confessions officially made (i.e., under torture).

† Nor does there seem to have been any general outcry. The chief complaint surviving from the period is that of the owners of the land on which de Molay and the rest were burned; the proprietors evidently felt that their rights had been violated.

saw no promising avenue of attack. Even at the shoreline, Edward's fleet, loaded with archers and armed with a few cannon, stood in so close that the French did not dare attempt an assault over the coastal downs—apparently the only piece of unobstructed ground around the town.[10] After considering the position for several days, Philip appears to have sent a message to Edward suggesting that he come out for a fair fight in the open. On the evidence of a letter Edward wrote at the time to the Archbishop of Canterbury, the English king, after parleys between representatives of both sides ("two cardinals assisting"[10]), agreed to this proposal and recommended that four English and four French knights choose a battle site. We cannot be absolutely certain that these negotiations took place, because shortly afterwards, to the astonishment of John de Vienne, if not of Edward, Philip and the French burned their tents and hastily withdrew, with the English in close pursuit, harassing their rear guard and capturing quantities of baggage. Given that the negotiations *may* have taken place, they reveal a type of military thinking which any commander today would consider idiotic. The fact is, however, that battles in the Middle Ages were sometimes fought by this kind of prearrangement.

One reason, as Oman unkindly points out, was that "the opposing armies, being guided by no very definite aims and invariably neglecting to keep in touch with each other by means of outposts and vedettes, might often miss each other altogether." Moreover, they found many problems in maneuver insuperable. Oman gives an example: "Bela IV of Hungary and Ottokar II of Bohemia were in arms in 1260 and both were equally bent on fighting; but when they sighted each other it was only to find that the river March was between them. To pass a stream in the face of an enemy was a task far beyond the ability of the average thirteenth-century general. . . . Accordingly it was reckoned nothing strange when the Bohemian courteously invited his adversary either to cross the March unhindered, and fight in due form on the west bank, or to give him the same opportunity and grant a free passage to the Hungarian side. Bela chose the former alternative, forded the river without molestation, and fought on the other side the disastrous battle of Kressenbrunn."[11]

Of course, at close quarters—except in tourneys, where all was run according to rule—almost anything went; and quite under-standably so, since battles come down to killing, and in that extreme situation, face to face with one's opponent, it becomes difficult to remember, let alone to stick to, any code of decent be-havior. This in fact is the paradox of chivalry, that all etiquette or scrupulousness, when it ultimately involves the destruction of someone else or his destruction of oneself, becomes absurd, cer-tainly from a realistic standpoint but not less from a moral one. Chivalric ideals aimed at christianizing or making more decent a form of ancient behavior which is itself indecent and unchristian. Not only was the chivalric idea doomed to peter out in disillusion-ment and a renewed "realism"; it was also bound to work poorly and inefficiently even in its heyday because of the peculiar prac-tical difficulties just mentioned. So for all that they may have been models of knightly comportment themselves, many a medieval warrior ended, like John of Chandos, by being killed in the shape-less, catch-as-catch-can modern manner. While on a reconnoiter-ing expedition in Poitou, in 1370, Chandos and his band came upon some dismounted French defending a bridge. Clad in a white surcoat and full armor, but without a visor, he leaped from his horse and advanced with sword drawn. As he did so he lost his footing on the slippery ground and fell. A French squire, Jacques de St. Martin, thereupon rushed up and stabbed him in the eye, piercing his brain. (Chandos had lost one eye in a pre-vious engagement and supposedly did not see his opponent in time to turn his head away.)[12]

In short, to paraphrase another writer's remark about the Tem-plars,[9] the wonder is not that chivalry as an ethic of warfare failed, but that it worked even to the extent it did. At its apogee, it only slightly mitigated the (inherent, basically immitigable) nastiness of combat while perhaps contributing substantially to the stupidity with which most battles of the time seem to have been fought.

The beginnings of the modern unsportsmanlike era in warfare can be arbitrarily dated from the Hussite Wars of the early fif-teenth century. Jan Hus, rector of the University of Prague and a follower of the heretical Wycliffe, was lured to Constance on a promise of safe conduct, in 1415, where he was condemned by a papal council and burned. Four years later his followers, the Hussites, under Jan Ziska (and later under the two Prokops, the Great and the Lesser) went to war, inflicting a succession of stunning defeats upon the armies sent against them. As heretical in tactics as in religion, they used massed wagon columns armed with small cannon, formations which proved highly effective against the feudal cavalry of the Germans, and which also enabled the Hussite armies to keep in a state of constant battle readiness while on the march. Ziska's *Wagenburgs* were the first European *Panzers,* although no doubt ungainly-looking and moving at speeds we would consider absurdly slow. They were nonetheless an innovation which apparently stumped the best commanders the Catholics were able to call upon at the time.

In the next two centuries various combinations were tried on the battlefields of Western Europe. These included "cartes with gonnes"[13]—a sort of light horse artillery—and composite formations of pikemen and arquebusiers. During the sixteenth century the arquebus, the larger and heavier musket, and the wheel-lock pistol (which first appeared around 1550) became standard weapons. The arquebus had a barrel about three feet long, and fired a one-ounce ball to an effective range of sixty to seventy yards. The musket, with a barrel around four and a half feet long, had to be fired from a rest; it threw a two-ounce ball, supposedly to an effective range of two hundred yards.[14] Both pieces were matchlocks, loaded by ramrod from the muzzle and discharged by a complicated mechanism which carried a bit of smoldering string ("match") to the firing pan at pull of the trigger. The odd thing was that in this same period archery began declining in England, although the longbow had about the same range as the musket and more than made up for its lower shocking power by its far higher firing rate and greater resistance to the weather. "Match" was almost useless in the rain and sometimes led to explosions of powder stores on the field even under the best of conditions. Bowmen, on the other hand, waterproofed their strings by oiling them, and usually carried spares.

The wheel-lock pistol was fired by a spring mechanism which, when released, caused a rotating burr to strike sparks from a small piece of pyrites, the sparks being intended to ignite the powder in the pan. To be effective against even lightly armored troops, these pieces had to be fired practically at point-blank range. Their stocks, though often elaborately worked and ornamented, were too slightly curved to make for handiness in aiming, which under the circumstances hardly mattered. They also suffered from fragility and crankiness. Their springs easily fatigued and broke; the lump of pyrites tended to slip out of position or to be knocked loose in the heat of a charge. Nevertheless, the pistol became quite a popular weapon. The shock troops with which Henry IV of Navarre won his greatest victories in the Huguenot Wars were cavalrymen armed with sword and pistol. His technique was to intersperse squadrons of this type with formations of musketeers and arquebusiers, those at the ends of the battle line being known as *enfants perdus* because of their exposed position. The front ranks of his arquebusiers fired from a kneeling position so as to permit bringing the largest possible number of pieces to bear in a single volley. Like Edward III, he invited attack, if possible on a narrow front with some natural protection for his flanks, and with his cavalry drawn up four to six ranks deep, as opposed to the usual two. He had in addition a few small cannon which he used sparingly but with effect at the important battle of Coutras (1587). They appear to have galled his late-feudal adversary, the Duke of Joyeuse, into making an ill-advised frontal assault. On another occasion (Arques, 1589) Henry tipped the balance of action in his favor by opening a flanking fire at the critical moment, this time using the guns of a nearby eleventh-century castle built by an uncle of William the Conqueror.

Coutras, which occurred the year before the Armada and figured, somewhat unfortunately as it turned out, in the grand strategy of Philip II of Spain, began with the odds heavily in favor of the Catholic League under Joyeuse.* The young duke and his armored noblemen came upon Henry by a surprise march, catching him in a difficult position and outnumbering him as well. Henry, whose original object had been to evade battle, now de-

---

* The duke had been a favorite of King Henry III of Valois, whose taste ran to handsome young men. Henry III, whose security depended upon maintaining a delicate balance of power, never seemed too anxious that the Catholic League and the house of Guise (which Spain subsidized) should totally defeat his Huguenot cousin, Henry of Navarre. Moreover, by the time of Coutras, he reportedly had a new favorite, Louis, Duke of Epernon.

cided to accept it. He placed his four squadrons of heavy cavalry, each several ranks deep, in the center, with arquebusiers in between, and his light cavalry and infantry on the wings. On a rise to his left he stationed his three cannon. His infantry, on the right, were behind thickets and a ditch, to protect them from direct attack by horse. By comparison with the host they faced, the Huguenot troops appeared dingy and workmanlike, but their dispositions, notwithstanding the little time they had had to make them, were excellent.

Opposite, drawn up *en haye*—in line, two ranks deep—with pennons fluttering from its lances, and an assortment of splendid gear reminiscent of the days of Charles the Bold, the army of Joyeuse dressed ranks and prepared to attack. As it did so, Henry's cannon opened an enfilading fire on the main line, causing considerable confusion. The duke's first charge on the left, against the Huguenot light cavalry, drove it back. Henry's infantry on both wings then engaged, and some of the forwardmost Catholic cavalry was caught in a flanking fire from his arquebusiers. The duke's right wing, evidently caught by surprise, also fell into disorder. At this point he ordered his main body in the center into a headlong assault. Singing their battle hymn, the 118th Psalm, the Huguenot heavy squadrons stood waiting for them. At twenty yards the arquebusiers let off a volley and Henry's sword-and-pistol cavaliers countercharged, breaking through the royalist line and wheeling upon its fragments.* Within minutes the Catholic army was annihilated. A few noblemen who offered to surrender were treated with chivalric courtesy, but Joyeuse was not among them. Having sworn to take no prisoners that day and having distinguished himself for bloodthirstiness in the past, he was shot dead, though not before trying to give himself up and calling out the amount of his ransom. Having fought by the methods, he appealed to the code of a bygone time—a code which he himself had

* It is clear that heavy cavalry armed with lances, once attacked in this way, is at a severe disadvantage, especially if their line is broken in a number of places and the enemy can come back at them while they are still discarding their lances in order to draw whatever close-quarter weapons they may be carrying. Moreover, the heavier mounts used by armored lancers must have been slow to turn round, even when there was room to do so. None of these points seems to have made much impression on the military thought of the time, especially that of the traditionalist upper classes in France.

honored rarely enough—and in both attempts failed. After he was dead, the Huguenots were so intent on wiping out his entire force that Henry was at some pains to stop them, an act perhaps less of mercy than of policy, since the evidence suggests that he was shortly in touch with Henry of Valois via Montaigne with a view to preventing the rift between himself and his Catholic sovereign from becoming too great.

Out of 10,000 men, the Duke lost 3500 hundred slain. Henry's force of 6300 reportedly lost only 200 in killed and wounded. His methods on the battlefield in general worked quite well, not only because sound in themselves but because they remained a puzzle to those who faced them. At Arques, for instance, with 9000 men he beat the Duke of Mayenne commanding 24,000. In his second battle with Mayenne, near Paris, in 1589, he had 9000 foot and 3000 horse, as against forces of the Catholic League numbering 25,000. Mayenne, though he had meanwhile introduced some tactical refinements and this time had his enemy on an open plain, was trounced again, losing 4000 men to Henry's 500. The League became so alarmed at this trend of events that they brought one of their best commanders, Alexander of Parma, from the Netherlands with his army. Parma showed great skill in maneuvering against Henry (now King of France), forcing him to raise the siege of Rouen, but in turn nearly getting trapped against the Seine himself. (He escaped by throwing up a bridge and marching his army over it and away by night. He never fought a standup engagement with the French king, and the strain of avoiding one is said shortly afterwards to have killed him.)

One of the refinements introduced by Mayenne at his second great defeat was the use of German *Reiters*, who practiced what was called the caracole—an attack of mounted pistoleers who rode up in close order to within a few feet of the enemy's ranks, fired into them pointblank and wheeled off in file, permitting the next wave of *Reiters* to do the same. This technique had had some success in breaking up phalanxes of pikemen *à la Suisse;* but when the ratio of "pike" to "shot" had fallen as low as it had in the armies of Henry IV (about one pikeman to four arquebusiers, as opposed to one to one in Mayenne's) the caracole technique failed because it could be stopped by arquebus fire before the attackers themselves had come close enough to be effective. (In this battle the *Reiters* were fired on in flank, fell into disorder, and disrupted Mayenne's main cavalry attack with the usual result.)

Since the days when the Swiss had perfected their system of fighting in great squares of pikemen, during their wars against the Hapsburgs and Charles the Bold (late fifteenth century), a kind of slow-moving struggle for tactical advantage had been going on between infantry of this type and the once predominant feudal cavalry. "Cartes with gonnes" and the much heavier pieces of artillery such as Charles VIII of France carried with him into Italy, at the end of the fifteenth century, offered a way of breaching pike formations, as did musket and arquebus fire. For their part, the tacticians of the pike added firepower in increasing ratio, in some cases placing arquebusiers on each corner of the square so that these could enfilade an attack on any of its sides, thus making the whole formation a kind of walking fortress with salients whose fire flanked its walls. Another system of organization allowed the arquebusiers to sally out from inside of the square (normally reserved for halberdiers and unarmored pikemen), fire, and run back in again to reload. The pike itself meanwhile reached enormous length—up to twenty feet—so that as many as six rows of points projected beyond the front rank. Adding "shot" to pikes obviously made it possible either to contest the enemy's own missile attack or to discourage his cavalry onslaught at a distance, or both.

Anyone today seeing those dense masses of pikemen would be apt to conclude that the likeliest weapon to use against them would be the fieldpiece. But while artillery figured quite promisingly in the Italian Wars of Charles VIII and his successors—for example, at the battle of Ravenna in 1512, when the French breached the enemy's line of trenches by enfilading it with twenty-four guns—its development both tactically and in a technological sense continued to be surprisingly slow and uneven. Most of the ideas embodied in modern firearms—including breach loading and rapid fire—were in fact hit upon very early and then abandoned, no doubt as "visionary." (For instance, Jan Ziska, in his *Wagenburgs*, used the ribaudequin, a multibarreled weapon something like a Gatling gun.) Field artillery, properly speaking and properly used, did not appear until, in the seventeenth century, Gustavus Adolphus devised the tactics and the weapon to match.* (It took two more centuries for the idea of the ribaude-quin to be picked up more or less where Ziska had left it.) It was as if professional military minds—not merely of the feudal type but true professionals from the *condottieri* on down to the Thirty Years' War and even after—boggled at a problem so intricate. To design a suitable fieldpiece and supply it in quantity required engineering and long-term preparation; maintenance of numbers of them in the field presented a formidable problem in supply and organization; to use them effectively involved training a special corps, preferably a permanent one rather than a body of short-term enlistees. All of this seems to have been quite beyond the leaders of the time. The combination of foresight and technical competence needed was to be found less in the military than in the artisan and burgher classes, it being for this reason perhaps that for "more than 300 years after the first employment of ordnance, the men working the guns and the transport drivers were still civilians." Even in Gustavus Adolphus' army, though a soldier (Lennart Torstensson) commanded his artillery, "the transport and the drivers were still hired, and even the gunners were chiefly concerned for the safety of their pieces. . . . These civilian 'artists,' as they were termed, owed no more duty to the prince than any other employees. . . . Soldiers as drivers do not appear until 150 years later, and in the meanwhile companies of 'firelocks' and 'fusiliers' . . . came into existence, as much to prevent the gunners and drivers from running away as to protect them from the enemy."†15

In England, in the sixteenth century, where the stimulus of continuous land fighting was lacking, the progress of artillery was even slower. The author just cited mentions that "in the reign of Elizabeth, some of the Tower gunners were over ninety years of

---

* Of course others had anticipated him, notably Maurice of Nassau, at the end of the preceding century; and the French in the same period had invented the limber, which Webster defines as "the detachable forepart of a gun carriage or caisson consisting of two wheels, an axle and a pole." True horse artillery appeared only with Frederick the Great, in the mid-eighteenth century.

† As late as the battle of Valmy (1792) this civilian element caused trouble. One of the critical moments in that engagement came when an ammunition dump on the French side was hit and blew up, causing the artillery wagoners to take flight—as it happened, without fatal consequences.

age. Complaints as to the inefficiency of these men were frequent. . . ."[15]

At the prompting of Machiavelli, not to say of brute necessity, the organization of other army personnel and the development of new tactics did go forward on the Continent during the same century. A comparable improvement did not, however, appear in statecraft. Monarchs like Charles V and his successor, Philip II of Spain, continued to act on the old proprietary theory of government; and it was this theory or instinct, combined with an implacable orthodoxy,* which appears to have determined Philip to retain and forcibly convert his Protestant people in the Netherlands ("his" by dynastic right, i.e., by inheritance).† The resulting war was a masterpiece of inept frightfulness, in the end reducing Spain to that position of inconsequence in world affairs which she has ever since occupied. Philip's career is worth mention as exemplifying a type of bad generalship so rigid in its principles and global in its scope as to seem almost of this century. A hard-willed, bustling bureaucrat, whose passion for paperwork is said to have set the style for generations of Spanish officials to come, he consistently assigned his commanders, good and bad, projects they could not hope to carry out. (Besides Parma, two others, Don Luis of Requesens and Don John of Austria, were reportedly driven to their graves by the vexations encountered in his service, not unlike laboratory rats confronted by what its inventor has aptly called the "no-solution problem.")

It was, one might add, simply through a whim of his father's that the Low Countries were made part of Philip's inheritance and so became victims of a catastrophe as arbitrary as an earthquake. (His other properties included Naples, Sicily, Franche

---

* Rather predictably, Philip II was an enthusiast of the Inquisition. At his instance three new branches were set up in the colonies, in Lima, Cartagena, and Mexico. He also persuaded the pope to create an itinerant "inquisition of the galleys" or of the "fleets and armies." To have been a galley slave accused of heresy by roving inquisitors must have come close to exhausting the possibilities of human misfortune.

† Philip was the son of Charles V by Isabella of Portugal. A certain violence of temperament seems to have run in his family. In 1497 his great-aunt Margaret married a Spaniard of the houses of Aragon and Castile, appropriately named Don Juan. She so maddened him with love of her that he died six months later, reportedly of exhaustion.[16]

Comté, the duchy of Milan, and, of course, huge territories in the New World, none of them in any very logical way related to Spain.* After Charles V's abdication in 1555, Philip seems slowly to have convinced himself that retention of the Netherlands and the forcible suppression there of heresy (Protestantism) were essential to the Spanish future. In a sense he was right. The Low Countries were rich, productive and forward-looking, whereas Spain was backward, barely unified, and dependent for its grandeur chiefly on what it could wring from its client states by taxation, or from its colonies by looting.† Under the circumstances any policy which seemed likely to bind the Netherlands more tightly to the Stepmother Country was, from the Spanish standpoint, only sense. The policy Philip chose, however, was ill suited to that end. He evidently felt that religious thought control, rather than more and better trade relations, was essential to the entente he had in mind. (Similarly, in our dealings with the Communists, we do not use business to undermine and neutralize ideology, but the other way around.)

So, having first appointed Margaret, Duchess of Parma—a woman on the whole of some sense and restraint—regent of the Netherlands, Philip repented of his choice, and in 1567 dispatched the Duke of Alva with an army and with full powers to deal with the situation as he saw fit. Alva lost no time. One of his first acts was to set up a tribunal known as the Council of Troubles (shortly rechristened the Council of Blood), at which he himself presided. Its function was to "try" supposed heretics. "A swarm of commissioners ransacked the provinces in search of delinquents, and the council sat daily for hours, condemning the accused, almost without a hearing, in batches together. The executioners were ceaselessly at work with stake, sword and gibbet."[18]

With this disastrous stroke of policy, Philip precipitated a war which was to last almost without remission from the battle of Heiligerlee (in May of 1568) until the truce of 1609, eleven years after his own death. By that time Dutch independence was a *fait*

---

* It is said that in Sicily the Mafia first came into existence as an anti-Spanish underground—in its later tactics, perhaps, profiting from the oppressor's example.

† "The mother-country herself produced little but wool, fruit and iron; her manufacturers were naught; her industries suffered; her population steadily decreased."[17]

accompli and Spanish power on the way to being broken. The same war, continued until 1648, or a total of eighty years, completed the process. By its end, Spain had lost a second Armada of seventy-seven ships and 24,000 men to the Dutch Admiral Tromp in the battle of the Downs (October, 1639); Portugal had regained its independence; and all that remained to the Spanish, besides their weak and ill-administered domains in the New World, was that reputation for fanatic savagery which the Duke of Alva, during his long service to two kings, had done so much to establish.*

Although Philip had had occasion to restrain Alva from excesses before (in Italy, after 1655), he allowed his commander six years in the Netherlands, first as Grand Inquisitor, later as the most bloody of field generals, before recalling him. Alva erected a statue in Antwerp representing himself standing on the necks of two smaller figures symbolic of the two estates of the Low Countries, and with the help of his still more brutal son, Don Frederick of Toledo, undertook to realize that image by the systematic reduction of the country. In one of the opening moves of this struggle, William of Orange issued letters of marque creating a body of privateers, the Sea Beggars,† who were to play an enormous part in the undoing of Spain and the emergence of Holland as a major naval power.

The success of the Sea Beggars (who in 1572 seized Brill, Flushing, and two other ports) inspired a general revolt. Alva's counteroffensive by land was of historic ferocity. He took Malines and punished it by abandoning the inhabitants to three days of sack and murder. This action was followed by the sack of Zutphen (under Don Frederick) and the Naarden affair. In the latter place, the townspeople surrendered on promises of clemency, and by order of the Spanish commander set out a banquet for his troops. As the banquet was ending a bell tolled, whereupon the

---

*Fernando Alvarez de Toledo, Duke of Alva (1508-1583), was first given a command by Charles V and fought at Mühlberg and in the wars against the French in Italy.

† Originally, the opponents of Spain in the Low Countries had taken the name *beggars* from a remark made to Margaret of Parma by one of her councilors: "What, Madam, is your Highness afraid of these beggars?" Their motto, worn on amulets, seemed to involve a pun: "Faithful to the king, *jusqu'à la besace*"—besace meaning either wallet or beggary.

presumably calmed and well-fed soldiers rose from their tables
and slaughtered their hosts almost to a man. In its sheer modernity, anticipating the sort of cold-blooded butchery practiced by
the Germans in World War II, this event stands out as an oddity
of bloodthirstiness even in that bloody age. The cumulative effect
of these acts, like that of the Nazi outrages in Russia, was to unify
the victim people as almost no other course could have done, so
that operations which were already difficult for the invader soon
became prohibitive. The attack on Haarlem, which started in the
winter of the same year (1572) and ended in July of the next, was
resisted by the Dutch with almost maniacal obstinacy. As at Leningrad, centuries later, virtually the whole populace mobilized.
A women's arquebus corps was formed. To inflict casualties and
keep the enemy off balance, the defenders made frequent sallies.
When the Spanish attempted to mine the walls, Dutch engineers
countermined and blew up their works. During assaults on the
town, the besieged flung hoops of burning pitch over the heads
of the oncoming Spaniards. Spanish prisoners were hung on the
walls in full view of their countrymen outside. The Dutch outdid
themselves. Alva had only the highest praise for them in his
letters to Philip. (The town was nonetheless given over to pillage
when it fell.) The capture of Haarlem cost the Spanish 12,000
killed.

It was during the early part of that siege that one of the oddi-
ties of war of the period occurred. Standing as it does on a promontory, Haarlem was, at the beginning of Spanish operations,
partly surrounded by ice. The Dutch put a party of arquebusiers
on skates. These rounded the point and swept suddenly inshore,
firing upon the besiegers at close range, no doubt achieving considerable surprise at very small risk of pursuit.

(A still stranger action took place in 1574, during the siege of
Leyden. There the dikes were opened, flooding the surrounding
country. Dutch attempts to relieve the town still failed for some
months. In the meantime, apparently, both sides constructed
fleets of flat-bottomed boats. When finally a storm raised the flood
level sufficiently, the Dutch Admiral Boisot's Sea Beggars, manning scows and armed with harpoons, fought an old-style hull-
to-hull naval engagement with a similar Spanish squadron some
miles inland among the half-submerged trees and farmhouses of

the Dutch countryside. The Dutch won and Leyden was relieved.)

Besides losing 12,000 men at Haarlem, Don Frederick allowed himself to be pinned down there for over seven months, which gained the Dutch time to prepare against him. The result was that the next Spanish attack, on the town of Alkmaar, was beaten off; the dikes were cut; and Don Frederick was forced to withdraw. Shortly afterwards (October, 1573) Alva's fleet was caught in the Zuyder Zee and destroyed by the Sea Beggars, its admiral being taken prisoner. By December of the same year, because of interruption of sea lines, Spanish troops were without pay and beginning to mutiny.* Alva was relieved of command and "left Brussels, carrying with him the curses of the people over whom he had tyrannized for six terrible years."[19] Arriving in Spain in some disfavor, he could not forbear boasting that besides those he had caused to be killed in or after battle, he had taken an additional 18,000 lives by formal execution.

Alva's successors were men of more moderation, but the change in policy (if it was that, and not simply a question of the generals who happened to be available) came too late. By then (1573) Philip appears to have put himself in a position in which he could neither withdraw with honor nor go forward with much hope of success. He chose to go forward, and not against one enemy at a time but against his two main enemies simultaneously. The decision was evidently dictated—as it has been in the case of several notable statesmen of our own day—by a combination of personal grandeur and ideological inflexibility.

Philip lived in a curious world in which the medieval system of rulership, based upon blood lines and nations conceived of as heritable properties, had come to exist side by side with a more modern type of politics in which "interests" aligned themselves not so much with houses as with religious doctrines (houses of course following suit, so that besides being the champions of themselves, they also became crusaders, dedicated to ridding the

---

* In 1576, Spain, now severely harassed by Dutch and English privateers, fell still further in arrears of pay. The troops mutinied, marched on Antwerp, and subjected the town to two days and nights of looting and massacre—an event remembered still as the Spanish Fury. Its effect was to complete the (official) unification of the Netherlands against Spain.

world of deviant fellow Christians). One can imagine the confusion which this dualism in matters of state might have added to events in the present century.

As it was, royalty, under the emergent system of state-craft, finally grew to be an irrelevance and, depending on the country, was politely or forcibly put aside; but the optimism engendered in Europe and especially in America by this change seems to have been premature. Having rid ourselves of an expensive and often incompetent warrior aristocracy, and replaced it with university-trained professionals, we find these to be, in many cases, no great improvement, particularly in point of cost. Nor has the secularization of the objectives of war made it more sane or infrequent. On the contrary; our wars are fully as ferocious and perhaps a thousand times as destructive as any ever inspired by the word of the Lord.

Philip was quite modern in the scale on which he tried to wage his, but medieval in the reasons he gave for doing so. The word of the Lord, as he construed it, was the foundation of his policy, not merely in the Lowlands but everywhere, including Spain itself. There, pursuant to his edict of 1568, he set out to uproot the Mohammedanism persisting among the Moriscos of Granada. (It had been all but persecuted out of existence after the conquest of Granada in 1492; but like our own domestic anticommunists, Philip may have felt that the faith had become the more dangerous for being vestigial and hidden.) The result was a rebellion which lasted two years and devastated the province. Arising just as Spain was becoming involved in the Netherlands, this upheaval could hardly have been provoked at a worse moment.* Nor did it end when the king's troops had restored quiet. Numbers of Moriscos fled to North Africa, took to the sea as pirates, and began raiding the Spanish coast, sometimes with the help of tipoffs from their kinsfolk back home. The whole affair dragged on for decades—to as late as 1610, when Henry IV of France, just before his assassination, entered into negotiations with the Moriscos with a view to mounting a combined attack on Spain. As with all Philip's mistakes, the consequences of this one seemed endless. Beyond

---

* Rather as if Johnson, having embroiled us in Vietnam, had decided to suppress blacks and student dissidents at home, if necessary by mass shootouts. Philip, however, had no voters to consider.

doubt, however, his worst misstep was to incur the enmity of England.

He first made himself violently unpopular in that country by marrying Bloody Mary (in 1557) and associating himself with an attempt to reconvert Englishmen to the True Faith by means of heresy trials and a few executions.* This program collapsed upon the untimely death of the queen in 1558, but it had already been carried far enough to put relations between the two countries on a footing of hatred and suspicion which was to become almost permanent.

Shortly after Elizabeth had ascended the throne, Philip made her a proposal of marriage. (She of course refused him.) From that point onward, with some temporary remissions, Anglo-Spanish relations deteriorated steadily. A prime instrument of Elizabeth's policy *vis-à-vis* Spain became her privateers, who enabled her to wage a covert war and to enrich her own realm at the same time. Philip for his part felt that he had found the instrument he needed in the person of Mary Queen of Scots, a woman for whom the world has since developed a mysterious affection. In countless histories and romantic novels she has come down to us as beautiful (which she probably was), romantic, courageous, and tragically abused. She was in fact something of a monster, and apparently stupid and headlong into the bargain. Having come to Scotland from Catherine de Medici's court, she so mismanaged her affairs that she was driven by her own subjects into protective custody in England. There, through the influence of Philip, she became involved in a succession of plots aimed at the dethronement of Elizabeth and the restoration of English catholicism. When the last of these intrigues—in which Mary had implicated her young lover and former page, Anthony Babington—was uncovered, Elizabeth and her councilors lost patience. Babington was executed in 1586 and a year afterward—quite belatedly, in the opinion of some—Mary herself bent her head to the axe.

It was entirely in character that Philip should have chosen as his agent for subversion a woman so incapable. Her heart was clearly not in politics, it was in bed. At least during her earlier

* In all about 300 were burned at the stake—a mere token.

years, her ferocity seems to have expended itself less upon enemies of the Church than upon lovers she had grown tired of, it
being this peculiarity which had aroused public wrath against
her and caused her to be expelled from Scotland.* Even as a
conspirator, one feels, her mind was not wholly on the job and
her choice of co-workers not as good as it might have been. To
the degree that she never managed to become more than an
egregious public nuisance, she was a positive liability to her patron, broadcasting his intentions to a nation already too well
aware of them, inflaming, by domestic alarms, a dislike of Spain
and "popery" already intense and likely to end in a most savage
conflict.

Perhaps the worst mistake an ambitious statesman can make is
to let those whom he intends to conquer know how little he
thinks of their fundamental beliefs, how he intends to reshape
these by force. For it is just here, in the realm of large vague
notions—theological or ideological as the fashion happens to be—
that men seem liable to the wildest fears and the most lunatic
intransigence. In matters of trade some degree of bargaining is
nearly always possible; over questions of religious or political
faith it almost never is. By the same logic, a commercial rival who
is likewise a heretic is by definition beyond the law, any atrocity
in war or chicanery in trade with him becoming perfectly permis-
sible, if not indeed an act of the highest patriotism. In England,
one consequence of Philip's aggressive orthodoxy was to turn
ordinary professional slave traders like John Hawkins and Francis
Drake into master buccaneers whose zeal and boldness were re-
doubled by the knowledge that every blow for themselves was
also one for the realm, possibly to be rewarded with a peerage.

* She was followed from France by the young poet Pierre de Chastelard,
who not long afterward was seized in her bedchamber and summarily
hanged. Her Italian secretary, David Rizzio, was then killed by Henry, Lord
Darnley, who happened to be her most recent *inamorato*. Next Mary took
up with James Hepburn, Fourth Earl of Bothwell, and Darnley's hour soon
struck. The little house in which she had installed him was blown up and
he, oddly enough, was found strangled in the garden outside. At this point
such a hullabaloo broke out that the new couple split up, Mary fleeing to
England and Bothwell into piracy in the North Sea. He ended up a prisoner
of King Frederick IV of Denmark, and his last letter from Mary was a request for a divorce so that she could marry the Duke of Norfolk. Bothwell
died in jail, insane. Norfolk was beheaded for treason.

(Hawkins was "granted a coat of arms with demi-Moor, or Negro, in chains, as his crest."[20]) They went into the business of buying blacks or hijacking them from Portuguese ships off the African coast and selling them in the New World, in defiance of Spain's proclaimed monopoly of that trade in her own colonies. The upshot was that Drake and Hawkins were, in a manner of speaking, ambushed by the Spanish in the harbor of San Juan de Ulloa in 1568, losing one of their ships (the *Jesus,* lent or chartered to them by the queen), and barely escaping with the other two. With these events, and the increasing numbers of English privateers engaged, under foreign letters of marque, in preying upon Spanish shipping to the Netherlands, small-scale naval warfare between the two countries became perennial, pending some more decisive encounter which might settle the whole matter. Neither Philip nor Elizabeth, however, was prepared to push hostilities further for the time being—Philip because of his preoccupation with the Netherlands and from a certain *folie de grandeur* which led him to underestimate England as a maritime rival.* Elizabeth for her part, almost up to the day the Armada appeared off her shores, remained opposed to war on grounds of thrift, continually checking her freebooters or countermanding orders to them which she had in the meantime come to consider rash. In 1572, when the Huguenot influence in France was abruptly checked and the Guise family returned to power by the Massacre of St. Bartholomew,† Elizabeth renewed relations with

---

* The Spanish appear to have gained much prestige from the naval battle of Lepanto in the Mediterranean, against the Turks, in 1571, even though their contribution in ships was small (twenty-four vessels out of a fleet of over two hundred). One of Philip's best commanders, the Marquis of Santa Cruz, fought in that battle and later, in the 1580s twice defeated the fleets sent against him by Catherine de Medici. From the Spanish standpoint it was an ominous mischance that he died early in 1588, while the Armada was still fitting out.

† Charles IX, who came to the French throne during the regency of his mother, Catherine de Medici, seems finally to have rebelled against her and favored the Huguenot cause in the person of Coligny, which in turn threatened to bring on war with Spain. The massacre, a *contrecoup* engineered by his mother, quickly went out of control, spreading from Paris through much of the country. In Paris alone the slaughter continued for upwards of three weeks (from Sunday, August 24, to September 17, 1572), and in the provinces until the beginning of October. The number killed has been estimated at 50,000, including Admiral Coligny and the antischolastic logician Pierre de la Ramée ("Everything that Aristotle taught was false"). Pope Gregory

Spain in the (possibly correct) belief that French occupation of the Lowlands, if it occurred, might be more menacing to England than the Spanish presence there. Philip briefly and tardily responded by sending an ambassador to London in 1576, but Parma's successes in the Netherlands seem to have encouraged him once more to suppose that he could handle both his principal enemies at once. The end result was of course the Armada (1588), an operation which involved the assembly of a vast fleet in Lisbon and of an invasion force (including landing craft for both infantry and cavalry) by Parma in the Netherlands. Drake's famous raids on Cádiz and Lisbon were made in 1587, while these preparations were under way. Knowing his queen, he sailed with her approval and before she had time to withdraw it. The raids were a great success; thousands of tons of Spanish shipping were destroyed, including stores most necessary to the invasion.* Elizabeth would not hear, however, of a repetition of them, but instead allowed herself to be decoyed into peace talks with Parma, with the result that when the English finally met the Armada they did so in their own waters in a defensive action, as Parma had intended.† Before the engagement Philip showed some hint of tactical sense, advising his naval commander in chief "especially to take notice that the enemy's object will be to engage at a distance on account of the advantage which they have from their artillery."[22]

Medina Sidonia, the Spanish admiral whom contemporaries and later historians held largely responsible for the failure of the expedition, seems in fact to have been a hard-working, intelligent, decent sort of man, who did as well as might have been

XIII ordered bonfires lit and a medal struck in recognition of this great triumph, the chief effect of which may have been to give Henry of Navarre the resolute Huguenot troops with which he eventually won the kingship of France.

* According to one writer, these included a large quantity of barrel staves and hoops. When the Armada sailed the following year, it was found that many of her water casks had been made of green lumber, which warped, causing them to leak. Water shortages were to cause the expedition great trouble.[21]

† As things turned out, Elizabeth's decision was probably the right one. For the English to have met the Armada off Spain might only have delayed the Spanish fleet, in the end permitting it easier entry into the Channel en route to its rendezvous with Parma's troops. How these might have been ferried out to join it is another question.

expected in the circumstances.* His predecessor, the Marquis of
Santa Cruz, had died (on February 9, 1588) "worn out at sixty-
two by his labors"[24] and by the gathering impatience of his king.
With his project for the Armada and the English invasion, Philip
appears to have undergone a character change which sometimes
overtakes men—older ones perhaps in particular—who have long
been balked in their grand designs. Instead of retrenching, he
made them grander; and in proportion as their grandeur placed
them further beyond hope of achievement, he intensified his resolve to go through with them, details be damned. The timetable
became an obsession with him. Ready or not, the fleet must sail
by the date he had set. Medina Sidonia did all he could to com-
ply, appointing able captains as his aides, struggling with the
innumerable problems left him by Santa Cruz, organizing and
reporting his efforts in minutest particulars. It was to no avail.
The fleet was still not really prepared when it put to sea in May,
and the weather, as predicted by Johann Müller in the fifteenth
century, and by others after him, turned exceedingly violent.†
The Armada had not cleared Spanish waters before it had to put
into port again to refit, repair leaking hulls, replace sprung water
casks and spoiling food, and take on new recruits to fill the places
of those already sick. During the fleet's stay at Coruña, Medina
Sidonia again asked to be relieved. Philip again refused him, and
the duke thereupon resigned himself to discharging his duties as
best he might, evidently in the belief that Parma was doing
likewise.

After further delays (partly due to the slow speed imposed on
the fleet by its attendant supply vessels, or hulks), the Armada at
length appeared off the Lizard, the peninsula that forms the
southernmost coast of England. The English, under command
of Lord Charles Howard, were caught at an initial disadvantage—

* When Philip appointed him, the Duke of Medina Sidonia had had little
experience of the sea; and such as it was he had not enjoyed it. He tried to
decline the appointment in a letter to the king, in which he pleaded inexperience and crushing family debts, adding that on shipboard "I am always
seasick and always catch cold."[23] The king would not accept his resignation.

† These prophecies included the prediction that in the same year an empire would fall—the question of course being whose. As 1588 approached, a
number of monarchs seem to have become occupied with this problem. Philip
forbade public discussion of it.[25]

in port or just out of it and with the enemy holding the weather gage (i.e., upwind of them), possibly the worst situation a fleet under sail could expect to find itself in. By clever handling of their craft Howard and his captains managed to extricate themselves and get upwind of the Spanish, who promptly took up their crescent formation.* There was then a late-medieval exchange of challenges[26] and battle was officially joined, although neither side seems to have been clear about what to do next. Taking the initiative, some ships under Howard presently attacked one of the Spanish wings, while a second group, under Drake in the *Revenge*, attacked the other. Their method, as Philip had foreseen in his memorandum to Medina Sidonia, was to stay just out of range of the heavier Spanish cannon while keeping up an intense fire from their own culverins. Although their seamanship and the speed with which they worked their guns was the admiration of the enemy, it does not seem to have resulted in much harm to him. For doing serious damage to hulls along the waterline or bringing down the masts and spars of ships as large and stoutly built as many of the Spanish galleons or the armed Portuguese carracks were, the seventeen-pound shot of a culverin, even when accurately aimed, appears to have been too light. At this early stage in the battle, although they had missed a chance of trapping Howard in Plymouth harbor and found themselves unable to close with the enemy by counterattacking, the Spanish may have felt that if only they could maintain formation, keep up a brisk counterfire, and be granted fair winds, they might still make their rendezvous with Parma, and possibly even get his force across with the English fleet still in being.†

* Aside from the persistent refusal of the English to come to close range or attempt boarding, this was almost the only definite tactic used by either side. The crescent was intended for defense against an enemy who held the weather gage. Its concavity faced into the wind, with the strongest ships in the horns, so that any ships attacking the center would meet flanking fire from two sides. This formation, which Medina Sidonia repeatedly relied on, even in late desperate stages of the battle, probably went far toward maintaining a standoff. As most historians agree, however, we have no connected account of the whole engagement, only successive glimpses of it, some of them contradictory.

† Parma himself may not have shared this view. As late as August 6, when the Armada was standing in to Calais, he had few barges ready nor

By one account, the order of their rear guard was disrupted by a panic which followed the first English onset, one of their ships, the *Gran Grin*, being isolated and badly shot up by Drake, Hawkins, and Frobisher before she could be rescued.[29] Not long afterwards, when Howard had suspended the action, two other mishaps befell the Spanish. A pair of their ships collided, shearing off the bowsprit of one. And aboard a third, the *San Salvador*, a tremendous explosion carried away her sterncastle, leaving her ablaze and her decks strewn with casualties. (Stories which circulated through Europe at the time attributed this disaster to a crewman who, to avenge an insult from a superior, had fired one of the magazines.) In view of the trouble Philip had had in the past with unpaid troops, it was ominous too that the *San Salvador* carried the fleet paymaster and the expedition's gold.

During the night after this engagement, Drake in the *Revenge* seems to have carried out a peculiar maneuver not unlike one he had made in the Azores some months before.* Having been assigned the position of watch, or lead ship, by Howard—a post in part honorary, in part quite essential—he was expected to follow the Spanish fleet, with the ships behind him steering to his stern lantern. Sometime in the later hours, it unaccountably went out. He afterwards told a complicated story of having been led astray by some passing German merchantmen. But whatever the events which brought him there, he appears to have ended up, at daybreak, some miles astern, close by the crippled *Nuestra Señora del Rosario*, whose commander, Don Pedro de Valdez, surrendered her with slight resistance and was most courteously received aboard the *Revenge*. Howard in the meantime, thinking Drake had sailed on ahead, pressed forward in the *Ark Royal*, accompanied by two other ships, until he did see a light, only to discover as the sky brightened that he had been following the stern lantern of a ship in the Spanish rear guard. His own fleet

---

any means of propelling them. Moreover, as he must have known, a fleet of shallow-draft Dutch flyboats under Justin of Nassau was waiting to intercept him on the way to deep water.[27] Reports on Parma's state of preparedness vary, however.[28]

* On that occasion, perhaps because of a confusion in orders, a number of his ships sailed for home while he went back to take a very valuable prize. The captains who had "deserted" him were court-martialed *in absentia* and awarded fearful penalties, none of which was ever put into effect.

by then was far away, some of it "half mast high" on the horizon.[30] The incident, which could have ended quite badly, aroused some indignation, most notably in Frobisher, who was chiefly exercised over the question of spoils. *

To this point the battle had been fought by the Spaniards in a somewhat more organized way than by the English (who had as yet not grouped their ships into squadrons or even fully assembled them). On the second day the Spanish were drawn into some disarray when they sighted Frobisher's *Triumph* and a few smaller ships anchored up the Channel near Portland Bill. Four galleasses (large three-masted galleys with high fore- and sterncastles) were sent to attack them, whereupon Howard dispatched a force to relieve Frobisher. Medina Sidonia in his turn made as if to intercept the relief, but in the process his own ship, the *San Martín*, became separated from the rest of his squadron and came under heavy attack from several of the English. No great damage seems to have been sustained by anyone in the tremendous cannonade which followed. The *San Martín* was presently rescued by others of the fleet, Howard as usual prudently drawing out of range as they came up. It had become evident by this time that, even with the weather gage, the Spanish were no match for their enemy in maneuver and so had no chance of boarding him or sinking him with their shorter-range heavy guns.

However, as a result of so much inconsequential shooting, both sides were running low on ammunition. Medina Sidonia decided to draw off across the Channel toward Calais, which he did very slowly and still in good order, although several times set upon. One ship, the *Gran Grifon*, seems to have straggled out of the crescent and been so badly mauled she went adrift. (The English made no attempt to board her, and the galleasses came presently and towed her away into the fleet, this sort of rescue work apparently being one of their chief functions.) That night, after four days of fighting, Howard held a council on shipboard and at last organized his force of some hundred ships into four squadrons.

On Saturday, just a week after its arrival off the Lizard, the

---

* "He thinketh to cozen us of our shares of fifteen thousand ducats but we will have our shares or I will make him spend the best blood in his belly."[31]

Armada dropped anchor in the roadstead at Calais and the English did the same just outside. This was to be the turning point
in the battle. Medina Sidonia's prime reason for putting into
Calais was to get more cannon balls and to establish contact with
Parma, whose forces were supposedly concentrating some thirty
miles up the coast at Dunkirk. Parma, who himself was in Bruges,
was able to be of little help. Justin of Nassau with a fleet of flyboats had him shut in, since his own fleet at Dunkirk consisted
mostly of sailless and oarless canal boats, without stores or guns
aboard, and had no covering ships at all. As one writer remarks:
"There is something strange in Parma's behavior in this whole
episode."*32 Nor, apparently, were any cannon balls available
in Calais. One imagines that Medina Sidonia was rather taken
aback at this turn of events, but worse was to follow.

On the night of Sunday, August 7, the English launched a fireship attack. The Spanish admiral had been expecting one and
issued appropriate orders to meet it, sending out a screen of
smaller boats to grapple with the fireships and tow them aside as
they drifted shoreward. If any got through, the ships in the
roadstead were ordered to leave buoys marking their anchorages
and slip out to sea until the hulks had burned themselves out.
When the attack actually began, these sensible commands were
not obeyed. On their fireships the English had put a few loaded
cannon which began to go off from the heat as the screen vessels
came out to intercept them. This event seems to have set off a
panic in the whole fleet,† which made helter-skelter for the open

* Parma, like others among Philip's commanders, was a man grown care-
worn in his king's service. (As already mentioned, he was soon to die in it.)
A most capable soldier, he had doubtless become accustomed to receiving
impossible orders and devised his own technique for dealing with them. As
the Armada began its slow progress up the English coast, Medina Sidonia
had made repeated attempts to get information from him, apparently without success. Having nothing of use to report and much that might be damaging to morale, Parma perhaps preferred to say nothing, only wishing his
colleague the happiest possible exit from his own difficulties.

† Several years before, the "hell-burner of Antwerp," a fireship lined with
brick and loaded with hundreds of pounds of powder and scrap iron, had
blown up, killing, it is said, a thousand of Parma's men. The incident had
made a considerable impression, and stories had later circulated that the
designer of that monstrous device had gone to England to work for the queen.
When the guns on Howard's fireships began going off, those who heard them
were no doubt primed for the worst and acted accordingly.

sea. Next morning Medina Sidonia, who, pursuant to his own orders, had anchored his flagship just outside Calais, was appalled to see that downwind of him "right along the coast toward Dunkirk the Armada lay scattered with no possibility of regaining Calais Road where stranded on the sand . . . lay the *Capitana* galleass with Don Hugo de Monçada and 800 men on board."[33] The fleet's order, so long and stubbornly maintained, was at last broken.

While Howard, as if acting on Drake's example, went inshore to make a prize of the *Capitana* (which cost him a stiff fight), the rest of the fleet, under Drake, Hawkins, and Frobisher, took out after the main body of ships straggling up the coast, coming in almost to arquebus range, as they could now safely do, and pouring a fearful fire upon them. Medina Sidonia, as he sailed toward Gravelines to catch up with his command, was attacked by Frobisher in the huge *Triumph* along with the rest of his squadron, which was shortly joined by Hawkins in the *Victory*. It is a wonder the poor duke himself survived, and perhaps by that time he hardly cared whether he did so. "The Spanish fought gallantly. Again and again one galleon or another struggled desperately to board. . . . Badly mangled as the *San Martín* had been in the first phase of the action, afterwards, twice at least, she thrust herself into the . . . melee to rescue a ship in trouble. The crew of one of the *urcas* saw Bertendona's great carrack drive past, her deck a shambles, her battery guns silent, and blood spilling out of her scuppers . . . but musketeers still ready in the tops and on her quarterdeck as she came back . . . to take her place in line. The *San Mateo* . . . was in even worse case. More than half her men, soldiers and sailors, were killed or disabled, her great guns were useless, she was . . . wallowing low in the water. . . . By this time Medina Sidonia could see his painfully re-established formation breaking up again before his eyes."[34]

The whole action lasted from around 9:00 A.M. off Gravelines, until evening, by which time it seemed the English must finally be about to annihilate the Armada, if not by cannonfire then by driving it onto the Zeeland Banks. A sudden rainsquall abruptly ended the battle at about 6:00 P.M. The *María Juan* thereupon foundered, probably as the result of battle damage, and later, in the freshening wind, three more ships, including the stricken

San Mateo, drove onto the coast of Zeeland and were lost. The
English waited upwind of their enemy through the night, doubtless expecting to see more catastrophes of the kind; but next day,
in the words of Medina Sidonia, "God was pleased to change the
wind to W.S.W." and his fleet got a reprieve. Even before that
occurred the Armada, beaten as it was, all but out of ammunition
and drifting toward the shoals, took up its demilune formation
and once more offered to do battle. The English merely stood
off, partly no doubt in hopes that the weather would finish the
job for them, but also because they were short of ammunition
themselves. In spite of being so close to home and in constant
touch with it by means of fast courier vessels or pinnaces, Howard had much difficulty in getting the supplies he needed, possibly because the queen, through her ministers, was even then
discouraging needless expense.

The action off Gravelines and Dunkirk was the last of the string
of battles known as the Armada. Once it was over the Spanish
were far past their rendezvous point with little hope of sailing
back to it because of the wind, the English, and their own condition. For reasons not entirely clear, but probably with a view to
avoiding the risk of a blockade, Medina Sidonia elected not to
put into Hamburg to refit, or into the Firth of Forth (where he
might have been well received), but decided instead to sail back
to Spain via the Sea of Norway and Ireland. Not a single Spanish
ship had been sunk during the fights, although the losses just
mentioned were very likely an indirect result of them. Other
ships on the passage home came to bad ends through a combination of injuries, short crews, and foul weather. On the first leg of
the voyage northward, three cargo hulks which had been making
heavy going of it turned as if to head for a port on the mainland
and were never heard from again. In all, out of some hundred
and thirty ships—hulks, pinnaces, galleasses, galleons, and armed
merchantmen—approximately half were destroyed, nineteen by
shipwreck, others by forlornly foundering in the open sea. The
survivors from those driven ashore in Ireland, where the English
authorities were fearful of anything likely to incite a Catholic
revolt, were hunted down and slaughtered. The ships "came in
without charts or pilots, often without anchors . . . and with
crews so weakened by privation and disease they could barely

work them, and split themselves on rocks or wedged themselves on reefs, or were torn from insecure anchorages and dashed against cliffs."[35] The galleass *Girona*, the last of a squadron of four, managed to take off some castaways[18] but later, according to another account, broke up in heavy seas, carrying all aboard to the bottom.

Medina Sidonia himself, having spent days together on deck during the battles, and had men killed all around him, fell sick with "fever" (typhus?) on the homeward voyage, and lay below, delirious. On his ships that still survived, men were dying of untended wounds or disease, some of thirst or starvation, to the point that a few of the vessels finally reaching Santander in October were so feebly manned they could scarcely maneuver in to anchorages. Nevertheless, out of the sixty-eight galleons and other first-line fighting craft he had had off the Lizard on July 31, he brought back forty-four—a far better record than one of his successors managed in 1639, when a whole Spanish fleet was surprised and annihilated by the Dutch Admiral Tromp off the coast of Flanders. Because that disaster, and the one inflicted a while later by Tromp in the battle of the Downs, were mere afterpieces to the main débâcle, they have received far less attention than the Armada, whose losses were due more to the weather than to gunfire and whose architect was not so much its nominal first officer as the king. In justice, it must be added that Philip did not punish his admiral. Medina Sidonia proceeded to his home in the south, more or less incognito for fear of public demonstrations, and for some years afterwards continued in the royal service, though never again afloat. He seems to have lived the remainder of his life unforgiven by numbers of his countrymen, a man marked and saddened by humiliating great events for which he was not in fact responsible. The same plea can probably not be made for certain of his more obvious counterparts today.

No sooner had the Armada drawn away into the North Sea, with only a few score casualties to the defenders, than English sailors themselves were dying of hunger and neglect—some, by Howard's testimony in the streets of Margate, evidently because the queen felt it unnecessary to provide funds for the relief of those of whom she had lately asked so much. Philip's response, when news finally reached him of the ruin of his fleet, was also

in character: "Great thanks do I render to Almighty God, by
whose hand I am gifted with such power that I could easily, if I
chose, place another fleet upon the sea. Nor is it of very great
importance that a running stream should be sometimes intercepted, so long as the fountain from which it flows remains inexhaustible."[36]

These comments are hardly less remarkable than the battles
themselves, in which the Spanish are said to have fired something
over 100,000 cannon balls without scoring a hit of any consequence. The latter must surely stand as something of a record in
bad gunnery. Their arquebusiers seem also to have kept up a
steady fire, the chief effect of which must have been to envelop
the enemy in a hail of spent bullets. The English on the other
hand made repeated hits but never saw a ship go down as a result of one. The racket of these encounters was undoubtedly
prodigious, and the lack of real damage all the more discouraging in light of the violent efforts being made to inflict it. Frustra-
tion on both sides must have been intense. Indeed, an observer
familiar with such earlier battles as Sluys and Lepanto might,
seeing this one, have concluded that naval tactics had spectacu-
larly deteriorated. The truth was that the tactics for this sort of
fighting had not yet been invented, and the odd disparity of
weapons and preconceived ideas which the combatants brought
to it created an impasse of roughly the same kind which developed between the *Monitor* and the *Merrimac* in our own Civil
War (see Chapter VII). In the latter case improvements in defense had made victory for either ironclad impossible. In the
case of the Armada, both sides relied on forms of offense which
could not be made to work.

The political consequences of the Armada were momentous
for Spain, although many were not evident at once. For some
weeks during and after the battles Europe was filled with rumors that the English had taken a frightful licking. And in England itself, even after the real news had been received, there
seems to have been a feeling of uneasiness and disappointment.
The reports of some English captains were modest to the point of
suggesting an actual reverse, and not until long afterwards did
the whole adventure acquire the aura of glorious total victory it
has today. In Paris, Philip's ambassador, at word of the English

defeat, caused a great bonfire to be prepared. It was never finally lit, and in December of the same year the Duke of Guise was murdered on orders of King Henry (III) of Valois. While the Catholic League, Philip's apparatus in France, was by no means liquidated in this *coup de main*, the balance was still tipped against it. Henry of Navarre undertook to defend the fugitive Henry of Valois and the next year, upon the latter's assassination, ascended the throne himself as Henry IV. So Coutras and the Armada combined to undo most of what Philip had spent so long and paid so much* to accomplish.

The longer-term consequences for his kingdom were far more serious than these. What was saddest, perhaps, about the men who died in the Armada was that they did so not for the glory of their country but only to begin its decline. In the centuries ahead it was to sink by degrees to the level of a village civilization not unlike that of its former colonies. Other powers were to fight for control of its royal succession and even of its land, as though Spain, in the sense in which Philip and his subjects conceived of it, no longer really existed. It no longer did. In the twentieth century the Spanish Civil War was, to a considerable extent, fought and paid for by foreigners who used it merely as a training exercise, preparatory to World War II. By his attempts to put his nation at the center of European history, Philip took her clean out of it. Except in a nuclear age, bad generalship can hardly go further.

His proselytizing policies sound odd to our ears, although with a few substitutions of terms they should not do so. One feels in fact that Philip would have fitted into our era quite well. The grandeur of his comments on his own worst defeat suggests those politicians who have recently been telling us that, far from resenting the taxes we pay for ill-advised and clumsily conducted wars, we should be glad to be so prosperous that we can afford them. It is obvious that they too consider the fountains of public riches and public patience inexhaustible. On these grounds Philip must, I think, be regarded as ahead of his time rather than behind

---

* When Guise was murdered, the draft of a letter was found on him in which he had said: "To keep up the civil war in France will cost 700,000 livres a month,"[37] a very considerable sum, particularly in view of the little it had bought.

it. He was entirely without the capriciousness of Philip VI of France, a man not lacking in consideration for his own people— even for his day something of a liberal paternalist. If he had no notion of the probable consequences of his actions, one must ask, in fairness, what statesman of his caliber ever does? What major power today is less doctrinaire, really, than Spain was at her apogee? For that matter what nation—short of immediate total disaster—ever knows its own worst leaders or chooses, even when it is able, to repudiate them? On the contrary, most are apt to die, as Philip did in 1598, mourned and honored, as splendid still in the eyes of their stupider subjects as they were throughout life in their own. History corrects such errors, but seldom soon enough.

Because Philip's actions were largely military it is by these he must be judged (and perhaps wished to be, as did his father Charles V, with somewhat more justification). As a commander he must surely rank among the worst—a man without tactical, strategic, or everyday political sense, devoid of insight, slow to change course, insufficiently informed or thorough in his preparations, and yet heroically stubborn, exhausting the possibilities of his own mistakes and even then waving them away as trivial (". . . gifted with such power that I could easily, if I chose, place another fleet upon the sea"). He cannot but seem familiar to us, particularly in being a commander in chief who never did more himself than sit at a desk devising the impossible.

CHAPTER V

The Tiny Lion and the Enormous Mouse

Everyone who knows anything at all (but preferably not a great deal) about history is apt to have his favorite period, that is, a time which he imagines it would have been much nicer to live in than his own. Some favor the thirteenth century because of the "medieval synthesis"*—a way of life and state of society which, they suggest, were far more "organic" than ours. In those days, it is said, God was present as He has not been since, so that men went about their daily affairs with an inner security we can never hope to enjoy or even understand. (The fact that this same age was disrupted by the slaughter of the Albigensians and the obliteration of the culture of Provence must perhaps be written off as part of the price some men have to pay for the spiritual tranquillity of their brothers. The formal establishment of the Inquisition shortly afterwards was then a way of institutionalizing such payments.)

Others prefer the eighteenth century on the ground that it was an Age of Reason. In a strict sense it was no more so—possibly somewhat less so—than the nineteenth century. The reasons the eighteenth seemed, to many of those who lived in it, comparatively sane and therefore of almost classic dignity were in part purely political and negative. Philip II was long dead. The wars

* Which Henry Adams seems to have thought was at its height in the twelfth.

of religion had worn themselves out in the dreary carnage of
1618-48, under Tilly and Wallenstein and Gustavus Adolphus (it
being this period, some think, which reduced Germany to a barbarity from which it has never quite recovered). By the end of
that century, faith as an ostensible motive for war was passé,
while the still more ancient system of statecraft, based upon rivalry among the hereditary proprietors of nations, survived in
some vigor. The result was a brief period of dynastic wars fought
by professionals, many of them of great skill (for instance, Marlborough and Prince Eugène and their nearly successful opponent
at Malplaquet, Marshal Boufflers; or Frederick the Great and
Marshal Saxe, in the War of the Austrian Succession). In effect
Europe was enjoying an interregnum in which the fanaticism of
sacred causes lay behind it while that of secular causes was yet
to come. Armies were large in comparison to those of feudal
times but small by modern standards; nor had they, in all likelihood, increased very much relative to the total population since
the Hundred Years' War.* This fact, together with the greater
prosperity of Europe in 1700, meant that war was scarcely more
noticeable a feature of daily life than it had ever been, and even
with the added expense of modern weapons and training, no
harder to pay for. The question is why the common man, given
the objectives of war at that time, or the earnings he might expect
as a mercenary, could be induced to fight at all. The fact that
he could—that for instance Maria Theresa was able, by direct appeal, to raise a Hungarian *levée en masse* during her war against
Frederick the Great—argues that in addition to our ancestral
ferocity, something of feudal devotion and feudal gullibility persisted in the rank and file. These traits were not to persist long
after the French Revolution and the Napoleonic Wars, although

---

* Very roughly, armies had grown from around 10,000 men at the time of
Crécy to 55-60,000 men at Blenheim (1704), 45-50,000 at Fontenoy (1745),
or the exceptionally large number of 90,000 men on either side at Malplaquet (1709). Population figures for the same period are conjectural, but
it seems probable that England had about 3,500,000 in the reign of Henry
VII, and perhaps double that number of 1688, as shown by Gregory King's
estimate of the per capita distribution of income for that year.[1] By projection
backward, England's population under Edward III may have been on the
order of 1,000,000, thus increasing sevenfold by about 1700, while the size of
armies increased four and a half to ninefold.

it is doubtful whether those which replaced them were an un-qualified improvement.

By contrast with Philip II's lurid attempts to overwhelm the Netherlands and England, the Wars of the Spanish and the Aus-trian Succession make dull, difficult reading, full of complex intrigues, odd-sounding place names, and battles fought with ex-emplary skill to no purpose. Here is a typical passage taken at random from a standard account of the War of the Austrian Suc-cession (1740-48): "Charles VII, whose territories were overrun by the Austrians, asked [Frederick II of Prussia] to make a diver-sion by invading Moravia. In December 1741, therefore, Schwerin had crossed the border and captured Olmütz. Glatz also was in-vested . . . A combined plan of operations was made by the French, Saxons and Prussians for the rescue of Linz. But Linz soon fell; Broglie on the Moldau, weakened by the departure of the Bavarians to oppose Khevenhüller, and of the Saxons to join . . . Frederick, was in no condition to take the offensive, and large forces under Prince Charles of Lorraine lay in his front from Budweis to Iglau. Frederick's march was made toward Iglau in the first place. Brünn was invested about the same time (Feb-ruary), but the direction of march was changed, and instead of moving against Prince Charles, Frederick pushed on southwards by Znaim and Nikolsburg. The extreme outposts of the Prussians appeared before Vienna. But Frederick's advance [we are now surprised to learn] was a mere foray, and Prince Charles, leaving a screen of troops in front of Broglie, marched to cut off the Prus-sians from Silesia, while the Hungarian levies poured into upper Silesia by the Jablunka pass."[2] And so on. The same writer con-cludes, "The special feature of the war . . . and of other wars of the time, is the extraordinary disparity between ends and means," and goes on to say that both were in fact defective—the ends being trivial, while the means, the "small standing army of the eighteenth century," could "conquer by degrees but could not deliver a decisive blow." In contrast to the allied armies of later Napoleonic times, "those of 1741 represented the divergent pri-vate interests of the several dynasties and achieved nothing." (The accompanying skirmishes at sea, between England and the Franco-Spanish allies, another writer describes as "languid and confused.") Perhaps the chief lesson to be learned from war as it was practiced in the age of the *philosophes* was that it could be nearly as expensive and inconsequential when waged by outstandingly good generals as when waged by the usual run of bad.

To the north, at the start of the same century, a far more bizarre struggle—no less rich in intrigue and odd place names, but certainly more momentous for the European future—was taking shape on the Baltic. The principals were Charles XII of Sweden (1682-1718) and Peter the Great of Russia (1672-1725); the former a tactical genius who, despite appalling mistakes in policy, and even in logistics, never lost a battle till his last; the latter a tenacious strategist with a tendency to flightiness in actual combat, who defeated his great opponent only once.

When Charles came to the Swedish throne in 1697, at age fifteen, he inherited an empire which encircled the Baltic but was perhaps too large for the home country—a relatively poor nation of some two and a half million—to hope to maintain. It had been bequeathed him by a succession of fighting kings* and included Finland, Karelia, the states of Ingria Esthonia and Livonia, a number of Baltic islands, Bremen and Stralsund together with much of West Pomerania, and the town of Wismar in Mecklenburg. Besides the mouth of the Weser, Sweden controlled those of the Elbe, Oder, Neva, and Dvina and considerable parts of Lakes Ladoga and Peipus. Her provinces—Ingria and Karelia in particular—had long shut Russia off from the sea. At Charles's ac-

---

* Charles was descended from John Casimir, Count Palatine of Zweibrucken, who fell in love with Gustavus Adolphus' sister and, over Gustavus' objections, married her. Charles Gustavus, John's son, and Charles XI, his grandson, were formidable warriors. Besides winning Sweden a commanding position in the first Great Northern War, Charles XI sternly fought corruption and the power of the baronage at home, and saw to it that his son, later Charles XII, was far better educated than he himself had been.

The one woman ruler in the line, Gustavus Adolphus' daughter Christina (who reigned from 1644 to 1654, when she was forced to abdicate), had much of the ferocity but none of the martial discipline of her male relatives. She was wildly extravagant, oblivious of public opinion to the point of contempt, rather masculine and assertive, but not indifferent to culture. She imported Descartes and is said to have killed him by her habit of summoning him to the palace at dawn for tutorial sessions during which the windows were left open. (He appears to have died of pneumonia.) During a trip to France, after her abdication, she ordered the murder of her major-domo Monaldischi, for reasons not clearly understood. As an old lady in Rome, she wrote letters to Charles XII in French, a language Charles understood but in later years disapproved of.

cession, Sweden was suffering from famine, but her army, which Gustavus Adolphus had dramatically modernized, was still among the best in Europe. It depended in part on a territorial system, organized by Charles XI, by which potential draftees were given a yearly stipend, a cabbage patch, and other perquisites for their interim maintenance. Its core was a small standing force of crack regiments, notably the Household Foot Guards of Stockholm, which included numbers of young nobles. Like commoners, these began their careers in the ranks and, if lacking ability, remained there. In addition the king had an elite corps of two hundred, the Drabants, who served as his personal guard or, in battle, as mounted shock troops which he sent on particularly difficult or critical missions. By royal order they wore "blue cloth coats with flat gilt buttons, three and seven twelfths dozen to each coat; and with gold braid on lapels and pockets."

Whereas Sweden was poor and small in numbers but modern, Russia, or Muscovy as it was then called, was vast in numbers, even poorer, and, at Peter's accession, medieval. Unlike Charles's ascent to the throne, which was assured and indeed carefully prepared for, Peter's, to the tsardom, was desperately threatened during much of his boyhood and early youth by the intrigues of his malignant half-sister Sofia. In contrast to Charles, who was instructed in Latin (which he later wrote and spoke), German, French, mathematics, and the art of war (at nine, he wrote an impressively erudite reply to his tutor's question concerning the best method of attacking a fortified position with infantry), Peter at a comparable age was learning to decipher devotional literature[3] with the help of one Nikita Zotov, who was more a companion than a preceptor and later became the young tsar's fool-in-residence and an outstanding member of his company of convivial spirits. (He was made prince-pope of Peter's All-joking-All-drunken Assembly, a group "with its own patriarch, metropolitans, archimandrites, deacons and priesthood, who wore ecclesiastical vestments and performed special rites."[4] Zotov's exalted position in these satires was evidently due less to his wit than to a phenomenal capacity for drink.) Peter's regular schooling was discontinued entirely before he was ten, and such education as he later had he appears to have picked up for himself.

Charles (to continue the comparison) was moderately tall, with an elegant wasp-waisted figure, a long Nordic head, and a fair, almost girlish complexion which shamed him to the point that he set out to ruin it by exposure, very probably with success. Few monarchs since Merovingian times had lived a more consistently rigorous life than he, once he took to the field at the age of eighteen. After his first three wild years in the kingship, when he and his cousin Frederick of Holstein-Gottorp amused themselves beheading calves and sheep in the palace or running a hare through the Swedish Diet, Charles became a model—one might almost say a monster—of self-control. In the same early period, informed that the queen dowager disapproved of his drinking, he had a last glass of wine to toast his abandonment of the habit, and never drank again. Like Stonewall Jackson, whom he tactically resembled, he was profoundly religious, once nearly going to war with the Austrian Empire because of its mistreatment of Protestants in Silesia. Nothing could have been more alien to his nature than the licentiousness and somewhat desperate foolery of which the tsar and his company were so fond. Charles was apparently without frivolity of any kind, and, until years of war had congealed his character, without much cruelty or malice either.* Through years of campaigning he seems to have carried about in his head something of the immaculate quiet of his boyhood days, maintaining for as long as he lived those swift imperturbable actions of mind which had made him a keen military analyst at nine.

Peter was nearly a foot taller than Charles and in proportion broader, a man of phenomenal energy, rather coarsely handsome, and anything but immaculately quiet. At ten he was elected by the boyars and the patriarch to succeed the late Tsar Feodor. His half-sister Sofia, who wished to rule indefinitely, first as regent and then as the power behind her full brother Ivan, attempted a

* He anticipated Feuerbach in recommending that torture as a means of obtaining confessions be given up, in part on the practical ground that such confessions were worthless. In his later campaigns in Poland, he pursued a ruthlessly extortionist policy and his punishment of the rebellious Livonian noble Patkul (who was broken, alive, on the wheel, and begged to be beheaded) was of classic ferocity. However, by then he had been years at war and Patkul, who first organized the alliance against him, was both technically a traitor and actually a great source of his troubles.

coup. The result was the so-called revolt of the *streltsi*,* which quickly became a St. Bartholomew's Massacre of the opposition. During it the palace was invaded by a mob of drunken soldiery intent upon slaughter, and Peter, as a terrified small boy clinging to his mother, Natalya, saw a good deal of it. Prince Mikhail Dolgoruky, himself a commander of the *streltsi*, had the tactlessness to abuse his troops from the head of the Red Staircase, whereupon he was seized and flung over the balustrade onto the pikes below. Natalya's minister and champion, Matveev, was then literally torn from her arms and, with Peter watching, butchered in the same way. The *streltsi* next conducted a hunt through the palace for boyars who had supported Peter's election, and these were also thrown to the pikes, their bodies then being dismembered by the mob. For some reason Peter himself and his mother were spared, but this gruesome episode is thought, quite understandably, to have marked him for life. It was reinforced by two later crises. The first occurred in 1689, the year of his accession, when he was warned that Sofia and the *streltsi* were plotting to kill him. He fled pell-mell to the Troitsa Monastery, rallied his personal troops to him, and after some jockeying for political advantage, forced Sofia into retirement in a nunnery. In 1698, during his Grand Embassy in Europe, he got word that Sofia from her retreat had contrived still another uprising of her praetorians against him, and this time, although he still forbore to kill her, he arrived home in a disturbed and savage state, prepared not only to settle with the *streltsi* once and for all but to deal summarily with anyone else who crossed or displeased him. Some years before, he had contracted a tic which periodically contorted his features, giving him the look of a man on the verge of seizure. The tic in fact corresponded to a profound perturbability which all his life inclined him to panic, often followed by proportionately dangerous rages. It seems to have been in this latter

---

* The *streltsi* were a standing force intended to protect the realm from attack while the militia mobilized. In Moscow they seem to have served as a combined police and fire department, though not a very effective one, since the city had a high murder and robbery rate and, being built largely of wood, was continually burning down, now a house at a time, now whole quarters. A contributing cause was undoubtedly the general drunkenness, which, according to European travelers of the period, reached the proportions of a major epidemic on Saints' days and just before Lent.

mood that at a revel in Moscow he suddenly threw his old friend
and drinking companion Lefort to the floor and began kicking
him. At another gathering he accused an aide, the boyar Shein,
of selling military commissions (which indeed Shein did), thereupon drawing his sword as if to kill him. Two of His Majesty's
Company intervened to save Shein and were slightly wounded
before Peter had been calmed down.

With the *streltsi*, things went much worse. On the tsar's order,
hundreds were arrested and put to torture. By the time the winter of 1798-99 had set in, some eight hundred had been executed,
several by Peter himself. "For nearly five months Moscow was
like a charnel house. Frozen corpses hung from the Kremlin walls
and over the gates through which people passed on their daily
business. On the Red Square, at the execution place, headless
bodies lay grotesquely in pools of frozen blood, while on the
wheel were bent those whom death had so slowly overtaken."[5]
The *streltsi* ceased to be a factor in his political life.

Unlike Charles, Peter declined to specialize but remained
something of the boyish enthusiast and dilettante until he died.
The fact is, however, that all his interests, save perhaps his fondness for shooting off fireworks, converged on the same end: the
improvement of his country.* He built her navy, in part with his
own hands, working as a shipwright in his yards at Voronezh. At
his accession Russia had but one seaport, Archangel, which was
open scarcely three months of the year and a long dangerous
journey from Europe under the best of conditions. He captured
Azov on the Black Sea from the Turks and, assisted by this victory and his new fleet, obtained a peace with them. His next
problem was to break through to the Baltic and build himself
the city which would be Russia's window on Europe.

In this project he was first encouraged by the Livonian nobleman Johann Patkul and by Frederick Augustus,† Elector of Sax-

* His concern over the backwardness of Russia turned him into the nation's leading student, apprentice, exemplar, professor, and pioneer. While in
England he had a go at watchmaking and sent home, among other items, a
coffin, evidently as a model for Muscovite craftsmen. His mania for fireworks
led to at least one sad incident when, during a five-hour display in Moscow,
a boyar was brained by a defective rocket said to have been made by the
tsar himself.

† Augustus, sometimes called the Strong because of his impressive size and
his ability to bend horseshoes with his bare hands, was an indifferent soldier

ony, who had of late also made himself King of Poland by a form of purchase. In 1699 a secret alliance was concluded between Peter, Augustus, and the King of Denmark with the object of seizing and redistributing Sweden's Baltic possessions. The moment seemed appropriate, since that country was still suffering from famine and from Charles's early extravagance, Charles himself having not yet turned eighteen. His abilities were unknown but his inexperience was certain, and the numbers he faced were far greater than his own. Peter, always one to bargain from strength, apparently felt these odds to be promising. In 1700, while the Danes threatened Sweden and Augustus, Riga, Peter moved against the town of Narva, which stands on the Narova River, some hundred miles west southwest of the present site of Leningrad (formerly St. Petersburg), in what was then the Swedish province of Ingria. The garrison of Narva was approximately 1500 and Peter's army, at the time of the later battle there, numbered about 40,000, including considerable artillery under European officership. The Swedes, however, withstood his siege with some success.

Charles's response to these threatening maneuvers was so swift that it astonished all of Europe, and not least the edgy Peter, in whose psychic life Charles was soon to fill the role lately vacated by the *streltsi*. In the spring of 1700, Charles mobilized his rustic army and his fleet, made an adroit descent on Denmark, and eliminated her from the war without a fight. He then reorganized his forces and proceeded across the Baltic to the town of Reval, which was strategically placed so that he could march upon either Riga or Narva as circumstances might dictate. He decided upon Narva and set out, as he was habitually to do, at top speed and under the worst possible conditions. By that time fall had come; the countryside was boggy and all but impassable. On the march, his troops were short of food, eating only on alternate days. Amounting to between 8500 and 10,000 men (authorities as usual disagree on the exact figure), they were outnumbered

---

and a politician of such intricate duplicity that he often outsmarted himself. According to household records found at his death, he had fathered 345 illegitimate children and one son born in wedlock. His natural son by Maria Aurora of Königsmarck became a soldier far better than he—Maurice, Marshal Saxe. An illegitimate daughter of *his* was said to have been the paternal grandmother of George Sand, who made much of the connection.

at least four to one by the Russians, who in addition occupied strong defense works. Two factors only were in Charles's favor. Peter's army, like his fleet, was a creation not of decades but of months. While some of its officers were European and capable enough, only a few units, such as the Preobrazhensky and Semyonovsky regiments, were of professional caliber. On the other hand, Charles's men were also untried, being mostly recruits who had been called up after years of peace and who had had no experience of action in the Denmark landing because the latter, to Charles's evident annoyance, had been bloodless. A crucial factor was perhaps the nearly lunatic self-assurance of the one commander and the nearly lunatic misgivings of the other—feelings which seem to have transmitted themselves to the ranks in both cases. On the Swedes in particular, the moral effect of their leader was remarkable.

To the end of his strange career, Charles's men followed him apparently without question into adventures so seemingly doomed and so fraught with hardship on the way that any other army, between desertion, battle losses, undernourishment, and sheer melancholy, would simply have fallen to pieces. Not Charles's Swedes. Just as the country-boy soldiers of Gustavus Adolphus, long before, had marched with their king into Germany and, after his death in the mists of Lützen, had died there themselves, a man or a unit at a time until nothing remained but their fighting name, so Charles's troops would never waver. He was their king and exemplar, invincible, a phenomenon beyond mistrust or argument. Thousands might die of frost, wounds, and disease but the rest trudged on, half-starving, to still worse privations or more terrible odds lying ahead. No one knew quite why, but it had to be done, was worth doing, and could never fail.

On the Russian side, no such unanimity prevailed. The troops, like their leader, combined an odd eclecticism in dress and military methods with a chaotic ferocity which was at times truly courageous and at others merely hysterical and cruel. As Charles advanced on Narva, Peter sent out his cavalry commander, General Scheremetyev, to maintain contact and if possible slow the Swedish advance. While committing various atrocities,* Schere-

---

* In a ravaged church in Livonia the Swedes came upon the corpse of a deacon or caretaker whose ears and nose had been sliced off and his cheeks

metyev's men showed a marked disinclination to engage the enemy en route, even when, as once happened, the Russians occupied a strong position in a pass and might have held up Charles's advance quite effectively. Scheremetyev at length fell back upon Narva with the report that 30,000 Swedes would soon be before the main Russian works. At this news Peter seems to have gone into something like an ambulatory nervous breakdown. Believing Charles to be only a few hours away, he suddenly offered the command of his army to the Duke de Croy,* an elderly Belgian mercenary who was appalled at the responsibility thrust upon him and tried to decline it. According to the report of Hallart, another of the tsar's European officers, Peter wept and kissed the duke and pled with him for the better part of the night, until the latter finally agreed to accept his startling promotion if he were given explicit orders as to how to proceed. Without further word, Peter left for Moscow, leaving de Croy to handle matters as he saw fit.

On the morning of November 19, 1700, not long after the tsar's departure, the Swedes appeared and the two sides exchanged cannon fire while Charles briefly considered the position. The Muscovites were dug in behind strong fortifications which ran in a semicircle around the town, the northern and southern ends of the arc reaching the Narova River. The only bridge to the other side lay within the Russian lines, on their right (north) flank. In this first battle Charles at once showed the tactical peculiarities which were to become his hallmark—an astonishingly quick eye for his adversary's weak points, a disregard for conventional rules of procedure, and a strong preference for surprise and speed over strategic maneuver and lengthy preparation.† His plan at Narva was simply to use his infantry to pierce the Russian line near its center bastion and then to roll up both segments so as to split the enemy in two. His cavalry on the right was under orders to pin the defenders inside their works so as to prevent them from making

---

burned with hot pincers. Such episodes were evidently commonplace. After Peter's capture of Narva, in 1704, he was horrified at the general slaughter, reportedly beheading one of his own soldiers with his sword in an effort to stop it.

* Also called the Duke von Croy or Prince de Croy.

† As Fuller puts it, Charles was an "assaulting" general, not a "bombarding" general.[6]

a sally and attacking his main force in flank or in rear. The Drabants were assigned the formidable task of penetrating the Russian right and blocking escape by the bridge.

The Russians meanwhile, and the uneasy de Croy, waited inside their fortifications, believing that what they saw before them was only the Swedish advance guard. Not long before 2:00 P.M. a blinding snowstorm moved up over the wood from which the Swedish army had just emerged, and Charles's generals advised a halt in operations. Charles would not hear of it, pointing out that the snow would be driving into the Russians' faces. Shortly afterwards, the blizzard closed in and at two o'clock the Swedes advanced swiftly and almost invisibly to the attack. The result was devastating. Within minutes a gap in the Russian center had been opened and the rollback in both directions had begun. The Drabants won through to the bridge, an unnecessary exertion as it turned out, since under the weight of fugitives that structure soon collapsed, leaving the bulk of the Russian army in a cul-de-sac. Units of it began falling apart, notably Scheremetyev's cavalry, who, headed by their commander, plunged in panic into the Narova River on the left end of the line and attempted to ride to safety. The general himself reached the far shore, but a thousand of his troopers were swept over some falls and drowned. Men of other contingents murdered officers who tried to check their flight, and then took to their heels, in most cases only to find they had nowhere to go. The Preobrazhensky and Semyonovsky regiments stood their ground, and a desperate last-ditch fight began around an improvised laager which the Russians had built out of smashed baggage wagons not far from the fallen bridge. By 8:00 P.M. most of the fighting was over. The remainder of the Russians surrendered the following morning, unaware that they might still have mounted an effective counterattack since the Swedes were exhausted and many had totally incapacitated themselves by drinking quantities of captured liquor (presumably vodka) on empty stomachs. The losses to either army are not exactly known, but the Russians are said to have lost 8000, besides the 1000 cavalrymen drowned in the Narova, as against about 1600 killed and wounded on the Swedish side. The Swedes took upwards of fifty top-ranking officers prisoner and captured something over a hundred and fifty Russian cannon but released the bulk of the enemy because they were simply too many to hold captive:* One can imagine the psychological earthquake which these events would have caused in Peter had he stayed to see them.† As it is, one can dimly read in his later conduct the reverberations of this terrible day.

Fortunately for the tsar's sanity, Charles elected not to press his advantage just then but instead turned against Augustus and his Saxons (including the Saxon Marshal Steinau, who in the next months was to make something of a career out of being defeated by the Swedish king). It was not long after this time that Charles's character appeared in certain ways to set. His strategic and political notions, perhaps always secondary to his extraordinary grasp of tactics, now began to lead him wholly astray. Instead of making an ally of Augustus, which the latter, after a number of startling reverses, was only too anxious to have him do,‡ Charles set about with almost fanatical stubbornness trying to force Augustus' abdication from the throne of Poland. In the course of these efforts, which to Peter's delight cost the Swedish king years in the "Polish bog" (enabling Peter to retrain and equip his own armies for a return engagement), Charles won a victory at Klissow (in 1702) which more clearly than Narva established him as one of the most brilliantly bad good generals of his age.

At Klissow, which lies to the south of Warsaw in the heart of the Polish bog, Field Marshal Steinau, upon learning of the Swedes' approach, placed himself in a strong position, with marshes on his left and center, and only a narrow segment of his right open to direct attack. Besides outnumbering Charles to begin with, he was expecting at any moment to be reinforced by a large body of Polish cavalry. He had moreover made the marsh on his left passable by means of causeways constructed of bun-

---

* According to one writer, 6000 more of these unhappy troops died of exposure and starvation en route to the interior.

† One of Peter's biographers, Grey, reports that at the news of Narva "he was neither depressed nor deterred." A biographer of Charles (Bengtsson) says that the tsar "rolled about in paroxysms of tears and terror" when word of Narva reached him in Novgorod.

‡ Augustus so little understood his adversary that at one time he sent his former mistress, the beautiful Maria Aurora of Königsmarck, on an embassy to Charles, with the idea that she should seduce him. Charles evaded her, only once seeing her at all, and then merely to tip his hat and ride on.

dles of sticks (fascines), over which he meant to launch an attack when the appropriate moment came.

Charles, advancing with his usual abruptness and taking in the scene at a glance, decided upon an exceedingly dangerous maneuver, invented centuries before by the Theban general Epaminondas and later executed with great success by Frederick the Great at Leuthen (1757). Approaching from the Saxon left, he made a flank march across his enemy's front with a view to attacking him where that seemed most feasible, on the right. Steinau's cavalry thereupon broke out of the marsh on the left as planned and began an attack on the Swedish flank and rear, the Swedish cavalry wheeling to meet it. At that moment the Polish mounted knights, the pick of that medieval land's "200,000 hereditary sovereigns" and an odd reminder of the days of Crécy, thundered into view on the Saxon right, their breastplates, feathered headgear, and fantastically caparisoned horses no doubt making an awesome spectacle.* As they closed for the charge they raised what Bengtsson describes as a great "screeching." Any general but Charles XII might have been severely shaken by these developments. He seems simply to have dealt with each as it arose. Steinau's surprise assault gave him no trouble. The Saxon cavalry still practiced the caracole, or close-range pistol attack, whereas the Swedish horse had been trained to ride in tight formations, relying on shock and steel. At Charles's order, they counterattacked and the Saxon squadrons vanished from the field. No sooner had they done so than the Swedes reversed direction and in perfect order rode against the next wave of attackers. The onslaught of the Poles was evidently as ineffective as the Saxons' had been. After the briefest collision with the enemy the whole glittering horde turned and racketed away across the plain, leaving Charles to concentrate on what was left of Steinau's army. Its right was rolled up; and after a stiff fight,

---

* This was the so-called Polish Crown Army, commanded by Hieronymus Lubomirski, in which the noblemen, as of old, rode with squires in attendance, wore chain mail and long scarlet coats, and carried an assortment of weapons including clubs, long swords, lances with pennons, and engraved muskets. The Poles, however, had not always been as manageable opponents as these. The only general who consistently defeated Gustavus Adolphus and several times nearly cost him his life was the Polish hetman Stanislaus Koniecpolski.

Major General Posse with four battalions of the Life Guards broke through the Saxon center. The Saxons lost 2000 dead and wounded, 1100 by capture, all their guns (as Charles had predicted), and a considerable supply train. Swedish losses were 300 killed and 800 wounded. Steinau himself and the disgruntled Augustus escaped, only to be defeated by Charles again, the following spring, at Pultusk.

This battle was quite typical of Charles's methods, and in several ways prophetic of troubles they were soon to cause him. In fact, Steinau's position and plan were good ones; and as seldom happens in any engagement, his various moves were well coordinated. Though the Polish Crown Army did not stay long, it at least arrived on time. The Saxon cavalry on the left moved into action along with it, and that at a moment when the Swedes were barely in control of the situation at the other end of their line and so inviting envelopment. Charles had moreover thrown himself into combat with hungry unrested troops, saying—when his aide Count Piper protested—"Hungry dogs bite well." The Saxon army numbered about 17,000, including artillery; the Poles about 10,000. Charles's force amounted to 8000 and was supported by only four small fieldpieces. (When this fact was pointed out to him the king said, "We shall soon capture the enemy's guns, and then we shall have more than we need.") Steinau's trick of making the marsh passable with slightly submerged causeways evidently caught Charles by surprise, but he was able to cope with it because his troops were superbly trained, flexible in maneuver, and keen to fight, while he himself had the sort of rapid, imperturbable grasp of oncoming events which enabled him, it seemed, to turn any emergency back upon the enemy and often to compound it with dazzling speed. Had he lived in the twentieth century he would almost certainly have been a virtuoso of *Panzer* warfare, for with the means available in his own time, he practiced it. Like Henry of Navarre, but by even more headlong methods, he pierced and scattered his opponents, concentrating on key points and staking everything on momentum.

Not only did Steinau deserve to win at Klissow; the *way* he failed to do so could scarcely have been more startling or demoralizing. One has the impression that Charles's psychological effect on the Europeans of his day was greater than Marlborough's for this reason: he was a master of the improbable. His victories were not ordinary, not even outstanding; they were prodigies. In the end he perhaps came to rely too heavily on naked intelligence, which is to say, on tactical virtuosity and the *coup d'œil*. He was a general who made his best plans on the spur of the moment. When it came to co-ordinating a campaign involving armies in widely separated theaters, or to deciding on a stratagem suited to his larger situation, his ideas appeared to go awry, either because he overestimated the capacity of distant subordinates to carry out his orders or because (in the case of politics) he failed entirely to grasp essentials. Even in battle, finally, he tended to overreach himself, asking more of his army and of his own strength than either could supply.

As the most spectacular commander of the age, Charles was uniquely suited to unhinge the tsar. He should have done so while he had the chance, since Peter, rather than Augustus, was the real enemy. Saxony was of no great consequence; and Augustus' kingship of Poland was a medieval formality, the same in a sense being true of Poland itself. Augustus was no more than a pliant politician who had got himself caught in the middle. To have spent years deposing him and putting a new puppet in his place, as Charles did, was a course more in character with the Hundred Years' War than with the Age of Reason. (It took him until 1704 to accomplish the dethronement; another year to install his man, Stanislaus; and until 1706 to obtain the peace of Altranstädt and the supposed reconciliation with Augustus—all meaningless events, soon to be undone.)

It was possibly just because Charles was a European sovereign so much in the tradition, a man trained on the one hand to his kingship and on the other to a Protestant firmness of character which ensured loyalty to the principles he had been taught, that he could *not* think clearly about large strategic issues or handle himself with effect in the amoral world of politics. One feels he set himself, not to deal with enemies in the usual pragmatic sense, but to make examples of them, cost what it cost. Peter, on the other hand, even more than Augustus, was something of an amorph. The same shapelessness which enabled him to take a succession of shapes—Admiral Peter, Peter Alexei the shipyard

worker or common sailor, Peter the watchmaker, reformer, cutup
—also made him a prey to terrible shyness,* uncertain in nerve,
and something of a bully. But whereas he was intelligent and
could see what needed doing, he was also fortunate in lacking
any constraints upon his choice of methods, bringing to his problems few of the odd old-fashioned notions which may so seriously
have hampered Charles. Peter *did* understand strategic matters,
and he handled them, at least from a distance, with the unclouded cunning of a primitive. Thus although he still became
jittery on hearing of Charles's approach, he stuck doggedly to his
master plan of forcing a passage to the Baltic. While Charles
frittered away his good luck defeating Steinau at Pultusk and
besieging the town of Thorn, Peter fought his way into Ingria and
began building St. Petersburg. Eventually, in 1704, the tsar
avenged his first defeat by taking Narva with great (though un-
intended) slaughter. For a time all his projects seemed to be
flourishing, but in 1705-06 the prospect again turned ominous.
Two expeditions—one under his old standby Scheremetyev, sent
to harass the Swedish General Lewenhaupt in Courland; the
other a combined Russian-Saxon force of 10,000 under a General
Paykul, sent to overwhelm a Swedish garrison-army of 2000 in
Warsaw—were simultaneously and totally defeated.

Later in the same year word got about that Charles was plan-
ning a winter campaign against Russia. Peter and Menshikov
(then his preferred general) were instantly in a flutter. Charles
presently crossed the Vistula, heading northeast toward Grodno,
whereupon Menshikov wrote to the tsar, "But your Excellency
should not be distressed; we are well prepared here.'"7 Peter
decided to join his army (January, 1706) and got as far as Smolensk before he learned that the Swedes had already come in
sight of Grodno. "The news shocked him and he was relieved to
meet Menshikov at the village of Dubrovna. But he was anxious
about his army and during the following two months sent a

---

* During his Grand Embassy in Europe, in 1697-98, he came to have an
intense dislike, almost a horror, of the crowds he drew; and when he met
the dazzling Sophia Charlotte, Electress of Brandenburg, he was overcome,
covering his face with his hands and muttering (in German), "I don't know
what to say." Old-fashioned psychiatric writers might have noted that the
beautiful electress, besides superbly representing the culture Peter held so in
awe, was also the namesake of his half-sister, the patroness of the *streltsi*.

stream of orders to Ogilvie to retreat to the Russian frontier."[8]
In the meantime he was hoping that a new Saxon army of 30,-
000 might defeat Charles's General Rehnskjold (who commanded a force of 8000) and relieve Grodno. But the Saxons
were trounced once more at Fraustadt (February, 1706) and
Peter's English General Ogilvie, in some chagrin, ordered his neglected, disease-ravaged men out of their entrenchments at
Grodno. They managed to escape across the Niemen, thus putting themselves out of Charles's reach; and on reaching Kiev,
Ogilvie, one of Peter's few capable officers, resigned in disgust.
A long, nerve-wracking period had begun for the tsar. Even so
sympathetic a biographer as Ian Grey shows clearly by his account how perturbed his subject had become. "Peter was relieved
and excited to learn that his army was safe" (April 29, 1706).
"Peter had not anticipated that Menshikov would advance so
rapidly and so far into Poland. . . . [and] had written warnings
to be on guard" (September 22, 1706). On this occasion Menshikov managed finally to defeat a Swedish army half the size of
his own under a General Mardefeld, at Kalicz, in October, 1706.
Peter received the news "'with indescribable joy'" (and doubtless not a little surprise). In the spring of 1707 Peter moved into
Poland with an army of 70,000, in expectation of a Swedish invasion, meanwhile ordering extensive defense works to be built
in Moscow. "He seemed in good spirits *but his moods were un-
predictable*. . . . He still had no further news of the Swedish
army. The suspense of waiting . . . imposed a strain on him and
he gave way to outbursts which he almost immediately regretted"
(August, 1707). (Italics added.)

In the same month Charles, with the largest army of his career,* began his fateful march eastward, mercilessly looting the
Poles as he went. (The Poles, in that era, seem to have become
"residue" in both Russian and Western eyes. While Charles
ground money and supplies out of them, Peter, up ahead, was
putting their whole countryside to the torch.) By December the
Swedes crossed the Vistula with some difficulty, the Russians having burned the bridges in their path. "Soon after learning that
the Swedish army had at last moved [into Poland] Peter left

---

* By one account, 20,000 foot and 24,000 horse.

Warsaw to go to St. Petersburg. He traveled slowly for he was waiting for some indication of his enemy's intentions."[8]

By January, 1708, Charles was again crossing the Niemen. Peter hastened back to Grodno and there, to his astonishment, found the garrison under attack from a small advance force commanded by Charles himself. "Hearing the gunfire, Peter thought that the whole Swedish army had reached Grodno. At dawn he hurriedly left with Menshikov. . . ." The Swedes pressed on, as did the tsar in a somewhat different sense. "Taking advantage of Charles's halt at Radoshkovichi, Peter decided to go off to St. Petersburg again" (March, 1708).[8]

By this time the Swedish king's plans were beginning to be seriously upset by the tactics of devastation and hit-and-run warfare that the Russians were later to use with such success against Napoleon and Adolf Hitler. It was there tactics which prevented Charles from catching up with the tsar, or at least with his army, directly after the brush at Grodno. Long before Charles went into winter quarters at Radoshkovichi, his men had begun to suffer severely from cold and hunger. By spring many were dying of disease. However, in April, 1708, "Menshikov reported that the Swedes were building bridges over the rivers in preparation for their advance to the Russian frontier. . . . Peter replied that he was not to be summoned back to the army unless there was completely reliable information that the enemy was advancing"— adding that, having recently been sick, he hoped to be permitted to remain in St. Petersburg for "five or six weeks longer."[8] Either because he was not yet well enough, or had failed to receive completely reliable information as to the Swedes' movements, Peter was fortunately not able to be with his troops when they attempted to block Charles's crossing of the river Wabis (or Bibich or Vabitch), near Holovzin (Holowczyn), on the fourth of July. The Russians were commanded by General Goltz, Prince Repnin, and the perennial Scheremetyev, and Charles was in such haste to attack them that he did so before his whole force had come up. The result was another Narva, less decisive for the Russians than the first, but fought if possible with still greater stupidity. All that summer it had been raining and continued to rain, delaying or spoiling the harvest and making forage almost nonexistent, even where the Russians had omitted to destroy it. Charles's earlier attempt to outflank the southern wing of their army under General Goltz had failed because he was slowed down by mud. The whole Russian force at length entrenched itself on the farther (eastern) bank of the Wabis, Scheremetyev with the main infantry group taking a position on the right, Prince Repnin with a second infantry group in the center, and Goltz commanding miscellaneous cavalry formations on the left (southern) end of the line.

Charles, having looked over these dispositions, decided that they could best be breached at a point between Scheremetyev's and Repnin's groups. At dawn on July 4, 1708, the Swedish artillery opened up on Repnin, surprise having already been lost because the rain and sodden roads had prevented the leather pontoons needed by Charles's engineers from being brought up in time. Instead of charging over bridges previously built in the dark, the Swedes were forced to wade across in chest-deep water, and the king's usual effect of speed was further lost because the ground on the other side turned out to be mushy. As he had on hand only his forward troops, amounting to some 12,000 men, he was also at his normal disadvantage in numbers—here probably about three to one. None of this seems to have fazed him in the least. He himself led the first attack unit, a battalion of grenadiers, across the river, where they, and the units of foot and horse which followed, found themselves struggling through heavy muck continuously made mushier by churning. Repnin meanwhile managed to shift a few of his cannon to the right and open up on the Swedes, some units having to stand still under this artillery attack while those behind labored up to close ranks with them. Fortunately for Charles, Repnin had no eye for military opportunity. Instead of counterattacking with his infantry while the odds were still good, he at once began to withdraw. The Swedes, impeded as they were and clearly vulnerable, nonetheless made frantic efforts to push forward to solid ground and catch up with them. Repnin (as he said later at his court-martial) had sent desperate messages to Scheremetyev on his right and Goltz on his left, but neither made a move to help him. Even some of his own troops slightly to the south seem to have done nothing until he ordered them into their entrenchments, whereupon, like Admiral Suffren's insubordinate captains in the action against

Hughes, off Ceylon, seventy-three years later, they opened fire at too long a range to have any effect, shooting, it seems, simply as a gesture of zeal or compliance.

The Swedes, having at last gained a surer footing, swung to the right and began briskly mopping up what remained of Repnin's infantrymen. Meanwhile they had got a few bridges built and their cavalry was pouring across the river, only to become stuck in the same flypaper as the infantry units had been. Two regiments of Goltz's Russian dragoons (which might have had a disastrous effect had they come into action even a few minutes sooner) now suddenly appeared and began to ride down the Swedish foot soldiers in Repnin's position. Charles's General Rehnskjold, with all the cavalry he could get together—two squadrons or about 400 men—rode furiously to the rescue, and was nearly engulfed himself until another squadron, the Drabants, joined him. Still a third Russian cavalry regiment appeared and the Swedes were again almost overwhelmed, to be saved once more by two squadrons of the Household Dragoons and finally by the arrival of the Household Regiment. These last reinforcements decided the matter. The front line of Russians broke and, in fleeing, rode into some of their own cavalry, throwing the relieving troops into disorder. A general rout followed. The remaining Russian horse, a brigade of four regiments under Prince Hesse-Darmstadt (the southernmost group) was surprised while riding placidly northward, and encircled and badly cut up before finally escaping. It was a brilliant if chancy victory for the Swedish cavalry, whose numbers engaged had begun at a mere 400, and risen to about 2500 as the battle developed. They had driven Goltz's entire command of 10,000 men from the field with Russian casualties in killed and missing reported to be about 2500.

Scheremetyev, meanwhile, on the far northern end of the Russian line, had been thinking, and had finally hit upon a plan. He would recross the river, get in Charles's rear, seize his baggage in Holovzin, and cut him off from the remainder of his army, which was yet to come up. It was a good idea conceived hours too late. As Scheremetyev was about to execute it a column of Swedish infantry suddenly appeared behind Holovzin, and he paused to reconsider. Charles, for his part, having dealt with Repnin and

Goltz, had made an about-face and was about to attack Scheremetyev in flank when he received an erroneous report that Rehnskjold was in trouble, and accordingly held up his advance. At no
time does it seem to have occurred to the Russian general to attack Charles, either then or earlier when he might have taken him
in the rear. Now that Holovzin was invested and general action at
a standstill, Scheremetyev decided not to tempt fate and quickly
withdrew up the muddy roads into the interior, by one account
dividing his force in three and dispersing it as he did so.

The Swedish losses amounted to some 267 killed and 1000
wounded, the Drabants losing 42 out of their total strength
(which had already by then dropped from 200 to 150). From the
standpoint of either side, it had been a disappointing encounter.
The risks the king took, even granted that he thoroughly understood his enemy, were insane. It was nothing short of miraculous
that Rehnskjold was able to save the situation as he did and that
the Russians remained so ill co-ordinated and ineffectual in the
face of an assault whose foolhardiness and total lack of surprise
should have been an inspiration to them.

It was Charles's last victory in pitched battle against them,
and had clearly come harder than his first.

However, as Ian Grey notes, "the Russian army, except for
certain of Repnin's regiments, had retreated in good order, and
the fact that one wing had stood up for so long against the
Swedes,* led by Charles himself, had a good effect on Russian
morale." In fact, after this heartening reverse the tempo of devastation across the countryside and of bush warfare against the
Swedes seems to have picked up. On August 31, at Meskowitz,
near the border, the Russians imitated Charles at Holovzin; they
crossed a marsh on fascines and made a surprise attack at dawn
on the rearmost Swedish army group, commanded by General
Roos. A bloody two-hour battle followed. The Russians, unable
to force a decision, then "made an orderly retreat, having inflicted heavy losses . . . Peter was elated. He wrote to Apraxin,
to Catherine and others about the actions, as well as preparing
a proclamation to his people." In fact, Grey adds, "his enthusiasm

---

* A fact as much attributable to Swedish difficulties with the terrain as to
the new Russian discipline, it would appear.

seemed quite out of proportion"[8]—but it is natural to rejoice in good omens, especially when these have been scarce.

It was at about this time that the omens for Charles began to turn bad. The summer had been a hard one. By the end of July pasture was becoming difficult to find and food was running short. By August 5 the king had crossed the Dnieper and started moving slowly southeastward, partly to forage, partly to convince the tsar that he intended taking the southern route to Moscow, through Briansk. By mid-August the outlook had improved slightly. The Swedes had come upon some late-ripening rye which the Guards threshed and ground. Charles had also succeeded in drawing Menshikov and the bulk of the Russian cavalry after him. The object of this maneuver was to keep the Russians away from a relieving force of 12,000 to 16,000 men, including a large train of supplies, which was supposed to be joining Charles from Riga. The commander of this operation was General Adam Ludvig Lewenhaupt, a man so queer and dilatory and given to grotesque blunders that he might well have been one of our own Civil War generals. Lewenhaupt was a soldier who fought by the book, for the most part ably and with great personal courage, leading his men into battle in lines whose straightness he had been known to boast about afterwards.* This same man apparently suffered from a touchy jealousy of all those close to him in rank, was prone to consuming fantasies of persecution, never forgave a slight or doubted his ability to judge one, and when in the grip of any one of his idiosyncrasies was capable of a quite suicidal incompetence.

Charles had called him down into Poland the previous spring, evidently having never met him before (Lewenhaupt is said to have felt unappreciated by His Majesty at once, because Charles did not make enough of the victories his general had won). There they had planned Lewenhaupt's march down from the Baltic. It was supposed to have started early in June, 1708, but in fact got off at the end of the month. Lewenhaupt himself, rather oddly, in view of the urgency of his mission, stayed back in Riga a month longer, his troops meanwhile making some 143 miles (4.7 miles per day), or just under half the progress Charles had ex-

---

* For instance, after his victory over Scheremetyev in Courland.

pected. By July 29 they had only got as far as Vilna in Poland. By the latter part of August, Charles, now close to the Russian frontier, was expecting word of them at any moment, and delaying his march accordingly. Their arrival was indeed crucial to his plans. For with the supplies Lewenhaupt would be bringing, and the weather still passably good, Charles would be in a position to change course and strike out for Moscow along the Smolensk road. Without Lewenhaupt, he not only had to operate with a substantially smaller army, but was forced into a continual hunt for food, an emergency which canceled all other plans, threatening to turn his invasion into a mere armed wandering.

By mid-September, two weeks or so after the action at Meskowitz, the king, evidently still thinking that Lewenhaupt could not be far off, had swerved from his earlier course, moving north again to Tatarsk, on the Russian border, not far from Smolensk and the main road to Moscow. If, as some have said, he expected to find less devastation ahead of him than he had all across Poland, he was disappointed. For miles into the Russian interior, fields and villages now lay in flames. (Before Smolensk itself, Scheremetyev, whose feeling for security exceeded even the tsar's, had created a roadblock by felling an entire forest.) No couriers had come from Lewenhaupt. The shortage of supplies was once more critical; and with cold weather coming on, a bare, hostile countryside to traverse, and no relieving columns in sight, an advance on Moscow was clearly unthinkable. For the first time in his eight years of war, Charles was at a standstill.

There are those who believe that a man's momentum is his luck. And while some who have had this ability to propel themselves unfailingly upward to greater and greater success have then had the misfortune to be deprived of it at a single mortal stroke, it is also true that many have shown an almost magical invulnerability on the way. One thinks of John F. Kennedy's war experiences; of the threats and scuffles which Martin Luther King survived without a scratch; or of the great Henry of Navarre, who for years led his men in the field, only to be killed by an assassin long after his campaigning days were over. Charles was not one of this tragic company. His career was not, like theirs, an arrow which kept its perfect flight until suddenly and finally stopped; but for a time it seemed to be, and for just that long,

everything he attempted was as if under a spell. He had the sort
of luck card players despair of in others. In battle he exposed
himself with utter recklessness, often fighting hand-to-hand in
the front ranks. Again and again the men beside him were killed.
He lost innumerable horses. At the siege of Thorn, cannon balls
rolled into his tent. Later he was involved in dangerous forward
actions in which he and his troopers were heavily outnumbered
and just managed to extricate themselves. Yet though the enemy
had seen him countless times, and a considerable premium must
have been put on his head, he was never even wounded. After
Narva, a musket ball was found in his neck cloth. And once while
he rode out to review his Valacks, the Polish light cavalry, his
horse tripped on a tent rope and threw him, breaking his leg.
Some six months later he had a serious bout of fever (apparently
the grippe). No other harm befell him. He seemed to be bullet-
proof, and his plans were as charmed as his person. In battle,
detachments always arrived just where they were needed; the
day was saved or the decision clinched by the perfectly timed
action of his field officers; none of his calculations ever turned
out to err in the realization. Of all the facts about him this one is
the most extraordinary, for as Clausewitz was later to remark,
it takes no great ability to draft an intelligent plan of battle, but
a phenomenal combination of intuition, personal force, nagging,
and luck to get an army to do what one has planned. It is still
harder for a commander to get his subordinates to understand
and promptly execute changes in plan which he sees to be necessary on the spot. Charles was *par excellence* this sort of spur-of-
the-moment general, and most of what he instantaneously
decided upon appears, by some miracle, to have been carried out.
It is no wonder that as a tactician he took insane risks; for nearly
a decade he had gained nothing but success from doing so. But
now that he had reached Tatarsk and come at last to a full stop,
everything was to be different. His momentum was gone. Though
he was to get some of it back, his luck would never return. He
was not even (or not quite) to be destroyed at a single great
blow, but rather worn down and chipped away and only long
afterwards done to death, whether by an assassin or merely by
a final quirk of chance we will probably never learn.

Short of giving up and going home, Charles had two courses open to him at Tatarsk. One was to retire on the Dnieper with a view to speeding up his junction with Lewenhaupt. The other was to move southward as rapidly as possible into a fertile and still untouched district of Russia known as Severia, where he might find victuals and fodder and take up winter quarters, pending a later attempt on Moscow by a more southerly route. According to that plan, which was the one Charles adopted, Lewenhaupt would have to be sent orders to meet him in Starodub, the capital of Severia. These orders were dispatched and reached the general within about two days, on September 18 (although he later rather inappropriately complained of the delay). Charles meanwhile set off for Severia and sent another of his commanders, General Anders Lagercrona, forward on a most vital mission, which was to proceed eastward to the Potyep Pass, and block it, so as to prevent the Russian armies from entering Severia and reaching its capital before the Swedes did. Lagercrona was given a map drafted by Charles's quartermaster general, Gyllenkrook, a man known for the infallibility of his geographical information as well as for his somewhat idiosyncratic account of this campaign.[9] The main army thereupon began a terrible march through a deep forest, sixty or more miles across, which lay in its path. Men and horses dropped dead from hunger, and hundreds were next to incapacitated by dysentery. Lagercrona, riding ahead, appears not to have trusted Gyllenkrook's map, and presently sent back word that he was following a better route. Cavalry groups which had gone forward to rendezvous with him could not find him. Sensing a disaster, the king sent on more cavalry with orders to reach the pass at any cost. It was too late. The Russians got there first. The king's remaining hope was then to reach the capital, Starodub, ahead of them, and he received the heartening news that Lagercrona had in some unaccountable way ended up near there himself, instead of far to the east, where he should have been. Unfortunately for Charles, Lagercrona was not as enterprising as his own colonels, who urged him to take the town at once. The general's one thought was to go ahead, however belatedly, and do as he had been ordered—proceed to the pass. While this matter was still being argued, almost to the point of bloodshed, between Lagercrona and his officers, the Russians themselves stole into Starodub and set fire to it. Almost before it had begun, Charles's operation against Severia was in ruins.

In the meantime, far to the rear, Lewenhaupt and his relief column had managed to get across the Dnieper (some five days after his orders to do so had arrived) and found themselves being shadowed by a sizable Russian army. Instead of putting out a rear guard and moving his main force onward with all speed, he sent his wagons on ahead, and put his troops in battle order facing the enemy, only to fight a minor action and lose a whole day's marching time. Two days later at Ljesna (Lesnaya), as he was weeding dispensable vehicles out of his train with a view to making it more mobile, he was attacked by another force, under the tsar himself. The battle was costly and the Swedes' disorderly night march to Propoisk after it almost more so. Men looted their own wagons, got drunk, straggled off in the dark (a thousand are said to have found their way back later to Riga). Out of the 12,900 effectives, foot, horse, and dragoons, that Lewenhaupt had started out with, Ensign Petré counted 6593 remaining the next day in Propoisk. The same day Lewenhaupt burned his wagon trains—six weeks' worth of supplies for the whole Swedish army —and, as destitute as his king, set out to join him. It is impossible to describe Peter's delight at this coup. (According to his biographer, Grey, Peter himself described it at some length "to his ministers and generals and even to Augustus,"* whom everyone apparently continued to like and confide in for reasons now not easy to see.) A week and a half later, Lewenhaupt, with the remnant of his army—his men having eaten horseflesh and cabbage stalks and seasoned their food with gunpowder on the way

---

* Shortly afterwards, on October 28, 1708, Peter was also able to write a letter congratulating his Admiral-General Feodor Apraxin on the withdrawal with loss of a Swedish expeditionary force which had come down from Finland with the object of dislodging the Russians from St. Petersburg and Ingria. Charles seems to have counted on this phase of his strategy to take care of itself—with no better luck than he had in the case of Lewenhaupt. Ever since Narva, nothing had gone well in that sector. In May, 1704, not long before the surrender of the town of Dorpat, a Swedish naval squadron in Lake Peipus had allowed itself to be caught in a river mouth and destroyed, its admiral, reportedly drunk at the time, blowing himself up in his ship, the *Carolus*. Charles's comment was that he had died "like a sailor but not like a Christian."

—made his rendezvous with the main force near Starodub. (Appropriately enough, the first unit he came into contact with was Lagercrona's.) The curious thing is that although Charles temporarily relieved Lewenhaupt of all serious duty, he not only failed to reprimand him but at Poltava, the climactic battle of the campaign, gave him a major field command, with what result need not be imagined since it is known.

Even before Lewenhaupt's troops arrived, some word of his disaster had reached Charles; and by the account of his quartermaster, Gyllenkrook, the king who by habit slept well, if briefly, every night now began to have insomnia. For the first time he appeared to be suffering a loss of what Napoleon called "two o'clock in the morning courage," and for good reason. The next course that suggested itself to him, more or less *faute de mieux,* was to push on into the Ukraine. The old Cossack hetman Mazeppa had at this time sent emissaries to the Swedes. These suggested that Mazeppa was ready to lead an uprising of his people, upon the appearance in the Ukraine of a Swedish covering force.* Mazeppa's capital, the city of Baturin, lay not far ahead to the south, and there Charles might logically expect to find supplies of food and gunpowder and, if only in terms of numbers, a considerable auxiliary force. The new strategic combination taking shape in his mind called for a junction with Mazeppa in the Ukraine and joint action by his man in Poland, King Stanislaus, who was supposed to send an army the following spring, under a General Krassow, to rendezvous with the already reinforced Swedes.

Unfortunately for this plan, Mazeppa was as idiotic a general

---

* Though picturesque and ferocious, the Cossacks, like their Mongol overlords of old, had no great reputation for personal courage. They had also failed to conserve anything of Mongol tactical virtuosity. In Europe they had proved difficult auxiliaries. The Swedes had particular reason to dislike them since at Latovice, near Warsaw, a detachment of 500 Swedes had surrendered to a Cossack troop, only to be slaughtered almost *in toto* after they had laid down their arms. This atrocity was avenged when, shortly after Charles's defeat of the learned General Schulenburg at Punitz (1704), some Swedish cavalry, riding ahead, came upon 2000 Cossacks whom their Saxon masters had sought to restrain by depriving them of their horses. Without further thought the Swedes surrounded them and cut them down or burned them alive in their billets, nearly to a man. In defense of Charles, it must be said that he was not much given to this sort of action. In the case mentioned the troops evidently acted on their own initiative.

as Lewenhaupt and Lagercrona. Instead of waiting in his well-supplied and fortified capital with his whole force (about 7000) for Charles's arrival, he left it, taking a part of his army (about 4000) and joined the king. He could hardly have made a worse move. The troops he brought were inadequate and those he left behind too demoralized to put up a fight. A race now began between Charles and the Russian general Menshikov, the fastest-moving of Peter's staff, to reach Baturin. En route, at the river Desna, Charles met a delaying force under General Hallart which he defeated with his usual ease; but, as was also becoming usual, this latest Russian defeat served its strategic purpose. Menshikov reached Baturin first, easily taking it and, as a matter of course, razing it and butchering the inhabitants. At a blow Mazeppa had lost not only most of his material resources but all of his prestige and his rallying power. (The next spring, when Charles in his extremity was hoping for help from the Zaporozhsky [Zaporog] Cossacks, Peter's Colonel Yakovlev made a similar descent on them, defeated them, and wiped out their capital, Perevolotnya.) Except for the men Mazeppa brought with him, many of whom later became double turncoats and disappeared, Charles was to have little help from the Ukrainian roughriders. His thoughts now began to turn to Turkey and to the Khan of the Crimea, both habitual enemies of Russia. If, say, by spring he could be joined by a combined force of Poles under Krassow, and of Crimean Tatars sent by the Khan . . .

At this juncture winter closed down. All across Europe, it was the worst in more than a century and in Russia unimaginably severe. The Baltic and the canals of Venice froze. Heavy wagons could be driven over the ice on the Seine and the Rhône. In the Ukraine birds were said to have dropped from the sky dead, and strong spirits froze solid in its casks. Firewood could not be ignited in the open; Charles's soldiers warmed themselves by burning straw. For a time they had the good luck to be quartered in Romne (Romni), a comfortable, well-provisioned town south of Baturin; but from there, according to Fuller, they were decoyed forward by the tsar to Gadiatz (Hadjatch), where accommodations were much poorer; Peter's armies then closed in on the rear and destroyed Romne.[10] On the march to Gadiatz, made by night, the Swedes suffered horribly. According to Ensign Petré, men lost feet, hands, noses, some even their genitals, by frostbite. Cavalrymen were found frozen to death in the saddle. One soldier, sitting down by the road to rest, underwent some sort of spinal contracture; the ligaments in his back parted with a crack "like a pistol shot" and he fell over dead. Several times Petré saw the king's cheeks and nose begin to whiten with frostbite, a condition Charles seems to have checked by massaging them with snow. By one account the Swedish army lost upwards of 3000 men in its fearful winter marches, though these sufferings did not prevent their small cavalry patrols from several times routing Russian forces larger than their own.

With the easing of the weather in spring, the army was deep in the Ukraine, its effectives having dropped from 32,000 to something over 20,000, 10 percent of these being still disabled by wounds, disease, or frost injuries. Charles's problem, as he thought, was even yet to lure the Russian army into a pitched battle, with or without the arrival of his Polish and Tatar allies. To this end he laid siege in May to the town of Poltava, which lies on the Vorskla some fifty miles north and east of the point at which that river empties into the Dnieper. It is believed he never meant to take the place, nor was he equipped to do so in any haste. The garrison of 5000 men under Hallart was well prepared for a siege, and Charles, besides his greatly reduced numbers and large sick list, had only thirty pieces of artillery and limited supplies of gunpowder, much of it partially spoiled. During the king's advance on Poltava in April (which he made against the advice of his generals, who were still for withdrawing into Poland), Tsar Peter seems suddenly to have felt an urge to visit his shipyards in Voronezh, on arrival there writing to Menshikov that he had fallen ill and might be detained into May. In the first week of that month Charles began the siege. During it he received crushing news, first of the liquidation of the Zaporozhsky Cossacks, second, of the defeat of Krassow in Poland by a Russian force under General Goltz. Thanks to energetic diplomatic work (chiefly threats) on the Russian side, the Turks and the Khan of the Crimea now gave no sign of coming to Charles's aid. In effect, his isolation was complete. As surely as Crassus had been, centuries before, on the sands of Mesopotamia, this far abler soldier was finally stranded in the middle of a vast desolate country, hundreds of miles from any sort of help, awaiting with the wreck of his army the assault of an enemy more tentative, perhaps, than the ancient Parthians, but in the end no less effectual.

By June, what with the events just mentioned and the flagging siege, the tsar evidently decided the outlook was improving and rejoined his army near Poltava. Just before the battle he issued a general order which said, among other things: "Of Peter it should be known that he does not value his own life but only that Russia should live, and Russian piety, glory and prosperity."[11]

Since the end of May Russian forces had been concentrating upriver, on the other side of the Vorskla from Poltava, and were in contact with Hallart, inside the fortress, by means of messages fired back and forth in bombs which had been emptied of their powder. Hallart reported he could hold out at the latest till the end of June. For some time, however, the tsar still made no move, although the army he had at hand was huge—over 45,000 by one estimate, 80,000 by another. At length, on June 17, 1709, Charles's birthday, a strong Russian cavalry detachment crossed the river to the Swedes' side, on the north, presumably to create a diversion, while Hallart began a move to break out of Poltava. The king rushed to block this attempt, at the head of a battalion, later reinforced by some Zaporozhsky Cossacks who opened on the enemy with "their handsome rifled muskets,"[12] a rather advanced weapon for that time, and especially for those troops. The king himself was caught in heavy fire and while riding away received a bad wound in his left foot, which was laid open diagonally from heel to toe by a musket ball. He ignored his injury for two and a half hours, only to fall from his horse in a faint when he came to dismount. Within minutes the whole army knew of this mishap, and not long afterwards word of it reached the Russian camp. Three days later the king's leg was swollen to the knee; he was in a high fever and at moments delirious. On the twentieth, as he lay close to death, the Russians stirred once again. Peter began moving troops across the river. The moment had at last come for him to confront his Nemesis. Even then he evidently felt it would not do to be hasty. Having brought his army over, he entrenched it in a strong camp, a mile or so north of the Swedes, and (leaving his communications exposed) sat down to await developments.

The first development—almost a miracle in view of the sweat-cure and the bloodletting to which he had been subjected—was that Charles began to recover,* though not before suffering a relapse on the twenty-fourth. By June 26 the Russians had completed their camp and were fortifying its approaches. The king decided that he must attack them forthwith; but being still able to get about only in a litter, he assigned the supreme command to Field Marshal Rehnskjold. The only open approach to the Russians' position, a little defile with woods on either side, had been blocked by a system of redoubts, six lying across the path of advance and four projecting forward from the center so as to form a salient like the stem of a T. Charles's plan was to rush the redoubts in a surprise assault at dawn, with the object of breaking through to the west and north side of the Russian position. There the Swedish army would have a chance to put itself across the Russian line of retreat; and would moreover have turned the enemy's flank, a move likely (Charles may have thought) to cause the usual amount of psychological havoc on the other side —enough, possibly, to permit his small army (by one estimate 12,500, by another about 18,000) to cut up the tsar's much larger one. General Roos was chosen to attack the redoubts opposite the Swedish center, Lewenhaupt those on the right. Sparre with foot, and Creutz and Hamilton with cavalry, were to penetrate the left and proceed on to the open ground to the north and west of the Russian camp, where the other wings would as quickly as possible join them. This plan appears to have been conveyed in its entirety to hardly anyone, Rehnskjold being as taciturn as the king. And because of his wound, Charles could not, as he had done in the past, move rapidly from place to place seeing to it himself that each unit commander did what he should when he was supposed to. Moreover, the Russian salient tended to cut the Swedish wings off from one another, dividing the army and hampering its communications from the outset.

The king's orders were for a general advance to begin just after

---

* While the king lay for several days recuperating, his old servant Hultman is said to have helped him pass the time by reciting Norse sagas. One wonders if Charles still had with him Quintus Curtius' *Alexander,* a book he had carried on his earlier campaigns; or if he recalled the Plutarch he must have read in the days of his scholarly youth.

midnight on June 27. A certain confusion set in at once, "from want," as one writer puts it, "of detailed instructions."[13] The result was that all units were late in coming into position, and by the time dawn had begun to break the Russians had got wind of what was up. A warning shot was fired, and sounds of hammering and sawing which had been coming from their redoubts abruptly died away. Very soon afterwards Peter drew a strong force of cavalry and foot out of his camp and placed it behind the redoubts. The Russian artillery opened fire.

The king was then in his litter with Sparre's infantry on the Swedish left, and there Rehnskjold came to him for the final conference at which the details of the attack were apparently decided on. If that is indeed how it happened, there was little time for others to be informed; and except for a few such as Colonel of the day Siegroth, attached to Roos's units in the center, none of the field officers seems to have known exactly what the plan was or what he was expected to do. Most unfortunately, Siegroth himself was killed just as the battle started. If any single death could be said to have decided the outcome it was probably his. At 4:00 A.M. the Swedish attack got under way.

On the left, where Charles evidently remained, borne along with the troops on his litter, the Russians were promptly routed, Creutz and Hamilton reaching the open ground to the north and west of the Russian camp as planned. Rehnskjold succeeded quite early in driving off Menshikov's cavalry, stationed behind the redoubts, and he then appears to have joined the others. All was so far going quite well. By 6:00 A.M. the Swedish units which had broken through were already forming up in their new position for the grand assault. But now a difficulty developed. Roos and Lewenhaupt had not arrived. And with the army so shrunken, their numbers could not be spared. No major attack was possible without them. Where were they? Couriers were dispatched to find out.

To his consternation, Rehnskjold presently learned that Lewenhaupt, in his usual straight-line way, had proceeded through the redoubts and on ahead far to the right, to a position under the palisades of the Russian camp, where, his mission accomplished, he had halted. He was ordered to rejoin the main body at once, and reasonably soon did so (whereupon the field marshal gave him a tongue-lashing*)—but already time was running against them all. The advantage Charles had always relied on in battle— had held even at the start of this one—was slipping away; he was losing his momentum. Almost his only hope of defeating the Russians lay in keeping them off balance—subjecting them to an unbroken succession of attacks which would annihilate their vast army, a unit or a wing at a time, and inspire the usual rapidly spreading disorder and vacillation in the rest of it. Instead, whole hours were passing in the search for Roos, while the enemy, as had never happened before, was being given time to regroup and to shore up his courage as best he might (which was somewhat better than formerly).

Roos's situation, it soon developed, was grave. Instead of bypassing the redoubts in the salient and pushing on, he had set about reducing them one by one. Immediately he lost headway, began to suffer stiff casualties, and fell out of contact with the units on either side of him. Siegroth, who might have prevented this disastrous blunder, lay somewhere in the melee dying. The tsar, meanwhile, seeing Roos's difficulty, sent a force of 10,000 under General Rensel to attack him and split him off from the main body completely. The Swedish General Schlippenbach, having also seen what was happening, tried to ride out for help but was intercepted by Rensel's men. To complete the confusion, a courier sent off by Roos, seeing Schlippenbach as he rode up among the Russians, mistook Rensel's men for Swedes and was captured himself. All lines of communication with the rest of the army were now cut. Roos's force was soon surrounded and slowly driven off southward, almost to the town of Poltava. By the time he surrendered he had only 400 men left out of 2600. It was then ten o'clock in the morning, and far away, the main engagement was just beginning. With Roos's surrender, one-third of the Swedish infantry had already been lost.

As soon as it became clear that Rensel's attack might succeed,

---

* This is Bengtsson's version. Fuller says that Lewenhaupt was blamed for not attacking the camp, having halted at the last moment on an order he later said he got "from a loyal servant of the king." According to Bengtsson, such an attack would have been impossible because of a ditch in Lewenhaupt's front, and was in any case never a part of Rehnskjold's plan. This seems the likelier account.

Peter (who by one account had been jittery and just on the point of bolting) took heart and, drawing the rest of his troops out of the camp, formed them into battle order. As he did, the Swedes appear to have made a flank march in column, across his front, looking for a place to make a stand. While this maneuver was proceeding, Lewenhaupt received, or thought he did, an order to halt and form front and, ignoring the units on either side of him, did so. The order was quickly countermanded and Lewenhaupt* violently rebuked, but too late. Seeing Lewenhaupt's move, the Russians evidently thought the Swedes were about to attack and speeded up their own preparations. More or less by accident, they had picked the perfect moment to strike. Half the Swedish cavalry, under Hamilton, was still floundering across a marsh to the rear, and the other half, under Creutz, had not yet brought itself into sufficient order to fight. The Swedish foot were just at a point where the Russians, with their much larger numbers, could easily envelop them on both flanks.

But now, seeing what was coming, the Swedes ceased maneuvering and prepared to do battle where they were. The infantry—ten battalions by the reckoning of that day, or some 4000 men—formed into battle order, leaving large gaps between units so as to stretch their line as far as possible. None of Charles's thirty guns was on hand, since the order to bring them up had been sent too late. For want of powder, most of the men would go in without firing a shot, relying on their bayonets. They had only their right-wing cavalry for support, Hamilton still being stuck in the mud to the rear.

Facing them stood 16,000 to 20,000 Russian foot soldiers, in an unbroken line which extended around the ends of their own. Particularly opposite the Swedish left, they had brought up a considerable number of field guns. As the tsar's army drew close, it halted and the guns went into action. Even then, it seems, he would not risk an assault without massive preparation. And even

---

* It is consistent with Lewenhaupt's character—especially in view of the fact that Rehnskjold, unlike the king, bluntly disliked him and held him responsible for the disaster of Lesnaya—that he should have half-unconsciously done things in this battle to foul up his superiors' plans. No longer the supreme commander he had once been in the Baltic states—now indeed a somewhat despised subordinate—he may have developed a strong will for others to fail. In modern armies his type is apparently not unfamiliar.

then, ill armed and already engulfed as they were, the Swedes would not wait for him. As the Russian cannon blasted into their thin ranks and the long volleys of musket fire began cutting them down, the remains of Charles's army—the veterans of Fraustadt and Klissow and Holovzin, a few perhaps even of Narva*—went in a last time to the attack, driving forward into the dense Russian masses and failing where they stood—"in heaps," as one survivor said: the Upplanders, Mannersvärd's and Gyllenstierna's Guards battalions, the Kalmar and Skaraborg regiments, "whom the enemy with pike, bayonet, and sword was eagerly slaughtering and massacring with all his might."[14] Out of the 4000 hardly a man escaped.

The king's litter was shattered by cannon fire and most of his bearers killed. As the battle was ending, about noon, Charles managed to commandeer a horse from one of his Drabants and, putting his wounded foot up on its neck, rode away, his wound, as he did so, opening again and beginning to bleed. Rehnskjold was last heard shouting to Count Piper that all was over—oddly enough in German ("*Alles ist verloren!*"). Shortly afterwards the Russians had him. Of the estimated 18,000 who had gone into action, the Swedes lost 300 officers, 16 Drabants, and 6600 of lower ranks killed. An additional 200 officers and 2600 men were taken prisoner. Rehnskjold was not to see his master again until 1718 on his release from Russia, and just before the death of Charles himself, by a gunshot wound during a siege in Norway.†

Whether the Russians were too elated to follow up with a pursuit, or simply felt it unnecessary, Charles and a part of his army (with Lewenhaupt, of all people, as its only remaining senior

* The Swedish army records of the period show that at least one veteran— Peter Paul Wulff—who had served in the Jönköping regiment in 1675, and later with Charles from 1703 on, fought as an ensign at Poltava at the incredible age of eighty. He was captured, returning to Jönköping from Siberia in 1722, and died, an ensign, retired, in 1725.

† It was long believed, and even, as a friend tells me, taught to Swedish schoolchildren, that Charles was shot by Captain André Sicre, a French mercenary who later confessed to the murder while in a delirium. The argument is that Charles was too far from the besieged fortress to have been hit from there. In camp with him at the time was Frederick of Hesse, his brother-in-law and heir apparent to the throne, who in fact became king of Sweden after his death. The story that Charles was killed for good dynastic reasons is said to have been discredited, but has a certain plausibility still.

officer) escaped and began making their way south to the Dnieper. The tsar meanwhile had Rehnskjold, Count Piper, and other high-ranking Swedes brought to his tent and held a great celebration. During it, after salutes of cannon fire, the tsar gallantly toasted his enemies, whom he called his "teachers in the art of war."[15]

Charles on the retreat became feverish and confused. At the Dnieper it was found the army could not get across. The king, however, with about 1000 troops, and the aged Mazeppa were able to do so, Lewenhaupt electing to stay behind and promising to give a good account of himself. A day or so later he surrendered his whole force—just over 14,000 men—to Menshikov. The army which had been the marvel of Europe was gone.

Charles himself pushed on into Turkey (which then included much of the Balkans), where his career deteriorated into somewhat sinister *opéra bouffe*. He spent years trying to engineer a major Turkish assault on Russia, and at one point almost managed it. In the spring of 1711 the Sultan put a gigantic army into the field (it supposedly numbered 100,000) under command of an hysterical incompetent known as Mehemet Pasha, or Baltaji (the Woodcutter). Peter advanced to meet it on the river Prut, assisted by his old comrades-in-arms Repnin, Hallart, and Scheremetyev. He had expected to receive help from a rebellious Turkish vassal in Moldavia but, like Charles before him, in his dealings with the Cossacks, the tsar was soon disappointed. His allies never materialized; while en route the Crimean Tatars relentlessly harassed and wore him down. At length, after grave losses, he and his force of 40,000 managed to get themselves trapped against the Prut by the Tatars and the Sultan's host.* Peter is said to have gone into an almost insane panic, running in tears about his camp, and ordering a tremendous underground bunker built for himself and the Tsarina Catherine, who had accompanied him on this calamitous expedition. While he had learned

* This mishap was in fact very serious. It was the Khan of the Crimea who trapped the Russians in the first place. Their army had already lost its baggage train and most of its horses to the Tatars, and was dug in without food behind whatever fortifications it could throw up—mostly its own dead mounts. While the Khan kept the Russians pinned down, the Turkish army crossed the river and joined him and the disaster was complete—or in any sensibly run campaign should have been.

something of the art of war from his teachers, it is clear that he was some way short of an advanced degree, and if only for psychiatric reasons might never make it. In the blackest moment of this crisis, at dawn of the day when all was ready for the great Turkish onslaught, some thought they saw a familiar figure—a solitary horseman wearing a dark blue greatcoat and saber, riding slowly along the far bank of the river—but it was only an illusion,* cast up in the tsar's disordered mind, or Repnin's or Scheremetyev's, by the power of long association.

As a desperate last move, Peter was urged by an aide to send a peace proposal to the Turkish commander. He did so, having little to lose including face; and to the consternation of all—the Khan of the Crimea not least, one imagines—the Turkish commander accepted it. Charles's last bid for an invasion by proxy had failed. He shortly fell out with his Turkish hosts and was attacked by them in force with only a small body of his veterans to defend him. The fighting quickly got to the hand-to-hand stage, the king with his enormous old saber (in its scabbard it reached from the ground almost up to his armpit) wading into the melee as he had so often done in the past. In Persia, where the Turks were not popular, pictures soon circulated showing Charles with two, or in some cases four, Turks impaled on his sword. But the encounter was hardly more than a scuffle—nothing the Turks did at that time seemed to come to much—and shortly afterwards Charles was making his way across Europe for a last go at restoring Sweden's fortunes. He might better have stayed away. Stralsund on the European mainland was reduced to rubble around him. The Swedes at home were exhausted, insolvent, and understandably wary of further adventures. Their old enemies the Danes were gaining on them with Russian help; and all their Baltic provinces, including Finland, were gone. Within slightly less than a century, the empire built by Gustavus Adolphus had ceased to exist. Poltava had been decisive, beyond question. It was the only major engagement Charles ever lost. He was twenty-seven when he lost it, and thirty-six at the time of his death in Norway, in 1718.

As for Peter, Poltava gained him much, and history, as it usu-

---

* Charles was far away, in Turkey.

ally does, honors the means in light of the result. But no one who saw that day and survived to recall it—especially no one who had also seen all that led up to it—would have been likely, I think, to take it for anything but the slightly seedy triumph it was. Much has been made of the Russian strategy in Charles's last campaign, but in reality it was little more than a crude and ruinously expensive substitute for competence. To ravage large areas of an already backward country, and one's own at that, to bleed out campaigns which should have been decided in weeks over months and years, are hardly acts of high military intelligence. The only excuse for them is an incapacity to do anything else, and that, Peter felt, perhaps correctly, he had. It is certain that most of his generals did.

Charles on the other hand was *too* competent, too much a *Wunderkind*. Without him his commanders were simply what they were—dull or mediocre or reasonably skilled professionals who could never on their own have undertaken a tenth of what they did in his company, and doubtless would not have dreamed of trying. A man of obvious ability and depth who might, under other conditions, have become a mathematician or a philosopher*—though possibly never a statesman—Charles was driven

---

* Coming back to Sweden after fifteen years of campaigning, Charles found himself in Lund, temporarily at leisure while new troops and more money were being raised from his depleted kingdom. He seems to have attended the university there, discussing mathematics and philosophy with, among others, Swedenborg, and setting down fourteen postulates as the basis for a philosophy of his own (needless to say never finished). Swedenborg had a high opinion of his intellectual gifts—which makes it all the more sad and puzzling that throughout his life he used them so narrowly. Perhaps the tiny lion soon came to see it could never defeat the enormous, if still timid and disorganized, mouse, but could not forbear trying. In fact, Charles's choices were few. He might have resigned himself to giving up piecemeal, by negotiation, what was taken from him in a lump, by force—but such a course was contrary to all that he was and had been trained to be. His solution to this impossible problem may have been to suppress his larger awareness of his position—which might account for his curious defects as a strategist and the enigmatic folly of his long foray into Russia. Once, late in that campaign, he instructed Quartermaster General Gyllenkrook to prepare him maps of Asia—this apparently being a complex joke designed to fluster his old officer while perhaps ridiculing his own ambition to emulate Alexander, an ambition even then not quite dead. Anders Alstrin, the student of Uppsala and later memoirist, said of him: "It is a strange thing that painters find it difficult to catch his likeness, for I never yet saw a portrait of him that hit it off."[16]

to specialize too soon. Of all the men he might have been, circumstances quickly forced him to choose one; and the hopelessness of the military problem he was called upon to solve, together with his early success in solving it, may then have made the choice irrevocable. He was (or perhaps became) medieval in that war was his obsession. Like Edward III he had little time, and possibly no liking, for administrative matters, leaving those to his slow-moving elderly ministers in Stockholm and showing few signs in his long, busy career that he understood the world which was growing around him—one in which numbers, wealth, and strategic position were to be everything and questions of honor and dynastic polity utterly forgotten. Not many others of his day understood it either, but one may suppose that Peter did. Of the two he was far the more modern—a psychically disheveled realist, given to brutal excesses and totally expedient in his use of power, but nonetheless a man who saw through to the issues that really concerned his country. In contrast to Charles's, the tsar's acts and preoccupations were of far greater scope, most of them converging on a common aim and a surprising number of them yielding substantial results. Just as he shaved his prelates' beards, discouraged traditional forms of dress as impractical, and defied the xenophobia of his people by openly favoring foreigners and their handiwork, so, for all his absurdity as a commander, he achieved in the field what he had set out to. One may find him too rapaciously "natural," too "sincere" in the naked animal fashion which we are trying in this century to accept as the right and necessary way for men to be; one may even object that in the interests of his beloved Russia, he killed too many of his beloved Russians. He still fell short of bad generalship in one essential— he did not kill people for absolutely nothing. In the end, Charles did.

CHAPTER VI

"Whose Blood Have I Shed?"*

The Wars of the Spanish, Polish, and Austrian Succession, the Seven Years' War, and even our War of Independence, were the last of the old-fashioned ones. The French Revolution, Valmy, and democracy's stepchild, Napoleon, among them began a new era in the combat of nations, although one perhaps not obvious as such until the time of our own Civil War. The armies of Charles XII's time were still small and personal, being made up of long-term enlistees from the home country, or of foreign mercenaries, many of whom were evidently more inspired by the skill of a particular leader than by zeal for a particular cause. Modern armies are large corporate ventures, exceedingly mixed in psychological make-up and labyrinthine in complexity. Some, like Caesar's, Napoleon's, Hitler's, or even McClellan's, are in a sense personal; but because of the sheer numbers involved, the Great Leader can never be real to his troops in quite the way that Charles was to his. Far from being a disadvantage, this remoteness permits a modern-style leader to create an "image" of himself often more attractive than the reality might be, the only problem then being to maintain it.

For while it may be easier to delude a large mass of men than

* Napoleon to Montholon, on St. Helena. The full quotation reads: "Whose blood have I shed? Who can boast that in my place he would have acted differently? What epoch confronted with similar difficulties, has ever come through with such blameless results? I believe it to be without parallel in history that a plain man should have attained such amazing power without committing a single crime."[1]

a small one, it is also proportionately harder to manage large masses in battle—i.e., to get the results necessary to one's "image" in the first place.* Clausewitz was quite aware of this problem. In a memorandum to Prince August just before going off to fight with the Russians against Napoleon, he remarked that although it takes no great intelligence to devise a sound battle plan, something like genius is needed to overcome the internal friction of the army intended to carry it out. He might have added that this difficulty increases not in direct ratio to the number of men involved but as some power of it. Unfortunately the opposite applies in the case of propaganda; the larger the group one is addressing, the bigger the lies one can get away with, at least for a while. This amounts to saying that distance lends credulity, that the further away an event is, the more unhesitatingly men will believe any report of it. As a companion problem to the unmanageability of large armies, this one may have gone far toward creating the lunatic atmosphere in which world affairs in our own day seem to be conducted.†

Napoleon may be regarded as the grandfather of these developments. He had a flair for the theatrical, apparently uncomplicated by any real warmth or sentiment. He knew the weaknesses of his own people and played upon them without compunction. Even as he rallied them for yet another outpouring of blood and money, he was clearheaded enough to see that the man they thought they adored was a figment, the personification of their own ferocious vanity. It is a tribute to his methods that millions of them venerate him to this day.‡

The same principle which worked for him in domestic affairs and recruitment acted steadily to compound his difficulties in

---

* Contrary to Bertrand Russell's suggestion that propaganda can make men believe absolutely anything, a modern military leader, it seems, must have *some* success to support his press releases. Back of the ad, somewhere, there must be a product.

† For instance the Cold War, or Hitler's War of Nerves in the 1930s. The basic fact seems to be that the media have not annihilated space in the sense of enabling men at last to think sensibly about distant events; quite the reverse. Thanks to radio, TV and the press we can now develop absurd misconceptions about peoples and governments we once hardly knew existed.

‡ To the point that during the presidency of De Gaulle the celebration of the 150th anniversary of Waterloo was, I believe, called off—a procedure which *le petit caporal* himself would certainly have approved. He followed it often enough himself, for instance after the campaign in Russia, when the French press reported the outcome with notable restraint.

warfare. He had inherited the already large armies of the Revolution and of necessity—as his foreign enemies increased—made them larger. In doing so he began a trend which reached its apogee in World War I, when the numbers and firepower of the men in the field clearly defied the ability of the high command on either side to handle them. The result was a conflict so ghastly that the whole western world staggered under the blow. One more like World War I and pacifism might have become a universal religion. Even now there is a certain rumbling in the ranks, but probably nothing will come of it. The old common sense which has kept us at each other's throats for centuries will doubtless prevail and the business of nations proceed as it always has, for however long circumstances may permit. One feels that Napoleon, with his callousness and personal courage, would have been quite at home in the Nuclear Age; while the problem which haunted him in his later career—absence of staffwork—he might have found if anything oversolved today.

It is not usual, I know, to classify him as a bad general, but in certain quite crucial ways he was one. In war, as in sport or chess, the final test is not superb form or brilliant conception; it is victory. To rate as a military genius, just as to be acknowledged champion in the prize ring, it is necessary to win the Big One. Not all great commanders meet this requirement, of course. Without question, Lee was a better general than Grant, at least in Grant's Wilderness period. Lee won all the Big Ones; he simply could not afford to go on winning and retreating, whereas Grant could afford to go on losing and advancing. Napoleon lost the Big Ones, and not from want of material advantage. At Waterloo, for most of the day, he outnumbered Wellington 74,000 to 67,600; more important, he had 246 guns to Wellington's 156. With a little of his earlier foresight and verve he might have outnumbered Wellington by far more. Instead, like a textbook bad general, he divided his forces, sending Marshal Grouchy off on a mission of no consequence which the latter faithfully accomplished within sound of the guns that were ending his own and his emperor's career.*

One explanation offered for Napoleon's later failures is his

* After Waterloo Grouchy was court-martialed. He escaped death but was exiled to America, a fate any Frenchman today would regard with horror; and though soon delivered from it, he was never afterward liked or favored.

health. The emperor is said to have suffered from cystitis, a recurrent inflammation of the urinary tract, often touched off in him by exposure to cold. He is believed to have had an attack of it at Borodino, during his Russian campaign in 1812. In that battle, for whatever reason, he evidently went into a kind of agitated fugue state, huddling silently by his campfire and leaving the conduct of operations to his marshals. It is a question whether cold and the physiology of discomfort could, of themselves, have produced this sudden blackout. After Moscow had gone up in flames, and the already decimated Grand Army was approaching the horrors of the Berezina crossing, Napoleon had a conference with his generals about the lines of retreat still open to him. According to one of his aides, General Philippe-Paul de Ségur: ". . . He pointed out on his staff map the portion of the Berezina just above Borisov, declaring that it was there he wished to cross. When the general reminded him that Tchitchakov occupied all the right bank, the emperor indicated another spot below the first and still a third, nearer the Dnieper. Realizing that he was approaching the country of the Cossacks, he desisted. 'Ah yes,' he cried, 'Poltava . . . Like Charles XII.' . . . And this similarity of his situation and the Swedish conqueror's threw him into such despair that he fell ill, afflicted even more cruelly than at Malo-Yaroslavetz.* In his distress he was heard to mutter, 'This is what happens when one heaps one mistake upon another.' "[2]

A year or so later, during the battle of Dresden (which he won), Napoleon had another of his "unaccountable attacks of apparent intellectual paralysis,"[3] and after crouching for a while by a fire, as at Borodino, left the field without further word to his subordinates. He seems to have remained in a confused state for some time, during it composing a memorandum which has puzzled military scholars ever since. In its odd antique language, the memorandum suggests that the emperor had suddenly reverted to his cadet days, expressing many of the military ideas "in which he had been brought up [and] which he himself had destroyed."[3]

It is well known that at Waterloo the emperor was not in the best of health. The problem, for historians, is what ailed him.

---

* At Malo-Yaroslavetz, the Russians attacked and badly cut up a part of the French army. Both sides then marched off in opposite directions.

One says "bladder trouble" and toothache,[4] another, cystitis and piles.[*5] After Ligny, one of the battles which preceded the main engagement, he seems to have been overcome by a strange inertia. Although he continued to chat with his staff, he was evidently somewhat disoriented and (as if waiting for this condition to pass) declined for some time to give any orders. According to some writers, he left much of the conduct of Waterloo to Marshal Ney.

The clue to Napoleon's fading powers and ultimate disaster is not, I suspect, to be found in his diseases or advancing age (he was forty-six at Waterloo); still less in an old-fashioned psychoanalysis which might explain his ailments as the result of "repressed conflicts." The clue may lie in what one could call his temperamental modernity. He was anything but repressed—far less so, indeed, than poor Freud. His earlier career suggests, not inner division, but a phenomenal readiness to "act out" his slightest intention. Nor did he do so blindly or in any doubt as to what he was really after. He enjoyed for the most part perfect clarity as to both aims and means; and in his actions, perfect freedom from timidity or moral reluctance. This is not to say he chose his career in the usual sense. His nature appears almost to have forced him to it. The "pleasure principle" drove him, in the same naked unapologetic way we now try to let it drive us, the "reality principle" being merely the faithful servant and formulator of policy which made his innumerable creature wishes come true. The chief of these was to rise, to head the butting order, to take all by being all. Numbers of men have of course set out to achieve the same thing, primevally by conquest, in more civilized ages through high politics or money. But primeval warriors, as in the Christian Middle Ages, tend to live by codes, however naïvely self-serving or often honored in the breach. Politicians and businessmen, however rapacious, are obliged at some point to consider the law, if only as an instrument of rival interests. Napoleon contrived to have it all ways, being the primeval conqueror who arises, not in the steppes, but in the heart of civilization itself. He was quite modern, as Emerson said, in the coldness and sophisti-

---

* Still another authority I read years ago said that in his last campaigns Napoleon suffered from severe gastric pains (ulcers?), which he relieved by taking hot baths.

cated precision with which he did the expedient. By good luck
he had had an excellent military education; and as an ambitious
colonial, walking in upon the collapse of the mother country, he
saw at once the splendid, in fact absolutely unique, opportunity
which she in her prostration and her neighbors in their senility
offered.*

When in the grip of his curiously feral genius, Napoleon
showed an astonishing quickness of mind, and sometimes, but by
no means always, great originality. In his earlier battles, including Marengo, "we can discern no trace of strategical innovation.
He was simply a master of the methods of his time. . . . Even in
1805, at Ulm and Austerlitz, it was still the excellence of the tactical instrument, the army, which the Revolution had bequeathed
to him that essentially produced the results."[6] The same writer
goes on to say that in 1806 Napoleon devised an order of march
for his army which *was* an innovation and highly successful. "Yet
it would seem that this invention of Napoleon's was intuitive
rather than reasoned; he never communicated it in its entirety
to his marshals, and seems to have been only capable of exercising it when in full possession of his health or under the excitement of action. . . . One is forced to the conclusion that there
existed in Napoleon's brain a dual capacity—one the normal and
reasoning one, developing only the ideas and conceptions of his
contemporaries, the other intuitive and capable only of work
under abnormal pressure. At such moments . . . it almost ex-
celled human comprehension."

It is this "dual capacity" which I believe may be the key to
him. In animals and tribal man it perhaps scarcely exists; there
is perfect unanimity of thought and feeling because mind depends for its impetus upon the Id, being propelled from task to
task simply by the machinery of fear or appetite. In the highly
civilized, mind tends in some degree to break free, to escape
into powers of its own.† Between these extremes there is still a
third group, the mock-civilized—men often of great native ca-

---

* He was quite aware of his debt to the Revolution, once saying: "My
son cannot replace me. I could not replace myself. I am a creature of circumstances."

† Which is possibly why some civilized men are capable of a coldly ra-
tional courage, whereas animals and human primitives depend for theirs on
frenzy or the "togetherness" of well-knit fighting gangs.

pacity and in full possession of the mental tools of their parent culture but impervious to its ideals or larger intentions and to the same degree without conscience. Like Napoleon, they are "compulsive" in a peculiar way. Only rather primal projects, closely connected with the safety or aggrandizement of the self, really command their interest. As that interest arises in the Id and is fed or served by their intelligence but never seriously contested by it, men of this psychic type readily develop intense tic-like ambitions. They have, as we say, terrific "drive." The other self, capable of more disinterested interests—more leisurely, affectionate, lucid, genuinely curious—scarcely exists in them except as a form of dilettantism or of useful mimicry. In the deepest sense they are actors who form or alter their identity as the Id and the script require. They are said to "create" their parts; but in reality it is the other way around. What identity they have depends on the roles available to them and ceases after each performance. In public they can be brilliant orators, strategists, improvisers, can cope with any conceivable enemy or emergency —only to collapse in private into the most depressing banality, often coming down to us, in the memoirs of their intimates, as men so tiresome and trivial that we can only think they have been slandered. In most cases, they probably have not been; nor were they the monsters of deceit we are apt to think them. They were simply true to their psychic type—not villains exactly, or juveniles; just not quite men, gaining by that fact an adaptive advantage which is often decisve for themselves and catastrophic for the rest of us. Napoleon had this sort of animal force and unity, whereas Charles XII, one feels, had the continuity of true character (as did Peter, in his chaotic way).

In public the emperor was a man of presence, with a fine commanding eye and a gift for the statesmanlike phrase. He even played a bit at culture, putting his savants philosophical conundrums as they sailed off to Egypt and at one point seeming to reproach them for their disregard of the Almighty.* This last was

---

* Years afterwards, on the retreat from Moscow, while his staff distracted themselves by considering the geometry of snowflakes or the reasons for the complex halo of the December sun, the emperor did not join them, having other things to occupy him. Culture by then, in the Grand Army, had become something else in any case—as illustrated by the old Count de Narbonne-Lara, who with "imperturbable gaiety" performed a complete toi-

almost certainly a bit of posturing. The Almighty played little enough part in his own plans, even in his rhetoric; nor was he later what one could call a patron of learning.* And just as his modern *reductio ad absurdum* Adolf Hitler was, in off hours, a doting, inane *petit bourgeois* and an indefatigable windbag, one finds the emperor at home to have been a *Jupiter scapin*, as Emerson rather grandly called him—a coarse, fanny-pinching *arriviste†* who read other people's mail, cheated at cards, and snubbed his old comrade Marshal Junot because he had become ashamed of him.‡

---

lette every day, even to putting on a curled and powdered wig, as he sat in the snow.[7] (He was then fifty-seven, and survived to become Napoleon's ambassador to Vienna the following year.)

* During his Home Improvement period—roughly 1804-08—Napoleon gave, among other things, precise instructions for the school at Ecouen to be set up for indigent daughters of members of the Legion of Honor. He provided carefully for their religious education. "The pupils must then also be taught arithmetic, writing, and the principles of the mother tongue. . . . They must be taught a little geography and history, but be careful not to teach them Latin or any foreign tongue. To the eldest may be taught a little botany or a slight course of physics or natural history, and even that may have a bad effect. They must be limited in physics to what is necessary to prevent gross ignorance or stupid superstition, and must keep to facts, *without reasonings which tend directly or indirectly to first causes.*"[8] (Italics added.)

† In 1807 this former libertarian and champion of the Little Man created twenty-six dukes. When poor ostracized Junot finally died of his wounds, Napoleon, like a nervous tycoon, had their correspondence—some five hundred letters—seized and presumably destroyed.

‡ In her memoirs Junot's widow, the Duchesse d'Abrantès, said of Napoleon: "Like all sovereigns [he] felt a pride in being beloved. Yet it is strange that in general he never thought of conferring any but worldly recompenses on the men who were most sincerely devoted to him"—which was no more than a mark of his honest modernity. He was, in fact, quite contemptuous of men who, as he remarked, were so easily controlled by the two levers (really the same lever) of fear and interest. For all the reasons she had to dislike him, Mme. Junot remained loyal to the emperor, saying at the close of her memoirs that he was a "tutelary Providence—a light which will shine during ages to come."[9]

She was quite a patriotic lady, who became indignant over events at the Berezina crossing, during the emperor's Russian retreat: "Twenty thousand prisoners were taken—the treasures of Moscow were wrested from us, and we lost one hundred and fifty pieces of cannon. In short, we in our turn were plundered—and ignominiously, like vile brigands!"

Far worse was to happen. A few weeks later, the remnants of the Grand Army were falling dead of starvation and cold in the streets of Vilna while the emperor, having left them, was trying to conceal their fate from the home folks by the usual methods. At one point he sought to minimize his casualties

Since the conquests of such men (like those of many financial wizards or geniuses of the boudoir) are dictated by instinct, rather than by reason or by any definable ideal, they have no logical limits. The conqueror does not decide for himself where to stop; he cannot. So circumstances do it for him. The Mongols of the thirteenth century were a co-operative psychic venture of this kind, they supplying the gross instinctive "drive" and their captive Chinese experts the "know-how." Had a political contretemps not called them home they would probably have continued campaigning indefinitely. Alexander was halted by a fever, Hitler by the sheer immensity of his enemies. Napoleon likewise was stopped, or at least critically slowed down, by the Russians. The evidence gives the impression that during this period a profound change was taking place inside the man himself; nor was it perhaps a purely physical one, brought on by his overt illnesses and the weather, or by the silent phase of the cancer which was later to kill him. Inflammatory disorders seem in fact to be aggravated by psychic turmoil; while Fernel, and others since, have suggested that one of the precipitating factors in cancer may be "melancholy."

There was reason enough for melancholy in the events which followed the French occupation of Moscow in September of 1812. The emperor's mixed French-German army had by that time shrunk from something like half a million to about 100,000 effectives. The burning of the city put him in an exceedingly difficult position, partly, as he said, because Moscow was as much a political as a military objective. It had ceased to be tenable, particularly in view of the season, but yet could not be given up without a critical loss of face. Having allowed his momentum to carry him too far, Napoleon now faced the possibility of being deprived of it altogether, and his agitation was understandably intense. According to Ségur: "He jumped up every minute, walked a few paces, sat down again. He crossed and recrossed

by saying that many of them were "only Germans"—a remark noted by his former allies.

But like the duchess and brave, foolish Stendhal, the French clung to their emperor. He appealed to their "realism" and their vanity. It was the *cachet* of his name that made possible his absurd successor Napoleon III, and has given much of French history, since, its air of pride embittered and anticlimax, most recently during the reign of De Gaulle.

his chambers with hurried step, his nervous choppy gestures betraying a tortured perplexity. He laid aside, took up, and laid aside again, some urgent piece of business, to run to the windows [of the Kremlin] and watch the progress of the conflagration."[10]

Still unable to make the decision demanded by his circumstances, the emperor, after the fire had subsided, reoccupied what was left of the city and sent peace proposals to the tsar in St. Petersburg. The tsar bided his time. No answer came back. A month of fine weather, from mid-September to mid-October, slipped by. Ségur's account continues: "Then, without warning, the first snowfall came. . . . And still Napoleon could not make up his mind whether to remain or flee. In the midst of the terrible confusion . . . that was building up around him . . . he spent those last days discussing the merits of a book of verse he had just received, or settling the accounts of the Comédie Française in Paris, which took three whole evenings. . . . We noticed . . . that he was prolonging his meals, which had until then been simple and brief. . . . Then, dull and heavy, he would slump down in his armchair and sit for hours as if benumbed, with a novel in his hands, waiting for the end of his terrible adventure. . . . We said among ourselves . . . that he had the presentiment that the first downward step would mark the beginning of his ruin, and was therefore clinging motionless to that summit for a last few minutes."

In this situation too, almost by definition, the old union of reason and impulse which had been the secret of his phenomenal effectiveness was being pulled apart. In lingering over poetry and the affairs of the Comédie, he was perhaps not merely taking a last few moments off from his troubles, but belatedly, almost wistfully, indulging a freedom in imagination which his deeper nature had seldom allowed him. If only one had had time to do justice to that other Higher self, to bring it on a bit more. And possibly in the years past, it *had* come on, rather more than he realized. With the rapid fulfillment of his early ambitions and the waning of his energy as he grew older, a slow dissolution of his "animal force and unity" may have set in, affecting his generalship if not his peace of mind long before Borodino.* His in-

* Wagram, for instance, in 1809, was wanting in the execution or clean-cut results of his earlier victories. And the battle which preceded it, at

telligence, though a captive faculty, was nonetheless a prodigious one, and having told him so much of use, may gradually have started telling him things he did not care to hear. Having formerly, in the press of emergencies, submitted totally to the practical needs of the moment and so pulled him through, it may now have begun, in the same circumstances, to assert a traitorous independence, plunging him, when he could least afford it, into a paralyzing confusion.*

It is hardly ever possible, of course, to say what occurs in the depths of a man, more especially in moments of the greatest turbulence or in someone as dedicated as Napoleon was to the maintenance of a façade. One has the feeling, however, that what he underwent in Russia was not unlike those crises of "insight" in the mentally ill which, rather than delivering them, throw them into blacker ecstasies of terror and bewilderment. What he may have had, and been horribly frightened and disconcerted by, was a momentary vision of his own slavery to himself—a self totally mindless and cruel which drove him and used him up as he drove and used up others, in the end to no purpose whatever, but simply from the blind energy of instinct. He, the personification of will, was in a sense will-less.

In the language of that day, Napoleon in 1812 began to doubt his "destiny"—in fact, perhaps, to turn the light of his devastating realism inward, and instead of thinking in the interests of his ambitions, to think for once *about* them. No situation could have

---

Aspern-Essling, was very nearly a disaster for the French. After being forced out of their bridgehead on the far side of the Danube they ended up, 100,-000 of them, with upwards of 20,000 wounded, jammed onto the island of Lobau scarcely a mile square, with few provisions and no medical facilities.

In comparing Napoleon and Charles XII, as is often done, one might note that whereas Charles's Russian opponents were ill organized and primitive, Napoleon's were, in a military sense, fossils. Some of the generals Charles faced—for instance Steinau and Schulenberg, even Menshikov—were perhaps better than Mack, whom Napoleon defeated at Ulm, or Weyrother, the loser at Austerlitz (whose co-commander, Kutuzov, fell asleep as Weyrother outlined his plan of attack). Under the circumstances, Napoleon could do with less originality, perhaps, than Charles; and it may have suited the nature of his genius to do so, since under more pressure he might have worn away much sooner. Unfortunately for Sweden, Charles was *not* of Napoleon's type, and except for the interlude of his wound at Poltava, never wore away at all.

* In effect, men of Napoleon's type, like film stars, cannot afford to get older, since age brings them neither peace nor wisdom; it merely dissolves the cement of sheer "ego" which once held them together.

been better suited to encourage this treason of the mind than the
lull after the burning of Moscow. Partly because he seldom suffered them, defeats never greatly troubled the emperor. Even
at Leipzig, a year later, the *fait accompli* seems to have put him
on his mettle, mobilizing his animal reserves and causing him to
become almost irrationally optimistic and unconcerned.* It was
at Dresden, where he was victorious, that he experienced the
strange flight from reality I have described—an episode apparently lasting several days, and preceded on the battlefield by a
display of the same rather forlorn bravado he had shown upon
leaving Moscow. (There, as the retreat began, he had pointed
to the sky, asking his aides if they could still see his star. At
Dresden, evidently just before he ceased functioning, he exclaimed, "I cannot be beaten!") It was not defeat which troubled
him so much as the prospect of an impasse, precluding any
prompt redress of matters on the morrow. The paradox of his
position was that he could not simply back down, give up his
illimitable projects and abdicate. For success, though increasingly
difficult to maintain and perhaps no longer even very attractive
to him, had become his last line of defense. From long habit, it
was so to speak his situation and sole stratagem. Others might
wrest it from him, but that was only a defeat, remediable as all
his others had been. To have surrendered it himself, casting his
mind adrift once and for all, denying his ferocious nature any
outlet, would have been to invite insanity. It is this condition
which I suspect may once or twice nearly have overtaken him,
producing those queer lapses which his contemporaries have reported. He was of such strength that it took an extraordinary
combination of reverses to bring him to that point, and he never
remained there long. In a subtler form, this same disorder, this
cleavage between his animal "will" and his reason, may have

---

* At Leipzig, after several days of violent fighting in its vicinity, the town
and much of the French army, which was then struggling through it, were
reduced to chaos. Civilians, cattle, carriages, and wounded or dying men
choked the thoroughfares. In the midst of this uproar, near the Lindenau
bridge, a General Château noticed "a man of peculiar dress and with only a
small retinue; he was whistling the air of *'Malbrook s'en va-t'-en guerre.'* . . .
It was the emperor, who, with his usual phlegm, seemed to be perfectly cal-
lous to the scenes of destruction which surrounded him."[11] Shortly afterwards, in Lindenau, a mile or so away, the emperor fell asleep. So much for
that day and the 40,000 to 70,000 casualties left behind.

acted gradually to undermine his generalship; and by adding to his stresses, perhaps caused him to age more rapidly than he should have, and to develop various chronic illnesses, as he approached his forties. One thing is certain. After 1812, although he had not lost his touch, it became far less dependable. His last battle was a case in point. The maneuvers by which he led up to it were on the whole excellent—very much in his old style.

In June of 1815, Wellington had his headquarters in Brussels, and his force of English and Dutch-Belgian troops (in all, approximately 100,000 men and 200 guns) was dispersed in bivouacs along the French frontier. His dispositions were made in particular with an eye to protecting his right flank on the sea. Off his left flank away to the east was another army of some 125,-000 Prussians and 300 guns under Marshal Blücher. Against these the emperor, only a few months returned from Elba, had mobilized five corps, or a total of 125,000 men and 350 guns.*[12] He seems to have understood the enemy's state of mind exactly, guessing that Wellington would have an *idée fixe* about his right flank and be looking for an attack there. To reinforce this notion, Napoleon reportedly put out word through his agents that he planned an advance toward the coast. His real intention was to move with all speed on the allied center, attacking Blücher and Wellington in detail, not only before they had joined but, with luck, before each had had time to gather his forces. By June 15, 1815, he had "perfected his arrangements. . . . His army was organized definitely into two wings and a reserve. . . . As circumstances dictated either wing would fasten upon one of the allied armies and detain it until the reserve had time to come up and complete its destruction; the other wing meantime detaining the other allied army. . . . The emperor was not in possession of the Namur-Nivelles road. The allies were thus afforded the opportunity of committing the very blunder which Napoleon longed for, namely to attempt a risky forward concentration. His dispositions . . . were skilfully calculated to encourage the allies

---

* He might have gathered a slightly larger force, but as Sutherland points out, there were the Russians and Austrians and the Spanish border to consider, for which Napoleon held out 50,000 men. Wellington and the allies, on the other hand, were spread over a front ninety miles long by thirty miles deep, which made for flexibility should they decide to move but for some danger should the emperor move against them first.

to mass at Quatre Bras [to the west] and Sombreffe [to the east].
. . . At nightfall the Army of the North lay concentrated 'in a
square whose sides measured 12 miles each; and it could with
equal facility swing against the Prussians [near Sombreffe] or the
Anglo-Dutch [at Quatre Bras] and was already placed between
them.' "[13]

Napoleon seems to have meant to fall upon Wellington first
and Blücher later. Certainly Wellington was likely to be the more
dangerous of the two. In years of fighting against the emperor's
marshals in Spain he had never been defeated; whereas Blücher,
a seventy-two-year-old ex-general of cavalry, Napoleon had met
often before.* Unfortunately for the emperor's strategy, however, Wellington was not quick enough. On the fifteenth his forward concentration at Quatre Bras had hardly begun and was
even then in a sense accidental. The few troops that held the
place were doing so against orders, because their commanders
had grasped the importance of the village crossroads, one arm of
which communicated with Blücher to the east. The duke's general orders on the fifteenth, issued many hours after the invasion
of Belgium had started, show that he still did not understand
what Napoleon intended—a lapse partly attributable to the fact
that a message from his agent in France, Colonel Colquhoun
Grant, had been intercepted by an officious subordinate. Blücher,
for his part, as his outlying troops were driven in at Gilly, concentrated with great vigor, determining, as the emperor had foreseen, to make a stand on the sixteenth at Ligny, a short distance
from Sombreffe. It was on that day that Napoleon's plans began
to go seriously astray. Marshal Ney, who might easily have taken
the crossroads at Quatre Bras, appears to have overestimated the
force defending it and delayed his attack through the morning.
Wellington, who arrived there during the same period, saw the
position at once and sent orders to rush up more troops. Napo-

---

* Except for a brief period when Frederick the Great separated him from
the service, evidently for riotous behavior, Blücher spent most of his life fighting for Prussia, and that mostly against the French. He was active in the
War of Liberation in 1813, precipitating Napoleon's defeat at Leipzig by
himself defeating Marmont at Mockern. In the following year Napoleon more
than evened the score by whipping him at Champaubert, Vauxchamps, and
Montmirail. As one writer remarks: ". . . The most conspicuous military
quality displayed by Blücher was his unrelenting energy."[14]

leon meanwhile concluded the allies would *not* after all risk a forward concentration and seems to have thought that Quatre Bras could be easily overrun (which for a short time was true). A message from him, which was dispatched at six in the morning and reached Ney at eleven, suggested that "one of Ney's divisions should be well north of Quatre Bras by the evening of the 16th so that Brussels could be taken the following morning,"[15] thereby splitting the allies. But as late as 2:00 P.M. Ney, "remembering the surprises that the battles in Spain had provided for the marshals opposed to the duke,"[16] and deceived by the enemy's skillful use of cover, was still massing almost a whole corps against a force of some 7500 men under the Prince of Orange. By the time his attack finally began substantial allied reinforcements were arriving to meet it, as were more dispatches from Napoleon insisting that the place be taken at once. By 5:00 P.M., on the defensive, with Wellington himself now facing him, and the allies still further reinforced, Ney sent a call for help to d'Erlon's corps. It was too late. Needing the corps for his battle with Blücher at Ligny, Napoleon countermanded Ney's order, and the chance for a breakthrough to Brussels was lost.

At Ligny things were, from the French standpoint, going much better. That morning, after his visit to Quatre Bras, Wellington had gone to see Blücher, to whom he promised help he could not possibly send, and whose dispositions he surveyed with some perturbation. "The old man had deployed his troops on the exposed slope. The main villages he was attempting to defend, Ligny and Brye, seemed to be too far apart. They were not within musket range of one another. . . . Consequently . . . Blücher's units . . . could only support one another with artillery fire."[17] "Everybody knows their own army best," the duke is supposed to have said, "but if I were to fight with mine here, I should expect to be beat."[18] Blücher was, quite severely, losing in the end 16,000 killed and wounded out of about 83,000 engaged.* The battle was fought with great fury and cries of "no quarter," and the men of d'Erlon's corps figured in it only to the extent that they appeared on the horizon rather late in the afternoon, causing a near-panic in the ranks of Vandamme's corps, who

---

* French casualties were about 12,000 out of a force of some 70,000.

thought they were a Prussian relief column. Napoleon himself was not sure who they were, and by the time he had had them reconnoitered, they had received a counterorder from Ney and were on their way back to Quatre Bras, where they arrived hours after dark, having marched all day and not fired a shot in either engagement.

While the French were outnumbered and had no easy time of it at Ligny, they were assisted by a fortunate mishap. In the evening, as Marshal Blücher led a desperate countercharge, his horse was shot, falling and rolling over on him. He was carried stunned to a cottage nearby and revived with gin. But his army from that point disintegrated rapidly. His chief of staff, General Gneisenau, tried to organize its retreat, deciding to retire on the village of Wavre, fourteen miles to the north. This line of withdrawal, chosen in entire ignorance of Wellington's position or plans, nevertheless left the Prussian army still close enough so that in the final engagement Blücher could with strenuous effort join his allies. By that fact, and by his earlier failure to break through the Prussians' center soon enough to be able to destroy their army totally in a pursuit, Napoleon was not merely balked; he was doomed. The confusion in orders to d'Erlon was doubtless a factor in the unsatisfactory outcome at Ligny, but the emperor must be held more than half responsible for that. It was the next morning, apparently, that he had the curious blank spell mentioned above, not emerging from his headquarters until 9:00 A.M., hours after sunup. By that time the main body of the Prussians was miles away, and an hour later the English, having learned of their allies' reverse, were also beginning to pull back from Quatre Bras. Napoleon meanwhile, "followed by a train of staff officers and commanders, including Marshal Grouchy, who desperately awaited their orders,"[19] conducted a leisurely review of his troops, not leaving off and ordering a move on Quatre Bras until eleven o'clock. At the latter place, Marshal Ney "had had Napoleon's orders since 9:00 A.M. but seemed stricken with the same disease which earlier had paralyzed Napoleon."[20] Not without some stiff skirmishes, the duke's men got away northward. Waterloo was now prepared.

That battle has been described often enough to require little further elaboration. As Edward III had done at Crécy, Wellington chose an excellent defensive position at Mont St. Jean, on a southward-facing ridge with two advanced strong points—the stone farm buildings of Hougoumont to his right, and the farm of La Haye Sainte in the center, a site which was to become critical in the battle. Still believing that Napoleon might try to turn his right flank, he placed much strength there.* Along the ridge behind some exposed Dutch-Belgian troops he concealed his main line, his men lying down along the bank of the road leading to Wavre. In terms of real strength, Wellington's situation was less favorable than numbers alone might suggest. He was, on paper, at some disadvantage, having 67,600 troops and 156 guns to Napoleon's 74,000 and 246 guns. (The emperor had sent Grouchy off with 33,000 men and 110 guns to pursue the Prussians, a serious mistake, since he gave up what might have been decisive reserves in the interests of a maneuver which that general, in part because of badly worded orders, failed to execute.† But in Wellington's army only some 29,000 troops were English, Scottish, or of the king's German Legions, the remainder being Dutch-Belgians whose capabilities and commitment to the allied cause were doubtful. Some of these did not later perform very well or even remain on the field, the brunt of the fighting being borne by the British. Wellington, not knowing about Grouchy's expedition, thought he faced the whole French army, or over 100,000 men. As it was, the force before him was somewhat more than a match for his own, while his only real reserve, the Prussians, were several hours' march away at Wavre. To complicate

* Too much strength—17,000 men, including some British troops, stationed eight miles away to his right, at Hal and Tubize.
† As usual, accounts disagree. According to one, Grouchy received orders too vague to make it clear that he was to put himself between Blücher and Wellington, the implication being that he was too stupid to have thought out this course for himself. Belatedly, he was told by the emperor to "proceed to Gembloux," an order which the marshal "only too literally obeyed. After an inconceivably slow and wearisome march, in one badly arranged column on one road, he only reached Gembloux on June 17, and halted there for the night." He then had the gleam of an idea, and in a message dated 10:00 P.M. informed the emperor that if he found the Prussians to be moving on Wavre, he would maneuver so as to prevent their junction with Wellington. "But a glance at the map shows that this was impossible. *By following the Prussians, Grouchy, who had taken up a position outside the Prussian left flank, would inevitably drive the allies together.*"21 (Italics added.)

matters, early on the eighteenth, the day of the battle, a fire broke out in Wavre. Between the time lost in putting it out and an unfortunate change in marching orders which called for the rearmost corps—Bülow's—to be put first, Blücher (now recovered and back in the saddle) did not get his army under way until rather late. Once en route, however, he pressed forward with his usual energy, having left Thielemann's corps (about 16,000 men) to deal with Grouchy. The latter, in perhaps the most absurd victory of the war, overwhelmed them the following day, long after Waterloo itself had been decided. His own commanders had apparently tried, on the eighteenth, to dissuade him from this engagement, knowing from the sound of the guns at Waterloo that their services were probably needed elsewhere and from the size of the force in front of them that it had been left there merely to detain them. Grouchy was adamant. Late as he had come to his task, he would not now give it up. "Instead of concentrating his force upon one bridge over the swampy and unfordable Dyle, Grouchy scattered it in attacks upon several; and when the emperor's dispatch arrived, saying that Bülow was in sight, the marshal was powerless to move westward."[22] It is hard to imagine an assignment worse handled; and were it not for the overshadowing catastrophe which befell the *Armée du Nord* on the same day, Grouchy's name would probably rank far higher than it does in the annals of bad generalship. He lacked perhaps the entire consistency of a Burnside (who would have been defeated outright at Wavre) or the scope, say, of Sir Ian Hamilton (see Chapters VIII and IX), but he obviously had all the essentials.

At Waterloo itself, Napoleon did not plan to attack Wellington's right flank, as the duke supposed, nor to concentrate against his left, as he possibly should have done. After a brisk action at the right outpost of Hougoumont, and at La Haye Sainte, the emperor made straight for the English center, first with massed infantry, then with cavalry, at last with his Ultimate Weapon, the Guard. Between these seemingly endless attacks, the French artillery fired with great effect upon the defenders. Except that it was a much nearer thing—in Wellington's phrase, "the nearest run thing you ever saw in your life"[23]—the battle as a whole had some striking resemblances to the great French defeats of the Middle Ages. As at Crécy, the action began late (11:00 A.M., a delay partly intentional, to let the ground dry after the rain of the night before); and as at Agincourt, heavy French troops, horse and foot, went to the attack across hundreds of yards of sodden ploughed earth. The infantry assault, which came first, was made in column, the men in ranks trudging forward through rye fields, their brilliant uniforms already soaked and mud-stained from having been slept in on the wet ground. The onset, like its medieval predecessors, was nonetheless impressive. In the face of an increasingly terrible fire, Napoleon's *enfants** came on "thousands after thousands, not deployed in battle line but marching like troops in review, an immense solid block of them. . . . It looked irresistible and that was the intention behind it. . . . But they were not a practical fighting formation. . . . At best only the front three ranks could open fire,"[24] though the men behind them could quite well be part of a whole swath cut down by a cannon ball.

As the French infantry assault began to falter, the Earl of Uxbridge, a lieutenant general of cavalry, led a devastating charge, of which he seems to have lost control, since it went much too far and was presently counterattacked by French horse, being forced to retire with heavy losses.† Later in the day this reverse could have had quite serious consequences since, pending the arrival of Blücher, it left Wellington's desperately battered center almost without a cavalry reserve.

When the French left off their infantry attacks and switched to cavalry (the reverse of the order of events at Agincourt), the British infantry formed in square, a formation which, as it presented a hedge of bayonets on all sides, and made a fire defense in any direction possible, was quite formidable to horsemen.

---

* The emperor often addressed his troops as *"mes enfants,"* a speaking style which Wellington, like Charles XII (whom he somewhat resembled in character), never used. I have read that this same gruesomely sentimental language is sometimes used in the Mafia, whose units are called "families."

† Uxbridge was by nature, apparently, rather headlong. Near Quatre Bras he had dashed out to meet some approaching squadrons, only to discover at the last minute that they were French. Later at Waterloo, he placed himself at the head of some Dutch cavalry, ordered a charge, and set out full speed for the enemy. His aide-de-camp caught up with him just in time to explain that the Dutch had not understood him and that the earl was riding alone into the French ranks. He lost a leg at Waterloo, which was buried under a gravestone in Brussels and became a paying tourist attraction.

When these retired however, the squares became better targets for artillery than the same men in line had been. For their part, to reach the squares, the French cavalry had to ride against English batteries firing grape or canister almost to pointblank ranges. The result of these repeated attacks was to deplete and exhaust, but not quite to break, the troops in Wellington's center; and at moments the action assumed an air of general bafflement and fatigue, the men in the squares merely maintaining their hedge of points while the French cavalrymen, carrying swords or lances, rode between them, uncertain what to do next. There was some outcry from the English troops when French lancers went about killing wounded, but on the whole there appears to have been less of that sort of thing than there was in the brutal engagement at Ligny, at which both sides slaughtered prisoners and gave little quarter in the fighting.

At 1:00 P.M. Napoleon and his officers had seen a cloud of dust to the north and east which told them that the Prussians were coming. By 4:00, it was clear that the cavalry attacks (which might have succeeded with infantry support) had failed. By 4:30, Bülow's corps was on hand, beginning an assault on the French right at Plancenoit. Wellington's center strong point, La Haye Sainte, still held. The situation, from Napoleon's standpoint, had become critical. He "now ordered Ney to carry La Haye Sainte at whatever cost, and this the marshal accomplished with the wrecks of d'Erlon's corps, soon after 6:00 P.M. The garrison [King's German Legion] had run out of ammunition. . . . This was the first decided advantage Napoleon had gained during the day. The key of the duke's position was now in Napoleon's hands. Wellington's center was dangerously shaken, the troops were exhausted, and the reserves inadequate."[25] But at this point, Bülow with reinforcements had taken Plancenoit and his artillery was firing on the Charleroi road, which ran through the center of the French position. Napoleon was forced to divert some of his Guards to push them back, and by the time that was done, more Prussians under Zieten were moving into line on Wellington's left. Because it had come hours too late, the opportunity offered by the capture of La Haye Sainte was lost, and so was the battle. Zieten's arrival made it possible for Wellington to move two cavalry brigades from the left to support his center. As if aware of how the balance had finally shifted, the French made a last desperate frontal attack with the Guard, in three echelons,[26] all of which were repulsed with fearful bloodshed. At about 8:00 P.M. Zieten and the English counterattacked, and the better part of the French army simply fell into ruins. It was indeed a near-run thing.

The gruesomeness of the aftermath was proportioned to the grandeur of the rest of the occasion. Thousands of wounded lay for days dying all over the field, some struggling to bandage themselves while coachloads of sightseers who had driven down from Brussels ate basket lunches and surveyed the scene as if it were already a battle canvas. By night looters, including a number of women, went among the fallen, stealing their valuables and killing those of the still living who protested too loudly.* Armies had already grown far too large, and battles too bloody, for the small, ill-equipped, ignorant medical corps on either side —the loser's especially—who were expected to handle their casualties. This situation was to reach a kind of apogee in our own Civil War, when a wounded man was often better off *not* getting the medical attention available to him.

As darkness fell on the eighteenth, the Prussian cavalry whooped off in pursuit of the enemy. Blücher was not to realize his dream of seeing the emperor hang, but somewhat later, in Paris, he caused a sensation by attempting to blow up a bridge named after a Prussian defeat (Jena). He then took another fall from a horse while performing evolutions for some English ladies, suffering a blow to the head which seems to have permanently deranged him.[27] Wellington after the battle "rode slowly back to Waterloo," where he and his staff sat down to supper. "The duke, who ate very little, kept looking at the door and Alava [his servant] knew that he was watching for the absent faces."[28] Later, when he read the casualty lists, he wept.

The emperor, meanwhile, was hurrying away through the night —Quitting the Stage of History, not à la Charles XII, with his wounded foot over the neck of a cavalryman's horse, but as an overweight, middle-aged adventurer unscathed except for his cystitis and piles and apparently no more inclined than he had

---

* Some were even stripped of their clothes and left to fend for themselves naked.

ever been, even in Russia, to weep* over those who had so lately fallen in his service. The Prussian pursuit and the press of his own defeated troops soon obliged him to transfer to horseback, and inside a cordon of his Guards he rode for Paris, leaving behind the imperial coach, a vehicle one writer describes as "pathetic in its intimate splendors." The latter included "a dinner service of gold, sanitary utensils of silver, perfumery, a writing desk, pistols, a folding bed, and a *nécessaire* containing nearly a hundred gold articles of toilet . . . the emperor's medals, and his clothes including a spare uniform which had diamonds to the value of 2,000,000 francs sewn into its lining."†[30]

These *nouveau riche* conveniences, the last in particular, are oddly out of character with the "image" of Napoleon evidently still vivid in the minds of many of his countrymen. So was his last-minute attempt at Waterloo to bolster morale by circulating the report that Grouchy and his men were close at hand. Almost for a certainty he must have known they could not be. Nor was it surprising that many French soldiers, after the battle, began declaring that they had been betrayed. They had been, but as much by that in themselves which they shared with their emperor as by the magic or the trickery of the man himself. Out of his army of 74,000, approximately 40,000 were lost—dead, wounded, captured, or fled—together with nearly all of its artillery and baggage. Wellington lost upwards of 15,000, the Prussians 7000. "So desperate was the fighting that some 45,000 killed and wounded lay on an area of roughly 3 square miles. At one point on the plateau 'the 27th (Inniskillings) were lying literally dead in square; and the position that the British infantry had held was plainly marked by the line of dead and wounded they left behind them.' "[32]

Accounts vary as to the emperor's condition and the degree to which he, rather than Marshal Ney, directed events during his

---

* However, even on this point authorities disagree. While some depict the emperor scurrying away, one has him standing "in the moonlight waiting in a little wood, waiting for troops that never came: his cheeks were wet with tears."[29]

† In 1969 the French celebrated the bicentenary of the emperor's birth with a six-month (June to December) exhibition of his personal belongings at the Grand Palais, attended by the usual rhetoric to the effect that "once the tears were dried and the dead forgotten" it was clear that he had founded modern France and done no end of indirect good. Many of the objects displayed, most notably Josephine's crown, were of surpassing gorgeousness.[31]

last battle. Some have said he was too stricken with piles to ride
a horse (though he clearly managed to do so that evening),
spending most of the day at Rossomme, morosely out of touch as
he had been at Borodino. Others write as though he was almost
as close to the action as he had been at Ulm or Austerlitz. Several mention his optimism on the morning of the eighteenth. All
that is certain is that he was fatally slow and made a succession
of tactical mistakes, the most serious having been to send his
cavalry unsupported into a grand attack. On the strength of that
last day he would never perhaps rate as a truly bad general, but
neither would he as a very good one. As at Borodino and Leipzig, his spur-of-the-moment capability had failed him, and with
that, apparently, the better part of his genius was gone.

Early one morning, in June of 1709, shortly before Poltava,
Ensign Petré passed by the little house where Charles had his
quarters. In the half-light he saw the king kneeling beside a tree
in the dooryard praying. And something he heard in the voice or
sensed in the bearing of that lonely man so moved the ensign that
he broke into tears. It is difficult to imagine such a story being
told about Napoleon; or if it were told it would at once set one
to wondering. For obvious reasons, the two men are often compared; both were good generals who lost the Big One, and both
might therefore be considered bad generals of the Fatal Flaw
type. But that is the extent of the resemblance. The odd thing is
that of the two, Napoleon is probably the more "sympathetic."
We understand his success mania, or think we do. The woods
today are full of him—the business world, the movies, politics,
even (though we had better hope not) the military. Charles is
the more opaque to us and, if only for that reason, suspect.* Many

---

* As is Wellington, who had been disliked and even hated for his aloofness
and his conservatism, his supposed lack of sympathy for the people. (He did
in fact oppose parliamentary reform and the Catholic Emancipation.) Like
Charles, Wellington was a shy man who had had the makings of an entirely
different career. In his youth he had wanted to be a violinist, but at twenty-
four, obedient to his mother's famous declaration that he was "food for
powder and nothing more," he burned his violin and resigned himself to life
in the army. There he was underrated for years, keeping to his plain-spoken
enigmatic style and doing his job far better than anyone seemed to realize.
Some of his victories in Spain were classic in their swiftness and economy.
He may never have loved his *enfants* (he was accused later of taking little
interest in pensions for his veterans), but he did them, or the common people
of his country, far less harm than Napoleon did to France. After Waterloo he

have in fact wondered about him—what his lifelong dedication to duty *really* meant, what that great saber he always wore may have symbolized. And what about his bachelorhood, his supposed asceticism? Was he a repressed or discreetly practicing homosexual perhaps? Or a sadist who *enjoyed* his years in the field because of all the destruction and bloodshed? Was his bravery simply a form of the death wish? And in contrast to Napoleon, who at his coronation in Nôtre Dame did the frank, healthy thing, taking the diadem from the pontiff's hands and crowning himself, Charles at his was all conformity and mock-submission, permitting himself to be crowned by others in the usual way. One can only, as a modern, ask why.

The difficulty is that while Napoleon may seem to us the more "human," Charles strikes us as the tragic figure and the man. He was even, I suspect, not as bad a general.

---

stood, almost alone, for a moderate settlement with the French, saying, apropos of Blücher's plan for hanging the emperor, "If the Sovereigns wish to put him to death they should appoint an executioner, which should not be me."[33] He was unlike Charles in not even caring very much for war. Nor did he lose the Big One. He never lost at all, and his unpopularity seems in some degree to have been proportioned to his success. During the occupation after Waterloo, the French quickly came to detest him, although he favored a liberal peace. "He was held responsible . . . for every untoward incident . . . even Blücher's attempt to blow up the Pont de Jéna was laid to his charge . . . Two attempts were made to assassinate him."

Chapter VII

State of the Union
1861-62

By the time the nineteenth century was half gone, the western world seemed to have broken with its own past, not merely in methods but in some deeper sense which for a while divided it as Protestantism had once split Christendom. History had begun another long jump, and many declined to jump with it, a fact which complicated the situation without in any material way changing it, as the French discovered at Sedan. We were becoming "modern," a condition we are still rather self-conscious about and continually redefining, usually not in a spirit of unqualified acclaim. The mid-Victorians were like us in that, regarding their age with an odd mixture of complacency and dejection. Officially they rejoiced in Progress, but there were signs of a general damping of spirits. By the 1840s the robust emotions of earlier times were turning maudlin and hysterical, and life assumed a funerary cast. Between the era of *Tom Jones* and that of *Bleak House* and *Oliver Twist*, it is as though the sun had slowly been going out.* In Daumier, or in the mezzotints and daguerreotypes of the period, the whole world appears gaslit. The Victorian parlor chokes out whatever natural light remains. Themes in literature and art become dark and hectic; clothing grows somber and at the

---

* By the end of the century, scientific pessimists were applying the Second Law of Thermodynamics to the solar system and predicting the literal extinction of the sun. They are still doing so.

same time curiously bulky, suggesting not austerity so much as a glum ostentation. No longer do men gaze out of their portraits, as in the eighteenth century, with a "fine eye," a certain well-ballasted composure. In the early photographs—particularly in the panoramic work of Brady—one sees the strangest assortment of faces: some quite mad, others almost unbelievably vain or vulnerable-looking, still others splendidly confused or of an antique handsomeness, and not a few which are recognizably of our own era.

The War between the States is sometimes described by military writers as the first modern one, which, in a primitive way, it was. Aerial spotting (by Professor Lowe in his balloon, during the Peninsular Campaign), trench warfare (Vicksburg; Petersburg), the movement of troops and matériel by rail (Second Manassas; Sherman's march), mass deportation (of civilians, from Atlanta), concentration camps (Andersonville; Elmira), and the draft all began for us then. With his strategy of '64-65 Grant pioneered the technique of victory by strangulation, the *ultima ratio* of bad modern generals, especially, as it were, rich ones.

In Europe, where the Old Order had been holding out with greater stubbornness, notably in the succession from Louis Philippe to Napoleon III, the tendency was for soldiers to retain the brilliant regalia which was their legacy from the days of Charles the Bold (who would doubtless have been horrified to see so much "residue" wearing it). At the start of the Civil War, our troops showed an inclination to trick themselves out in the same way. In '61-62, recruits often had their pictures taken wearing fanciful Zouave uniforms, and some of the first regiments to go into action were quite dandified. Our terrible roads and the demands of battle soon put an end to that. As months went by the uniforms in both armies became grubbier and more miscellaneous; men threw away much of the gear they had been issued* and skinned their pack loads down to essentials, learning to replace lost clothing or to eke out scanty rations with "liberated" items as they went. Many wore slouch hats and (like the Union

---

* Including knapsacks, coats, and various cooking and fighting utensils. After Antietam in particular, the Union army divested itself of huge amounts of matériel. As Bruce Catton puts it, the war began the American soldier's habit of waste, some time, apparently, before our civilians had acquired it.

gunners photographed before Petersburg in '64) worked in shirts and suspenders. So for all the talk of glory and the incredibly brave things some of these men did, they were hardly distinguishable from the civilian labor force of their day—the farmers and factory workers and pick-and-shovel men from whom they had largely been recruited.

Their officers were in some cases smartly, or at least neatly, turned out, but continental extravagance was avoided. There were none of the plumes and vivid colors which both sides, and nearly all ranks, had worn at Waterloo. With their dark blue brassbuttoned coats and long trousers, the Union officers looked like nothing so much as turn-of-the-century policemen. General Burnside, indeed, wore the helmet later made famous by the Keystone Kops. I do not recall seeing a picture of any other officer in this particular headgear and can think of only a few it might have suited as well.* The more dashing, such as Fighting Joe Hooker, favored black leather boots which reached to the knee or higher. But baggy pants seem to have been more generally the rule; and as in wars now, the closer a unit got to the front the worse it began to look. In a photograph of a railroad gun crew of nine, taken during a pause in the fighting before Petersburg in '64, I counted five regulation Union kepis, one broad-brimmed bowler, two varieties of slouch hat, and one long-visored carpenter's cap. The rest are simply in civvies. One has on a trim three-button striped shirt; another, black pants, gray shirt with bow tie and a black vest; the others are in regulation shirt and suspenders (no tie). The age range of the group, at a fair guess, is from seventeen (the kid in the carpenter's cap) to sixty-five (broad-brimmed slouch). The caption of the picture says: ". . . A glance at them shows that they were men picked for the job—men in the prime of life, brawny and strong—they

---

* There is perhaps some connection between military incompetence and a fondness for *outré* forms of headdress. Bruce Catton mentions that General Irvin McDowell, the loser at First Bull Run, had a "special hat . . . devised for his summer comfort, a cool but rather weird-looking contrivance of bamboo and cloth," which cost him much ridicule in the ranks and seems somehow to have lent strength to the rumors of his treason.[1] In a photograph of him, taken with McClellan, he wears a kepi twice as tall as McClellan's.[2] McClellan, however, sports a tasseled gold sash, has his hand in his bosom à la Napoleon, and looks far more stern and pulled together.

were slaves of their monster."[3] They may have been slaves of their monster, right enough, but only the wildest patriotic enthusiasm could have generated the rest of that description. The point is not, of course, to ridicule the men in blue (so to speak) but to underscore the extreme functionalism which had overtaken warfare since the days of the Iron Duke.

The civilians whom Brady and other photographers of the time show us, while often tidier and more formal in their attire, were hardly what we would call sporty. It is clear that their notion of the "image," though strong, was quite different from our own. There is—to take an example at random—a photograph of clerks and officials of the War Department which, but for the few caps and uniforms present, might have been snapped during a convention of undertakers (in this case appropriately enough, in view of the contributions of such stay-at-homes as General Halleck).[4] Lincoln and his Cabinet made an outstandingly lugubrious group,* and even so handsome a woman as Kate Chase Sprague seemed, at least in still-life, rather dimmed and smothered by what she had on.

Aside from its nostalgic appeal for us, its twentieth-century heirs, and from the fact that it was the first war to be photographed, the Civil War is fascinating for the reason that, like the age, it was transitional. Its commanders were forced to cope with the multitude of problems which Napoleon, in his haste, had created and left unsolved, the chief of these, in modern armies, being simply the problem of size.† For America, a relatively unmartial and industrially second-class nation in 1860, the demands of an army of 100,000 in the field were apparently as exacting as

---

* A psychiatrist friend recently told me, in some earnestness, that Lincoln was a "known" manic-depressive. One may doubt that, though it is certain that he was melancholy at times, and for good reason. The point is that, thanks to his clothes and surroundings, Lincoln *looked* melancholy even when he may not have been.

† One can trace the growth of this problem in the emperor's campaigns. At Austerlitz (1805) he had, in round figures, 65,000 men. Four years later, at Aspern (where he was defeated), he had 95,000; and at Wagram, a dubious victory, 220,000. Borodino (1812): 125,000; Leipzig (1813): 150,000. The critical number seems to have been around 100,000. Armies larger than that tended to be too big for the staff work and liaison of that day, and Napoleon himself was too much the prima donna, perhaps, to adapt to this new fact of war.

those of 220,000 had been for Napoleon at Wagram, half a century earlier. Whereas he had taken over an existing force, and a very good one, at the start of his career, both sides, in the Civil War, had to create theirs overnight, from a small nucleus of regulars and West Pointers, and a vast miscellany of state militiamen and volunteers, including, in the North, some exceedingly unfortunate political generals, like McClernand, Banks, and Butler, whom nobody seemed able to dislodge. Once they had taken the field, we were stuck with them for the duration.

States' rights being far more a reality then, and federal power far weaker, it was considerably harder for Lincoln in '61 than for Franklin Roosevelt in 1940 to organize the national effort. Lincoln had, for want of clear precedents, to rely on trial and error and make strange, intricate compromises to the point that even now we can scarcely appreciate the difficulty of his position. Everything else appeared to be in the same uneasy emergent state. At the start of the war, the old smooth-bore musket—with an effective range, by one account, of about ninety feet—was still used, but muzzle-loading rifles—the Springfield, shooting a minie (Minié) ball—were coming in, and even a few breechloaders. (Burnside, just before the war, is said to have invented one of the latter, which, perhaps fortunately, never found its way into the firing line.) Artillery was also beginning to be rifled, one Confederate piece imported from England having a range of around six miles. Range-finding methods were in no way equal to the newer weapons; and the design of shells was so faulty that some exploded in the mouth of the gun or just beyond it, and a considerable percentage never went off at all. While far more help was available to the wounded than had been at Waterloo, antisepsis was still to come, so that many a man who had a bullet extracted might better have left it where it was. An outfit's musicians often doubled as its stretcher bearers, and a minor crisis occurred during McClellan's tenure, just before the Peninsular Campaign in '62, when some musicians of the Fifteenth Massachusetts refused to submit to ambulance drill.*

* They were placed in a stockade on no rations until they complied. The 79th New York, in the same period, refused one morning to obey orders. They were promptly faced by a regiment of regulars and a battery, all of whom clearly intended to shoot. They backed down.

Railroads were to hand for mass transport of men and supplies, but there were not enough of them and the state of the art was primitive. (For instance, the Westinghouse air brake was not patented until 1869. Until it came into use, stopping heavy trains at high speeds was a tricky business, sometimes causing the rear cars to telescope with those ahead of them, or the whole train to be derailed by jackknifing.) Roads were very bad—perhaps nearly as bad as in the days of the Revolution—whereas the increased demand for ammunition and medical paraphernalia had greatly added to the military transportation load. In his memoirs Sherman estimated that a *corps d'armée*—on paper 27,000-30,000 men; in fact usually far less—required a train of 600 wagons.[5] Allowing about 25 feet per wagon, a train of this size, in single file (as it would probably often have to be, given the roads available) would stretch some three miles; and by Sherman's estimate, its speed was 2-2.5 miles an hour. Had the firepower of the same force been increased by the issue of breechloading rifles and fieldpieces, the size and slowness of its train might well have paralyzed it—one reason, perhaps, that the improvement of weapons during the war came almost to a halt after the first year or two.

Both armies were highly miscellaneous in make-up. Some Texas regiments consisted of Poles, Irish, Germans, and even a few Mexicans. One New York outfit consisted mainly of Bowery toughs and Dead Rabbits (i.e., members of the Irish fighting gang of that name); to join it, recruits were said to need a prison record.

The German community in St. Louis furnished a Union contingent commanded by a former European revolutionary, Franz Sigel. These men prided themselves on having been trained in the superior military "science" of the Continent, but by Civil War standards their record was somewhat spotty. After retreating with creditable skill at the battle (or skirmish) of Carthage, Sigel and his troops failed completely at Wilson's Creek (August 10, '61), spoiling General Lyon's plan for taking the Confederates by combined surprise attacks. The divided Union force was to strike at dawn, Lyon on the Southerners' front and Sigel at their right flank and rear. The Germans, after an initial success, rushed in and began eating the routed Confederates' breakfasts. Meanwhile the enemy formed up again in the brush and counterattacked, and the Germans, caught stuffing themselves or looting the camp, were rapidly scattered. Sigel extricated a part of his force and continued his march around the Southern army, only to mistake some approaching Confederates for Federals and be almost totally annihilated. He escaped to command again (which Lyon unfortunately did not; he was defeated and killed), but the reputation of the Germans as fighters in this war remained poor, and after the battle of Pea Ridge the Southern commander Van Dorn accused them of having shot unarmed prisoners.* From the tone of some of his remarks in a letter to Sherman, it is clear that Grant regarded Sigel as something of an idiot, though one of the dependable rather than the catastrophic type. He was however, a good artillerist, as the Confederates presently learned at Pea Ridge.

Indians fought on the Southern side in that battle, and for the Union as well, in other engagements in the West, but their military conduct—and indeed the Indian situation as a whole—was extremely peculiar. Just before Sumter, large blocks of them—mostly Cherokees and Creeks—had been evicted by forced sale from their lands in the South and moved out to Indian Territory, below Kansas and just west of Arkansas. These tribes, which also included Choctaws, Chickasaws, and Seminoles, were quite different from the still wild plains Indians, such as the Apaches, Arapaho, and Cheyenne, who lived beyond the Mississippi. The tribes of the Southeast had developed a white-style aristocracy who were planters and gentlemen. John Ross, the nominal chief of the Cherokees, owned slaves (as did many of his class), habitually wore a frock coat and stovepipe hat, and lived in a big plantation house, apparently in some fear of being bushwhacked by his subjects. John Ross was mostly Scottish. His archrival, Stand Watie, who later became a Confederate general of sorts, was the leader of a faction of discontented landless mixed-bloods. Below these were the so-called "pin" Indians†—mostly pure-

---

* He need not have been too indignant on this point. For shortly before, some proslavery militiamen had come upon a party of Germans asleep in a barn, disarmed and murdered them, and made off with their guns.

† I do not know the origin of this term. It is clear, however, that the "pins" were in a sense the Black Muslims of their day, who distrusted the mixed-bloods and regarded John Ross and his kind as turncoats.

bloods who lived in the hills in the new lands, where they formed a secret society, the Keetoowah, to revive ancient tribal ways.

It is hard to understand why anyone might suppose a people as divided and ill used as these to be a military asset, especially to their oppressors. But as soon as the Confederacy was formed, emissaries were sent out to the Creeks, Seminoles, and Cherokees seeking their help. Stand Watie's faction appears to have joined the Southern cause for pay. John Ross signed on not only as a slaveowner but for fear that if he did not, Watie might get the upper hand of him in tribal affairs. The reaction in other tribes was mixed. Some of the Creeks, under Danny and Chilly McIntosh, became Confederates, as did the Seminole chief Johnny Jumper. Two other Seminoles, Billy Bowlegs and Alligator, threw in their lot with a pathetic old Creek chieftain who feared white duplicity and would not sign. Families of both tribes were meanwhile fleeing to the North, and some formed delegations to beseech protection from President Lincoln for the loyalists back home. Unfortunately the White Father was in no position to help them just then, so Opothleyoholo and his band of miscellaneous refugees decided to make a run for it, their hope being to reach "free" Kansas. The result was one of the saddest and most pointless "campaigns" of the whole war.

The old chief's wagon trains were immediately pursued by a mixed force of whites and Indians under the command of a boozy Texas Indian agent named Douglas Cooper. The pursuers, about 1500 to Opothleyoholo's 700, finally caught up with him on the night of November 19, 1861, at a place known as Round Mounds. The fugitives' fires suggested that they had been caught napping. The Texas contingent, intent apparently on being first to the charge, formed up on a nearby ridge and whooped down into the wooded hollow where Opothleyoholo's people were encamped. Alas for their pride and ardor, they rode straight into an ambush, being met by a volley of arrows and minie balls and turned back with heavy losses. Many of their casualties were found scalped the next day. (Scalping was much practiced by Indian troops during the war. One bald victim had his beard removed in lieu of head hair, and some Choctaw troopers are said to have mailed scalps home to relatives in Mississippi.)

Cooper made a second attempt to stop the fleeing Indians and was again stood off, farther north at Bird Creek. Far from helping Opothleyoholo, these victories proved his undoing. Confederate newspapers played him up as an "abolitionist" chief heading a force of thousands, who would now very likely be emboldened to turn back and ravage the South. A (white) general named James McIntosh, with 1400 veterans of the battle of Wilson's Creek, was sent to reinforce Cooper and that did the trick. On a bitter day in late December of '61, this overwhelming force charged up an icy slope, dispersing the old man's warriors and capturing his camp, including all the party's supplies, its women-folk, and a number of Negroes, presumably slaves. Stand Watie's cavalry hunted down and killed those warriors who had escaped, among them the Seminole Alligator. Almost the entire band of 700 was wiped out.

Something about this victory—aside from the clumsiness with which it was accomplished—makes it hard to forget, as it seems to lay bare with particular clarity the cat-mouse instinct that lies at the bottom of war. No one, it appears, had bothered to ascertain what Opothleyoholo's intentions really were or how dangerous he and his people were likely to be to the Southern cause. It was enough that he had refused to throw in with the Great White tribe and tried to flee; the pouncing reflex did the rest. After the fact it was no doubt easy to see the whole affair as a triumph over dangerous renegades and free-staters. In reality it was a massacre of pitiful refugees who had simply been hoping to make it to some place where they might be allowed to live in peace. And as a military adventure it was, in its small way, almost perfectly superfluous. Stand Watie, by a kind of poetic justice, went on to give the Confederate General Van Dorn a push over the edge into total defeat at Pea Ridge.

Before that battle, the Union commander, S. R. Curtis, a capable veteran of the Mexican War, had been moving southward with a small army of about 10,000 to retake the territory which Sigel and Frémont had recently helped to lose. He was opposed by Van Dorn, a Mississippian related to the late Andrew Jackson, a dashing sort who was shot later in the war, supposedly by one of the husbands he had cuckolded. To meet Curtis, he assembled a much larger force—somewhere between 16,000 and 25,000 men.

The South's Ambassador-to-the-Indians-in-General, Albert Pike, accompanied the expedition with his native troops (whose pay he was withholding, evidently for fear that when paid they would desert). Pike himself wore leggings, moccasins, and a feather headdress, as if to stress a solidarity theme. Old Chief John Ross also came along, dressed, as usual, in a frock coat and top hat. There were also twelve hundred "pin" Indians, who were mostly looking to change sides, and a sizable contingent of mixed-bloods under Stand Watie. The main force was white and brought along sixty pieces of artillery.

Van Dorn and his strange army made contact with the Federals on the evening of March 6, '62, Curtis having entrenched himself on a ridge more or less à la Wellington, with Sigel's Germans on his right and his left based on the Elk Horn Tavern, which stood by a road that dropped abruptly down into a narrow gully. He dug in his artillery behind log bunkers—a practice not yet generally followed in the East. Van Dorn, in the valley below, decided Curtis' position was too tough to assault frontally and, leaving his campfires burning, moved by night around both ends of the Federal line—a very promising maneuver in view of his superiority in numbers. Next morning Curtis found himself under attack from two sides and driven to deciding, as the battle developed, which end of his line to risk his scanty reserves on. The German cavalry on his right was quickly demoralized by the queer-looking Indian-Texan force coming on at them, and broke. Their commander called for help. Meanwhile, on the extreme left, Confederate guns silenced the Yankee batteries and a massive infantry assault began on General Carr's position, threatening to overrun it. He sent couriers to headquarters prophesying disaster if he were not reinforced at once. At this juncture the Confederate General McCulloch started an attack on the Union center. The outlook, from Curtis' standpoint, had become very poor.

The Confederates' difficulties began with the Indians. A group of them, having captured a Union gun, heaped up straw around it, set it on fire, and commenced a somewhat premature victory dance. Between this and other distractions, Albert Pike was not able to get their attack rolling again. "He discovered that the red men were uncontrollable under artillery fire. They refused to lie down and let the shells pass harmlessly overhead. Most of the Indians wanted to fight individually—to climb trees or shoot from behind rocks." The advantage gained by their first onslaught was rapidly turning into an emergency. McCulloch threw some Arkansas troops in, to bolster the disintegrating left wing, but an Illinois unit repulsed them and McCulloch, in his bright blue trousers and shiny Wellingtons, was shot dead. Toward nightfall Curtis finally felt free enough of the Indian menace to reinforce Carr on the other end of the line, and the day was saved. Next morning Sigel, with forty guns and relatively fresh troops, opened up on the Southern artillery and what was left of the Indians. Union morale began to rise. The battle ended in a great charge which collapsed the whole tattered Confederate line. At his next roll call Van Dorn counted 2894 men out of his original 16,000-25,000 (although many not present were simply lost or straggling, and most of the "pin" Indians had deserted). Curtis lost 1384, killed, wounded, and missing.[6]

Poor Curtis was a bad-luck general, a good man but without guile or push, totally lacking in tribal finesse. He seems to have gotten little thanks for his victory at Pea Ridge,* though the Northern politicians needed one badly enough at the time. In 1863 Lincoln removed him as department commander of Missouri to please a difficult governor, Curtis in the meantime having lost a son in action and a daughter who died while serving as a nurse. Later, as commander of the Department of Kansas—a post awarded him as an honorary afterthought—he had the misfortune to harry General Sterling ("Old Pap") Price and his army off into Indian Territory just at a time when Sherman was creating a sensation in Georgia—so once again he went unnoticed. His dismissal by Lincoln is said to have undermined his morale and his generalship, a result not only understandable but quite typical of this muddled, intensely political war. On both sides, but especially in the North, everything done on the field was apt to have the most complicated consequences, if not actually at the ballot box, at least in the press and in the minds of those holding office or anxious to do so. To complicate matters further, we had also developed the beginnings of our present vast military

---

* Which was not only outstandingly complete, but one of the few any Union commander won against a force half again or twice the size of his own.

bureaucracy, which meant that field generals were driven nearly to distraction between wondering what the newspapers and the politicians might do to them if they so much as faltered on their way to glory, and how service rivals in high place might contrive to outwit and sidetrack them, particularly if they *did* show signs of succeeding. Rosecrans, for one, was apparently a general of this type—a man continually harried and worn down by his own paranoia, certain that he was being undermined, double-crossed, cheated of his due. He was set up for his climactic defeat at Chickamauga by far more than Braxton Bragg. Halleck, of all the Union generals, was the man best fitted to inspire such feelings in his subordinates. As general in chief in Washington, and a failed field commander himself, with sound motives for wanting to obstruct others, and a naturally devious, opaque way of expressing himself, he had them all at his mercy. His position was a bureaucrat's dream. Lincoln trusted him. He had risen with the blessing of old General Winfield Scott. He was even thought intelligent, being called "Old Brains," evidently without intended sarcasm.

To add to the possibilities inherent in this situation, the country itself was only half-organized—the Indians half-subdued, Kansas and Missouri half-civilized (though intensely, not to say murderously, political).* The result in the border states was an odd half-official war fought by grab-bag armies composed (on the Southern side) usually of a nucleus of regulars and large corps of "residue"—Indian contingents like Watie's, or troops of white bushwhackers commanded by such men as Charles Quantrill, Dave Pool, Holtzclaw, John Thrailkill, or Bloody Bill Anderson. These last committed horrible atrocities—notably the Lawrence (Kansas) massacre, Quantrill's masterpiece—but true to the iron sexual code of the age, they never molested women

---

* In *The Look of the West, 1860* (University of Nebraska Press, 1963), Sir Richard Burton, who traveled through the country at that time, quotes a speech made by a General Stringfellow in the Kansas Legislature:

" 'I advise you one and all to enter every election district in Kansas and vote at the point of the bowie-knife and revolver. Neither give nor take quarter, as our case demands it.

" 'I tell you mark every scoundrel among you that is the least tainted with freesoilism or abolitionism, and exterminate him. Neither give nor take quarter from them.' "

except to the extent of stealing their valuables and shooting down their menfolk before their eyes. Frank and Jesse James and the Youngers fought in the proslavery ranks, while Wild Bill Hickok served the North, half the time apparently as a spy, marching with "Pap" Price's Southern troops. As the war dragged on and Federal forces came to be transferred to Grant's and Sherman's commands, the Plains Indians, with Southern encouragement, began attacking white settlers and interrupting the stage lines to the Far West.

The Civil War in the West and the earlier border war between Kansas and Missouri, which overlapped it, seem to have established, or at least given a strong impetus to, the barbarous, frowzy style of life which prevailed on the frontier through the seventies and eighties. (Jesse James died in 1882.) And by inciting the Indians to fight white men, both sides helped to speed up the extermination of that luckless race in the postwar years when nobody needed them any longer. In fact, nobody needed them very much at the time. Watie's men, as they showed at Pea Ridge, could be a liability in real battle, and were little more than bloodthirsty nuisances the rest of the time, excelling in swooping down on lightly guarded wagon trains and slaughtering military captives or Negro work gangs. Those who served in the Indian Home Guard in the North made equally chancy soldiers, idle and messy in camp and uncontrollably zealous in action.

"A Union captain told of receiving a detail of Indians from the Fifth Wisconsin Regiment to help him destroy Confederate stores in Jackson, Mississippi. 'No sooner had they comprehended the nature of the work we had to do,' he wrote, 'than they put their warpaint on and with demoniac yells . . . began putting the torch to every house they came to.' The fire engines were summoned to put out the flames . . . but the . . . Indians blocked the firemen's efforts by jabbing their bayonets into the hoses."[7] Other Union troops were finally called in to suppress them. In the West, at Honey Springs, a Southern force of whites and Indians fought a Northern one composed of Indians and a Negro unit, the First Kansas Cavalry. (The Federals apparently won, losing 77 dead and wounded to the Confederates' 550.) Some Indians were excellent officers and one, Colonel Ely S. Parker, served on Grant's staff. On the whole, however, their contribution was not invaluable, the surprising thing being that, under the circumstances, anyone could have supposed it might be.

In view of the state of the military at the start of the war, it is also surprising that some of the white troops performed as well as they did in the early battles. The London *Times* correspondent William Russell described the sorry volunteer units he saw drilling in Washington in the spring of '61. ". . . I had seen that day [April 4] an assemblage of men doing a goose-step march forth dressed in blue tunics, and grey trousers, shakoes and cross-belts, armed with musket and bayonet, cheering and hurrahing in the square before the War Department. . . . They had indeed been visible in various forms, parading, marching, and trumpeting about town with a poor imitation of French *pas* and *élan,* but they did not, to the eye of a soldier, give any appearance of military efficiency, or to the eye of the anxious statesman any indication of the *animus pugnandi.* Starved, washed-out creatures most of them, interpolated with Irish and flatfooted stumpy Germans . . ."[8]

The state of the armed forces in the supposedly more martial South did not strike him as much better. While in Jackson, Mississippi, Russell was invited by the Confederate General Gideon J. Pillow to come along on an inspection tour of Fort Randolph, a short way up the river. "It is scarcely worthwhile to transcribe from my diary a description of the [defense] works. . . . A more extraordinary maze could not be conceived, even in the dreams of a sick engineer. A number of mad beavers might possibly construct such dams. They were so ingeniously made as to prevent the troops engaged in their defence from resisting the enemy's attacks, or getting away from them when the assailants had got inside. . . . The General ordered some practice to be made with round shot down the river. An old forty-two-pound carronade was loaded with some difficulty and pointed at a tree about seventeen hundred yards . . . distant. The General and his staff took their posts on the parapet to the leeward, and I ventured to say, 'I think, General, the smoke will prevent your seeing the shot.' To which the General replied, 'No Sir' in a tone which indicated 'I beg you to understand I have been wounded in Mexico and know all about this kind of thing.' "

The general then gave the order to fire, and the piece failed to go off. On the second try, it fired, "but where the ball went no one could say, as the smoke drifted right into our eyes. . . . Gun No. 3 was next fired. Off went the ball down the river, but off went the gun too, and with a frantic leap it jumped, carriage and all, clean off the platform. . . . Most of us felt relieved when the firing was over, and, for my own part, I would much rather have been close to the target than to the battery."

After these ceremonies, General Pillow addressed his troops. But as he "wound up with a florid peroration . . . assuring them that 'When the hour of danger comes I will be with you,' the effect was by no means equal to his expectations. The men did not seem to care much whether General Pillow was with them or not. . . ."[9]

Particularly during this stage of the war, the military dress on both sides tended to be gaudy, or at times downright peculiar. Russell describes a young general he saw on the steamer, en route to Fort Randolph—"redolent of tobacco, his chin and shirt slavered by its foul juices, dressed in a green cutaway coat and white jean trousers strapped under a pair of prunella slippers. . . . This strange figure was topped by a tremendous black felt sombrero, looped up at one side by a gilt eagle, in which was stuck a plume of ostrich feathers, and from the other side dangled a heavy gold tassel. This decrepit young warrior's name was Ruggles or Struggles, who came from Arkansas where he passed, I was told, for 'quite a leading citizen.' "[9]

From these and other of his descriptions, it is difficult to see why Russell felt the South had such a good chance of winning. It is still more remarkable that this half-organized, insubordinate, often drunken soldiery fought as well as it did—at times with a disciplined ferocity and a mad courage perhaps not easy to duplicate today.

The war seems also to have inflamed that passion for paperwork which has been characteristic of our own and other armies ever since. Thanks to the records that were kept (more fully on the Union side because it could better afford the effort), we know all sorts of odd things which may or may not have been typical of other wars past. In the Union army, for example, several women,

posing as men, managed to enlist and reach the fighting front.*
One, an Irish lady named Hodgers (pseudonym, "Albert Cashier"), served for three years as a private (Company G, 95th Illinois), participating in such major actions as Vicksburg and
Nashville. (There are reasons to believe, however, that Miss
Hodgers may have been hermaphroditic, passing for most of her
life simply as a dramatically undersexed male.) Another, Sarah
Seelye ("Franklin Thompson"), did two years of active service,
including First Bull Run and the Seven Days, but was sufficiently
feminine that, when she was hospitalized with malaria, her im-
posture was discovered. She spent the rest of the war as a
nurse.[10] One reason these women were accepted into the service
in the first place was that recruiting proceeded on the "warm
body" principle (the phrase then was "sound of wind and limb").
If a man looked hale, and especially if he seemed fired with zeal
to fight, it was thought unnecessary to undress him, thump his
chest, take urine samples, and the like. Indeed, in the existing
state of medicine, it would scarcely have been worth the trouble.
The real medical test in those days was camp life. If you failed to
break under drill, constant exposure, the scorbutic diet, and bad
sanitation, you were fit; and if only because of this speeded-up
natural selection, units which were on campaign were generally
far healthier than those still in training.† For the same reason
most regiments, sometimes long before seeing action, dropped
from a paper strength of about 1200 to 500-700 men, or even less.
The whole war, as Bruce Catton remarked, was fought with skele-
ton outfits. Instead of replacements for old regiments, new (but
already depleted) ones were sent up—from the veteran's stand-

---

* One lady, a Mrs. Reynolds, was commissioned major by the Governor of
Illinois. Pauline Cushman, the spy who just escaped hanging by the Confederates, was called "major" by the Federal soldiers and apparently wore
the appropriate insignia. Still another lady became a regimental chaplain.
And in the South a few soubrette types attached themselves briefly to the
army by wearing the gray and posing as recruits. A devoted young wife
joined up to be near her husband.

† The going diseases included malaria, typhoid, various nonspecific types
of dysentery, measles (which sometimes killed men by complications such
as pneumonia), and scurvy. Years afterwards, a doctor diagnosed the disease
prevalent in one outfit as pellagra. There is a record of Southern and Northern skirmishers fighting for control of a blackberry patch, dietetically a quite
sound engagement (blackberries contain Vitamin C and are hence anti-
scorbutic). In both armies venereal disease rates were high.

point, a very poor system, since it meant that instead of having
a few green men in his own unit he might find a whole green outfit in line next to him.

Religion in the service was in the same transitional state as
much else. While officially still Christian, we were even then
ceasing to be so, at least in the way of Charles XII and his men
(whose battle cry was "With God's help!"—in contrast to Schulenberg's more realistic Saxons, who cried "*Machet alles nieder!*"
or roughly, "Smash them all down!"). A certain primitive dubiety,
a flickering sense of commitment, appears to have seized the men
of the cloth once they came under fire, or sometimes merely
within earshot of it. "'Our chaplain is not very popular,' wrote
Private C. B. Thurston from Louisiana in 1863; 'he hardly ever
has any religious exercises and spends a great part of his time in
New Orleans getting the mail. . . .' Private Edward Edes, writing from Fredericksburg in 1862, said, 'I have lost all confidence
in the chaplain . . . He lied to me about carrying the mail and
does nothing at all but hang around the tent and sort the mail.
He never goes around any amongst the men and I think he is
nothing but a confounded humbug and nuisance.'"[11] A few units
carried their disdain of the clergy to the point of holding highly
sacrilegious mock services. According to another writer: "Chaplains the army had in plenty—one for each regiment . . . Yet as
one reads the memoirs and diaries there is a distinct impression
that as a group, and with honorable exceptions, the chaplains
. . . did not quite measure up. . . . A Massachusetts regiment
had a first lieutenant who was a minister in private life; he pulled
wires to get himself made regimental chaplain, failed, and wound
up by absconding with ninety dollars. . . ."[12] A colonel of the
Eleventh Massachusetts pressed his chaplain into service as a full-
time cook.

At sea modernity of a more strictly technological sort was just
setting in. The changeover from wooden hulls to iron, and from
sail to steam, had already begun, but not noticeably in the United
States navy. At the start of hostilities the fleet consisted chiefly of
square-riggers of the kind which had fought in the War of 1812.
Plans for ironclads had been around for some time,* and now,

---

* In fact since that war. In 1812 John Stevens, of Hoboken, New Jersey,
submitted a design for one to the government, which ignored the whole

rather belatedly, commenced being acted upon, some including the ancient principle of the beak, by which a ship could poke a hole in its adversary. The two fleets produced by this fever of in-novation were surely among the queerest-looking in the history of war at sea. They included ponderous rams like the *Albemarle;* armored side-wheelers (carrying masts and sails just in case); hastily converted ships like the *Unadilla* or the New York harbor ferryboat *Commodore Perry;* and *Monitor-* or *Merrimac-*like river gunboats, some of which rode so low in the water that one feels the wash of a passing steamer might have swamped them. In-deed, a class of small Monitors intended for river duty was, through some miscalculation, unable to float at all, the first one launched going immediately to the bottom.[14] Three of the series were drastically lightened and put into service on the James River, but the jinx persisted, their crews for the duration unani-mously cursing and denouncing them. They seem to have been to Civil War sailors what the Eagle boat was to the men of World War I—one of those mysterious freaks of engineering which mod-ern governments foist upon their services and then, in the face of the most violent protests or dramatic failure, go on with for as long as possible, as if from some afterthought of thrift.

Both sides used torpedoes—another novelty—stationary or "de-fensive" torpedoes being what we would call mines. (Farragut's "damn the torpedoes" refers to these.) And in the South, some experiments of truly desperate bravery were tried with a hand-crank-propelled submarine invented by H. B. Hunley, of Mobile, Alabama. She sank a number of times; once, I believe, while ly-ing at the dock with her hatch open and her crew of six asleep below. Hunley himself took her for a trial run off Charleston and was drowned with all hands. Finally, under command of Lieu-tenant George Dixon, the *Hunley,* which carried a torpedo on a spar mounted on her bow, managed to reach the Union sloop of

matter for another fifty years. In the '50s, however, some experiments with strips of armor plating were apparently made. John Ericsson's *Monitor* (the design of which was one of many submitted on competitive bid to the Navy Department; estimated cost, $275,000) was anticipated by Theodore R. Timby, of New York, who in 1841 proposed an almost identical "floating battery" with a revolving iron turret. He addressed his proposal to the War Department, evidently without result.[13] Ericsson's backers thought it wise to buy up Timby's patents.

war *Housatonic,* blowing it literally out of the water and, not unexpectedly, failing to return herself. For the time there were no further experiments in submarine warfare.

The famous *Merrimac* (or *"Virginia"*) was constructed upon the wooden hull of a Union frigate which had been burned to the water's edge and sunk. Captain William H. Parker, C.S.N., in his *Recollections* noted that she looked "like the roof of a house. Saw off the top . . . at the eaves (supposing it to be an ordinary gable-ended shelving-sided roof), pass a plane parallel to the first through the roof some feet beneath the ridge, and you have the *Merrimac.* . . . When she was not in action her people stood on top of this roof which was, in fact, her spar deck."[15] She was able to do perhaps five knots and was so unwieldy that tugs were sometimes called in to guide her. She drew twenty-six feet—an enormous draft even by modern standards, and most inconvenient in the shoal waters off Norfolk, in which she had to operate. She was equipped with a beak so she could double as a ram, and in Captain Parker's opinion was totally unseaworthy. Her sudden appearance, with two gunboats, before the Union squadron off Newport News on March 8, 1862, was nonetheless ominous for the enemy and caused great consternation. For although miserably engineered in most respects she was invulnerable to cannon fire, driving forward, through clouds of shot, to ram the old frigate *Cumberland,* which instantly began to sink, taking the *Merrimac* with her. The latter was spared this low-comedy disaster by the fact that her beak was so poorly constructed that it broke off, enabling her to back away and escape with no more than a few serious leaks.

One result of this episode was that the *Merrimac,* which was dramatically met by the *Monitor* the very next morning, as she sailed out to mop up the rest of the Federal fleet, could not hope to ram her new adversary but had to try for a decision by shooting it out. (In view of her own clumsiness, it is doubtful if she could have run down the *Monitor* in any case.) The famous battle between them chiefly served to show what the new rifled musket was already showing on land—that the defensive had gained one of its periodic advantages over the offense. The two ironclads blasted away at each other for five or six hours with no effect other than a few impressive dents in their superstructures and a few cases of concussion or acute headache caused by the tremendous clangor of projectiles striking their plates. Commander Worden of the *Monitor* was temporarily blinded when a shell burst near a peephole in his armored pilothouse. The *Monitor* at last made for shoal water and the *Merrimac* then broke off the engagement, by one account because she had begun leaking too badly to continue. Her success the day before, however, threw the whole North into a stew. "The moral effect," wrote Captain Parker, "was most marvellous. . . . The people of New York and Washington were in hourly expectation of the Merrimac's appearance off those cities."[16] Secretary Stanton, never the coolest of heads, came near to equaling Peter the Great on this occasion. Another writer reports: "With a glance out of the White House window, [the Secretary of War] stated he was sure the monster was at that moment on her way to Washington. 'Not unlikely we shall have a shell or a cannon ball from one of her guns in the White House before we leave this room!' The cabinet and even Mr. Lincoln himself were much depressed."[17] But to go back to Captain Parker's account, "As to the Merrimac going to New York, she would have foundered as soon as she got outside of Cape Henry. She could not have lived in Hampton Roads in a moderate sea. She was just buoyant enough to float when she had a few days' coal and water aboard."[18]

Alas for the *Monitor* and some of her brave volunteer crew, she *did* founder not long afterwards, in a storm off Cape Hatteras. In passing, those men left a document which must read strangely to servicemen of today—a letter written to their commander, Lieutenant Worden, who was ashore convalescing: "To our Dear and honored Captain:—Dear Sir: These few lines is from your own Crew of the 'Monitor,' Hoping to God they will have the Pleasure of Welcoming you Back to us again Soon, for we are all Ready, able, and willing to meet Death or any thing else, only give us Back our own Captain again. Dear Captain we have got your Pilot-house fixed and all ready for you when you get well again. . . . But we all join in with our Kindest love to you hoping that God will restore you to us again and hoping that your Sufferings is at an end and we are all so glad to hear that your eye Sight will be Spaired to you again. . . . We remain until death, your Affectionate Crew, the 'Monitor' Boys."[19]

Picturesque and touching as it sometimes was, the War between the States, from a strictly naval standpoint, lacked interest.* However, from photographs of the ships and their crews, one gets the same impression as one does from the pictures taken on land—the posed shots of officers trying to look grand and fierce; the Sanitary Commission officials and trim, glassy-eyed nurses pausing a frozen moment from their work; the groups of oddly assorted common soldiers, caught in camp just before or just after some bloody engagement, smoking their pipes and lounging about, a few posturing a bit, others staring into the camera with a wild, blank intensity. One senses in them all a curious kind of naïveté, as if, by our standards, each were too unguardedly himself, the villains obviously and totally villainous, the virtuous cleareyed and straight as strings, the country boys so rustic and simple one cannot believe them. One feels they must have caught the theatricality of the age, the Victorian passion for *tableaux*. The drummer boys were clearly not taken from life; they were snapped in a studio, as illustrations for some pathetic tale of the period. Among the sailors, many appear to be grizzled tars in their fifties or sixties who want us to believe they once sailed as cabin boys with Commodore Perry. Young or old, old-fashioned or new, they are apt to strike us as extras who have just gotten the casting director's pep talk and are working too hard at their parts. Those "Monitor Boys," what were they after, really? Did any group of A.B.s ever seriously write such a letter to their captain? (In fact, that group probably did.)

One gets the same impression of staginess, looking at the portrait photos of the generals on either side. Each seems to wear his career or his character on his face—far too much so. Old General Winfield Scott looks frankly cracked; Jackson has the eerie pale eyes of a seer—one with whom one would not care to argue points of faith. Ben Butler is a wirepuller, the personification of brilliantined guile; Hooker a *bon vivant* and loudmouth; Slocum a worried second-stringer; Sumner† a man totally upright and

---

* Experts will protest. There were all those "firsts." True, but there were few full-scale actions à la Farragut, and many of the technical innovations were too new to work very well (or, in the case of submarines, at all).

† The general Edwin Vose, not the statesman Charles. The latter (whom Lincoln called "my idea of a bishop") was not without his own sort of heroism. As a fiery antislavery orator in the U. S. Senate, he was once nearly

staunch; Wadsworth likewise. Sherman is a Terrible-Tempered Mister Bangs (but a capable one); Fitz John Porter a tragic cavalier; Rosecrans a stately, rather martyred officer, not up to the grand emergencies; Pope a sort of effigy, whose whiskers look pasted on; Phil Sheridan a bang-up cheery fighter and ladies' man; Grant an entrepreneur type (booze, cigars, iron will); Jubal Early a religious maniac; Kearny* a medieval warrior; Halleck a slow-witted dyspeptic who would be pitiable were it not for something sneaky and pompous in his expression. Lee is obviously an eighteenth-century ideal, lucid, decent, profoundly solid and self-possessed (and like Meade, perhaps liverish); Beauregard a man wizened by a peculiar kind of pride; and McClellan a preincarnation of Thomas E. Dewey.

It is obvious that some of these impressions are wildly unfair,†

beaten to death in his office by Representative Preston S. Brooks of South Carolina, spending three years in convalescence. After the war, in 1870, he aroused in Grant an unusual vindictiveness when the latter, anticipating President Johnson, endorsed a scheme for the annexation of Santo Domingo. Sumner opposed it, and in consequence was forced out of the chairmanship of the Senate Committee on Foreign Relations, which he had held since 1861 —a maneuver also quite in the Johnsonian spirit. The combination of this and other reverses seems to have killed him a few years afterwards.

General Sumner, who was in his middle sixties, was wounded during the Seven Days, and again at Antietam (where his II Corps all but gave McClellan a decisive victory). His corps also bore the brunt of the battle at Fredericksburg under Burnside. He died some months afterwards, having requested, and been given, a transfer. In battle he was famous for removing his upper dental plate before shouting "Charge!"

* Kearny was evidently a man not only of some ability (he was unfortunately killed at Chantilly in '62) but also of unbelievable valor. He reminds one a little of Uxbridge, having ridden by mistake into the Confederate lines, and then been shot attempting to ride out again—by one account, saber in hand and with the reins in his teeth.

He was a formidable example to his men. Noticing that one of his aides, following Second Bull Run, was still shaking he said: "You must never be frightened of anything!" Out of respect, the Confederates, after Chantilly, sent his body back to the Union lines. He would have made a superb knight officer to Edward III.

† Jubal Early, for instance, far from being a religious maniac, had been the Franklin County Attorney in Virginia before the war. During the battle at Fredericksburg he teased a chaplain he caught going to the rear: "I have known you for the past thirty years, and all that time you have been trying to get to Heaven, and now that the opportunity is offered, you are fleeing from it, sir. I am surprised." In 1869 he and General Beauregard presided over the Louisiana Lottery. By all accounts he was fierce and crabbed enough to be a practicing fanatic. He simply didn't happen to be religious.

Grant was entrepreneurial only in certain of his pictures. In others he has but also that some are reasonably accurate. What one is seeing, I think, in this curious war, is the emergence of certain new psychological types. In the case of bad generals, it was not simply a matter of the new institutions which in the '60s were producing them—democratic politics giving us the ambitious incompetent who hoped to run later on his war record, and West Point the touchy, overcautious career man who might equally well (better, in some cases) have served in the post office. One of the new psychological products of the time was the "image" general, the man overwhelmingly concerned not with results as such, but with how they can be made to look. The primary objective of this sort of officer is no longer to win wars but to play them as a complicated game of prestige. (Of course it is better not to lose, just as in business it is better for one's firm not to go bankrupt, although the really shrewd officer-executive can sometimes survive and do well by himself even then.) If he wins a battle, can he take all the credit? If he loses can he dump all the blame on others? Can he work things so that his own balance sheet, at the end of hostilities, shows a huge total in his favor? Can he at the same time manage to make his closest rivals come out the losers, not to the enemy, necessarily, but to him (which may sometimes of course entail their losing to both)? Long before, in Charles XII's army in Russia, General Lewenhaupt foreshadowed this unpleasant professional type, one which no doubt would also have been reported in the armies of Scipio Africanus and Caesar, had

---

a remarkably worn, defenseless look, and his face is oddly split, one half seeming far more drawn down and sad and disorganized than the other. There is much to suggest that in a part of his nature he was excessively sensitive and vulnerable, requiring a considerable exercise of his famous determination simply to hold himself together.

General Winfield Scott, according to Grant (who served with him in the Mexican War of 1846-48), was a fine commander but an overpowering conversationalist, whose style suggests the late Douglas MacArthur. By 1861-62, when the London *Times* correspondent William Russell made his acquaintance, the old general's compulsion to express himself, and especially to illustrate every point by an excursion into reminiscence, had reached debilitating proportions. He was moreover literally debilitated and so, fortunately, unable to be present at First Bull Run. As titular commander in chief, he kept giving out hopeful bulletins on McDowell's progress in that action until the returning rabble of soldiery made further reports unnecessary. The first thing these troops did, according to Russell, was to besiege the liquor stores in Washington and environs and get themselves stunningly drunk—a move one can sympathize with, although it is clear that Russell did not.

there been historians of a mind then to note such fine points of human character in any but the most exalted.

More is involved here, I suspect, than the timeless human inclination to duck responsibility, sabotage rivals, and claim credit for achievements not really one's own. It is not even, perhaps, a matter of the expanding scale on which, in "modern" eras, every enterprise including war comes to be conducted, giving more scope to supple political types and more *Lebensraum* to the incapable. The basic question is the degree to which certain ideals of behavior and accomplishment actually have a hold on men, which in turn may be reflected in the degree of order and steadiness and as it were objectivity which they bring to their actions. One would hesitate to call Stonewall Jackson objective in a modern sense,* yet he was profoundly so in that his intense religiousness and sense of principle apparently acted to keep *himself* out of his calculations as a commander. And by that single-minded attention to the Problem, he achieved prodigies, being not only an idealist but highly intelligent into the bargain. Except that his ideals were perhaps somewhat more secular, the same description might be applied to Lee.

The psychological antithesis of both was McClellan, a commander whom generations of historians seem to have found quite irritating. McClellan was *par excellence* an "image" general. In his middle thirties, he rose swiftly to fame and the supreme command by winning a tiny victory in West Virginia just at a moment when Union military competence nearly everywhere else was in doubt. It is clear that he had great ability, that he was not a coward in the ordinary way, and that he had a certain natural charm, or "charisma." His men never ceased to love him. Even after the Seven Days in '62 his prestige among them remained high, his veterans maintaining to the end of their days that Little

---

* Not only because of his strong faith but because his Christianity was oddly at variance with his defense of slavery. But I am here not speaking of the objectivity of ideals themselves—which may, as in Jackson's case, contain many contradictions or concealed concessions to an amoral practicality. I mean objectivity in the special sense that strong commitment to certain ideals may make men totally disregard all ordinary concerns of self, including reputation and safety, enabling them to concentrate on tasks in hand with the least possible interference from distracting second thoughts.

Mac had never been given a proper chance. When he was assigned the command of Pope's force during its retreat at Second Manassas—dramatically riding up to that general and his staff and himself announcing the change in appointment—the whole Union army, defeated and half-mutinous as it was, burst into tremendous cheers. The Confederate Kyd Douglas wrote of him: "The attitude of our officers and men toward McClellan was peculiar. We seemed to understand his limitations and defects of character, and yet we were invariably relieved when he was relieved, for we unquestionably always believed him to be a stronger and more dangerous man than anyone who might be his successor. His great professional ability was never questioned. . . . The appointment of General Burnside [just after Antietam in 1862] created no apprehension."[20]

Whatever was wrong with Little Mac, it seldom showed through his façade, at least when he was on duty. It seemed to attack him in those private hours when he was considering what to do next or composing the strange missives he sent to his wife and to President Lincoln. Some have suggested that his paranoia —his astonishing insolence to the President, the tone of the injured and unappreciated great man which he often adopted in his letters to Mrs. McClellan—was due to the fact that too much was asked of him too quickly. Grant, in his memoirs, magnanimously said as much: ". . . If he did not succeed it was because the conditions of success were so trying. If McClellan had gone into the war as Sherman, Thomas, or Meade; had fought his way along and up, I have no reason to suppose that he would not have won as high distinction as any of us."[21] The *Times* correspondent Russell described him as ". . . A very squarely built, thick-throated broadchested man, under middle height, with slightly bowed legs, a tendency to *embonpoint*. His head, covered with a closely cut crop of dark auburn hair, is well set on his shoulders. His features are regular and prepossessing. . . . The President confides in him and 'George's' him; the press fawn upon him; the people trust him; he is 'the little corporal' of unfought fields. . . . He looks like a stout little captain of dragoons but for his American seat and saddle. The latter is adapted to a man who cannot ride; if a squadron so mounted were to attempt a fence or ditch, half of them would be ruptured or spilled. The seat is a marvel to any European."*

Somewhat later, Russell said: "For my own part I confess that General McClellan does not appear to me a man of action, or at least, a man who intends to act as speedily as the crisis demands."[23] This estimate, made September 2, 1861, shortly after First Bull's Run, proved quite accurate (although four days later he was to be judging Halleck our topmost military brain, a mistake others were just then making).

But all the existing appraisals of McClellan seem somehow unsatisfactory. They describe more or less what he was but give no clue as to why he turned out quite that way. Certainly, as Grant said, he was not seasoned enough. But perhaps the most telling thing about him is that the queer note of grandeur which he so often struck in writing appeared *before* his elevation to the supreme command—in an order of the day composed after his

---

* Like many a visitor, Mr. Russell found certain of our customs surprising and got some of our names wrong. He speaks, for instance, of the battle of Bull's Run, of the Southern General Joe Johnson, and of Southern bands playing their national anthem "Dixie's Land." (Some eighty years later, in her American recollections, Simone de Beauvoir was to refer to McClellan as General Max Ellen.) Nevertheless, Russell's report of his travels, which took him through New York and Washington into the deep South and back, in the year between Sumter and the Peninsular Campaign, gives a remarkable insight into the state of the nation at the time. Not only was the Federal power extraordinarily problematical, *vis-à-vis* that of the states; the tenor of everyday life and the "facilities" were rather like those of a boom town on the frontier. Even in New York and Washington the streets were miserably paved. Russell complains repeatedly of the smells and the "drainage," the continual fire alarms, the terrible hotel accommodations in the South, the filthy restaurants and ill-cooked food, the vast amount of drinking which went on at all hours from 7:00 A.M. onwards, and our national habit (which had so appalled his countrywoman Mrs. Trollope) of chewing tobacco. He endured several nightmarish train trips—one from New York during which a party of drunken prize fighters kept the whole car awake most of the night; another on a troop train in the deep South, aboard which a contingent of Irish soldiers got violently intoxicated on "forty-rod" (so called from the distance at which it was supposed to kill) only to wake the next morning groaning and crying out for water. En route, the Englishman was introduced to Governor Pettus of Mississippi, a Davy Crockett type who dropped "a portentous plug of tobacco just outside the spittoon with the air of a man who wished to show he could have hit the centre if he liked." At that time, Russell adds, there were "more outrages on the person in this State, nay more murders perpetrated in the very capital, than were known in the worst days of Medieval Venice."[22] Which may have been only a slight exaggeration.

first triumph in West Virginia. He was, to be sure, back in service after spending some years out of it as a railroad man. But he had been at West Point, had served creditably in the Mexican War, and gone to the Crimea as an official observer, so the excitement and the horrors of campaigning were not new to him. (However, he seems to have arrived in the Crimea after the fighting was over, and merely toured the battlefields.) In the Civil War, he began as a major general of volunteers in Ohio, leading his force into West Virginia to stop the rebels there who were tearing up the tracks of the Baltimore and Ohio. He quickly routed and mopped up two small Confederate detachments (Union losses, less than 30 men; Confederate, less than 100), then paused in the town of Beverly to tell his men they had "annihilated two armies, commanded by educated and experienced soldiers, entrenched in mountain fastnesses fortified at their leisure."[24] This order, and his speech to the troops just before the battle ("Soldiers! I have heard there is danger here. I have come to place myself at your head and share it with you," etc.),* were, as he no doubt intended, circulated through the North and gave him his instant reputation.

But it quickly developed that something was wrong. The Little Corporal was not up to his role—perhaps because it was just that. Not that he was a fake in the usual sense. One feels he simply hadn't the objectivity, couldn't keep himself out of his calculations sufficiently to perform well, the more so the greater the occasion. He was neither intensely principled, like Lee or Jackson— or like Charles XII, who went to war as an untried general of

---

* However, this speaking style was rather the vogue. Before his trouncing at Pea Ridge, Van Dorn addressed his troops as follows:
"Soldiers! Behold your leader! He comes to show you the way to glory and immortal renown. . . . Awake young men of Arkansas . . . Beautiful maidens of Louisiana, smile not on the craven youth who may linger by your hearth . . . Texas chivalry, to arms!" (Why he was apostrophizing the beautiful maidens of Louisiana on this occasion is not clear.)
It is obvious that the impression left by Napoleon lingered on in countries other than France. In the Civil War photographs, a great many men, including some fairly tacky-looking noncoms, adopted the hand-in-bosom pose; and other things, for instance the kepi and the Zouave uniform and a certain stance with the back curved and the rump thrust out, suggest strong French influence. The Spanish-American War appears to have ended all that, and by the world wars we had developed our own military style, as represented by the doughboy and the G.I.

eighteen—nor intensely "modern" in the way that Caesar and Napoleon, or Bismarck and his successors were. He was a transitional man—in the fashionable phrase of a few years ago, "other-directed"—unable to be the pure egoist driven without second thoughts by his instincts, and equally incapable of devoting himself single-mindedly to a moral idea or cause.

Half taken in by the cant which they use every day as a means of getting along in the world, yet not really sure what they *do* believe in—lacking the courage either of faith or of a whole-hearted animality—men of this psychic type suffer from a perpetual wavering and inconstancy which is sometimes interpreted as shiftiness. It is not that, exactly, but a peculiar restless sort of dependence. Unable to settle the question of who they are, they try to make external circumstances do it for them. They are ambitious not in the ordinary sense but because, far more than most, they need some form of success to define them, to fix the outlines of their character. And to achieve that they depend not so much on self-discipline and real achievement as on performances and audience participation.

In McClellan's case this may have meant that he was content to *look* the superb soldier. Having quickly established this "image" with his West Virginia victory and the help of a press desperate for good news, he found himself in a paradoxical position. Great things were expected of him whereas in secret, without even being quite aware of it perhaps, his one anxiety may now have been to take no further risks, to do nothing which might destroy his precious new identity. So he prepared for battle with great energy and panache, but when the time came to march, he was overcome by strange misgivings. During the Seven Days, in the spring of '62, the personality of the Little Napoleon, so snappy and vigorous in camp, underwent a remarkable change. At Fair Oaks—despite his earlier battle experience—he was reportedly quite upset by the sight of all the Union dead. His movements in the field became unaccountably slow. And almost from the first he wildly overestimated the numbers facing him,*

---

* While McClellan had the help of cavalry scouts and of Professor Lowe in his balloon, he was also told, by his intelligence chief Allan Pinkerton, that Lee's forces numbered something over 120,000. (The Pinkertons, in the Civil War, evidently filled the role since taken over by the CIA.) The odd

supposing Lee's forces to be about twice their actual size and applying repeatedly to Washington for more support. The odd tone in his letters to his wife and the President dates from this period.

His best battle, Malvern Hill, he fought by a kind of prearrangement, knowing, as a good artilleryman and engineer, how strong his position was and how little chance Lee had of carrying it by direct assault. The significant point is that, having fought off the Confederates and caused them heavy loss, he did not try to clinch matters by counterattacking.* On the contrary, he continued his retreat (having, after all, protected and even somewhat improved his "image"). At Antietam, his last fight, he had the enormous advantage of having come into possession of the Confederate battle plan, which called for a convergence of Jackson, Walker, and McLaws on Harper's Ferry, this move to be followed by a junction with Lee and Longstreet to the north. Fortunately also, that plan, as so many strategic coups do in the execution, was already falling behind schedule by the time McClellan learned of it. And at the moment he himself was under some pressure to retrieve his reputation, which had not, on balance, profited in the Peninsula. His "image" needed fixing, and by luck he had been given an inside track for accomplishing just that. But then at Antietam, having maneuvered Lee into an action more or less on his own terms, he faltered again. Hooker on the right, and Sumner on the right and in the center, were finally beginning to prevail and Lee's line was all but punched in. McClellan seems never to have realized it.† Overestimating his enemy and playing it safe as usual, he evidently could not believe that a decisive victory was within his reach despite all of

thing is that McClellan, a professional soldier with other information to hand, was quite willing to believe him. We intuitively know, and psychological experiments have shown, that fear or intense anxiety causes us to overestimate the size of whatever is alarming us. One writer has suggested that Pinkerton was only telling his chief what he surmised the man wanted to hear.

* Three of his generals, Porter, Hunt, and E. V. Sumner, urged him to do so.

† Sumner on the field, discouraged by his own heavy losses, some of them due to his tactical mistake, sent back word that his and Hooker's commands were shattered, thus apparently deciding McClellan *not* to throw in his 10,000 fresh troops.

Burnside's efforts, on the Union left, to prevent one. So, as if unaware of how critical and promising the moment was, he withheld his reserves and Lee, although beaten, escaped. The battle which might have cut three years from the war ended up just another battle, more favorable to the Union than most but nonetheless exasperating to those who understood it. McClellan was almost immediately relieved, not because he had failed exactly (he hadn't), but to punish him for the disappointment he had caused so many—a punishment soon to recoil horribly on the Union army at Fredericksburg. Antietam was the end of his military career. It is clear that on the whole—by his own lights—he had done well. His veterans never forgot him, and his military strengths and shortcomings are argued to this day. He created an "image," beyond question, but the protection of it then taxed him to the limit, driving him to prodigies of delay and underperformance and giving him, at best, a paradoxical sort of fame—but fame nonetheless. He was, if I have gauged him correctly, a highly contemporary phenomenon: the nihilistic professional, too conventional, still, to break with the existing order but too skeptical to believe any longer in what it supposedly stands for. He was not the man to have accepted the dictatorship which is said to have been offered him in 1861. It was enough for McClellan that his own secret doubts of himself should never be confirmed and played back to him in the shape of some climactic public failure. They never were, but his "defenses" (as psychiatrists might say) were so good they took him clean out of the battle.

The same, unfortunately, cannot be said of Burnside, one of his subordinates at Antietam and his successor in command after it. In Burnside's case there was nothing ambiguous about either the man or his accomplishments. He was as old-fashioned and "inner-directed" as could be, an officer of strong, if usually mistaken views, who never shrank from seeing them through to a conclusion, no matter how foregone. He curried no favor with history, apparently having little of the self-consciousness which seemed to eat up the Little Napoleon (not to say the big one). Burnside might have been written by Balzac and played on the screen by Oliver Hardy. At thirty-eight, he had a portly figure and a great domed bald head, wore the policeman's helmet I have mentioned, sat a horse with tremendous grandeur, and after the war did famously in politics. A photograph of him taken at Fredericksburg shows him—rather too casually, one might suppose—reading a newspaper, like a police lieutenant relaxing after a busy day on the desk. This incredible man, who hardly won a victory after his first, and often came close to costing his colleagues theirs, fought throughout the Civil War in positions of the highest responsibility until he literally blasted himself out of the service with the affair of the Crater, on July 30, 1864. His history is one of those wonders of modern soldiering which show, among other things, the extraordinary amount of stupidity advanced populous nations will put up with in their "qualified" officials. A part of the reason is ingrained in the social organization, or rather in the habits of mind which hold it together. If a man is *regular*, doing all the right things at the right time, rising by the rules, people tend to respect him, if only because it is easier to read credentials than character. The vanity of his peers becomes involved in any question as to his competence which may then arise. An executive who reaches a certain level in the business world can never be fired, since any such public humiliation would be a breach of class etiquette—really, a reflection on the good sense of those who promoted him in the first place. Similarly, in military life—which since Napoleon's time has ceased to be a feudal amusement outright and become a profession with its own universities and degree-rating system—quite bad generals, provided they are "U," are often extremely difficult to get rid of. Burnside was a good example of the type. For years his colleagues belittled him but he held his job until he committed a *faux pas* so spectacular that no one could afford to overlook it. One could wish that some of our more recent commanders had done us the favor of being *that* bad. Burnside was never granted the power of, say, a Westmoreland; but within the scope allowed him he achieved miracles. Because no account of bad generals would be complete without him and because of the unique, almost classic unity of his career, I have given him a chapter to himself.

CHAPTER VIII

From the Jaws of Victory

The careers of some men can be quite adequately covered by the entries in an index. Here for instance is Rosecrans', as given in the index to Volume IV of Rhodes's *History of the United States:* "Rosecrans [Major General William Starke, U.S.M.A. 1842] placed in command of the Army of the Ohio . . . reply of, to impatience of Halleck . . . encounters Bragg at Stone's River . . . claims the victory . . . inactivity of . . . inaugurates a brilliant campaign . . . maneuvers Bragg out of middle Tennessee . . . enters Chattanooga . . . demoralization of . . . at the battle of Chickamauga . . . despondent despatch of . . . inability of, to cope with the situation . . . superseded by Thomas. . . ."

The career of "Beast" (Major General Benjamin Franklin) Butler, who earned his nickname while commander of the Department of the Gulf, is even more succinctly put: "Butler, B. F., order of, regarding women of New Orleans . . . City Point and Bermuda Hundred occupied by . . . inactivity of . . . delay of, in moving on Petersburg . . . strange influence of, over Grant, in connection with his [Butler's] removal . . ."

No such presentation would do justice to the military accomplishments of Burnside (Major General Ambrose Everett, U.S.M.A., 1847). The general was born at Liberty, Union County, Indiana, May 23, 1824, of Scottish-English ancestry. His great-grandfather, Robert Burnside, having been a supporter of Bonnie Prince Charlie, fled to South Carolina following the defeat of the Young Pretender at Culloden in 1746. (It is not clear from most accounts whether Robert served in that action; or if so, in what capacity.) Ambrose's grandfather, James Burnside, married a Miss Edghill (an English girl). Their son, Edghill Burnside, "appears to have sympathized with the . . . repugnance to slavery which, even at that early day, had been aroused in the Carolinas, for he freed his slaves and accompanied the 'Quaker Emigration' to the West. . . . In his new home he maintained a character of high respectability and influence; was for a long time clerk of the county court, an associate justice of the same, and a senator in the legislature of the state. Ambrose was his youngest son. He gave him a good English education in the schools of the neighborhood; and in 1843 he [Ambrose] entered as a cadet at West Point. [In the interim, while bucking for West Point, he seems to have worked as a tailor.] At the Academy he was not a hard student. With exuberant animal spirits, of vigorous bodily strength, he became an expert in military and athletic exercises, while his aptitude in mathematics . . . compensated for his deficiency of literary application. . . . He graduated [eighteenth] in a class of thirty-eight. . . . Among his fellow students were Generals McClellan, Hancock, Pleasonton, Fitz John Porter . . . Jackson (Stonewall) . . . Pickett. . . ."[1]

In 1853 Burnside, "having just invented a breech-loading rifle which, although since superseded, was a great improvement over any then in use . . . resigned his commission and engaged in the manufacture of this new weapon in Bristol [Rhode Island]. The enterprise proved unfortunate. . . ," not, his biographer says, from "lack of merit in the invention, but from his indignant refusal to employ the intervention of a lobbyist . . . who enjoyed the favor of the War Department."* Leaving Bristol for the time, he "entered the service of the Illinois Central Railroad Company, of which his friend and fellow-student, McClellan, was vice-president, and where he soon rose to the important position of treasurer."[3]

At the outbreak of the war he "promptly and without a moment's hesitation offered to his country the sword that she had

---

* Another biographer says that he "had the assistance of some of our leading capitalists, but the negotiations at Washington failed . . . and the enterprise ended in complete disaster. . . . Burnside sold his uniform and his sword, gave up all to his creditors and sought occupation elsewhere."[2]

taught him to use. He was selected for the command of the First
Rhode Island Regiment. . . . In the Battle of Bull Run . . . Colonel Burnside commanded a brigade and, as was justly said in a
memoir read before the Loyal Legion by Colonel William God-
dard, who served under him, 'no share in the disasters of that
conflict can be assigned to him or his troops.' "[4] In fact, after the
engagement Burnside and his men were welcomed in Providence
as heroes because theirs was among the few outfits which had
not run.*

"Burnside received a merited approval in his appointment as
brigadier-general, August 6, 1861. His first duty was to his friend
McClellan in reorganizing the Army of the Potomac."[5]

"One evening" (Burnside himself speaking) "in the following
October, General McClellan and I were chatting together. . . .
I mentioned to him a plan I had given some thought to. . . ." It
called for 12,000-15,000 troops and "a goodly number of mechanics, to fit out a fleet of light-draught steamers, sailing vessels
and barges, large enough to transport the division . . . so that it
could be rapidly thrown from point to point on the coast with a
view to establishing lodgments . . . landing troops, and penetrating into the interior, thereby threatening the lines of transportation in the rear of the main [Confederate] army then
concentrating in Virginia."[6]

What could be more sound or up-to-date in conception than
that? His friend McClellan asked for the plan in writing and approved it, and Burnside began assembling his forces. He had
some difficulty with the marine end of the project, ships of all
kinds being just then at a premium. By January 4, 1862, after (as
he puts it) "most mortifying and vexatious delays,"[7] his little
armada had gathered at Annapolis harbor. It consisted of eleven
transport steamers of various sizes and degrees of seaworthiness,
thirty-five sailing vessels (to carry stores, ordnance, etc.) some
barges or "propellers" (self-propelled steam craft) converted into
floating batteries, and a few tugs and ferryboats. Coal and water
ships were chartered out of Baltimore, and the troops numbered

* Had the men at that time known their commander better, they might
have acted differently. Unfortunately for all concerned, Burnside was only
too faithfully served throughout the war, at least by the common soldiers in
his commands.

about 12,000. When orders for sailing were given out on January 4, Burnside reports, "they were received from one end of the camp to the other with most enthusiastic cheers." Other reports suggest that the men had serious doubts about some of the craft they were going to be setting sail in.* "It may be well to state here that I had been notified by General McClellan that our destination would be Hatteras Inlet, with a view to operations in the inland waters of North Carolina."[8] After a rendezvous in Hampton Roads the whole force, with sealed orders, put to sea on January 11 and 12. For ten days nothing was heard of it. Then came news of a bad storm off Hatteras. "There were croakers," says one of the general's biographers, ". . . who prophesied disaster and failure. . . . Cape Hatteras is not an inviting place in the best of weather, and Hatteras Inlet is hardly more than a swash-channel of varying depth. The tempest came down upon the fleet while it was attempting to make an entrance by this doubtful passage into Pamlico Sound. . . . The channel was finally passed with the loss of two steamers, one gunboat, one floating battery and one or two supply schooners."[9] As some of Burnside's later losses were to go, these were trivial. Almost nobody drowned. On the voyage he was, by all accounts including his own, a model of courage and of solicitude for his men.

The dominant note in McClellan's orders to him was briskness mingled with circumspection:

GENERAL McCLELLAN'S ORDER
Headquarters of the Army
Washington January 7, 1862

(To)   Brigadier-General Ambrose E. Burnside,

COMMANDING EXPEDITION

General: . . . Your first point of attack will be Roanoke Island. . . . Having occupied the island and its dependencies you will at once proceed to the erection of batteries and other defences. . . . Having completed your arrangements you will please at once

---

* And as if to bolster their morale by example (and belie his later recollections of this, the most glorious adventure of his career), Burnside declined the well-fitted-out steamer he was supposed to have sailed in and transferred his floating headquarters to a small "propeller," the *Picket*, which came close to foundering in the ensuing storm.

make a descent on New Berne, having gained possession of which and the railroad passing through it you will at once throw a sufficient force upon Beaufort. . . . I would advise great caution in moving so far into the interior as upon Raleigh . . . I would urge great caution in regard to proclamation. In no case would I go beyond a moderate joint proclamation with the naval commander, which should say as little as possible about politics or the negro. Merely state that the true issue for which we are fighting is the preservation of the Union. . . .*

With my best wishes for your success, I am &c.,

Geo. B. McClellan,

Major-General, Commanding-in-Chief[10]

It took until the fourth of February to get the whole fleet from the inlet into Pamlico Sound, and until the seventh (because of more bad weather) to start the reduction of Roanoke Island and the shoreward garrison. On the thirteenth of March the attack on New Bern(e) began. Troops were put ashore, but "about this time rain began to fall, and the road became almost impassable. No ammunition could be carried except what the men could carry themselves. No artillery could be taken except the small howitzers, which were hauled by the troops. . . . A most dreary bivouac followed that night. Early the next morning, notwithstanding the fog, the disposition for the attack was made."[11] The enemy had about 8,000 men and sixty-six guns. ". . . Burnside deployed his lines with a simple faith in the Army regulations that would have given joy to . . . Von Moltke or Frederick. The rebels were admirably protected . . . Great fields of yellow furze with a thin growth of pines separated their works from the river. These works, beginning with an enormous railway embankment . . . that reached the dimensions of bastions at certain points, were calculated to hold an army in check until field-guns and regular approaches should demolish them. Burnside, though timid in peace and diffident in war, was never cautious in battle. . . . Heckman, the dashing commander of the Ninth New Jersey

* This interesting adjuration makes one wonder about a current item of faith in the history books. How much in fact was the North fighting for preservation of the Union, and how much was that issue used as a political dodge, designed to minimize Southern wrath and resistance? Is McClellan here simply echoing conversations he had recently had with Lincoln and others? Knowing the man one might guess so.

Infantry, took the lead, and the regiment tore across the field on a run. They found the men behind the works as full of ardor as themselves. The *élan* of the Jerseymen, however had caught the Conncticut troops and the New Yorkers, and the line, though mowed down and almost annihilated, reached the railway . . . crossed the ditch on the side, and in a few minutes the astonished . . . rebels were prisoners."[12]

In this engagement (which the writer just quoted called an "admirably complete military diversion") Burnside had no reserves, either of ammunition or of men. Had his first rush failed he would have been in grave trouble. As it was, he had temporarily disrupted an important Confederate railroad junction and won one of the earliest Union victories, a sort of miniature Narva, except with the odds the other way around. In the North, "the name of Burnside was in every mouth."[13] Unfortunately for Northern arms, if not for the man himself, who had won the far more hard-fought and substantial victory of Pea Ridge only a week before, the name of General Curtis was *not* in every mouth, nor would it ever come to be in quite the way Burnside's finally was. A part of the reason was probably geographical: Burnside was closer to the eastern seaboard and its newspapers. And, of course, he was a friend and old West Point-mate of McClellan's. He was relatively young and in; Curtis was old and out.

It was at Antietam, six months later, in mid-September of '62, that Burnside first showed his true mettle. One of his biographers, Augustus Woodbury,[14] reports that just before it, at South Mountain, Burnside, under McClellan's eye, ably cleared the passes of D. H. Hill's men as the Union army moved through for the big engagement.* However that may be, it is certain that he played a big part in the latter.

The battle of Antietam, from the reports of those who fought it, not to mention the casualty figures, was one of the most frightful and heartbreaking of the war. It also came at a most critical time. Having already been disappointed that spring by McClel-

---

* I do not find him mentioned, however, in Douglas Southall Freeman or other standard accounts, as having taken a significant part in this action, or indeed any part. After Major General Jesse Reno had been killed at South Mountain, Burnside at Antietam inherited his IX Corps, leading it for some two years thereafter.

lan's showing in the Peninsula, the North was staggered by the
disaster which overtook Pope at Second Bull Run (August 27,
'62). Pope had since been got rid of, but as his replacement
McClellan seems to have inspired no little uneasiness, particularly on the part of various legislators and high officials who felt
that their careers as well as their country were gravely threatened. By restoring him to command, after Pope's débâcle, Lincoln had acted in defiance of the Republican majority in
Congress, the War Department, and some of his own Cabinet.[15]
Moreover, McClellan had no definite orders to fight this particular battle. As I have mentioned, he had been emboldened to do
so after reading an intercepted Southern staff order which gave
him Lee's troop dispositions and put him in the way of attacking
a part of Lee's forces with all of his own. He did not move fast
enough or along the right routes to accomplish that—though in
fairness it should be added that Lee had learned within twenty-
four hours of McClellan's interception of Staff Order 191, Army
of Northern Virginia,[16] so that some of McClellan's initial advantage was quickly lost. Lee might still be outmaneuvered but
he could not be surprised. Having been slowed down at South
Mountain by what he took to be a huge force, the Northern general now found himself facing (by his own estimate) 100,000
Confederates at Sharpsburg, on Antietam Creek in Maryland.
(Even with A. P. Hill's troops, who arrived late by forced march
from Harper's Ferry, Lee had about 40,000 men against 70,000-
85,000 on the Union side.) McClellan appears to have believed
that if he failed to win—and in particular if he was decisively
defeated—Stanton and others would take extraordinary puni-
tive measures against him. As he melodramatically said, he fought
Antietam with a noose around his neck; but from what one can
surmise of Stanton, the general for once may not have been
exaggerating.

In any event he chose his position reasonably well and disposed his artillery with his usual skill. His plan was to attack Lee
first on the Southern left, then probe the center, and when these
actions were well under way, to begin an attack across Antietam
Creek against Lee's right, aimed at his base of operations in
Sharpsburg. The only trouble with this plan was that it was not
properly co-ordinated. In prize-ring jargon, McClellan intended

a three-punch "combination," but, chiefly because of Burnside, his timing was off. The struggle, which lasted twelve terrible hours, began with Hooker's famous attack on the Southerners in the cornfield, near the Dunker Church (the Confederate left wing). After this had been going on for some time, with Union artillery catching the Confederates in a converging fire, and the hard-pressed Confederate infantry, in the cornfield, mowing down the advancing Federals, Sumner's attack on the center, at Bloody Lane, commenced, with much the same results.

It was at this stage that Burnside's mission against Lee's right became of critical importance. If he could get across the creek and move up the slope toward Sharpsburg, the pressure on these other sectors might be relieved. For want of reserves, one or another of the defending Southern lines might collapse and Lee's army be cut up and overwhelmed. The original plan apparently called for Burnside's move to follow closely on Hooker's. But it did not. Burnside had evidently begun the day in something of a huff, having first been given, and then denied, command of Hooker's I Corps. There even remained some question as to the exact chain of command in his own corps. In any case, none of the impetuosity he had shown at New Bern developed here. Though the creek was shallow enough in most places to wade across, no one seems to have thought of that, and one unit under General Rodman spent hours looking for a ford which was supposed to be just downstream. After some hesitation another began an attack on what has since come to be known as Burnside's Bridge. The bridge was of course well defended—almost as though it had been left standing just to decoy a bad commander into trying to take it. When several not very vigorous attempts had been beaten back by heavy artillery and rifle fire, the Federals brought up guns and laid down a barrage. By this time it was past noon. In contrast, Hooker's attack had been fully under way by seven-thirty and his men, having long since suffered horrible casualties, were almost unfit for action. Sumner's troops in the center were by this time bearing the brunt of the battle and, thanks to Burnside's delays, Lee had been able to strip his right wing down to a mere screen of riflemen in order to reinforce his desperately threatened left and center. McClellan via one of his staff colonels sent a brusque order to Burnside, who said to the colonel: "McClellan appears to think I am not trying my best to carry this bridge; you are the third or fourth one who has been to me this morning. . . ."[17]

At last a Colonel Ferrero and two regiments, the 51st Pennsylvania and the 51st New York, under heavy covering fire managed to get across the bridge and gain the hilltop beyond, where they saw nothing but a retreating skirmish line and, in the distance, a few Confederate batteries. Leaving pickets, they moved back down over the brow of the hill, lit fires and made coffee, apparently unaware that what they had just routed was not an advance guard but almost the whole Confederate force on their front. At this point the Federal General Sturgis with his division prepared to move up in support of them, only to discover at the last minute that as result of the morning's exchange of fire, his men were out of ammunition. A jam then developed at the bridge as another division came up to go in in place of Sturgis', the Confederate gunners meanwhile keeping the crossing under a brisk fire. As matters now stood, out of four divisions amounting to 12,000 men, Burnside had one resting up and replenishing its ammo, another in reserve, a third hunting for an imaginary ford, and only the fourth, some 3000 men out of twelve, rather confusedly going to the attack. Off in another part of the field, near Bloody Lane, Sumner, whose advance had been more energetic, sent back word that his units were too shattered to undertake another assault. It was this report which seems to have decided McClellan against making a final all-out attempt to overrun the Confederates. Coming precisely at the moment when Lee's whole line was on the verge of collapse, that decision was the worst (and last) McClellan ever made in battle, for with it all chance of a decisive Union victory was lost.* Dawn to dusk, in killed, wounded, and missing, the Union casualties were 12,390 men out of perhaps 65,000 actually engaged, while Southern losses were 13,524 out of 40,000. No other battle of the war seems to me quite so sad as this one. The Union army was then at its peak, composed mainly of volunteers (in contrast to the con-

---

* Around 4:00 P.M. Burnside's men did get to the outskirts of Sharpsburg. But by then nothing was happening anywhere else and A. P. Hill's troops, arriving from Harper's Ferry, were able to concentrate against this last Federal assault and beat it back. Rodman's division, still hunting for the ford, was enfiladed and routed and Rodman was killed.

scripts and paid substitutes of '64-65)—men who adored and had absolute faith in their commander in chief. Nor had the South, by then, gotten its second wind. Though effective enough as a fighting force, many of Lee's men were already without shoes; and one senses that the Confederacy had not yet hardened itself to its situation, as it had done by the time of Gettysburg, ten months later. At Antietam both sides were still hoping for a quick knockout, and the morale of both was accordingly volatile. To have destroyed Lee's army at that moment might well have overwhelmed the South in a psychic as well as a practical sense, and so ended the war. As much as any man on the field except McClellan himself, Burnside, by his own "most mortifying and vexatious delays," had prevented that outcome. What was the reason for them? Where was the verve he had shown at New Bern? Was the problem of the bridge simply too much for him? Or was he perhaps, more or less consciously, trying to frustrate his rival Joe Hooker by withholding support? Later events suggest that might have been the case. Whatever his motives, he should have been relieved at once, as was his superior, McClellan. Instead, over his own strong protests, he was appointed to *replace* him. Of all Lincoln's decisions, this one was surely the most opaque. It was rather as if, after the battle of Holovzin, Prince Repnin, instead of being court-martialed for allowing Charles XII to bypass his position, had been promoted by Peter to the supreme command. If the price of Antietam had been stiff, it was nothing to that of the battle of Fredericksburg, fought under Burnside's tenure immediately afterwards.

The change in command of the Army of the Potomac was accomplished in the queer crabwise fashion in which everything on the Northern side seems to have been done. For a time, nothing happened at all. McClellan stayed at Antietam; Washington was silent about his future. McClellan himself is said to have been rather puffed up over his deliverance or near-success in the battle. And he and Fitz John Porter were quite angry with Lincoln for issuing the Emancipation Proclamation just after it.*18 As

---

* While slavery was for Lincoln a major, if politically touchy, issue, it could not be expected to appeal to many professional officers. The latter—as McClellan did in his order to Burnside cited above—naturally inclined to go along with the President when he followed a tactful line on the Negro question, and as naturally balked when he abandoned it. This episode appears to

weeks went by and Little Mac did nothing, the President in his turn became irritated, perhaps for more than one reason. (McClellan, in an order of the day to his troops shortly after the Emancipation Proclamation, had urged submission of the military to the civilian authority, but gone on to say that those who did not like the existing state of things could always vote to change them.) With his keen political sense, it is unlikely that Lincoln overlooked that remark, particularly as McClellan himself was a Democrat, already considered by some a promising candidate for the next presidential election. On October 1, 1862, Lincoln came to McClellan's headquarters at Antietam for several days of talks. Their tone was supposedly cordial, but during them Lincoln and a friend took time out to stroll to a nearby hill overlooking the encampment. "Lincoln asked his friend if he knew what the sight before them was. The friend, surprised, said that it was the Army of the Potomac . . . Lincoln replied: 'So it is called, but that is a mistake; it is only McClellan's bodyguard.'"[19] A little more than a week later, Jeb Stuart and a picked force of 1800 cavalrymen, led by such stalwarts as Wade Hampton, "Rooney" Lee, and "Grumble" Jones, rode completely around McClellan's bodyguard, commandeering a number of horses from farmers in southern Pennsylvania (the troop passed only a few miles from Gettysburg) and frustrating a feeble effort on the part of Union cavalry and foot troops to prevent their recrossing of the Potomac near Barnesville, in Maryland.

McClellan had hoped to head off this force at the river with Stoneman's and Pleasonton's cavalry, backed up by two brigades of Burnside's which were put on a train "and told to stay [there] with steam up, so that the troops might be sent up or down the B. & O. on the click of the telegraph."[20] These men never saw action; and the only ones who did—a hundred or two of cavalry under a Lieutenant Colonel Edwin R. Biles—gave way after a short fight, abandoning a strong position in a quarry and letting Stuart get across into Virginia with no one killed. "Subsequently, with all the evidence before him, McClellan decided that the principal error was made by Burnside's infantry in going to Fred-

show that the spirit of the authoritarian *arriviste*, though muffled in the Little Napoleon, was still definitely there. His first public *gaffe* was in a speech made in western Virginia in which he referred to slaves as "property."

erick instead of remaining on the train . . ."21 as they had been ordered. Strike two.

Lincoln's communiqués to his field commander now became quite sharp, and Little Mac was depressed. ("'Lincoln is down on me,' he told a friend."22) He began applying to Halleck for more horses and for a clarification of his orders, that general replying with his usual bewildering vagueness. At last, in early November, McClellan began crossing the Potomac. On the night of the seventh, as his forces were gathering on the other side, in Warrenton, he was met by a staff officer from Washington, General Buckingham, who summarily relieved him, the only sop to his dignity being that he was told to go home and "await orders." (He of course never got any; his military career was over.) "Buckingham had been instructed by Stanton to see Burnside first and offer him the command"23—why, it is hard to imagine.

Burnside, who at least had moments of self-doubt, demurred, on grounds of loyalty to McClellan and of his own incompetence. The news that Joe Hooker was to have the command if he refused it seems to have changed his mind. The fact that he accepted was not, in these circumstances, the unmitigated disaster it must soon have seemed. For bad as Burnside was, Hooker, as he showed at Chancellorsville the next April, was, if anything, worse, attempting more and taking far greater risks before he lost his nerve and his wits and 16,792 men. Besides, there were *some* reasons for choosing Burnside. He had done well in North Carolina commanding his own expedition (provided one did not look too closely into the details), and was, as much as Hooker, a bluff, impressive-looking officer, sometimes, indeed, quite dashingly turned out. ("When he rode before the troops, he wore large buckskin gauntlets and a loose pistol belt that allowed his holster to swing at his hip."24) People liked him.

Once he had allowed his rivalry with Hooker to force him into the command of McClellan's army, however, Burnside's usual hearty good humor failed him and he began slipping into a state reminiscent of Peter the Great at Narva, with the difference that, unlike Peter, he could take no sudden leaves of absence to recover himself. Trapped with his new responsibilities, he "fretted, drove himself to long hours of work, went almost without sleep, and became physically ill."25 The plan he came up with called for a cessation of action around the Blue Ridge and a move, instead, directly upon Richmond. Since Lincoln had favored the former course, Halleck found himself in the middle, and came down for a conference with "Burn" in Warrenton, the chief result of this meeting being much subsequent confusion as to just who had authorized what. "Old Brains's" concern seems as usual to have been to get himself off the hook, if necessary at the cost of muddling everyone still further; while Lincoln appears to have felt that if the march on Fredericksburg were made fast enough, it might succeed. Of course it was not.

A part of the reason was that, as Fredericksburg lay on the far side of the Rappahannock, Burnside needed pontoon bridges to get across to it. These he ordered through Halleck and the delivery was made eight days late. By the first week in December, when the Federals, fully equipped at last, were moving up on the town, Lee's whole army had dug itself in on the heights behind Fredericksburg, with its artillery commanding the place and the crossings of the Rappahannock just beyond. It had become a question of whether, in the face of these defense works, the Federals could get over the river at all. From the account given by Freeman, it appears that although Burnside's men had some help from the long nights and the fog, the Southerners in effect invited them to cross, being confident that they themselves could not be dislodged, especially by that commander. ("The appointment of Burnside created no apprehension. . . .") While that was to prove horribly the case, it need not have done so, for their position in fact included a serious weakness which any other general might have exploited to great advantage.

The army that Burnside brought to this engagement was a very fine one, thanks mainly to the work of McClellan. Its artillery, most of which concentrated on Stafford Heights, on the Federals' side (east) of the river, was excellent. Its fire outranged the Confederates' and was as accurate and handily directed. Morale in the infantry seems to have been good.* If not wildly confident,

---

* A British military commentator wrote: ". . . That vast array, so formidable of aspect, lacked that moral force without which physical power, even in its most terrible form, is but an idle show. . . . Northern writers have recorded that the Army of the Potomac never went down to battle with less alacrity than on this day. . . ."[26] There are reasons to think this appraisal is

the men were at least ready to obey their new commander, as events were soon to show.

On the night of December 10-11, Federal pontoniers began putting bridges across the Rappahannock. The next day Confederate riflemen in Fredericksburg went to work on them. Burnside ordered a massive bombardment and followed it with crossings of troops in "bateaux."[27] By the end of the day his men occupied the town, and three out of four of his pontoon bridges were completed. The Confederates knew now, even if they had not already guessed, that the Federal attack was not a feint. On the twelfth both sides shuffled their forces. The strongest part of the Southerners' line was directly behind the town, in the sunken road up on Marye's and Willis's Heights. The right of their line extended some distance south of Fredericksburg, to a point a mile or more below the southernmost of the Federals' bridges. In this sector (Jackson's) there was a gap in their defenses of some five or six hundred yards—a piece of dense, swampy woodland which Jackson, on the twelfth, appears not to have known about. Arrangements were made by the Southern commanders on the spot to put troops behind it and to command it by artillery, but the gap itself remained. During the same day, Union troops were subjecting Fredericksburg to a spectacular sack. According to a Northern officer: "Splendid alabaster vases and pieces of statuary were thrown at 6 and 700 dollar mirrors. Closets of the very finest china were broken into and their contents smashed onto the floor and stamped to pieces . . . rosewood pianos piled in the street and burned, or soldiers would get on top of them and kick the keyboard and internal machinery all to pieces . . . wine cellars broken into and the soldiers drinking all they could and then opening the faucets and let[ting] the rest run out. . . . Libraries worth thousands of dollars . . . thrown on the floor and in the streets. . . ."[28] Burnside seems to have done nothing to check this French Revolutionary exuberance and may, in his distraction, not even have noticed it.

---

inaccurate, a matter perhaps of judging events in the light of their outcome. As the Confederates saw it, the Federal attack was far from lacking in vigor. And it is doubtful if any demoralized army could have flung itself, as the Northern one repeatedly did, against positions so well chosen and fire so deadly. On that day, indeed, a little slackness, a touch of mutiny in the ranks, might have saved thousands of Union lives.

The next morning, December 13, either because his reconnaissance had informed him of the gap on the Confederate right or simply by chance, he launched his first attack on that front, and it soon showed signs of succeeding. The Federal guns laid down an intense barrage. Then, with the Confederate artillery still silent, waiting for the range, "those long awe-inspiring lines of blue began to move."[29] Not a shot was fired until they had come within eight hundred yards, when the Confederate artillery opened on them with solid shot and shells. The line reeled, pushed on again, reeled once more, and finally withdrew out of range to re-form. The Union "artillery never ceased to fire. There was no hurry, no loitering in the Federal ranks. . . . About 1:00 P.M. across the fields the Federals advanced in three long massive lines. This time evidently a general assault was to be delivered . . . supported by every gun the Federals could bring to bear. . . . On the neck of the woodland . . . the woods that represented part of the gap in the lines of [A. P. Hill's] Light Division—the first blow would fall."*[30]

It fell with very good effect. After being staggered once again by the Southern artillery, the Unionists renewed the charge and got to within rifle range, and the fighting began in earnest. By an accident of terrain, their charge was in part funneled into the gap between General Lane's and General Archer's Southern brigades. Archer's men found themselves flanked by the Federals in the boggy wood. They broke, and Archer was barely able to maintain his position by moving in fresh troops to take their place. He applied urgently to Hill for reinforcements. On the other side of the gap, to the northwest, Union soldiers broke through and began forcing some of Lane's units apart by attacking them from the rear, threatening part of that wing with envelopment. Maxcy Gregg's men, behind the gap, had been caught with their arms stacked and a number of them bolted. The gap, in short, had been penetrated. The moment was everything an enterprising commander might have hoped for. Up to it (except for the intense artillery preparation) the battle had gone ex-

---

* As one of the Federal commanders of this operation was the very capable Reynolds (later killed at Gettysburg), it is probable that the attack on the gap was in fact made in full awareness that a breakthrough was feasible at that point. G.H.Q. was still not impressed, and the reinforcements requested later were never sent.

actly as Charles XII might have fought it, singling out his opponent's most vulnerable point, concentrating his full force upon
it, then bursting through and re-forming so as to take the enemy
in flank.

Freeman, the most detailed of battle historians, seems to
think the Federals, at least momentarily, had that opportunity.
"Through the gap," he says, "the enemy could now pour thousands of men."[31] However, while the Confederates, with soldierly
speed, ordered up reinforcements and prepared to plug the hole
in their line, the Federal High Command did nothing, in effect
leaving its men stranded, to be driven back at the enemy's leisure. "Gallantly the Unionists had thrust, but now they could not
push farther the spearhead of their attack."[32] Jubal Early and
his troops counterattacked. The Federals soon lost their foothold
in the boggy wood and by 2:00 P.M., their advantage lost, they
had given up the battle in that part of the field,* retreating under the same punishing fire they had so bravely charged into a
short while before. Burnside later blamed Franklin for his failure
to press the attack. The real question is what Burnside himself
was doing at the time. If Franklin was really hesitating, Burnside, his superior, and presumably well enough informed to sense
at least the beginnings of victory on his left, should have ridden
at once to that part of the field and if necessary seen to the conduct of the battle himself. It was never clear *what* Burnside was
doing through most of that terrible day.

Between eleven o'clock and noon, while the assault on the
Southern right was proceeding, the main Union attack, out of
Fredericksburg and up Marye's and Willis's Heights, began. If
only because the action on the other end of the line had been
going somewhat favorably, and because the Confederate position
on the Heights was obviously so strong, this second assault should
have been no more than a demonstration, aimed at pinning down
Confederate troops while the full weight of Federal attacks
fell elsewhere. It was nothing of the kind, of course, but Burnside's *chef d'œuvre*—an attempt perhaps to re-enact his head-on

---

* By another account, Franklin, in command of the Federal Grand Division in this sector, applied as late as 2:45 P.M. to Burnside for reinforcements,
without success.[9] A second dispatch shows him to be fighting hopelessly on
at 3:45.

triumph at New Bern, this time against an enemy forewarned and in every way better prepared than that small garrison had been. The results were so frightful that they stand out even among the slaughters of that singularly bloody war.

On orders to advance, the men of Sumner's Grand Division, crying "Hi hi hi," ran or stumbled through the littered streets on the edge of Fredericksburg and started over more open ground toward the Heights, where the Southerners, behind the wall in the sunken road and on the crest above it, were waiting with their rifles cocked. The Confederate batteries had been placed so that, as one of their gunners remarked, "A chicken could not live in that field when we open on it."[33] The Federal guns on Stafford Heights, across the river, and a few in the town, laid down a heavy advance fire while the Union infantry, kicking down a board fence "as if it had been paper,"[34] came on at the double. Apparently the Confederates held their fire until the enemy had got within rifle and canister* range. Their artillery opened first, with such fearful effect that General Cobb's men, in the sunken road, and Cooke's, above them, had only time to let off one volley before the first Federal assault was shattered. (Cobb himself, however, fell a moment later, mortally wounded by a sniper. He was a good amateur soldier, whose remark about West Pointers deserves to be remembered, as a commentary not so much on that institution as on the type of the professional in modern warfare generally: "They are very sociable fellows . . . but never have I seen men who had so little appreciation of merit in others. Self-sufficiency and self-aggrandizement are their . . . controlling characteristics."[35])

When the smoke of that first cannonade lifted, the remnants of Sumner's first wave had retreated to cover, leaving the ground strewn with hundreds of casualties. Within minutes the attack

* Canister consisted of numbers of small cannon shot or grape, in a container. An artillery piece used this way was in effect a huge sawed-off shotgun—its range being about 250 yards, or just beyond the 100-200 yards optimal for the large-caliber (e.g., 0.57) muzzle-loading rifles of that day. The so-called minie ball was not a ball but a slug, hollow at the hind end so that the explosion of the powder would make it expand and take the rifling. A firing rate of two rounds a minute was usual, up to fifty rounds or so, when heat and fouling of the rifle barrel often forced a pause. Hence in twenty-five to thirty-five minutes of action a firing line, otherwise intact, might suddenly begin to lose its firepower and need reinforcements.

was begun again with the same hideous results; and, after another pause, again; and again. With almost insane bravery, the Union infantry threw itself up the slope, trying to carry out its impossible orders. Time after time it dashed out into that bloody chaos, over the stiffening bodies of its own dead, only to be scythed down by canister or massacred in blocks by the volleys of rifle fire.* "The whole plain was covered with men, prostrate and dropping, the live men running here and there, and in front closing upon each other [i.e., trying to form ranks and push on] and the wounded coming back. I had never before seen fighting like that, nothing approaching it in terrible uproar and destruction."[36] Later in the battle, the Union General Couch, just quoted, was overheard by a fellow officer exclaiming: "Oh great God, see how our men, our poor fellows, are falling!"[37] The only thing, probably, that saved the Federals from even worse slaughter was the clouds of smoke made by the black powder used in those days. Now and again it seems to have shrouded the attackers, giving them momentary cover. As the day wore on, the dead, in the biting cold, became quite rigid. A few of the living used their bodies as shields, either on the ground where they lay or stood up, like waxworks.

The Federal assault was so unbelievably stubborn that at one moment Lee evidently felt his men on the heights might be overrun. Reinforcements were sent to Cobb's brigade in the sunken road. Along most of that line the formation was then four deep. As Freeman remarks, "Never had Lee presented so many muskets on so narrow a front."[38] Once the move effecting this concentration of men had been made, any chance that Confederate firepower might fall off to the point that the Federals could carry their position had vanished, and the Burnside attack was for a certainty doomed. It still continued, as though of itself—as if in the horror of the moment no one had thought to give an order stopping it. At last even Burnside gave way. As Sumner's Grand Division withdrew at dusk, leaving 5444 killed and wounded be-

---

* Being soft lead and of large caliber, the "minie ball" had terrific shocking power even when spent; and the wounds that it inflicted at effective ranges were often dreadful, shivering bone to splinters or almost eviscerating men hit in the midriff. There is a record of one Confederate general who, wounded in this way at the battle of Cedar Mountain, persuaded his surgeon to put his entrails back and sew him up. Incredibly, he lived.

hind them, their commander in chief cried out, "Oh those men, those men over there! I cannot get them out of my mind." It was almost as if they had been overtaken by some great natural calamity, at which Burnside, like everyone else present, had simply been a stunned spectator. One can only wonder again what on earth had been going on in his mind during the earlier hours of that day. Had he no battle reports, or trusted aides to persuade him to reconsider; no telescope to see for himself, from his headquarters in the Phillips House, how badly his hopes had miscarried? Why was the slaughter allowed to go on and on? Can he really have been *that* stupid. One senses that some other element —perhaps not unlike the one which underlay Grant's refusal to permit a truce for the relief of the wounded at Cold Harbor— may have caused him to act as he did.

Cold Harbor was in fact quite like Fredericksburg. There too Lee had moved faster than his opponent and installed himself in a formidable position. And there, with a brutal lack of finesse unusual even for him, Grant attacked head-on—three of his corps diverging in their advance so as gradually to expose themselves to flanking, as well as to direct, fire.[39] Misinformed as to the fearful outcome of this effort, Meade, the nominal commander, continued the order for an advance; one of his officers in the field was so outraged that he flatly disobeyed, saying in effect that the order was ridiculous. Under such fire further movement in any direction was impossible. At Cold Harbor, which was fought on June 3, 1864, the Union lost 12,000 men, many of them in the first fifteen minutes. The truce to remove the wounded was acceded to by General Grant only on the seventh, by which time all but two of the Union wounded had died. Southern losses in the battle are not accurately known, but were evidently small.*

The same cruel exasperation, if that is what it was, which caused Grant, not ordinarily a cruel man, to allow the wounded at Cold Harbor to lie untended for days in the summer's heat, slowly dying before the eyes of the men on either side, may have driven Burnside into a kind of crisis of obstinacy at Fredericksburg. Stubbornness is, in fact, only a dull man's substitute for resolution. It is natural for men who do not come by ideas easily

* Figures in the official records are: Union, 1844 killed, 9077 wounded, 1816 missing; Confederate, 1200 killed and wounded, 500 missing.

to cling to those they have; and just in proportion as they do so, it becomes even more difficult for them to acquire new ones or to correct the old. There is not the slightest sign that as the battle of Fredericksburg developed Burnside was following events in any precise way, or grasped what had gone wrong. It is rather as though he had come to that action with a clear crude image of how it *should* go; and having formed his "idea" and given the appropriate orders for making it come true, had sat back fully expecting it to do so. His frame of mind was not such as to admit the unforeseen. Balked by events, he tried to turn his back on them.

It is quite probable that he was well informed as to Reynolds' breakthrough at the boggy wood, on the Confederate right. The reason he failed to support it may well have been that it was simply not in his plans to win a victory there. In his mind's eye, the main assault had been, and by God still would be, a triumphant charge straight up and over the main Confederate works. *That* was how he'd conceived it and *that* was how it would be done, and why all the damn delay? Get on with it then. Attack, attack! So Reynolds' assault was allowed to peter out and Sumner's was pushed to the limit. But then as each wave of men washed up the slope of Marye's Heights, broke and melted back, what could the commanding general do but look away and repeat his order, angrily determined that they should try again, and keep trying, until the wave reached the top. Only when none were left to try—when darkness was falling and the remains of Sumner's Grand Division were retiring into the town—may the truth of his mistake finally have gotten through to Burnside. For a moment he seems to have dissolved in anguish ("Oh those men, those men over there . . ."), only to bring himself up once more, indulging in yet another round of wild fantasies, convincing himself that one last attack, the next morning, would do the trick.* That was it! He'd lead it himself, on his great charger—at the head of his old IX Corps! How sadly and disgustedly one can imagine, his officers dissuaded him from this mad scheme.

Fredericksburg cost the Federals 12,653 casualties,[40] including 9600 wounded, of whom a good percentage probably died. South-

---

* He actually proposed making one, with himself at its head.

ern losses were 595 killed, 4061 wounded, and 653 missing—a total of 5309. Of these, many of the "missing" and possibly of the wounded were men making unauthorized trips home for the Christmas holidays.[41] Almost no major battle in the war, excepting Grant's masterpiece at Cold Harbor, was as lopsided in its losses.

Having recovered himself, Burnside made a last attempt to retrieve the situation by his famous "mud march," which was intended to flank Lee and force him into a position more suited to the Northern general's tactics. It failed, as its name suggests, because of the weather; and Lincoln, with some regret, fired him. Burnside was transferred to an apparently safe post, as commander of the Department of the Ohio. Before leaving to assume it, he showed a side of his nature not so much as hinted at in the funerary orations delivered in his honor many years afterwards.*

According to an article published in *Harper's New Monthly* in 1865: "When Burnside was in command of the Army of the Potomac, he executed an order, which was afterward suppressed by the President, dismissing several officers of his army from the service for various reasons. Among the number was General Hooker, dismissed . . . for having criticised the action of his commanding general at Fredericksburg. The order . . . known as 'General Order No. 8' was not carried into effect and only saw the light through the treachery of a clerk in the Adjutant-General's office. . . ."[42] The supposedly warmhearted Burnside seems to have meant business, for according to another report, "Henry J. Raymond, the publisher of the *New York Times*, was in camp, and Burnside showed him the order. Raymond asked what Burnside would do if Hooker resisted the order. Burnside replied with satisfaction that he would swing Hooker before sundown. The astonished and alarmed Raymond rushed to Washington to tell Lincoln. . . . The President said sadly that he would

* In the United States Senate.[1] At the time of his death in 1881, he was a senator from Rhode Island—a man who all admitted had been a moderately poor orator and a controversial commander, but whom all praised as the soul of honor, hospitality, and simple good-heartedness. None failed to mention that right after Fredericksburg, in his dispatch to Lincoln, he had assumed all responsibility for the disaster. He could hardly have done otherwise, and in any case had a change of heart later, to the extent of holding Franklin to blame for the failure of the attack on Lee's right.

stop Burnside from issuing the order but that he feared he would have to relieve him and appoint . . . Hooker to the command. Hooker, said Lincoln, was stronger with the country than any other general."*

One would have thought that as commander of a military district in Ohio, Burnside would have been well out of harm's way. It seems probable Lincoln made the appointment with that in mind, but if so he had misgauged his man. The anti-Unionist Copperhead movement was quite active in Ohio at the time. One of its busiest representatives was Clement L. Vallandigham, who besides being a rabble-rouser and morally rather unattractive was a Democrat. "Better had it been," says the historian Rhodes, "to leave his punishment to public opinion."[43] But Burnside, he continues, was "smarting under his defeat at Fredericksburg and the criticisms to which he was subject . . . and when he came in contact with the Copperheads . . . he began literally to breathe out threatenings." On April 13, 1863, from his headquarters in Cincinnati, "he issued his famous General Order No. 38 in which . . . he said: 'The habit of declaring sympathy for the enemy will not be allowed. . . . It must be distinctly understood that treason, expressed or implied, will not be tolerated in this department.'" And it was not. On May 1, 1863, Vallandigham, who was campaigning for the gubernatorial nomination, addressed a gathering of obviously seditious Democrats at Mount Vernon. "Two of Burnside's captains, in citizens' clothes, were taking notes. . . . The captains' reports were sufficient to convince Burnside that his General Order No. 38 had been grossly violated. Without consulting his subordinates or an attorney, he ordered his aide-de-camp to go to Dayton and arrest Vallandigham. The aide with a

---

* And bloodier than most, losing 4139 more men at Chancellorsville than Burnside did at Fredericksburg. His strategic plan that led to the battle was excellent, and he gave out advance notices of its success to the press, in very vivid language. Lee of course outwitted him, sending Jackson around his flank and rear and throwing the Union army into confusion by an attack at nightfall. Jackson was killed—mourned, it is said, by the men on both sides— while Hooker, perhaps no longer so strong with the country, became what he had been all along—a second-string general, fit to be a divisional commander or (if closely watched) to lead a corps. His failure at Chancellorsville began not with Jackson's attack but with Lee's, on his front, which apparently caused him to lose his nerve and cede the initiative. Having done so he was lost.

company of soldiers took a special train and reached his house at half past two in the morning. . . . They broke into the house, seized Vallandigham in his bed-chamber, and took him quickly to Cincinnati where he was incarcerated in a military prison. May 6 he was brought before a military commission for trial. . . . It lasted two days."[44] His lawyer applied to the U. S. Circuit Court for a writ of *habeas corpus* and was turned down. He was sentenced to imprisonment at Fort Warren for the duration of the war.

This extraordinary proceeding converted Vallandigham from a local nuisance into a potential *cause célèbre*, capable of reaching the Supreme Court and possibly of influencing the next presidential election. Lincoln at once commuted his sentence to banishment "within the limits of the Confederacy."[45] (The Southerners, upon receiving Vallandigham, evoked their own Alien Enemies Act and deported him to Canada. From there he soon made his way back to Ohio and subsequently was not bothered.) The issues Burnside had raised, however, were not so easily disposed of. The only ground upon which his summary treatment of a civilian could be justified was that Ohio was a part of the theater of war at the time. And that argument, says Rhodes, "cannot be maintained. The only safe rule is as old as the Parliament of Edward III: 'When the King's courts are open, it is a time of peace in judgment of the law.' The United States Courts were regularly open in the Southern District of Ohio. . . . The Secretary of War should have reported the arrest of Vallandigham to the United States judge of that jurisdiction, and if the grand jury found no indictment against him . . . it became the duty of the judge to discharge the prisoner."[46] Stanton, of course, was no more the man than Burnside for this sort of legal hairsplitting. And even Lincoln's commutation of the sentence, as it implied acquiescence in the military court's conviction, likewise implied condonement of the whole proceeding, including invasion of a civil jurisdiction by the army, denial of trial by jury, and suspension of *habeas corpus*. With everything else he had to trouble him, it is not surprising that Lincoln took the easy way out in the Vallandigham case. It is also true that the amiable warmhearted Burnside—who might, one feels, have made a fine bustling aide to Barry Goldwater or the late Senator Joe McCarthy—had managed to put the President himself in a quite awkward position, if not actually to compromise him.

'62-'63 was just not "Burn's" year. Better times were coming, though, for he soon received another military assignment in which he not only did not fail but even distinguished himself by winning a small victory. On orders to hold the place at all costs, he dug himself in at Knoxville behind superbly strong breastworks. Longstreet tried to carry them, lost a thousand men or so in the attempt, and then was forced for other reasons to abandon the siege. (Besides being well fortified, Burnside outnumbered him two to one.) At last, in the spring of '64, Burnside, at the head of his old IX Corps, was ordered to join Grant in that general's long, clumsy advance from the Wilderness to Spotsylvania to Cold Harbor to Petersburg.

But now, after a considerable quiet spell, marred only by certain routine inadequacies, "Burn" was about to Do It Again. On May 4, 1864, as Grant began his advance from Germanna ford on the Rapidan, Burnside unbeknownst to everyone was only twelve weeks away from his masterpiece, the tactical blunder which would end his military career with a bang heard literally for miles.

What in the world made him do it—and just when things had been going so well, too? As his military colleagues seem to have dealt rather offhandedly with him in their memoirs, and historians since have mostly followed their example, all one has in reconstructing "Burn's" motives are a few bald facts. One is that he came of a family evidently of some pretensions (witness their carefully preserved genealogy) whose fortunes, by the time of Burnside *père*, had somewhat declined. Perhaps Ambrose was expected to retrieve them. And as the son of parents whom "reduced circumstances" had made defensively proud and talkative, he may have been brought up to believe he was innately Somebody, a *Burnside*—it being just a question then of finding the proper métier in which to display his extraordinary endowments. The choices open to him were limited enough, but he appears to have been a strapping energetic lad regarded by his contemporaries, then and later, as quite handsome. If only on these grounds, and because money for his higher education was lacking, he was a likely candidate for West Point. It was either soldiering for "Burn" or tailoring; and to a young fellow with lots of muscle and pep and pride of lineage, life in the tailor shop must have seemed a nightmare. He *had* to get that appointment to the Academy—and unfortunately did so. With that his career was assured. More important, his training as an officer may have lent strength to the conviction—already so long dinned into him as perhaps to be habitual or hardly conscious—that he, "Burn," was one of Nature's aristocrats, a man destined to reach the top, never mind just how; *some*how; through sheer natural justice.

He was, note, an officer of little battle experience, who had never commanded a large force, when he proposed his New Bern expedition to McClellan. But ever since the success of that adventure nothing had gone right for him. At Antietam he had been affronted by having his command at the last minute drastically reduced; possibly this blow to his *amour-propre* combined with jealousy of Hooker to undermine his generalship that day —rather the way, one suspects, that Lewenhaupt's, at Poltava, was undermined by his resentment of Field Marshal Rehnskjold. Worse still, there had been the awful Fredericksburg affair, and all the lip he had had to take from Hooker and others after it.* The damage to his self-esteem on that occasion was the worse because he himself had inflicted most of it. By the same logic, *just* to be one of Grant's corps commanders in '64 (and rather a second-stringer at that, compared to Hancock or Sedgwick), must have grated intolerably on "Burn," not because he did not merit that status, but because he did.

His problem was less, one feels, that he had come to doubt his own intelligence than that he found himself disappointed in certain ill-founded hopes which had been overstimulated in him in the first place. Intelligence, in a sense, was neither here nor there. "Burn" would probably have been the first to admit he wasn't all brains; but in his private deliberations he may have given that fact too little real weight.† Bad and humiliating as his perform-

---

* And with no redress either, thanks to Lincoln's suppression of his General Order No. 8.

† It is perhaps asking too much of a naturally stupid man to expect him to make proper allowance for his own stupidity. Nevertheless, many who are not overmotivated in the way Burnside was seem able to do just that. Conversely, of course, many quite intelligent men are driven by a kind of animal vanity to overestimate themselves, and end up as even more spectacular fail-

ance often was, he neither managed by taking thought to improve it nor learned a discretion proportioned to his actual abilities. From the beginning he evidently ran more on push than sense. That business venture of his before the war, for instance; on the testimony of a fellow officer it failed because Burnside's breech-loading rifle was one of several entered in a $100,000 government-sponsored contest which was crookedly run. In Washington, his friend reports, Burnside was approached by a man close to the Buchanan Administration who told him that for $5000 he, the insider, could guarantee that the Burnside rifle would win. Burnside rejected the suggestion with violence, saying afterwards he wished he'd thrashed the fellow, and soon was obliged to sell his factory and personal belongings to pay his debts. Very creditable; but was it good sense to have gone into factory production of a weapon whose market, from the outset, was so uncertain? Possibly, as the insider may have intimated to him, the rifle itself was not of outstandingly good design, so that the only way it could have won was through chicanery.

The essential point is that "Burn" obviously thought big. He saw himself, with no difficulty, as an arms tycoon or, later, as a general of armies. He had, if nothing else, a thoroughly developed urge to rise and many of the animal assets to help him do so. Like Warren Gamaliel Harding, he *looked* right. People were impressed and trusted him, up to a point. Beyond that point everyone suddenly seemed to feel that a mistake had been made —that they had somehow been hoodwinked into accepting as first-rate, a man who was in fact, barely second—, but by that time it was usually too late; "Burn" was in the saddle again, riding off on some new doomed adventure. The bad morale in the army before Fredericksburg may have developed first among the officers close to him who began to see in their distracted leader qualities which had up to then escaped them. Burnside seems to have had the same startling revelations himself. No sooner had he allowed his jealousy of Hooker to trick him into accepting the command than he sensed he had put himself in a hopelessly exposed position, and so "fretted" and "drove himself" and ended up performing far below even his modest standard.

---

ures—this being possibly the only hint of similarity between Burnside and Napoleon.

It is not after all brains which make the world go round—or rather, it is only on the sly or in supreme emergencies that they do. Most of the time it is instinct, with just enough brains thrown in to get the immediate job done. And the man who happens to house great mental capabilities in the wrong sort of face and body, or to join them to the wrong sort of temperament (the right sorts varying according to the era), may never be called upon in great crises or enjoy more than a marginal life at the best of times. Conversely, the man who is by temperament and physique close to the going tribal norms tends to rise no matter how stupid he is, it being only in the eleventh hour that his unfitness comes to be seen, to the consternation and loss of all concerned. This is, I believe, a fair description of the nature and career of Burnside, who was a sort of Victorian beau ideal, looking like the photographs of many of our own grandfathers. (He is memorialized for *appearance*, of course, having given his name, slightly reshuffled, to a style of whiskers.) It is easy to visualize him as a Morgan partner of 1900; and in fact after the war he was consistently successful in politics, having, as many strongly instinctive men do and all politicians must, a hearty warmth and affability, especially toward those who in some way represented his own upward progress.* It is such as he who do most of the world's important business, and sheer good luck for the rest of us when the same men happen to be reasonably intelligent. They represent the persistence of an ancient psychological type in modern eras—a sort of New Feudalism whose aristocracy, while more fluid than the old, is fully as biological in principle. Its members, like Burnside, are perfectly confident of their "image." Their jealousy is of rank.

In Grant's Big Push of '64, beginning with the battle of the Wilderness, Burnside's IX Corps appears to have played a special role, in that it and he were treated as not quite on a par with the rest of the army. It seems to have been taken for granted by Meade and Grant that Burnside was hardly of the stature of Hancock or Sedgwick, and that he and his men should when possible be given less critical or supporting assignments. The first battle

* And also of course the converse, a savage dislike of those who would oppose or criticize him—notably Hooker and William Swinton. (The Swinton affair is described farther on.)

of that campaign is interesting in that it occurred hardly a year after Hooker's defeat at Chancellorsville (which took place quite nearby); and Grant began it by making the same mistake Hooker had. He left his right flank "in the air" (and his left one too, as Longstreet soon discovered).

This time, however, luck was with the Federals. Longstreet, before he could organize his attack, was carried to the rear so severely wounded that many thought him dead. The attack he had planned was delivered at 4:15 P.M. and failed. On the other end of the Confederate line, General Gordon, who had early learned of the exposed Union right flank and reconnoitered it himself, was unable to persuade his superiors to act on his information.[47] The irascible Jube Early had contrary reports and refused to believe Gordon; and Ewell, Gordon's immediate superior, would not make a decision. So the chance of rolling up the Union right was let slip. When the Confederates finally attacked, as Gordon had wanted, it was nightfall and the height of the fighting elsewhere had passed; nor was there time enough before dark for their attack to develop much momentum. The horrors of the Wilderness, fought as it was in dense woods and underbrush, almost blind and at pointblank ranges, with forest fires later sweeping the ground and burning alive many of the wounded, need not be redescribed here. The Union lost 17,666 men.[*48] Burnside's corps fought with Hancock's, the latter commander distinguishing himself for bravery and presence of mind on that hideously confused field. Burnside's conduct during the engagement seems to have attracted little notice.

Grant's next move was by his left flank southward toward Spotsylvania Court House. Lee anticipated it, and his General Dick Anderson, by a night march, established himself on the ground first. As both armies maneuvered into position, Lee arranged his forces in a prominent north-facing salient, known to his men as the "Mule Shoe" and later to historians as the Bloody Angle. Grant's first surprise attack (made by Hancock) on this position was quite successful, resulting in a substantial capture of men and guns† and forcing the Confederates after a desperate fight

* Southern losses are not officially known, but were probably heavy—on the order of 13,000.

† Some 2000 men, twenty guns, several thousand stand of arms and two Confederate generals.

back to a supporting line. The battle went on, at close quarters and under enfilading fire of canister from the Federal guns, until three o'clock the next morning. The trenches became piled full of dead, trees were cut down by rifle slugs, men shot or stabbed each other across parapets or through holes in the log breast-works in a perfect frenzy of killing, until some of the survivors became staring-eyed and speechless as though struck mad. "Battle line after battle line, bravely obeying orders, was annihilated. . . . Lee hurled his army with unparalleled vigor against his opponent five times during the day, but each time was repulsed. . . . All the fighting" (this writer goes on to say) "on the 12th [of May, '64] was not done at the 'Bloody Angle.' Burnside on the left of Hancock [now known as Hancock the Superb] engaged Early's troops and was defeated, while on the other side of the salient [the Federal General] Wright succeeded in driving Anderson back."[49] Here, while all were distinguishing themselves, "Burn" was flubbing again.

Except for an abortive attack by Hancock on the same salient on May 18 and 19, the battle had ended. One might suspect, though perhaps wrongly, that the tactical possibilities offered by Lee's rather exposed position at Spotsylvania had been taken minimal advantage of by his opponent, who once he had caved in the front of the Mule Shoe seemed to have run out of ideas. (Lee on this occasion did scarcely better, wasting men as recklessly as Grant.) Sherman (who was just then beginning his long series of battles with Joe Johnston and Hood in the South) might, after the successful dawn attack at Spotsylvania, have been more apt to shift his offensive so as to try taking Lee in flank or in rear, thus following the first surprise with a second. But Grant, in this campaign was never one for fine points. Even six days later, all that occurred to him was to try the same approach again. As his old friend, the correspondent Cadwallader, said of him: "His plans . . . were clearly outlined to his Adjutant and Chief-of-Staff and every detail . . . quite apt to be thereafter wholly left to them for execution."[50] He was a Big Picture general, not a *coup d'œil* general. Where some men cannot see the woods for the trees, he was almost totally the other way round. He had strategic sweep, that breadth of vision which some of us, inundated as we are by details, can achieve only now and then, sometimes when drinking.* But from the Wilderness on, his tactics were as good as accidental and almost never, even by accident, a success. The cost of this second engagement was appalling—by one report, 18,399 killed, wounded, and missing, as against Confederate casualties of about 9000. (Some 2000 of the Union casualties were incurred when the frontal assault on Lee's position was renewed on the eighteenth and nineteenth of May. The Union lost General Sedgwick, killed, and the South, Generals Johnson and Stuart, captured.) After Spotsylvania Grant began moving by his left flank, toward the North Anna River, and almost immediately found himself in difficulties.

"On the day after the start, Hancock crossed the Mattapony River at one point and Warren at another. Hancock was ordered to take position on the right bank and, if practicable, to attack the Confederates. . . . By the 22nd [of May] Wright and Burnside came up and the march proceeded. But the vigilant Lee had again detected the plans of his adversary. . . . As on the march from the Wilderness to Spotsylvania, Lee's troops took the shorter route, along the main roads, and reached the North Anna ahead of the Federals. Warren's corps was the first of Meade's army to reach the north bank of the river. . . . Lee was already on the south bank but Warren crossed without opposition. No sooner had he gotten over, however, than he was attacked by the Confederates. . . . The next morning [the 24th] Hancock and Wright put their troops across at places some miles apart, and before these two wings of the army could be joined, Lee made a brilliant stroke by marching in between them, forming a wedge whose point rested on the bank of the river, *opposite the Union center, under Burnside, which had not yet crossed the river.* The Army of the Potomac was now in three badly separated parts. *Burnside could not get over in sufficient strength* to re-enforce the wings, and all attempts by the latter to aid him in so doing met with considerable disaster. The loss in these en-

---

* Cadwallader gives perhaps the best account of this aspect of the general. From it, it would appear that Grant was a spree drinker—most difficult to control at times—but a teetotaler betweenwhiles. My own theory is that he had developed a drinker's all-inclusive way of looking at things, and indifference to minutiae even when sober. Hence his peculiarities as a commander. He had never, as he says, wanted to be a soldier anyway—still less President, one imagines. The particulars of either job bored him.

gagements approximated two thousand on each side."[51] (Italics added.) Grant, who had earlier complimented Burnside on his "remarkable march"[52] which had brought the IX Corps to the Wilderness in time to engage Longstreet with some success, must have wondered what had delayed "Burn" this time. The commander in chief was in any case able to extricate himself from the trap which Lee, with "Burn's" help, had laid for him, proceeding to Cold Harbor, where a far worse disaster awaited him and his already ravaged army.

Why was Burnside, after a considerable interval of good behavior, getting the "slows" again? Was he possibly having another attack of Lewenhaupt's disease, the Will for Others to Fail? Was the North Anna affair a repetition, perhaps, of his behavior at the bridge over Antietam Creek, a case of grumpy noncompliance on the part of an officer who, in comparison to colleagues like Hancock the Superb, had commenced to feel underrated and pushed aside? Certainly it is clear that the Knoxville expedition had greatly bolstered Burnside's self-esteem. As Sherman was later to do in Georgia, Burnside had marched to Knoxville crosscountry, cut off from his base of supplies; and having worsted the Confederates in two minor engagements before holing up in the town itself, completed his mission by repulsing Longstreet's attempt to carry his defense works. The whole action was even of some strategic value, as it served to draw Southern troops away from Bragg in Chattanooga, just before the latter was about to be attacked (and defeated) by Grant and Sherman. In the expansiveness which may have set in with his new success, Burnside, as early as September of '63, sent a proposal to Washington that he be authorized to make a march through the deep South to the sea, more or less along the route later taken by Sherman— only to be coldly advised by Halleck that "distant expeditions into Georgia are not now contemplated." (Burnside's biographer, Woodbury, adds: "For some reason which I have not been able to ascertain, General Halleck conceived a strong feeling of distrust toward Burnside.")

Worse still, as far as its psychological effect on him was concerned, was the fact that after Knoxville Burnside had been temporarily relieved and gone home to Rhode Island. However, on January 7, 1864, he was reassigned the command of his old IX

Corps, to which he added a Negro division, bringing it to a strength of four divisions or a nominal 50,000 men.* With that, his spirits seem to have risen and his thoughts to have turned back to the days of his first great triumph. Woodbury says: "He submitted a plan on the 26th of January for a coastwise expedition to North Carolina, to complete the work which he had so well begun in 1862. . . ." He apparently received no reply, and continued training and fitting out his corps, uncertain to the last minute as to just where he was to be sent. The orders he finally got to join Grant's army across the Rapidan can only have been something of a disappointment, setting him up for a second attack of Lewenhaupt's disease. His defeat, then, by Early at Spotsylvania, at a time when Wright was pushing back the other end of the Confederate line and Hancock in the center was performing prodigies, may have completed his embitterment. Partly by his own intention, as it were, he was once more the fuming nonentity and low man on the team he had been at Antietam and during the troop-train incident just after it.

It is not that "Burn" *meant* to sabotage anyone, any more than he was aware, in any very clear way, of his irrational need to be top dog. The machinery of his never very swift or varied intellect may simply have begun, after the Wilderness, to grind and overheat; and quite unconsciously, under the pressure of jealous wrathful daydreams, he may have begun doing things intended to be more damaging to colleagues whom he hated than to the enemy for whom he had a purely professional animosity. Having vindicated himself at Knoxville and proposed a brilliant plan to cut the Confederacy in half, here he was, a subordinate again, not only robbed of the chance to repeat his great Roanoke expedition but compelled to sit obscurely by while Sherman marched on into Georgia as he had wanted to do. Could any turn of events have been more ironic? Even after Fredericksburg or the Vallandigham business, people had at least *noticed* him. His General Orders No. 8 and 38 had roiled the waters, all right. These reflections may have set him casting about for new ways to distinguish himself, and he shortly came up with one which looked surefire. In the meantime, his bad temper

---

* Its actual strength was about half that number.

manifested itself rather startlingly in the case of William Swinton.

Swinton was an evidently odious Englishman who had been with the Army of the Potomac as a correspondent for *The New York Times,* at the battles of Fredericksburg and Chancellorsville. His comments on Burnside and Hooker in those engagements had been highly uncomplimentary, and during Hooker's tenure he was banished from the field. He turned up again at Grant's headquarters during the spring offensive of '64, this time as a sort of literary aide to Elihu B. Washburne, a congressman from Illinois. Shortly after the Union army had crossed the Rapidan, Grant was startled to read his orders for that day reprinted almost verbatim in a Richmond newspaper. Not long afterwards Swinton was caught hanging around headquarters as though listening in on a conversation between Grant and Meade. (The latter was nominally commander in chief, actually Grant's chief of staff, an arrangement designed to honor Meade for his services at Gettysburg while giving control to the man thought to be the better general. The truth was perhaps that Grant *would* have been the better general had he had Sherman, instead of Meade, as his chief tactician.) From Cadwallader's report of this episode it appears that Swinton was "exposed" and reprimanded but that no further action was taken against him.[53] News of all this, however, soon reached Burnside, and he was only too ready to act.

"We heard little more about Swinton until we arrived at Cold Harbor, when about the time Meade was having his trouble with Crapsey,* Meade came to Grant's headquarters to tell him that Burnside had arrested Swinton for some of his past offences, and had ordered him to be shot that afternoon! Grant thought this would be unwarranted, and ordered him released on the condi-

---

* By Cold Harbor, it seems, all the generals were getting a bit touchy. Crapsey, correspondent for the *Philadelphia Inquirer,* had been highly critical of the victor of Gettysburg during the Wilderness campaign. Meade turned him over to his "brutal, tyrannical" provost marshal General Patrick, who lashed him to the back of an army mule with his head hanging over its rump and paraded him, to a roll of drums, "for hours" through the ranks. The press responded quickly. . . . "After the Crapsey affair at Cold Harbor all newspaper correspondents with the army (excepting myself) and those in Washington . . . united in ignoring Gen. Meade's official existence. His name never appeared in print if they could prevent it. At the end of three or four months of such treatment, Gen. Meade became very restive. . . ."[17]

tion that he should be expelled from the Army. . . . If Burnside had not been overridden, he would certainly have had his order executed."[54]

At this juncture, the great Northern offensive was a little over a month old. The plan had called for a three-pronged movement, beginning the first week in May—Grant to advance south upon Richmond, Sherman to strike into Georgia toward Atlanta, and a third Union force, of 40,000 men, to steam up the James River to the vicinity of City Point, from which it would move by land to attack Petersburg, a railroad junction just south of the Confederate capital. This last operation was strategically sound and indeed of the greatest importance, since most of the supplies and reinforcements reaching Richmond did so by rail, through Petersburg. If that city could be promptly taken, the position of Lee's army, not to say of the whole Confederacy, would become critical.

It is difficult, though perhaps not impossible, to guess why an assignment as vital as this one should have been entrusted to a general of the caliber of Benjamin Franklin Butler. He was, by profession, a criminal lawyer and politician, and 1864 was of course an election year. (In '66 Butler was elected a Republican congressman from Massachusetts, and in '83 he became governor of the state.) It is fair to say that the war might have been shortened by as much as ten months had almost anyone besides Butler been in charge of the expedition up the James. As it was the 40,000 Union troops in his command, after a farcical defeat near Richmond on May 16, 1864, were "bottled up"* at Bermuda Hundred, in a sharp bend of the James River, not only failing in their mission but robbing the Union of men desperately needed elsewhere. (By then, in two battles, Grant had lost nearly 40,000.)

Almost from the first, Ben Butler seems to have been able to write his own military ticket. In May of '61 he was created, as if by magic, a major general of volunteers, assisting in the capture of Forts Clark and Hatteras shortly afterwards (August). His first action seems, however, to have been at Big Bethel Church, Vir-

---

* The phrase that Butler had let himself be stoppered up in a bottle was coined, appropriately enough, by Grant.

ginia, on June 10, 1861—a dismal little foray against Colonel (later General) D. H. Hill in which the Federals were defeated, with losses of 16 killed and 34 wounded, vs. 1 killed and 7 wounded on the other side.[55] "With [General] Magruder* directing a few changes in his dispositions Hill met and repulsed . . . some feeble, poorly handled assaults by Federals who already had sustained casualties by firing wildly into one another."[56] Nothing Butler did later belied this early promise.

The London *Times* correspondent William Russell mentions Butler's mishap at "Great Bethel," going on to describe the general's manner as "quick, decided and abrupt. He is a stout middle-aged man, strongly built with coarse limbs, his features indicative of great shrewdness . . . his forehead high, the elevation being in some degree due to the want of hair; with a strong obliquity of vision, which may have been caused by an injury, as the eyelid hangs with a peculiar droop. . . ." Russell discussed with him the current Confederate project of raising the *Merrimac* and other sunken Federal ships and making ironclads of them. "The General said: 'It is not by these great masses of iron this contest is to be decided: we must bring sharp points of steel, directed by superior intelligence' "[57]—the only question, as in the old joke, being whose? The question was as pressing in May of '64 as it had been three years earlier on the day of "Great Bethel."

Had they only known it, Butler's men in the James offensive were facing an enemy not only far weaker in numbers but hardly less mismanaged than themselves. As the Union forces landed up the James River in May of '64 and began feeble demonstrations at City Point and Port Walthall Junction, wild confusion prevailed in the upper Confederate ranks. General Pickett, never the clearest of heads, was in charge at Petersburg. Bragg, relieved of field duty after Chattanooga, commanded at Richmond (where he was evidently the Southern counterpart of Halleck, having President Davis' ear and theoretically overriding authority *vis-à-vis* Pickett and others in the field); while P. G. T. Beauregard, the hero of Sumter and First Bull Run, was on his way

---

* General Magruder became famous overnight for this small victory, and was quickly promoted to be brigadier. He is the same General Magruder who a year or so later, after the Confederate defeat at Malvern Hill, was accused of drinking on duty and subsequently transferred, after much wrangling, to another theater.

from Charleston to take command of the defense against Butler.*
His arrival was delayed first by sickness, and second, Freeman's
account suggests, by the general's habitual fondness for making
an entrance.[58] Like Napoleon, Beauregard was a great *metteur
en scène;* and in addition had a Napoleonic flair for battles conceived on a grand scale. Sizing up the problem presented by
Butler, he at once hit upon a plan. Lee (then en route from the
Wilderness to Spotsylvania) should detach a division or so to his
aid, and the capital should send him 5000 of its own defending
troops. With these, and the regiments to hand, he would annihilate Butler and, moving swiftly northward, open a devastating
attack on Grant's left flank—the result of which, in his own words,
would be to "open the way to Washington where we might dictate *Peace!*"[59] Another result, of course, would have been to
make Beauregard rather than Lee the supreme Confederate commander.

Bragg was immediately put in a difficult position. He knew
that if he countermanded Beauregard, and if the latter had only
an indifferent success in a smaller operation, the Louisiana general would almost certainly try to blame Bragg and cover himself
by filing elaborate reports stating what he had meant to do and
how others had prevented him from doing it. On the other hand,
Bragg knew that the Beauregard plan was not practicable. Lee
had too few men as it was; and even if he sent part of the number asked for it would take too long for them to get where they
were needed. Bragg's problem was then to cover *himself* and
also to see that Beauregard did not somehow evade his orders,
taking more authority and attempting more than Bragg and
Davis thought wise. Beauregard lost no time in trying to do just
that. Among other things he gave his subordinate, General Whiting, a blanket order negating in advance any instructions Whiting
might receive from other quarters. In the meantime, despite
alarms and interruptions of the line by Union cavalry, trainloads

---

* At which point it became a question as to just who was responsible to
whom. Did Beauregard override Bragg; was Pickett directly responsible to
Beauregard? In the midst of these uncertainties, Union cavalry under Kautz
began cutting the rail lines from the South, delaying the flow of troops into
the area and complicating everyone's plans. At one point telegraph lines were
also cut and Beauregard, the approaching commander, was out of touch with
his capital and his army.

of troops were hurried into Petersburg from the south, a small contingent passing through the town and arriving at Port Walthall Junction *just* in time to keep the road from being cut by the Federals at that point. Had a strong Union advance been made during this chaotic period, Petersburg might well have fallen, and Richmond soon after it.

But Beauregard's opponent was Ben Butler. Instead of promptly committing the better part of his sizable army, Butler made only a few halfhearted demonstrations, the last with the X and XVIII Corps under Generals Gillmore and "Baldy" Smith, before Drewry's Bluff toward the middle of May. Beauregard, thwarted in the grand design he had sketched out to Bragg, devised a new strategy to "annihilate" the Federals, or so he said, at least, after the fact. On the sixteenth of May his chosen subordinate, Whiting, was to advance northward with about two brigades from Dunlop's Station, on sound of the guns at Drewry's Bluff, the idea being that they would arrive, like Blücher, but of course earlier in the day, to take the hard-pressed Federals in flank and rear, as Beauregard himself was attacking them frontally. The distance involved was about ten miles, so that with a 4:00 A.M. start—6:00 at the latest—and a column speed of two miles an hour Whiting's force should have reached the field by ten or eleven in the forenoon. Moreover, by a stroke of luck, the capable D. H. Hill had turned up, seemingly out of semiretirement, and agreed to act as Whiting's "adviser."

Unfortunately, the morning of the sixteenth dawned foggy. Beauregard's first attack had some success; but partly due to the fog and partly to ill-trained brigade commanders who failed to execute certain maneuvers promptly or in good order, the main Confederate assault under General Ransom, on the left, soon floundered to a halt. By 8:00 A.M., after some three hours of murky action, that part of the front became quiet. Meanwhile, in the center, the Federals had attacked and overrun a part of General Hoke's line. After hard fighting they had finally been driven back again, only to open a new assault on the Southerners' right. Beauregard ordered up reinforcements which succeeded in checking the enemy but also opened a gap in his own lines. His commanders on the spot ordered a withdrawal which, far from repairing matters, left two Confederate brigades isolated and out of the battle thereafter.[60]

Bad as their own top leadership was, the Federals, it appears, were fresh spirited troops whose corps commanders were quite competent. While the orders they were receiving from General Butler were "incessant" and for the most part fantastic, these officers were not disposed, nor were their men, to let the Confederates gun them down without a fight. For his part, Beauregard had evidently concluded, by eight or nine o'clock, that without some additional help, some *deus ex machina*, his offensive would be unable to go further; and it was at this point, Freeman suggests, rather than before the battle, that the general's great strategic stroke may have occurred to him. Whiting and his 1500 or 2000 men became the key to the whole operation; it was they who would clinch the victory for him. ("Press on and press over everything in your front, and the day will be complete."*)[61] But although sounds of firing had been heard from the south, in Whiting's direction, at around 8:00 A.M., there was still no sign of him. By about 9:00 President Davis arrived at Beauregard's headquarters to watch the progress of the action, but alas, there was none—less and less, in fact, as the hours went by. Pending Whiting's arrival, the commanding general seems to have issued no further orders to Hoke or Ransom; while the Federals, no doubt as puzzled by the enemy as by their own chief, let matters lie.

"About 1:45, while the President and General Beauregard were standing on the works, the long-awaited sound of renewed firing was heard. . . . 'Ah, at last!' said Davis with a smile. . . . Not another sound came from the south. . . ."[62]

Whiting, of course, never showed up. He seems to have gotten about two miles, or nearly to Port Walthall Junction, when a small Federal unit, a regiment of a few hundred men, began to contest his advance. D. H. Hill, acting together with a General Wise, who commanded one of Whiting's brigades, was repulsing the Federals quite handily when he was astounded to see Wise's men, up ahead, break off the engagement and start to withdraw. Whiting, he was told, had ordered it. Nothing Whiting did from that time on made the slightest sense. Having halted his troops,

* Beauregard to Whiting, by courier; at 9:00 A.M. Repeated, 9:30 A.M.

and with the enemy still somewhere in his front, he called in his skirmishers. When Hill asked how he expected to hold his position without them, Whiting replied "You don't think I intend to remain here?" following this remarkable *non sequitur* with a retreat so confused that it "soon resulted in a wretched tangle of wagons and troops, artillery and ambulances, on the Petersburg road."[63] Fortunately for Whiting's command, the Federals did not stay to reconnoiter, or their one regiment might have routed two or so Southern brigades and captured a considerable baggage train. If Whiting received any of Beauregard's dispatches during this period, he either disregarded or instantly forgot them.

By midday or somewhat later Hill gave up and resigned as Whiting's adviser in chief. Not until 7:00 P.M. did General Whiting finally answer a late-afternoon message of Beauregard's—saying, somewhat superfluously: "Too late for action on my part."[64] All during the day he had suffered odd lapses of memory, forgetting orders he had just issued or talks he had just had. At one point he evidently became convinced that Petersburg, to his rear, was threatened, and immediately held up his advance. It would never do to leave the city exposed; besides, Beauregard had told him to move to Drewry's Bluff when he heard *heavy* firing—and the firing from there by that time (around 9:00 A.M.) was already petering out. Afterwards some officers maintained that Whiting on this disastrous day had been drunk. One, unable to smell alcohol on his breath, suspected narcotics. The truth, as Freeman suggests, may have been that Whiting was in a state of walking mental breakdown.* Whiting himself reported later that for the three nights preceding the battle he had not taken off his clothes or been to bed.

As for Drewry's Bluff, that absurd engagement ended when, after hours of inaction on both sides, the Confederates attempted at 4:00 P.M., during a violent rainstorm, to enfilade the enemy with artillery. The attempt failed; and after nightfall the Federal X and XVIII Corps withdrew, rejoining the rest of the army in

* "He may have been of the type . . . familiar in war, that loses through prolonged loss of sleep, all grip on the mental faculties"[65]—these being men, perhaps, in whom fear, repressed, results in insomnia and finally fear unrepressed. The Confederate General Gustavus Smith may have been a casualty of this sort.

Bermuda Hundred.* Beauregard was thus able to save some face by dashing forward the following day and stationing his whole force in front of Butler's across the neck of the promontory—it being perhaps chiefly because of this maneuver, which Butler all but forced upon him, that Drewry's Bluff is listed in most history books as a victory for Beauregard and the Confederates. (Union: 390 killed, 2380 wounded. Confederacy: 400 killed, 2000 wounded.) It is hard really to know *how* to describe it, though some apt phrases may have occurred to President Davis during his ride back to Richmond the previous afternoon.

The chief effect of Butler's ineptitude in this brief campaign was to make Grant's advance on Petersburg, after the battle of Cold Harbor, far more difficult and in the end more abortive than it need have been. Indeed, at Cold Harbor Grant for once outmaneuvered Lee, getting most of his army away and across the James before Lee realized what he was up to. But thanks to Butler, Petersburg was still in Southern hands, so a race for the city now began. The Federals as usual lost it. Beauregard in effect acted as Lee's advance guard, while Butler was in theory Grant's. Grant visited the camp in Bermuda Hundred and it was arranged that "Baldy" Smith's XVIII Corps should make the first assault. On June 15 it attacked Beauregard's men in their works northeast of the city, and was repulsed. On the sixteenth the main Union forces began to appear, and for three days in increasing strength they flung themselves at the Confederate entrenchments with fearful losses and no success. By the eighteenth Lee's army had completed its junction with Beauregard before Petersburg, both sides were digging in for a long siege à la Verdun, and still another chance for a decisive Union victory had gone by. On June 19, First Assistant Secretary of War Dana, then with the Union army, wrote that Grant "has directed that no more assaults shall be made. He will now manoeuvre."†[67] The news, if it reached Lee, cannot have perturbed him very much.

In fact for some time no one did anything. The Army of the

* "Both Corps probably had plenty of fight left in them when the bewildered commanding general ordered them to withdraw to fortified lines."[66]

† Dana seems originally to have been sent to the army at Vicksburg to report on Grant's behavior to Stanton, a role in which Stanton decided to keep him.

Potomac was as exhausted and broken in morale as it had probably ever been, even after Fredericksburg. In four calamitous encounters including Petersburg (which cost the North some 10,000 casualties) its losses in killed, wounded, and missing had been about 60,000, or slightly better than 50 percent. The heavy loss in officers had made the Union attacks at Petersburg, if possible, clumsier and more bloody than they had been, except at Cold Harbor. The quality of the troops was poor in comparison to the days of Antietam, the men now being mostly conscripts or paid substitutes. Even had Grant's soldiers been of the caliber of McClellan's, it is doubtful if they could have felt as keen an enthusiasm for their commander after the string of "victories" he had just obliged them to win. And in this same period Grant himself seems to have become dejected to the point that he fell off the wagon. (Cadwallader in his memoirs loyally overlooks this incident, so just how drunk the general got, or whether he rivaled his earlier performance at Vicksburg, we will probably never know.) It appears that news of his binge quickly reached Bermuda Hundred. Shortly after it, being understandably put out by Butler's performance on the James, Grant began taking steps to have him removed from command. The precipitating episode was apparently a dispute which had arisen between Butler and "Baldy" Smith.

On July 1, 1864, "Grant wrote to Halleck: 'I have feared it might become necessary to separate General Butler and General Smith. The latter is really one of the most efficient officers in service . . .' He went on to say that 'the good of the service would be subserved'" if a post could be found for Butler where "'there are no great battles to be fought.'"[68] Halleck agreed on Butler's unfitness to command in the field but would not at first order his transfer out of it. He suggested that Grant take the responsibility for this politically touchy move. Grant acceded, on July 6; and on the seventh, after a meeting between Halleck, Stanton and Lincoln, an order was prepared by which Grant effectively kicked Butler upstairs. "Butler, learning of this order, paid a visit July 9th, to Grant at his headquarters, the outcome of which was seen the next day when Grant telegraphed Halleck that he had suspended the order depriving Butler of his active command, thus leaving him in the same position which he had held. . . ."[68]

"Baldy" Smith was shortly afterwards relieved himself, having made the double mistake of quarreling with Butler and (by his own account) criticizing the conduct of Cold Harbor to General Grant, speaking as though Meade rather than Grant had been the officer responsible. Not surprisingly, his military career, despite Grant's expressed high opinion of him, was at an end. Also not surprisingly, it might be added that Beauregard, after his "victory" at Drewry's Bluff, praised Ransom to the skies in an order transferring that general to another post. "Almost a month later, in Beauregard's report of the engagement, Ransom's conduct was presented coldly and, at the end, was described along with Whiting's delay, as one of the two reasons 'more glorious results' were not obtained."[69]

So the first phase of Grant's Peninsular Campaign came to a close. A long, dreary period of trench warfare set in, the end of which, the next spring, was the death by strangulation of the Confederacy. Both sides had hardly settled down to the siege at Petersburg when Burnside was offered the chance at personal glory for which he may have been looking. His IX Corps included the 48th Pennsylvania Regiment, "made up mostly of miners from the upper Schuylkill coal district."[70] Lieutenant Colonel Henry Pleasants, a mining engineer then with the 48th, proposed to Burnside that his men dig a tunnel out across no man's land and under the opposing Confederate lines. In galleries off the main tunnel, the men would then put some four tons of gunpowder connected back to the Union side by a 510-foot fuse. On the night before the mine was to be set off Burnside would assemble troops whose job would then be to rush into the breach created by the explosion and start attacking the Confederates. In this way Burnside hoped a stunning surprise might be achieved; before the Southerners had grasped what was happening, their lines might be rolled up and their whole position possibly made untenable.

There was, in principle, nothing at all wrong with this scheme and Burnside approved it at once. Work on the tunnel was begun June 25, hardly a week after Grant had called off his last attack. Progress was slow because the men mostly had to work with improvised tools. Meanwhile, of course, Burnside had ob-

tained consent from Grant and Meade to go ahead with the whole
project, although contemporary reports suggest that neither of the
top generals—Meade in particular—was very enthusiastic about it.
(However, on Detonation Day, Grant made a feint with Hancock's II Corps so as to draw Confederate troops away from
Burnside's front just before the mine went off. He also ordered
a general artillery preparation. Meade is said to have refused to
come forward to view the main event at all.) Burnside's original
intention had been to use his Negro division to spearhead the attack, but G.H.Q. appears to have talked him out of that plan. So
the (white) Second Brigade, under a Colonel Marshal, was
picked to go in first, and a General Ledlie was to direct and ac-
company the assault, whose second or third waves would be
Negro.

At last on July 29 everything was ready—the powder in place,
the fuse laid, the troops alerted. The match was applied at four
o'clock the following morning—but nothing happened. After about
an hour a sergeant of the 48th Pennsylvania offered to go into
the tunnel and see what was wrong. He did so, spliced the fuse,
which had broken, and the match was applied again. At about
five, with a stupendous *whoof,* the mine blew up. "Contrary to
the usual expectation," said Cadwallader, who was there, "the
noise . . . is not the first thing to break on the senses. . . . My
first perception was that of seeing the earth commencing to rise
on a line a hundred yards in length; then to split open by fissures,
from which emerged a dense volume of smoke . . . followed by
sulphurous flames. . . . The smoke and flames rose perpendicu-
larly at first; then spread out into a great sheet; and commenced
slowly to fall in the form of a great water spout. . . . The sound
of the explosion did not equal my expectations."[71] A battery of
Confederate guns and several hundred men went up with the
mushroom-shaped cloud. Even though they had heard the Union
sappers working under them, the Southerners evidently did not
expect a blast of this magnitude and had not gotten wind of
Union troop movements in their front, so the surprise was considerable. Now came the attack through the crater (which Cadwallader described as 150 yards long, and others put at 170 feet
long by 60 wide), preceded by a Federal cannonade for a mile
along the lines on either side of it.

No one, it appears, had thought to train the assault troops to climb out quickly over their own works, or alternatively made arrangements to flatten the works ahead of time. As a result the attack was slow in getting under way and the men lost formation almost at once. General Ledlie was nowhere to be seen, and Burnside himself remained far to the rear. Even so, the first few units made an attempt to go in with dash. One line of Federals reached the far end of the crater and climbed to the top, only to withdraw again for no apparent reason and pile up on those coming from behind. By the time the Southerners had recovered from their shock and begun rushing troops forward to block the gap in their lines, they found themselves not under flank attack but looking down into an immense hole in the earth full to its upper slopes with black and white soldiers struggling back and forth in wild disorder. Such an opportunity for massacre—and of black troops at that—was seldom given the Confederates, even by a military spendthrift like Grant. They opened up with every cannon and musket that could be brought within range. On the Union side, no units to the right or left of the doomed men in the crater made the slightest move to help them. "Huge missiles from Confederate mortars rained down into the awful chasm. The muskets left by the retreating Federals were thrown like pitchforks among the retreating troops. The shouts, the screams, the explosions, added to the horror. . . . The Southerners pushed in from both sides of the crater, forming a cordon of bayonets about it. . . . Both of Ledlie's brigade commanders were captured."[72] By the time Burnside called off this insane action, at about 2:00 P.M., the Federals had lost 4000 men and their enemies 1000. Grant said, "It was the saddest affair I have witnessed in the war."[73] Cadwallader quotes him as remarking that the action of the crater was "a positive benefit to the enemy."[74] "One good result followed not long after," Cadwallader adds, "Gen. Burnside ceased to command the Ninth Corps."

That summer of '64 seems to have featured big explosions. Ben Butler, in his "bottle," undertook to dig a canal at Dutch Gap which would bypass a part of the James River blocked by obstacles he himself had sunk in it. His Negro troops, under continual Southern artillery fire, completed the work, and a retaining dam was thereupon blown up in order to flood the channel. The charge went off but was not placed right, leaving the canal itself blocked by the remains of the dam. The project was thereupon abandoned. Finally, at City Point on the James, where Grant had his headquarters and where most of the Union ammunition was landed from river steamers, a dockworker, toward the end of August, "dropped something which exploded. This fired all the cargo in an instant, destroying a large number of vessels . . . killing many men, and destroying over a million dollars worth of property. Fragments of flesh, hands, feet, and other parts of human bodies were literally gathered by the basketful, one-fourth of a mile distant. Showers of shot, shell, grape and canister, minie balls and other missiles were rained down in every direction. The ridge pole of my tent was snapped in two by a solid shot. . . . Singularly, no one connected with headquarters was injured."[75] The blast might have been taken as a sort of ghastly last salute to General Burnside, who on August 13 had received a leave of absence from the army, luckily never to command again.

He seems, after 1866, to have begun failing once more in business—this time as a manufacturer of locomotives. By a strange quirk of circumstances he turned up at the siege of Paris in 1870, acting briefly as an unofficial mediator between Bismarck and the French representative, M. Jules Favre. "His interviews," says his biographer, ". . . although comparatively resultless, were yet very agreeable to all parties concerned, and he left upon these able diplomatists a deeply-marked impression. . . ."[76] It is perhaps best that we do not know precisely what their impression was, although at that, he may have done the national "image" far less damage than have some of our high officials since, including many who never left Washington.

Burnside spent his last years (he died in 1881) as a twice-elected Senator from Rhode Island, apparently well liked, full of hearty good cheer, and disposed as always to let the dead bury their dead. Butler was defeated once more, at Fort Fisher, in December of 1864, by which time Grant felt strong enough politically and otherwise to fire him. In the 1880s he turned Democrat and at last ran unsuccessfully for the presidency as the candidate of the Greenback-Labor and Antimonopolist party. Beauregard in the postwar years was for a while an officer of the Louisiana lottery. From the history of these and other generals of our Civil

War days, one is led to wonder if a talent for politics may not be synonymous with a lack of it in military matters, if not in almost everything else.

Of all the wrack of terrible commanders which that conflict cast up, Burnside I think deserves the highest mention. In sheer consistency of performance, however, Butler was perhaps worse—worse than anyone including Banks, McClernand, and even the frightful Sickles. Butler was also clearly "Burn's" superior in meanness and chicanery, and in the boldness with which he was prepared to push any personal advantage. "Burn" would probably have hanged Hooker or shot Swinton, had he been allowed to, but one doubts that he would have had the gall, let alone the presence of mind, to blackmail General Grant. Butler was a worse commander but an amateur. Burnside was after all a pro—a *trained* bad general—and as one of the newer style of "school" soldiers he must surely rank with such monumental disasters as Sir John French of World War I. In the military, as on the frontier, we were pioneering back in the 1860s. Not until a hundred years later would we see, in our armed forces, the likes of "Burn" again. In a way he achieved his life's ambition; he made the top in something.

As for Grant, anyone familiar only with his Wilderness Campaign would be apt to think the President's loyalty to him misguided. The fact is, however, that before he came east to take charge of the Union's last great offensive, Grant had performed brilliantly, far more so than he was ever to do again. Even at Shiloh, although caught in a bad position, he managed to extricate himself and to win besides. And in the maneuvers that led to the fall of Vicksburg, he behaved with a daring and prescience which would have done credit to Charles XII.* His management

---

* Grant transferred his whole army by night down the Mississippi, past the batteries at Vicksburg, putting it ashore in hostile territory, miles from his base of supplies. His problem was then to prevent Joe Johnston from moving westward from Jackson, Mississippi, so as to make a junction with Pemberton in Vicksburg—thereby creating a combined force which might easily have crushed his own. By swift, skillful action he liquidated his enemies in detail, moving first against the town of Jackson, where he defeated the Confederates and interrupted the rail line to Vicksburg; then turning against Pemberton, defeating *him* and forcing him back into his siege works. Grant's only mis-

of the battle of Chattanooga was on the whole excellent—especially as he was under continual pressure from Washington to "remember Burnside," who was then being attacked by Longstreet at Knoxville. For once "Burn" did not need to be remembered, but accomplished his mission as ordered, drawing off and engaging a part of Bragg's army while Grant and his corps commanders, Sherman, Thomas, and Hooker, defeated the rest of it at Chattanooga.

When one compares Grant's generalship, from Fort Donelson and Shiloh to Vicksburg, in '62-'63, with his conduct of the drive toward Richmond in '64, it is almost as if one were following the careers of two different officers. In the former campaign, he seldom made a serious mistake or persisted in those he had made, and his casualties were comparatively light. In five battles fought in and around Vicksburg he lost in killed, wounded, and missing a total of 8873 men as against about 10,000 killed and wounded, and 37,000 captured, on the Confederate side. At Chattanooga he lost 5800 men out of about 60,000, while Bragg (whose force, minus Longstreet, numbered 33,000) lost 3000 killed and wounded as well as 5400 men, 40 guns, and 6000 stands of arms, captured.

From the day he crossed the Rapidan, almost ten months later, beginning that campaign by leaving both his flanks "in the air" at the battle of the Wilderness, Grant seems hardly to have done anything right; and the few things he did do properly, such as his passage of the James River before Lee could head him off, were neutralized by the ineptitude of his subordinates (in that case, Butler's). Was it simply because Lee was so much better than any of the other generals Grant had faced? Some commentators, I am sure, would say so. But that is perhaps not the whole explanation; nor probably was drink, since others besides Cadwallader have reported that Grant was not a drinker in the way Joe Hooker appears to have been. The tradition is that in '64 Grant went off his good behavior only once, at the start of the Petersburg siege, and heaven knows he had reason enough to by that time.

It is entirely possible that the remarkable change in Grant's

take was to try to carry these by mass assault, as at Petersburg. His assault having failed, the town was starved out and surrendered July 4, 1863.

generalship after he joined the Army of the Potomac was due to the peculiar command arrangements which Stanton and others had seen fit to wish upon him. In its usual awkward way, trying to please everyone, Washington had given the heroes of Vicksburg and Gettysburg nearly equal billing; so that whereas before Grant had dealt directly with his corps commanders, his orders now reached them through Meade. In other words, Grant's habit of sketching out his grand plan and leaving the details of execution to others may not have been typical of his earlier campaigns,* and perhaps developed in this one only as a form of tact —out of deference to the rather delicate problems in protocol presented by Meade, who was after all his senior and the displaced commander in chief.

Meade had fought one good defensive battle—Gettysburg—failing to clinch his victory by a determined pursuit. (Lieutenant, later Colonel, Frank Haskell, who served under him in that battle, defended Meade on the ground that a majority of his generals were against trying to follow Lee and destroy his army, because of the exhaustion of their own.[78] A stronger military intelligence might, however, have overridden them.†) He appears to have been a soldier's soldier whose appointment to the command at Gettysburg delighted his fellow officers but was "distasteful" to the men in the ranks.[79] He was evidently a punctilious, sniffish sort of man, exacting in matters of routine and given to grumpiness or outbursts of wrath when things went contrary to his lik-

* Besides mentioning this habit of Grant's, Cadwallader seems to qualify his description of it. In the last few days of the war, in April '65, Meade was incapacitated by sickness and Grant, in order to trap Lee, moved the VI Corps from his right clear around to the other end of the line. "The transfer of this corps was the only direct command which I ever knew Gen. Grant to give any body of troops *after assuming command as Lieutenant-General.*"[77] (Italics added.)

† Interestingly enough, Meade was criticized not only by Lincoln but by Dwight Eisenhower and Field Marshal Viscount Montgomery, for having let Lee's badly mauled army escape. For all his fiery talk Montgomery seems to have been a general rather like Meade—one who prepared and prepared, never moving until the last detail had been attended to. Charles XII was exactly not this sort of commander, knowing very well that once one is in the field thoroughness is better sacrificed to timing than the other way around. Grant showed a perfect understanding of the same principle in his Vicksburg campaign, incessantly urging his commanders forward, impressing upon them the importance of speed and, as Fuller says, infusing the whole army with the energy of his resolve.

ing. One writer speaks of his "flaming temper,"[80] which was shown clearly enough in the Crapsey affair. One wonders too if on the day of Burnside's last disaster it was Meade who, having refused to come forward to witness a project he had never approved of, also let "Burn's" men fall in the crater by the thousands while keeping fresh troops to the right and left of them inactive during the nine hours that the slaughter lasted. Grant seems rarely to have been vindictive, and indeed there was a side to him quite at odds with the character eventually created for him by events and the press—a streak of the compassionate and oversensitive, even of dreaminess, which caused him to read novels instead of studying his algebra at West Point, or to give a deserter's wife at Petersburg a kindly interview and finally to pardon the man himself.[81] The order forbidding the relief of the wounded between the lines at Cold Harbor, and the pressing of the attack itself on that occasion, do not seem in character, and may not, in fact, have originated with Grant. When "Baldy" Smith criticized Meade for his conduct of that terrible battle, he may have spoken from a sounder knowledge than historians have given him credit for. The same instinct of loyalty which caused Grant to relieve General Smith for that breach of etiquette may likewise have prevented him from ever trying to repair his own reputation by revealing how much of his supposed clumsiness, his irate persistence in certain tactical blunders, were in reality Meade's.

The impression one is left with is that Meade may have been Field Marshal Rehnskjold to Grant's Charles XII, the former behaving as though, in point of command at least, every engagement were another Poltava, and in several cases contriving to produce nearly the same outcome.* Possibly thanks to him, but certainly with the help of Butler and Burnside, the Union army in the summer of '64 managed to wrest from the jaws of victory a last string of defeats as bloody as any it had ever suffered. The odd thing is that by then the quality of the men was in theory too low, and that of their supreme commander too high, to permit either the ordering of such dreadful mistakes as Cold Harbor

---

* Had the odds been those of Poltava, instead of two to one in his favor, he might have succeeded entirely.

or, if ordered, their execution with such incredible hopeless valor. Nor is it every general who could ultimately win under these strange conditions and there were many at the time who doubted that Grant would do so. Only Lincoln seems to have known his man.

So this saddest of all our wars trudged to a conclusion. As the summer passed, Grant gradually extended his lines around Petersburg until they reached more than thirty miles, forcing Lee to distribute his own dwindling forces along the same length of front. Even then the Federals' attempts to cut the enemy's rail connections were only partially successful.* By fall Sherman had taken Atlanta, giving the Administration the victory it desperately needed, not only in the field but subsequently at the polls. By midwinter he made Lincoln a Christmas present of Savannah. The collapse of the South now became a matter of weeks. The next spring Phil Sheridan turned the Confederate right, defeating Pickett at Five Forks and cutting the Southside Railway, which connected Petersburg and Lynchburg. Grant then launched an attack that split Lee's army in two, Sheridan driving off the Southern right across the Appomattox River, while Grant drove the left into Petersburg and took Richmond. Less than a week later, at Appomattox Courthouse, " 'in a naked little parlor containing a table and two or three chairs,' Robert E. Lee, at the head of 7872 infantry with arms, 2100 cavalry, 63 guns, and not a single ration, surrendered to Ulysses S. Grant."[82]

The Big Event was over, and the "image" of everyone concerned froze into the form in which history, with the help of photographer Brady, would remember it—Lee the fallen knight, Grant the iron-jawed conqueror, Lincoln the patient countryman, the "rail splitter,"† McClellan the Napoleon *manqué* beloved by

---

* However, despite Ben Butler's success in not taking it, Fort Fisher at last fell to the North in mid-January, 1865. The South lost the port of Wilmington, North Carolina, and was cut off from all help by sea; and with that the war was as good as over.

† Which he never was. In an interview published in *Harper's New Monthly* in 1865 (Vol. 31, pp. 224, 227) he said: ". . . If there is anything in this world that I am a judge of, it is of good felling of timber, but I don't remember having worked by myself at splitting rails for one whole day in my life."

In the same interview the President mentioned an incident which had occurred just after his election in '60, when he had gone into his room to lie

his men long after he had gone, Butler the greasy politician,
Burnside the amiable Total Flop. Of them all, only Lincoln stood
somehow apart, radiating melancholy, as though he understood
his people and his time more deeply than he ever cared to say.

He was soon dead; the South was staggering under the Reconstruction and the rest of the nation rushing heedlessly away
in pursuit of the goods and powers and pleasures which have
occupied it ever since. Photographer Brady, having spent $100,-
000 or nearly all of the fortune he had made as a portraitist before the war (he had once been a student of Daguerre's), was
forced to give up his negatives in lieu of cash to his photographic
supplier in New York. Many of them were subsequently broken
or mislaid. A number have turned up since in private collections,
but what percentage of his work was totally lost we will probably never know. Congress in time voted him $25,000, this typi-
cally stingy tribute to the merely cultural and historic coming
years too late. Brady died broke and forgotten, in a New York
rooming house, in 1896. Sherman, who is now remembered less
for his military brilliance than as the inventor of Total War,* died
in the winter of 1891; his old adversary Joe Johnston came north
to his funeral, caught cold, and died himself a month or so later.

As for the war, it was perhaps as vitiated by compromise as
any we have ever fought, even including Vietnam (which was not
so much a matter of compromise as of doctrinaire rigidity). Its
real objective was scarcely made public until after the battle of

---

down. "Opposite where I lay was a bureau with a swinging glass on it . . .
and looking in that glass I saw myself reflected, nearly at full length; but
my face I noticed had *two* separate and distinct images, the tip of the nose of
one being about three inches from the tip of the other. I was a little bothered,
perhaps startled, and got up and looked in the glass, but the illusion vanished. On lying down I saw it a second time—if possible plainer than before;
and then I noticed that one of the faces was a little paler, say five shades,
than the other. I got up and the thing melted away, and I went off and in
the excitement of the hour forgot all about it—nearly but not quite, for the
thing would once in a while come up and give me a little pang, as though
something uncomfortable had happened . . . I tried the experiment again
when . . . sure enough, the thing came again; but I never succeeded in
bringing the ghost back after that, though I once tried very industriously to
show it to my wife, who was worried about it somewhat. She thought it was
a 'sign' . . . and that the paleness of one of the faces was an omen that I
should not see life through the last term."

* Which in a sense he was, the chief difference between him and the Germans being in the literalness with which the latter acted out his ideas.

Antietam, in September, 1862, when the President appears to have felt secure enough politically to tip his hand. Before or after the Emancipation Proclamation, emancipation itself was probably favored by no more than a small minority in the North, whose citizens were even less fond than they are now of their black brothers. When we began hostilities, there was some doubt that the federal government, under the Constitution, had any right to undertake them, given that the enemy was not a foreign power but a bloc of our own states. The declared aim of the Administration—preservation of the Union—was a type of political abstraction which one might suppose, particularly in that head-long "individualistic" age, would have stirred the electorate hardly at all. Why shouldn't the South have seceded and the continent been divided between two sister nations, either one of which was bigger than most European countries, and shielded furthermore from the rest of the world by two huge oceans? In the absence of any clear practical need for it, what was the great appeal of union? Presumably something deeper than everyday reason, for the North was able to raise large volunteer armies, many of which fought with desperate valor and under the worst possible leadership to preserve it. Why did they do so? We are still not sure except that, when all the rhetoric is swept away, the question of union reduces to one of tribal common sense—stay unified, which is to say as big as possible, and you stay safe. Stated in plain language, that program seems reasonable enough, but not one likely to inspire most men to lay down their lives or to ravage the country they have determined to keep whole. Apart from the role which instinct played in the matter—the same instinct, for instance, which provided recruits for the inconsequential dynastic wars of the eighteenth century or for the hopeless campaigns of Philip II—it is hard to understand why, even after the South had seceded, years more of negotiation and debate, instead of years of murder and destruction, did not follow. It is conceivable that, if only to improve its economy, the South would in a few decades have abandoned slavery. As a production system the latter was already failing in the '60s. For that and other reasons the two halves of the Republic would quite probably in time have rejoined, sparing us not only the ghastly loss in life and goods, but the less visible and longer-lasting wounds which the resort to force cost us. In short, while the Civil War is usually supposed—in common with other modern wars—to have had a far more sensible basis than those of the past, it may in fact have been as needless and as blind.

There is a curious principle in human affairs according to which the larger the number of people who can be persuaded or forced into certain beliefs or courses of action, the more stubbornly they will then persist in them. Religious dogmas, ideologies, and wars tend, by this principle, to develop an almost lunatic momentum, until nothing can stop them except some equally lunatic counterforce. Communist fanatics breed anticommunist fanatics. Catholicism bred Luther. The South, frightened, turned militant. The North, frightened by the South's militancy, began to arm. Sumter fell. The war was already past stopping. Perhaps two-thirds of recorded history, and a good many legends and ballads as well, are concerned with collisions of this sort. We feel them to be tragic, which is to say inexorable or somehow fated, when in fact they are no more so—no grander or more mysterious—than the collision of two bulls in a pasture. Behind them lies simply the ancestral push of instinct—those few bald automatic theorems incorporated in all of us which guarantee that in the pinches we will act "adaptively." Set this apparatus in motion in the right direction in large enough numbers and you will soon have at your disposal thousands or millions of men who, however civilized, can be induced to do practically anything.

In our own Civil War there was little of the atrocious intended cruelty of World War II, but nonetheless much barbarity which resulted because, a war being on, authorities on both sides felt they must be "realistic." At Elmira, and still more so at Andersonville, it was not feasible, or at least not easy, to give prisoners the food and medical attention and quarters needed to keep them from dying off at a high rate. The photographs, especially of Andersonville, are a forecast of Belsen and Auschwitz, though nobody *meant* those places to be anything like that. It is this ingenuous quality of the War between the States—the same ingenuousness one sees in many of the photographs of the men who fought it—that makes it touching rather than merely horrible. And caught up as they were in the momentum of the event, some still wondered if it was really as necessary as the oratory of the day made it seem. A Union soldier, who had spent the night before fraternizing with Confederate pickets across the Rappahannock, wrote home to his wife: "If the war had been left to us, we would have settled it in fifteen minutes." But wars are not of course settled in that way; they are mostly left to bad generals and clumsy-minded statesmen who prolong them beyond all endurance and guarantee that each is as nearly as possible fought for nothing.

CHAPTER IX

The German Century

PART 1: BISMARCK AND FRANCE

In the period since Lee's surrender, in the "naked little parlor" in Victorian Virginia, the world has changed beyond anyone's imagining, even our own of thirty years ago—and most radically perhaps through the agency of war.* For seventy-five years the Germans were the great wellspring of this sort of change (for which no doubt they have some grandiose compound word—*Weltkriegsangebildungenheit*) the chief result of which has been to enfeeble their old enemies Britain and France, while raising up two new ones, the United States and the U.S.S.R., who are today capable of wiping out not only the bipartite Reich but possibly

---

* Modern historians probably will not agree. The present view seems to be that social phenomena—language, mating customs, techniques of manufacture and exchange, and the like—are the real stuff of history while battles are simply among its more spectacular byproducts. But if one judges human undertakings according to the extent and as it were the gratuitousness of their consequences, war must surely rate as outstanding. For every one which has turned out as any of the parties to it intended, there have been ten which went wholly astray, often in quite bizarre ways—witness the results of the allied "victory" in the 1914-18 war, or those of the Germans' second attempt at world conquest in 1939. (Witness also the Hundred Years' War and the campaigns of Philip II.) Battles are, in this sense, frequently far more decisive than anyone at the time imagines. And in proportion as it has become modern and nuclear, the "objectives" of war, national security included, have become almost pure nonsense. One can only suppose that historians who still regard it as epiphenomenal do so for good subjective reasons, rather like men pretending not to see a lion which has just entered the room.

most of mankind, and that at the push of a few buttons. Such, you may say—the Germans themselves have said it often enough —are the rewards of good generalship. And such indeed they are, when statecraft and high military policy are of a ferocity so unremitting and an arrogance so puerile as to guarantee the nation opponents it need never have had.

From this standpoint Bismarck, the original architect of twentieth-century Germany, was also its most circumspect. Unlike Kaiser Wilhelm, he meant not to crush his enemies utterly but to reduce them to a manageable weakness. Nor was he such a fool as to take them all on at once. He drew Austria's few teeth first (at Königgrätz in 1866) and then, ignoring England, did the same for Napoleon III and France in 1870-71. And as the North had done in our Civil War, he fought, in a sense, for union. The idea seems to have been in the air at the time. Mere prosperity, it appears, was not enough. Any people worth its salt must also cultivate "national consciousness," must consolidate, knit itself up into a great complex of railroads and navies and munitions-production systems and prepare not merely to trade but—as of old, inevitably—to fight. The desirability of being Big and One is self-evident, at least to those in the process of becoming so. To their neighbors, who already are, the same urge is apt to seem quite unattractive, on the principle that anything foreigners do is *ipso facto* suspect. In this case, of course, it is. Stay big and you stay safe is a perfectly sound maxim, but the matter is seldom allowed to rest there; for once you are big enough, safety is taken for granted and the question becomes how much to risk toward making yourself even bigger (or biggest). This was the course Germany set out on with the Kaiser in 1914, and elected to have another whack at in 1939. It was a fatal one for all concerned. By means of three increasingly terrible wars, from Bismarck's liquidation of the *opéra bouffe* France of 1870 to the collapse of the Thousand-Year Reich, 994 years ahead of schedule in 1945, the Germans managed to raze the old European order practically *in toto*—not only its physical "plant" but its metaphysical foundations. Thanks to Hitler we learned, far sooner than we might have, what modern machines and modern men are capable of; nor was the lesson lost on those statesmen who have dominated world affairs since.

The first of the great German wars—the Franco-Prussian—is of interest chiefly as illustrating the weaknesses, or (on the French side) the downright decrepitude, often shown by university-trained officer corps. France at the time was in the phase of retrogression known as the Second Empire. Like many of his contemporaries who led armies in our Civil War, the emperor, Napoleon III, had a gift for politicking and apparently little else. As a young man he gave an impression of being "grave and dreamy"[1] but he happened to be only moderately intelligent. He seems to have lacked wit or magnetism, to have been small and swarthy, somewhat cold by nature, and transparently unscrupulous. His shrewdness extended only to domestic politics; his grasp of world affairs was on the whole very poor. Like his uncle and stepgrandfather Napoleon Bonaparte, he suffered from a bladder ailment (eventually fatal), but that was the extent of the resemblance. His success in attaining power seems to have depended essentially upon two things—his own ambition, stimulated from boyhood by his mother and others who hoped to profit by his name; and the pride of the French people in their Napoleonic past. Despite its bourgeois tone—in part perhaps just because of it —Victorian France evidently felt a strong nostalgia for the days of autocracy and *la gloire*.* At the same time many Frenchmen, possibly most, were not really prepared for such a revival. The despotic phase of the Second Empire was short—roughly from 1852 to 1859. After that the emperor was driven to all sorts of strange maneuvers and compromises, now favoring business at the expense of labor, now labor at the expense of business, now free trade at everyone's expense, now a revived parliamentarianism at his own, until by 1870 the Empire, so called, was in reality an unstable coalition far more like the France of Paul Reynaud than that of 1807. Throughout these ups and downs, the Emperor

---

* A part of that nostalgia no doubt being for a unity of feeling and purpose long since lost. As recent upheavals, especially of 1848, had clearly shown, the bourgeoisie lacked popularity. *Enrichissez-vous*, the slogan of Louis Philippe's day, might have patriotic overtones in war—industry being the backbone of armies—but in peacetime it was purely an incentive to riot. The nostalgia for the unanimity of war, if dangerous, is understandable. A French Resistance leader after World War II spoke sadly of each person having to "go back to the littleness of himself." Erich Maria Remarque and "Sapper" said much the same thing at the end of World War I.

and his beautiful brainless strong-willed consort maintained a sort of perpetual *bal masqué* at their court in Compiègne, as if through this display of late-medieval brilliance to convince everyone including themselves of the reality of the régime. The course of events abroad was less reassuring. Whereas Napoleon I, up to his Russian campaign, had had plans of aggrandizement which were clear and feasible, Napoleon III seems to have misread his situation and fumbled his chances almost from the first. Instead of concentrating on Germany, the real enemy, he took Austria at her face value, fought inconsequential wars in the Crimea and Italy, and dabbled in intrigue with Bismarck (who consistently got the better of him) or in overseas expansion with Maximilian. The fact that he picked the latter, an Austrian nobleman, instead of some capable commoner to head his Mexican expedition not only foredoomed that adventure but gave the Prussians still another measure of their opponent. (It was in this period, or about 1866, that the Prussian general staff worked out its invasion plan for France, revising it annually until *der Tag*.)

In America in the 1860s, the rifle was *the* weapon on the battlefield because of its range. In Europe that was even more the case; as early as 1841 the Prussians had introduced the Dreyse needle gun, a breechloader which took a paper cartridge. It could be easily loaded by an infantryman in the prone position and could deliver seven rounds a minute (vs. the American muzzle-loader's two). It had an extreme range of about 500 yards. The French *chassepot*, a better design, had a similar firing rate and perhaps double the range. These new arms made old-fashioned smoothbore artillery (whose range, when loaded with canister, was around 250 yards) next to useless. The Prussians accordingly developed rifled artillery which far outreached infantry weapons, perfecting its use with their customary thoroughness. The French inspired by their emperor took a different tack.

"Napoleon III, a keen student of artillery, maintained a private arsenal at the château of Meudon and in 1866, in the alarm following upon Königgrätz [Moltke's crushing, if confused, victory over the Austrians] he ordered Commandant Reffye (1821-1880), the artillery officer he had placed in charge of it, to produce a machine-gun."[2] The result was a new secret weapon—the *mitrailleuse*. It consisted of twenty-five large-caliber rifle barrels

concentrically arranged, the whole being mounted on a carriage
like an ordinary field gun. It was said to have a firing rate as high
as 125 rounds a minute, and to be effective against infantry in
close order at 1500-2000 yards, or against artillery at 2000-2700
yards.* In essence it was a device for delivering case shot at more
than ten times the old range, and with considerably greater ac-
curacy. The difficulty was to prevent the enemy's learning of it
and making a similar weapon himself. With that in mind, the
emperor took care that the *mitrailleuse* was not issued to his
armies and that no one was shown how to handle it until almost
the day that war with Prussia began. It was thereupon used, in
Reffye's phrase, "in a perfectly idiotic fashion."[2] He had intended
it to be massed in batteries, behind the main body, just as other
artillery was, but the officers in the field could not bring themselves to accept this idea. To them the new weapon was a *rifle,*
which should go where it belonged, up with the other rifles in the
front lines. But it was *not* a rifle—not even an ancestor of the
machine gun. It was a fieldpiece weighing 645 pounds by itself
and just over a ton when mounted, with a carriage and limber,
to be drawn by a team. To keep it supplied with ammunition in
a forward position must have been difficult enough. In addition,
to put such a cumbrous machine—which must certainly have attracted a maximum of return fire—within range of the enemy's
rifles as well as of his cannon, was absolute lunacy. Its horses
and crews were often, no doubt, instant casualties, and the potential of the arm, as its inventor bitterly remarked, was largely
wasted. Its development had other consequences. Before the war
the French, knowing they had the *mitrailleuse,* left the rest of
their artillery as was, taking the field when the time came with
bronze muzzle-loaders which were hardly a match for the Dreyse
needle gun, let alone for Moltke's rifled fieldpieces. It was these
last which dominated the field at Sedan, beginning a new era in
long-range murder which has since produced the drumfire barrage, the mass-bombing assault and the ICBM. (At the start of
World War I the British General Sir Douglas Haig nevertheless

---

* It was sighted to 3300 yards and had a high muzzle velocity for those
days—1558 feet per second. Its chief advantage over artillery was in speed
of zeroing in on target.

gave it as his opinion that artillery would chiefly be of use against green troops.)

The fundamental reasons for the Franco-Prussian War were quite clear. From Bismarck's standpoint, it had a double purpose: to finish the process, begun by Wellington and the Allies (and long before by Marlborough), of reducing France to a second-class power, and to use the emergency which that enterprise would entail, to fire up German nationalism and complete the unification of the country, presumably with a view to still greater triumphs in the future. The army and the plan of attack were ready. All that was needed was an incident which would let loose a storm of French wrath and goad their absurd emperor into declaring war. The year 1870 was next to perfect because, although alarm in France had been rising since Königgrätz, military preparations there were still far behind schedule, so that the Germans could put 380,000 men in the field against a probable total of 250,000 for the enemy. What they may also have guessed from their intelligence reports was that even these troops were likely to be badly trained, miscellaneously equipped, and commanded by men many of whom might better have been in politics or the civil service. All these expectations proved quite accurate.

The precipitating incident was itself absurd, involving an impasse in Spanish politics which the parties involved were trying to break by a maneuver reminiscent of the reign of Edward III. The Spanish fleet having mutinied and the queen forced into exile, the pro tem ruler, Marshal Prim, finding the people still monarchically minded, was offering the throne of Spain to various qualified persons abroad. In secret parleys Bismarck proposed Prince Leopold of Hohenzollern-Sigmaringen. When the kaiser learned of these negotiations, he was upset and tried to stop them, without success. Word of the talks finally leaked to the Spanish press and caused a sensation in France, where a revival of the empire of Charles V was foreseen, this time of course with its center of gravity in Berlin. Napoleon III intervened, demanding that Leopold's candidature be withdrawn, that the kaiser cooperate to that end, that France be given full assurances from all parties etc., etc. . . . Bismarck then pleaded with the German emperor to stop his "irregular personal interviews"[3] with the French ambassador. The emperor complied, sending Bismarck a dispatch to that effect. Bismarck, who had discretion in the matter, elected to publish this dispatch in the form of the "Ems telegram," whose wording made it sound as though the French ambassador had been rudely turned away. Mobs took to the streets in Paris, and on July 19, 1870, France declared war.

The details of the campaign which followed are of interest chiefly as showing not only the lamentable state of the French army but some rather startling defects in the Prussian as well. As Fuller remarks, the Prussian field marshal and chief of staff, Count Helmuth von Moltke, was a general who "ran on rails." Policy and strategy were thoroughly worked out but the details of the execution were almost necessarily left to commanders in the field (again the problem of size—how to get close tactical control of armies of hundreds of thousands of men—a problem never really solved until aerial surveillance and radio communication were introduced). An early result was that one of the German commanders, General Steinmetz, received conflicting orders—from Moltke to retreat, and from the commander of the II Army, Prince Frederick Charles, to get out of the latter's road of advance. "Steinmetz telegraphed for instructions direct to the king, over Moltke's head. In reply he received a telegram from Moltke, ordering him to clear the road at once, and couched in terms which he considered as a severe reprimand."[4]

Meanwhile the French, in considerable confusion both as to means and intentions, were concentrating around Metz and Strasbourg as Moltke had foreseen. What the Prussian general had not foreseen was that they would manage to concentrate as fast as they did. ". . . By the 28th of July the troops had received all that was absolutely indispensable and might well have been led against the enemy who, thanks to Moltke's premature action, were for the moment at a very serious disadvantage . . . Had the great Napoleon and his marshals been in command, they would have made light of the want of cookingpots, cholera belts, etc., and by a series of rapid marches . . . concentrated odds of at least three to one upon the heads of the Prussian columns as they struggled through the defiles of the Hardt [mountains], and won a victory whose political results might well have proved decisive."[4]

"Fortunately for the Germans," the same writer continues, "the

French intelligence service not only failed to inform the staff of this extraordinary opportunity, but it allowed itself to be hypnotized by the most amazing rumors. In imagination they saw armies of 100,000 men behind every forest, and to guard against these dangers, the French troops were marched and countermarched along the frontiers, in the vain hope of discovering an ideal defensive position which should afford full power to their new weapons [the *chassepot* and the *mitrailleuse*]. As these delays were exerting a most unfavorable effect on public opinion*
. . . the emperor decided on the 1st of August [when his own mobilization was still incomplete but after most of his early advantage over the enemy had been lost] to initiate a movement toward the Saar."

The French advance on Saarbrücken, as it involved five divisions, startled the Prussian staff into taking steps to meet it, of which Moltke (who was then in Mainz) heard nothing until two days later. (It was at this time that the confusion in Steinmetz's orders occurred.) On August 3 one division of French Marshal MacMahon's command moved into Weissenburg, to the east and south of Saarbrücken, where it collided with the Prussian III Army and was driven back. Moltke was by now devising a grand plan of action in the Saar basin, a plan instantly derailed by two other accidental engagements, Wörth and Spicheren. In the former the Prussians defeated MacMahon but were too unorganized to pursue him. In the latter, Steinmetz, "quite unaware of the scheme for a great battle on the Saar about the 12th of August,"[6] advanced on Saarbrücken on the sixth, found its bridges intact, and proceeded to attack the French who were established a short distance to the south at Spicheren, under command of General Frossard. It happened that Frossard's position was a strong one and that, with other French forces nearby, he had numerical superiority. He decided to stand, but when he tried to call in other units to his aid, his fellow generals would not move (". . . The other generals had not been trained to mutual support and thought only of their own security"[7]). Frossard,

---

* Fuller puts the case more strongly: "Hesitation at once handed strategy over to the Paris mob. The boulevards were thronged, and shouts were raised demanding the instant invasion of Germany. This clamor forced the Emperor's hand . . ."[5]

"left to his own devices," was finally forced to withdraw when he found his left flank being turned. For their part, the Prussians "were scarcely aware of their victory,"[7] the troops bivouacking where they stood and Steinmetz returning to headquarters without issuing further orders. Of 42,000 men and 120 guns available, he had committed 27,000 and 78. The French, out of 64,000 men and 210 guns, had used only 24,000 and 90. From a professional's standpoint the war was off to a poor start, especially since it was professionals of the most up-to-date sort who had started it.

The eye of the storm which developed next was Marshal Achille Bazaine. After Spicheren and Wörth, the French high command grew jittery and ordered a general withdrawal on Châlons. The empress, then acting as regent in Paris, vetoed this move on the ground that it would precipitate a political catastrophe. The plan was changed, calling now for a stand around Metz, but not all the field commanders seem to have heard about it. Bazaine stood his ground, while MacMahon continued to pull back. The same day the existing ministry in Paris fell, to be replaced by a General Palikao, who, besides leaving decisions in the field more than ever at the mercy of Assembly politics, was soon to make an odd undercover move which would in effect destroy the Empire entirely.

Bazaine, meanwhile, isolated from MacMahon and finding his position unfavorable, tried to withdraw. He was prevented by heavy rains and ended up making a stand to the southwest of Metz, where, in the battle of Vionville, he fought the Prussians to a standstill. He then withdrew toward the city, and at Gravelotte-St. Privat did battle with them again, they having 200,000 troops to his 140,000. The result was bloody and by no means an overwhelming victory for the Germans. After it, Bazaine saw no course but to withdraw into the town. He was heavily outnumbered and could expect soon to be even more so. His staff disliked him; his decisions were made chancy by the presence of the emperor at headquarters; he had no faith in his corps commanders; and the enemy army lay between him and Paris. By holing up in Metz he might expect not only to escape annihilation but also to pin down numbers of Prussian troops, thereby taking some of the pressure off the surviving French forces. After the war he was court-martialed, but not for this maneuver so much as for his peculiar conduct shortly after it.*

With Bazaine's entrapment, the French situation became precarious, since their only remaining force in the field was MacMahon's and he was nowhere near the commander that Bazaine, for all his defects, had proved to be. "Given seven corps, each capable of averaging 15 miles a day for a week in succession, opposed to four corps only, shaken by defeat and unable as a whole to cover more than 5 miles a day, the result could hardly be doubtful."[8]

MacMahon sensibly decided that his best move would be to withdraw on Paris, leaving Bazaine to pin down a few thousand Prussians and stalling for time himself by fighting rear-guard actions until he could be reinforced. His force consisted of something over 100,000 men, including "a number of Parisian *Gardes Mobiles*, then in a state of mutiny . . . Many [of the army's] units were so untrained that General Lebrun informs us he allotted five rounds to each of his men to enable the officers and noncommissioned officers to show them how to load and sight their rifles."[9] MacMahon sent word of his proposed retreat to Palikao. The emperor, in the meantime, had decided to return to Paris and take charge, but his strong-minded consort bade him stay where he was, partly it seems from a well-grounded fear that his return might precipitate a general revolt. He acquiesced, as he usually did, and remained with his troops. General Palikao considered MacMahon's plan and dismissed it as foolishness. The important thing, especially from a political standpoint, was to relieve Bazaine in Metz. It was never clear how MacMahon, with the forces available to him, could have accomplished that. He had a try at it anyway, moving eastward in an attempt to get

---

* Bazaine was a period Frenchman and military man so pat that in fiction he would seem overdone. Out of jealousy of Frossard, and by the device of adhering quite literally to that general's dogma of "strong positions" Bazaine robbed him of a probable victory at Spicheren, moving as if to Frossard's aid and then taking up a "strong position" himself, just out of reach of the action. After being bottled up in Metz, he appears to have entered into somewhat shady negotiations with the Germans, proposing through intermediaries that he and his troops might help the enemy "save" his country. It is not absolutely certain that he made such a proposal, but his surrender of Metz came at a time when just a few more days of resistance would have made it far less useful to the Prussians than it turned out in fact to be. Bazaine's years in Mexico were thought by some to have undermined his character.

past the right flank of his faster-moving opponent. Meanwhile a curious actor now added himself to the cast—Emmanuel Félix de Wimpffen, a French soldier and graduate of St. Cyr (1811-1884) who had distinguished himself in the Crimea and by the summer of 1870 was serving as a field general in Algeria. On August 22 of that year, Palikao ordered him home posthaste. On the twenty-eighth, in Paris, he was given a fanciful briefing on the state of the war by Palikao and told to proceed to MacMahon's army to replace a General de Failly in command of the V Corps.

"He was then handed a roll of maps of the wrong locality and, on the morning of August 29, as he was about to enter his railway carriage . . . a messenger rushed up and thrust into his hand the following letter signed by Palikao: 'In the event of Marshal MacMahon being incapacitated, you will take over the command of the troops actually placed under his orders. I will send you an official letter . . . which you will make use of as occasion demands.' "[10]

Armed with what another writer calls this "dormant commission" de Wimpffen went, via Rheims, to Sedan (actually to Bazeilles, right nearby) where after a meandering march the French army had pocketed itself a few thousand yards from the Belgian frontier. There was some fuss when he displaced de Failly as a corps commander but that was all. No one knew of Palikao's last-minute arrangement with him, nor did he speak of it. It remained as a time bomb, due to go off at the worst possible moment. Meanwhile there was too much else going on for him to attract anyone's notice. The town of Sedan was jammed with army vehicles, short of supplies, and surrounded by hills from which it could be, and soon was, combed by artillery fire. The Meuse provided some natural defense against the Prussian advance from the south and west, but this was largely canceled by the fact that the railway bridge at Bazeilles and two others— one at Douzy to the southeast, the other at Donchéry to the west —were not blown up. ". . . A party of engineers," says Fuller, "were sent out to destroy [the bridge at Douzy], but while they were inspecting it the train which had brought them steamed off to Mézières with their tools and powder. Everywhere confusion reigned. When General Douay set about to entrench his position, MacMahon stopped him and said: 'What, entrenching! But I do

not intend to shut myself up as in Metz. I mean to maneuver.'"
(Which ominously recalls Dana's bulletin* from Petersburg, in
'64, not long before the battle of the Crater.) "Little wonder that
that evening [General] Ducrot was in despair. He turned to Dr.
Sarazin and exclaimed: *Nous sommes dans un pot de chambre
et nous y serons emmerdés.'"[11] It was too true, but not strictly
for geographic reasons, or even for military ones.

For while the town of Sedan proper was highly vulnerable,
especially from Frénois to the southwest, where the king of Prussia was presently to make his headquarters, nevertheless there
were good defensive positions around it—notably the plateau of
Illy and the Fond de Givonne close by to the north and east.
Moreover, throughout August 31, the day before the battle, Mac-
Mahon's road and rail communications to Mézières (lying westward) remained open, and there another French corps, the XIII,
under Vinoy, was forming. The bridgehead at Torcy, just west of
Sedan, and the open country beyond it provided an excellent
battleground, over which, had he thought of it, MacMahon could
have attempted a major drive, either with the object of splitting
off the Prussian III Army from the main body (the so-called
Army of the Meuse), or simply to permit him to escape westward
and make a junction with Vinoy. The latter move was the most
promising under the circumstances and Moltke evidently thought
he would make it.

"But MacMahon seems to have been too despondent to con-
template anything further than a battle for the honor of the army
. . . He neither sent orders to [Vinoy's corps in Mézières] nor
made any arrangements to meet the coming danger."[12] The chief
defect of the French position, aside from the psychological one,
was that it was too crowded—not merely Sedan itself, but the
whole area comprising a rough triangle formed by three rivers,
the Floing to the north, the Meuse to the west, and the Givonne
to the east. Besides being difficult to maneuver in, it exposed the
defenders to artillery fire from almost any quarter.

The German attack on the morning of September 1 began with
the Bavarians, who forded the Meuse at the southern end of the
French triangle, and in a thick mist, without artillery support,

* About Grant: "He will now maneuver."

launched an assault on Bazeilles. They were met by Vassoigne's division of the XII Corps, including several marine battalions, who more than stood their ground. By 6:00 A.M. the mist cleared and the German artillery opened up. Almost at once MacMahon was hit by a shell fragment and so seriously wounded that he turned over his command to General Ducrot, apparently one of the few capable officers in his army and a man, besides, thoroughly familiar with the terrain. Ducrot's immediate decision was to proceed to Torcy and, fighting a rear-guard action, to retire on Mézières, where he might strengthen his forces and dispose them in a better way. It is probable that this move had better than an even chance of success, since by that early hour the German III Army had not had time to move up from the south so as to threaten the western exits from Sedan. Ducrot had issued orders setting this plan in motion when, about 9:00 A.M., after a mysterious delay, de Wimpffen appeared at headquarters, produced his "dormant commission," assumed the command, and canceled all that his predecessor had just ordered. The sensible course, he declared, was not to retire on Mézières, but to attempt a breakthrough in the *other* direction, toward Metz and Bazaine.* To do so, of course, involved meeting the Prussian main body head-on, and were that move to succeed, it would put all of the French forces except Vinoy's corps on the other side of the enemy from their own lines of supply, leaving Paris completely unprotected and themselves without support. One can imagine the astonishment which this daring strategy must have caused the officers to whom it was outlined. Under the circumstances, it was perhaps the only plan which, even if successful, would have failed.

In the meantime Ducrot's orders were already being carried out. French troops to the north and east, at Fond de Givonne, were just beginning their withdrawal when de Wimpffen's directive to the contrary arrived, throwing the whole front into disorder. Moreover, by then the Saxon XII Corps had driven off the French rear guard and carried the ridge, a move which in turn threatened to cut off Vassoigne's division to the south in Bazeilles. Vassoigne for his part was already fighting a holding

---

* No doubt an echo of Palikao's concern for political appearances, which required that Bazaine be sprung at the earliest possible moment.

action, since by Ducrot's order Lebrun's corps, the main force in that sector, was also pulling back. The new commander in chief was quite angry at this news, as he had felt the stand at Bazeilles to be promising. It was there (he had told the emperor) that he intended to "drive the enemy into the Meuse." The net result of these developments was to confuse and disarray the French forces still further, squeezing them into an area even smaller than the one they had occupied at the start.

The German III Army, with little opposition, had meanwhile moved swiftly in an arc around Sedan from the south up along its western side and across the Mézières road, until by 10:00 A.M. seven battalions had reached the plateau of Illy to the north and were forming front. Shortly afterwards they opened a devastating fire from 62 field guns. A French charge, intended to break up these dispositions, was itself broken up and repulsed with severe losses. The number of Prussian guns near Illy, in the wood of Hattoy, was soon doubled, their fire converging with that of the guns of the German Army of the Meuse on the other side, roughly in the Fond de Givonne sector. The French artillery—hardly a match for the Prussian under the best of conditions—was quickly annihilated. On the northeast end of the French position, the I Corps on the Givonne had been flanked by a Prussian unit, which brought up 120 guns and forced the French infantry back in confusion into the wood of Garenne. What had begun as a series of blows aimed at knocking out the French artillery now turned into a slaughter of their infantry by short-range cannon fire. According to Prince Hohenlohe: ". . . The spectacle of the carnage was horrible; the fearful cries of the victims of our shells reached as far as where we stood [on the rise at Frénois]. Our superiority . . . was so overwhelming we suffered no loss at all."[13]

Surrounded as they finally were and without a hope of deliverance the French fought, as usual, with heroic *élan*. The Prussians to the east, between Daigny and the town of Givonne, were forming up and deploying their artillery "when suddenly a great column of French infantry, 6000 strong . . . in pursuance of de Wimpffen's orders, came over the eastern border of the valley and charged down at full speed towards the guns. Then followed one of the most dramatic spectacles of the entire war. The whole of the corps artillery of the [Prussian] Guard turned upon these devoted men and tore the column in half, shrouding it in dense clouds of smoke and dust above which could be seen the trunks and limbs of men flung upwards by their explosion. The head of the column . . . nevertheless kept on its way, but under the combined fire of the Guard rifle battalion and the flanking fire from other guns its impetus died out and its débris by degrees disappeared under convenient cover."[14]

By midafternoon, their encirclement long since complete, the French gave up any attempt to carry out de Wimpffen's original battle plan and began trying for a breakout in whatever direction they happened to be facing. In some cases they counterattacked merely in a frantic effort to hold their positions. Cavalry General Marguerite and General Gallifet (infantry), on orders from Ducrot, made a sally of this kind near Floing, which lies a mile or two north of Torcy, the point on which Ducrot, seven hours earlier, had evidently planned to concentrate his attack. Now (through no fault of Ducrot's) it was much too late. General Marguerite was killed at the outset while reconnoitering. General Gallifet gallantly took over his cavalry squadrons and led three charges himself. "In spite of the heroism shown, each failed, but Gallifet, accompanied by a few officers and chasseurs, penetrated to the enemy reserves. On their return, when they were within pistol shot of a Prussian battalion, its commander was so filled with admiration that he ordered a cease fire. The French troopers shouted '*Vive l'Empereur!*' at which the German officers saluted as they galloped past."*[15] The German wars to come were not to produce many other incidents of this kind.

De Wimpffen meanwhile had been riding around inside the French lines with a view to making his military know-how available wherever it might be most urgently needed. About midday he spoke to General Douay on the Illy ridge to the north. Douay had had some success there with a counterattack, and requested

---

* It was a brigade of Gallifet's Chasseurs d'Afrique which some hours earlier had charged the German III Army's artillery before the ridge of Illy. While these guns were apparently not yet adequately supported by infantry, the idea of trying to rush them with mounted troops seems wildly anachronistic, suggesting that the French commander was not only desperate (which he was) but trained to antiquated methods as well. Gallifet, to do him justice, later made a brilliant counterattack with infantry from the same position, failing partly from want of support from his befuddled commander in chief.

reinforcements. There were still a few intact units of the I Corps in the Wood of Garenne, and de Wimpffen agreed to send him these. Next the commander in chief proceeded south of Sedan to the village of Balan, into which the XII Corps had retired under pressure from the Bavarians. De Wimpffen at once sent back to Douay asking *him* for reinforcements to shore up the defense of Balan. The two contingents—of the I Corps, marching to Douay's help, and of Douay's men, marching to the relief of Balan—intersected en route and fell into a tangle. The delay and disorder of both were greatly aggravated by the Prussian shells which were raining in upon the close-packed French from several directions, as well as by the stragglers and runaway horses from other, already shattered units which were by then beginning to choke the roads. In consequence, Douay's front, where reinforcements might conceivably have made a breakout to the west possible, was *weakened*, it being in this grave and quite unnecessary emergency that the valiant Gallifet made his charge with a pathetic force of barely 2000 sabers.

Two results followed from these moves. After Gallifet had been turned back, the Germans, sensing the straitened condition of the enemy in their front, moved out in a general attack; and sometime between 3:00 and 4:00 P.M., though bitterly fought off, they managed to carry the ridge. South of the town, meanwhile, in the Balan-Bazeilles sector, de Wimpffen had succeeded in getting a counteroffensive going and was driving the Bavarians back. This success emboldened him to send further word to Douay ordering him to start a rear-guard action, withdrawing and reorganizing his forces in the wood of Garenne, so as to protect his own (de Wimpffen's) breakthrough. Neither of these projected events of course took place. The order to withdraw was unnecessary, for the ruins of Douay's VII Corps were even then legging it back to Sedan through a downpour of German shells. At this stage of the battle the havoc wrought by the Prussian guns probably reached its climax, particularly since the situation of the town made it ideal for artillery spotting and since their target was by now a vast jumble of men, horses, artillery, and miscellaneous transport, whose helplessness every shell burst only served to increase. The scene as described by those who were part of it outdid even Leipzig on the day of Napoleon's defeat, fifty-seven years before. The slaughter was the more horrible because it was inflicted at random, from every direction, driving those who still survived into the sort of insane behavior which sometimes seizes a crowd in a burning building.* Except for a small part of it, around Bazeilles, the Army of Châlons had ceased to exist. And even at Bazeilles, de Wimpffen's attack was doomed, for behind the Bavarians stood the Prussian IV Corps, ready to deliver the decisive counterstroke.

Realizing finally that there was no escape, but still dreaming of one, de Wimpffen started back to Sedan to gather up reinforcements. On the way he saw a white flag go up on the town's church tower, and shortly afterwards come down again.[16] The same confusion evidently prevailed at G.H.Q. as elsewhere. Having ordered the flag of truce raised, the emperor demanded to know why the fighting continued. He next told Ducrot to write a cease-fire order but the latter, having done so, declined to sign it, on the ground that he was not commander in chief. By the time de Wimpffen arrived, the white flag had been hauled back up again. He, however, would not hear of surrender, and (like Napoleon at Waterloo announcing the last-minute arrival of Grouchy) tried to rally troops around him by shouting "Bazaine approaches!"[17] He actually started back for Balan with a small contingent of men and guns, but this force had barely got outside the town walls before it went to pieces under the Prussian fire. De Wimpffen thereupon gave up and handed over the supreme command to General Lebrun, who refused it. The emperor offered it to Ducrot, and to Douay, neither of whom would accept it either. De Wimpffen then followed the course customary among bad generals of denouncing his immediate subordinates for his defeat, and the whole sorry day ended in a "wordy dispute"[18] at imperial headquarters.

The capitulation took place at about 6:30 P.M., and the following morning Napoleon III quietly surrendered his person to the Germans. He was interned for the remainder of the war at the castle of Wilhelmshöhe; and with him into captivity went 82,000 men and 558 guns of the Army of Châlons. Its losses that day

---

* And here, as at Waterloo, the cry went up: "We have been betrayed!" Here too the emperor, unable to sit a horse because of his bladder trouble, remained at headquarters while his generals undid him.

came to 17,000 killed and wounded as against about 9000 for the enemy. It only remained for the Second Empire to be officially pronounced dead in France, which occurred promptly and with the usual uproar. The war, which should have ended with Sedan, dragged on some months more—rather miraculously in view of the state of the country as a whole and of the military in particular. (One French force, in a campaign that winter, was badly handicapped by the issue of 50,000 pairs of English-made shoes which turned out to have paper soles.) While few of the other French generals were quite as bad as the absurdly named de Wimpffen, a number were outstandingly clumsy and hesitant. The majority, as cautious professionals, seemed disinclined to risk any full-scale engagement, offering no plans of campaign and moving only when pushed. The consequence was almost to force the conduct of the war upon politicians such as Gambetta, who, though quite ready to have a go at it, were lacking in the necessary perspective. One of the later crop of commanding generals, Bourbaki, was so downcast by his own lack of success (the Germans drove him and the remnants of his army into Switzerland) that he tried to commit suicide—also unsuccessfully. He even failed after the war in politics. The impression one gets is that whereas in our Civil War we had one McClellan, France in 1870 had dozens, possibly hundreds of them.* And while McClellan's men were at least well trained and equipped, those of his French equivalents were not even that, which makes their bravery all the more incredible and touching. Sad as that conflict was, however, a sadder was shortly to follow. And when it came, the French had naturally evolved new, most logical, concepts by which they hoped to gain the victory. They did the latter, after a fashion, but with little help from the former.

---

* Needless to say with Gallic peculiarities, of which Bazaine will do as an example. Like McClellan, he would fight on occasion, and fairly capably, but he was neither a sufficiently convinced nihilist to aim for the whole prize nor sufficiently an idealist to serve his country and to co-operate with his military peers in good faith. His character, as well as that of Napoleon III, reminds one of Queen Victoria's description of Louis Philippe: ". . . *thoroughly French.* . . . a man who in great as well as in small things took a pleasure in being cleverer and more cunning than others, often when there was no advantage to be gained by it. . . ."[19] Unfortunately for all three, their inclination to intrigue far exceeded their skill at it.

PART 2: THE KAISER AND EUROPE

The origins of the First World War are usually said to have been commercial. Germany, by her gathering industrial power, threatened England and France, who gave up, or rather postponed, their quarrels and arrived at a *rapprochement* with secret military clauses. It was only natural for Russia to complete Germany's "encirclement" by joining this entente. Since Peter's day French had become almost the first language of the Russian upper classes. (Turgeniev, for instance, received a French and German education. His mother reportedly spoke Russian only to the servants.) Moreover, France was farther away, and from medieval times had been less consistently a menace to the Slavs than were the Teutonic knights* or their descendants. Russia was also anxious to increase her security by diminishing Turkish and Austro-Hungarian influence in the Balkans, a policy which, with suitable adjustments and extensions, she has followed ever since.

It is less clear why Germany's booming economy made war inevitable, although Balfour, among others, evidently thought it did, and many, including Balfour, seem to have considered deliberately precipitating one with a view to reducing the upstart Germans before they had become too much of a threat. The question is what *sort* of threat? Was it simply that Germany might outproduce and undersell her rivals? Or was it also that her industries would put into the hands of the German military caste instruments so formidable that before long they could not forbear to use them? Conservatives and political cynics incline toward the first opinion, liberals and anti-Germans toward the second. It is true that in the nineteenth century trade followed the flag; great numbers of customers, especially in the Orient, were obtained less by salesmanship than by a form of stickup. Japan and the Treaty Ports were literally jimmied open. British go-getters created the opium business. Africa became a vast company store and Panama an American province.

---

* Who made annual forays, almost like hunts, into Slavic lands such as Poland—a custom still not extinct in the time of Charles XII and Augustus.

As countries become productive and rich, it is perhaps not so much their manufacturers and merchants and financiers as their military and political people who begin to see the attractions of war. The reason they do so is that they, far more, perhaps, than the tycoon type, are latter-day equivalents of the lords who dominated Europe throughout the Middle Ages, often to the point of making commerce next to impossible. Their interest, like that of their sword-swinging predecessors, is not to *produce* anything; it is to offer "protection," which, in the case of a nation growing as rapidly as Germany was by 1900, is apt to mean conquest. The latter is always, of course, in the interests of defense. It is not a wanton attack upon neighbors—far from it. The peace-loving fatherland is being hemmed in, stifled, denied its right of lording it over others. The business community is as open-minded as any other to this sort of talk, and besides is quick to see some benefit from taking it to heart, which is more than can be said of the ordinary citizen who ends up at the fighting front. *His* reward lies in the glory of a dirty job well done, which may seem thankless enough to those who survive the performance of it.

If the foregoing is a fair appraisal of the matter, it is a drastic oversimplification to say, as one writer does, that "the Industrial Revolution had led to the establishment of an economic struggle for existence in which self-preservation dictated a return to the ways of the jungle."[20] The ways of the jungle have always been with us, and while business is certainly ruthless enough, it tends to stick to its own methods, preferring the legal and surreptitious to the overt and forcible, not for moral reasons so much as for practical ones. Given too much social commotion, it simply cannot function.* It does not *produce* the "struggle for existence"; it merely gives it new dimensions. The sort of business done at gun point by adventurers in colonial lands cannot be taken as the model of businesses at home; and indeed, as types, the freebooter à la Lord Jim and the homegrown Robber Baron à la Jay Gould are quite different. The former would hardly think of swindling natives by selling them watered stock and the latter

---

* As the history of late Roman or early Christian times clearly shows. In business itself, as Walter Gutman has pointed out, a tough customer or "Mr. Hyde" may be necessary in the early precarious stages but a liability to management once the corporation is established.

would look down on trading in slaves or ivory as *déclassé* and small potatoes.*

In short, the difficulty in modern nations is not businessmen or commerce as such; it is that a class of men inclined to far more brutal and destructive methods continues to be their dominant political and military element—men who in many cases would have been quite incapable of success in business themselves but who as of old are quick to avail themselves of the wealth which it generates, and of the terrible weapons which modern technology puts at their disposal. As Thyssen did in Nazi Germany and McNamara in Johnson's America, a number of business people think they can play the same game as their primordial betters, and one way or another (like Crassus) they almost always lose. Certainly those who backed the kaiser did. Contrary to what historians in recent decades have said, the force which drove Germany, and dragged her allies, to war in 1914, was not the Germans' industrial might, nor even those industrialists eager to play at *Realpolitik*. It was Germany's still dominant primitives— her Junkers, her officer corps, and her medieval king (whose first address, at his accession, was made not to his people but to the armed forces). Meanwhile, on the other side of the Channel and in France, primitives like General Sir Douglas Haig and Papa Joffre were preparing, to the best of their modest abilities, to forestall him.

Of all modern nations in 1914, the Germany of Wilhelm II was perhaps the most antiquated in structure and if only for that reason the most likely to take up arms.† Its "system of govern-

---

* It is even a question whether the older style of imperialism pays any longer, the real profit today being in trade between nations (or within nations) of high technology. Harrison Salisbury was not believed when he made this point to high officials of North Vietnam. Our own Left doesn't grasp it either.

† In *The End of Economic Man*, Peter Drucker points out that unlike the French bourgeoisie, the German "did not attain power by its own revolutionary efforts . . . it was liberated from above. Its emancipation . . . was effected for the purpose of national unification. Politically and socially the bourgeoisie . . . never became a ruling class. The aristocracy and the hereditary, though often untitled, nobility of civil servants remained . . . master."[22] This implies support for the earlier argument here that Germany's motives for going to war were not economic by modern standards, although they were in a sense which would have been understood by Edward III and Louis of Nevers. The latter found in the burghers of Flanders a useful semi-

ment was an anachronism . . . It was a federation of twenty-seven kingdoms, duchies, principalities and 'free and imperial cities.' By far the largest of these components was Prussia whose Hohenzollern king, under . . . the imperial Constitution of 1871, also bore the title of German Emperor."[21] While the constituent states were to some extent self-governed, "the more important questions—foreign affairs, the Navy, the direction of the Army in wartime, imperial finance and foreign trade—were all under control of the Empire . . . The Emperor . . . appointed his own Imperial Chancellor, who in turn appointed his own 'secretaries of state'" who effectively ran things. "The Prussian Army swore an oath of fealty to the Emperor personally, not to the German nation,"[21] while the lower house of the Reichstag had no powers of initiation; it could only "approve" laws or military appropriations decided on elsewhere. Its function, as Bismarck no doubt intended when he set matters up in 1871, was to make the empire appear a parliamentary state and to provide the government a convenient means of gauging the trend of popular feeling without any necessity of conforming to it. The kaiser theoretically ruled this establishment and by a kind of inadvertence often decided its position on foreign affairs.

From his accession (upon the death of his father, Frederick III, in 1888) this talkative man had kept Europe in a continual hubbub. Accounts of him written just before or during World War I show that he was quite misread abroad. The reputation of Sedan and the Iron Chancellor clung to him, as did, in present fact, the younger Moltke and the military. He packed a wallop, if only by bequest, and his intemperate language and strange zigzags of policy created much nervousness.* What the world

subject class, whom Edward wished to protect for the good of his own realm, and Louis to loot for the glory of France and the defrayment of certain personal expenses. Futuristic as they tried to be, the Nazis had the same primitive view of economics, as Drucker in his book makes clear. It now appears Economic Man is far from dead, in particular in the land which once seemed bent upon his assassination.

* It was he who built the "image" later used against him by Allied propagandists, a fact which the Germans, in their postwar self-pity, wholly lost sight of. For instance, at the time of the Boxer Rebellion, in 1900, the Kaiser addressed his troops as follows:

"You must know, my men, that you are about to meet a crafty, well-armed cruel foe. Meet him and beat him! Give no quarter! Take no prisoners! Kill did not know was his utter incompetence. He was incapable even of working faithfully at his own mistakes as Philip II had done. His notion of how to be a good bureaucrat was confined to making marginal notes in state papers—exclamations such as "Swine!" or little exultations over his own cleverness: "So it works! This is very gratifying."[25] But in fact he had no very clear ideas on policy, and the few he had were erroneous. For the most part he allowed himself to be blown about by his emotions and (as if symbolizing his own unanchored mentality) wandered endlessly over the land on the imperial train or across the seas on his yacht. On these junkets his courtiers entertained him with *lieder* and antique foolery and it would have been better for the realm had he never left their company. Out of spite for Bismarck (and at the urging of the sinister Baron von Holstein,* who succeeded the old chancellor) the kaiser allowed a secret treaty with the Russians to lapse, thereby setting up his own "encirclement." Some years later he had fits of being overtly, insultingly anti-British, only to change his mood and visit England as if in all amity. At one point he sent their War Office a plan he had devised for a campaign against the Boers. It did not apparently

---

him, when he falls into your hands! Even as, a thousand years ago, the Huns under their King Attila made such a name for themselves as still resounds in terror . . . so may the name of German resound through Chinese history a thousand years from now, and you so conduct yourselves that no Chinaman will ever again so much as dare to look crooked [slantwise?] at a German!"[23]

Past or to come, the millennium seemed to fascinate German orators. Hitler was continually talking about the Thousand-Year Reich. When he took over Czechoslovakia, by establishing the protectorate of Bohemia and Moravia in March of 1939, he issued a proclamation which said, in part: "For a thousand years the provinces of Bohemia and Moravia formed part of the *Lebensraum* of the German people . . . The German Reich cannot tolerate continuous disturbances in these areas . . . Therefore the German Reich . . . is now resolved to intervene . . . For in the thousand years of its history it had already proved that thanks to the greatness and the qualities of the German people, it alone is called upon to undertake this task."[24]

To talk of the German Reich of 939 A.D. was of course nonsense, since Germany was then, like the rest of Europe, a chaos of baronies "the greatness and the qualities" of whose people consisted chiefly in an ability to scratch out some sort of existence despite their own ignorance and the climate of unending violence in which they were obliged to live.

* Holstein worked in semiseclusion and was so intensely paranoid that he never went out without a revolver in his pocket. Bismarck called him "the man with the hyena eyes."

evoke any response, which is hardly surprising in view of the opinion his own officers held of his military ability. *Their* dread, as one of his intimates records, was that he might one day decide to assume command himself in the field. He never did so, being somewhat hesitant when it came to taking real action or to exposing himself to danger. For the rest he was a thoroughly medieval sovereign,* brutally domineering toward his wife and his subordinates. He had a particular fondness for hunting driven game, a sport which reminds one of St. Simon's description of the ghastly slaughters practiced daily by Philip V of Spain. One of the Kaiser's courtiers (possibly with St. Simon in mind) has left an account of His Highness at the chase:

". . . The shoots were horrible . . . Strangely enough no one at Court has any sort of sense that it adds nothing to the glory of a sovereign to cause these hapless wild creatures to be driven into enclosures, in the center of which the noble sportsmen are posted, pouring their shots upon the desperate panting brutes . . . till all are dead or else dragging mortally wounded on the ground, until at the end of the day they are put out of their agony."[27]

There was, however, a modern aspect to the business. Instead of arranging things so he might have to show some degree of bravery in the face of a savage creature—a practice now considered unnecessary and perhaps barbarous—the hunter aimed at mass production. When he reached forty-three, the kaiser had a granite marker erected in the State Forest of Rominten bearing the following inscription in gold: "Here His Majesty William II brought down His Most High's fifty-thousandth animal, a white cock pheasant."[27] Compared to the blood sports popular in other nations at the time—for instance, the fox hunts and grouse shoots in England—those of the kaiser and his coterie were characteristically to the fore, which is to say behind. Much the same primal spirit was to show itself in the *Freikorps*, or unemployed German shock troops of 1919, who stamped out the Spartacist uprising

---

* At Pröckelwitz, according to an intimate, H.R.H. would shoot every day until noon, sleep till three, give an hour to state business, and then, after dinner, "it would amuse the Emperor to look for thunderbolts in the garden —many were to be found under the gravel, most of which had been scattered there beforehand by Eberhard" (Count Eberhard von Dohna, apparently a hunting companion of the Kaiser's).[26]

and murdered Karl Liebknecht and Rosa Luxemburg. In effect these patriots began the work of the Nazis in clubbing to death any semblance of an opposition,* loyal or disloyal, and did so, it would appear, as much from a love of human blood sports as from any particular political conviction. As the S.A. troopers later sang: "*Und willst du nicht genosse sein, so schlag wir dir den Schädel ein.*" (Roughly: "If you won't be nice we'll smash your skull in.") The kaiser himself shared these virile attitudes. Writing to Tsar "Nicky" of Russia, whom he had long since estranged, he warned that monarchs of the world should unite before it was too late. Observe, said he, the situation in France, in which the upper orders and representatives of the people mingle at public functions. "But what would be the result of this sort of thing at home, in our own countries? Republicans are by nature revolutionary, logically to be regarded as people who will one day have to be shot or hanged."[28]

Long before, Tsar "Nicky" had written of him—in a dispatch which Bismarck, to humiliate the young kaiser, had let him see— "*Il est fou. C'est un garçon mal élevé et de mauvaise foi.*"[28] The appraisal was on the whole quite accurate. The kaiser, grandson of the "old Emperor" William I, and son of the discontented Frederick III by Victoria, daughter of the English queen, had been born not breathing and, probably when the doctors spanked him to life, suffered an incurable injury to his left arm. The procedure, if not the injury, will do as a metaphor of his later condition. He seems to have been disliked by his parents, and exposed to much Prussian rigor during his boyhood, the effect of which was to brutalize without really toughening him. As most of Germany had done, he hated his mother and the English, and no doubt partly for that reason fell into a second great error in policy which was to cost him his throne. One of his ministers, Caprivi, urged that Germany should not undertake to build a navy equal to England's but concentrate instead on becoming the first military nation on the Continent. "With such a naval power [as the kaiser and others were then advocating] they en-

---

* Various *Freikorps* groups, devoted to particular leaders and resembling the private armies of late Roman times, existed through the twenties in Germany. Having used the *Freikorps* to rise to power, Hitler liquidated his most dangerous lieutenants among them in the horrible Blood Purge of 1934.

feeble our defensive power on land and will end by bringing us into conflict with England, our natural ally . . . The only naval question is how small our Fleet can be—not how big."[29] Given as he was to visceral logic, the kaiser of course paid no attention to this counsel, and the fleet grew apace. What with the man he was, and still more the man he sounded, war came to be felt inevitable, breaking out finally in 1914 not so much for good reason nor because any high command had planned it, but simply from the accumulated force of conviction on both sides. Britain, France, and Russia were menaced, Germany encircled. Resolution of the matter could not be put off a moment longer.

Unlike the war of 1870, which Bismarck carefully engineered, this one started almost by accident.* Given the pretext of a routine political assassination, all parties plunged into a melee, the British and French with no plan, the Germans with one they bungled. What followed was a conflict more gruesome and stupid, more incredibly pointlessly destructive, than any which the professional military, in their long, bloody tenure, have ever fought,† even including the one they stumbled into only twenty years afterwards.

The root of their difficulty was not, as in Ye Olden Time, simple ignorance, but the sort of university-trained doctrinaire backwardness which seems to result when men with no natural aptitude for ideas are nonetheless obliged to stuff their heads with them. Add to that the fact that the teachers of future generals are often men of the same type and it becomes easy to see how modern wars can exceed any in sheer frightfulness, since they put instruments of unexampled power at the disposal of a small special caste who left to themselves would probably have

---

* Almost but not quite. Alan Moorehead writes: "It was apparent . . . that the Kaiser had acted very wisely in precipitating the war in 1914. His military experts had estimated that the French and Russian armies if left in peace would have reached their maximum strength by 1917. To have waited therefore would have been fatal; relatively German power was declining with every year that went by. 'Now or never' the Kaiser had written on the margin of one of his state papers in 1914."[30]

† Some might argue that the Thirty Years War was worse, or Philip's Netherlands campaigns as bad. But it took far longer to achieve the same amount of devastation in those days; and for sheer grinding brutality, for degradation and discomfort and attrition of men's sanity, nothing approaches modern trench warfare.

been hard put to devise the stone ax; or having done so would have needed centuries more to work out the tactics for using it. (Witness the trouble medieval commanders had with the problem of the pike.) The lesson of Sedan, and still more of the Russo-Japanese War of 1904-05, was that firepower had created a potential impasse in which each side was impregnable on the defensive and doomed when it switched to the attack.

As early as the 1870s, an English military writer foresaw that deadlock and proposed a kind of mobile, armored artillery which might break it. He had, on paper, invented the tank. The idea naturally evoked no response. On the contrary, by 1910 the French, under the influence of Colonel Ardant du Picq's *Études sur le combat,* had come to the extraordinary conclusion that the key to success in modern war was *élan*—the overwhelming "moral" force of a mass onslaught. Far from acknowledging the increased power of the defensive, they began to neglect the fortifications they had built in the years since 1870 and succeeded moreover in talking themselves into the belief that the Germans would not attack through Belgium but would use roughly the same avenues as they had before Sedan.*

The English, at this time, had no army to speak of (six to eight divisions) while the Germans (who had eighty-seven divisions of infantry to sixty-two for France) were still under the influence of the older Moltke's tactical ideas. That is, they had not yet solved the problem of controlling an army of this magnitude by a centralized command. Headquarters laid down strategy, but the commanders on the spot had to devise the means of carrying it out. Moreover, they were as much at a loss as the Allies when it came to dealing with the situation which quickly developed. Once their advance had carried them through Belgium, their attack lost headway while defective liaison caused a gap to open in their front.† The English, under Haig and Sir John French, moved slowly into it. Gallieni sent out his Taxicab Army from Paris; and on September 5, 1914, the Battle of the Marne began.

* General Michel, who *had* foreseen what the Germans would do and who was in line for the chief command, was forced to resign just before the war in favor of Joffre, whom the staff regarded as a better team man.

† Apparently first discovered by General Franchet d'Esperey, an officer of some ability who unfortunately—one might say inevitably—was soon transferred to a secondary theater.

Within a week the invaders had been stopped and driven a short distance in retreat. The engagement was decisive in that it meant, as Fuller puts it, "that Germany had lost her one and only chance to defeat France before she engaged Russia *au fond.*"[31]

It meant more than that. From this point forward, both sides, thanks to the nearly total inability of their commanding officers to invent new tactics, were condemned to over three years of grinding trench warfare, compared to which the siege of Petersburg of '64-65, and even that of Port Arthur* in the Russo-Japanese War, were mere rehearsals. By 1914 the combined power of field artillery, machine guns, and the magazine rifle was literally annihilating. The fire fields between the combatants' lines became vast tracts of bloodied mud, strewn with the human debris of past attacks and made next to impassable by thousands of shell craters. Not a man could live, not a house or farm animal remained, in this waste, which stretched from the Vosges to the Channel coast. The Germans' attempt to break the deadlock by the use of poisonous or lung-blistering gases (which caused some men to die by internal drowning, their lungs filling slowly with fluid as medics stood by, unable to help them) proved indecisive thanks to the speedy development of the gas mask.† Early versions of the latter, however, were so clumsy that attacking troops, forced to wear them, often could not see where they were going and became better targets than ever as they stumbled hundreds of yards over ghastly broken ground toward barbed-wire entanglements (some of them electrified) behind which, in bunkers, stood the enemy, ready to let loose sheets of rifle and machine-gun bullets or (at fifty to seventy-five yards) showers of grenades. To break up this sort of defensive position, the drumfire artillery barrage was widely used. It consisted of a slowly advancing curtain of fire from hundreds, or even thousands, of guns. Preparatory bombardments of this intensity went on for hours, or sometimes days, before an assault. To meet them men dug deeper, reinforced their works with concrete, made their lines zigzag to avoid enfilading fire or to limit the success of howitzer and small-mortar attacks, and lived for weeks together below

---

* At which a kind of gas warfare was tried out by the Japanese.

† And also because gas proved a tricky weapon, sometimes blowing back upon those who had released it.

ground, often in partially flooded trenches or blockhouses. In this constant siege, food and ammunition often ran short, men caught flu or dysentery or "trench foot," died of neglected minor wounds or from "psychosomatic" causes or simply went insane.

In the whole history of warfare no one had ever devised a system of combat quite so ineffectual, so destructive of man's always precarious humanity, above all so mercilessly drawn out. In the past—even as recently as Sedan—battles had necessarily been episodic. Armies drilled, marched, maneuvered, and finally, after weeks, took up positions and had it out—usually in a matter of hours—after which there would be more drilling, marching, and maneuvering, sometimes by the same forces, sometimes by new ones. Though potential disaster hung over them all, the men in the ranks were not exposed to it continuously, for months or years together, except in rare campaigns such as Napoleon's in Russia or Charles XII's in the Ukraine. If only for that reason, the soldier's life retained much of its glamor, even for those who, like Stendhal, had actually lived it. The Civil War began a change in this ancestral attitude, but it was only an intimation, a vague stirring in a few minds, including of course Sherman's. For at Petersburg life in the trenches was nothing to what it would presently become, and the more protracted battles of that war— for instance Spotsylvania—lasted scarcely twenty-four hours. Perhaps in our innocence we imagined that human flesh and nerves could endure no more. But like all supposed natural limits—like the four-minute mile—this one was finally exceeded, with what effects on man in general we are even now just beginning to see. It was in 1914 that war really and truly became hell.

As the months dragged by the Allies' firepower, though not their tactical finesse, picked up. Himself a German veteran, Erich Maria Remarque describes an action in which the artillery preparation lasted for days: "We wake up in the middle of the night. The earth booms. Heavy fire is falling on us. We crouch into corners. We distinguish shells of every calibre. Every man lays hold of his things and looks again every minute to reassure himself that they are still there . . . Already by morning a few of the recruits are green and vomiting . . . Slowly the grey light trickles into the post . . . The explosion of mines mingles with the gunfire. That is the most dementing convulsion of all. The whole region where they go up becomes one grave. The reliefs go out, the observers stagger in, covered with dirt and trembling. One lies down in silence in the corner and eats, the other, a reservist-reinforcement, sobs; twice he has been flung over the parapet by the blast of the explosions without getting any more than shell-shock.

"The recruits are eying him. We must watch them, these things are catching, already some lips begin to quiver. It is good that it is growing daylight; perhaps the attack will come before noon."

But it doesn't. The shelling goes on that day, and through the next night, and the day following, before the French finally move out. At last the barrage moves off behind them; there is a pause, and then the attack begins:

"No one would believe that in this howling waste there could still be men; but steel helmets now appear on all sides, out of the trench, and fifty yards from us a machine-gun is already in position and barking. The wire entanglements are torn to pieces. Yet they offer some obstacle. We see the storm troops coming. Our artillery opens fire. Machine-guns rattle, rifles crack. The charge works its way across. Haie and Kropp begin with the hand grenades. They throw as fast as they can . . . Haie throws seventy-five yards, Kropp sixty, it has been measured, distance is important . . . A whole line has gone down before our machine-guns; then we have a lot of stoppages and they come nearer. I see one of them, his face upturned, fall into a wire cradle. His body collapses, his hands remain suspended as though he were praying. Then his body drops clean away and only his hands with the stumps of . . . arms, shot off, now hang in the wire . . . We make for the rear, pull wire cradles into the trench and leave bombs behind us with the string pulled, which ensure us a fiery retreat. The machine-guns are already firing from the next position . . . The forward trenches have been abandoned. Are they still trenches? They have been blown to pieces, annihilated . . . but the enemy's casualties increase. They did not count on so much resistance."[32]

Absolutely remarkable! After years of failure—after millions of shells and billions in money and hundreds upon hundreds of thousands of lives had been spent in proving that artillery could not after all reduce a garrison dug in like woodchucks—*they did not count on so much resistance!* Surely imbecility can go no further. In World War I it reached a pinnacle perhaps only to be exceeded on the day that the same sort of brain addresses itself to the problem of waging a nuclear war, when, no doubt, no one will survive at all, and the last cry heard will be: *"We did not count on so much resistance!"*

In the meantime, it is hard for a connoisseur of bad generalship, surveying the gray wastes of World War I, to single out any one commander as especially awful. There were dozens of them on both sides. True to the modern spirit, the war was a team enterprise. At its best it was run by men as systematic and unimaginative as truck dispatchers whose main concern seemed to be to replace the units which never came back. At its worst, as in the British campaign against Gallipoli or the Russian Samsonov's invasion of Poland, it was as perfect a disaster as Sedan. A general as bad as Sir John French might eventually be replaced, but the man who replaced him—Haig—was fully as stupid, and an unattractive, wire-pulling, shifty sort into the bargain, whose expressed military opinions all too accurately forecast his performance. (Besides his prewar views that cavalry was far from outmoded and that artillery would chiefly be of use against green troops, he stated, as late as April of 1915, in a minute to the War Council, that "the machine-gun is a much over-rated weapon and two per battalion is more than sufficient."[33]) Haig's chief assets were social, not military. Having failed his Staff College examinations he appealed to the Duke of Cambridge, a friend of his sister Henrietta's, who exercised his medieval prerogative and nominated Haig over the heads of his examiners. Already no doubt convinced of the value of aristocratic connections, Haig* put himself in the way of any number of them by marrying a maid of honor to the queen. However, unlike some under-talented and over-promoted men, he was not able in his profession to improve markedly with practice; nor did he readily forget those who had correctly appraised him in the first place.

"For example General Grierson, his fellow corps commander in the B.E.F., had completely outmaneuvered Haig at the au-

---

* Who was of the Scotch whiskey-making family. He is said originally to have ingratiated himself with Sir John French by lending him money, Sir John having expensive tastes traceable in part to a fondness for the ladies.

tumn exercises of 1912, to the embarrassment of all concerned, and to such an extent that the maneuvers had to be closed a day early. On arrival in France Grierson had died of a heart attack and Sir John French's choice as his successor was General Plumer, the erstwhile Staff College examiner who had taken such a poor view of Haig's performance. At the last moment . . . this decision was altered and Sir Horace Smith-Dorrien was appointed in his place."[34]

For months after its landing in France, the British Expeditionary Force was pathetically undersupplied. For want of grenades it improvised suicidal bombs of its own, and at one point a British officer desperately in need of trench mortars "managed to do a private deal with the French, paying cash for a number of old Coehorn siege-mortars which were found to bear the cypher of Louis-Philippe."[35] One battle, Loos (September, 1915), will do as an example of Haig's tactical style. On the first day the encounter began with a bungled gas attack which seems to have done more harm to the English than to the enemy. On Day Two (September 26) Haig sent some twelve battalions, or close to 10,000 men, out into "No man's land in broad daylight with no gas or smoke cloud to cover them," and preceded only by "a desultory pattern of artillery fire." The Germans, entrenched behind barbed wire (which the feeble bombardment had not disturbed), could hardly believe their eyes. "Ten columns of extended line," one of their men wrote in his diary ". . . offering such a target as had never been seen before." In three hours and a half it was wiped out. "One of the German battalion commanders spoke later of the revolting and nauseating impression made on them all as they watched the slaughter, so much so that after the retreat had begun they ceased fire."[36] The loss to the British was 385 officers and 7861 men—better than 80 percent. The Germans lost none—not a single man. By comparison, Fredericksburg seems almost a Union victory and Crécy a trifle. The German Field Marshal Falkenhayn, himself not the greatest of military intellects, said of the English: "In spite of undeniable bravery and endurance on the part of the men, [they, or rather their commanders] have proved so clumsy in action that they offer no prospect of accomplishing anything decisive . . . in the immediate future."[36] It was Falkenhayn's good fortune that that

was so, and the misfortune of the common soldier on both sides
to be led by men such as these. And just as Burnside, having
helped to sabotage McClellan at Antietam, was appointed by
Lincoln to succeed him, so Haig succeeded French in the fall of
1915, in part, naturally enough, because of the "rumblings from
London at the massacre of the 26th of September."[36]

Nineteen fifteen was a bad year for the Allies, though perhaps
only a little worse than '16 and '17, or even parts of '18. Its outstanding events included the first German gas attack (in April, at
Ypres), the yearlong failure of Joffre's strategy of pinching off
the great German salient in France by combined offensives (of
which Haig's action at Loos was a part), and last and most dismal, the Gallipoli campaign.

The objective of the latter was Constantinople, which stands
at the western end of the Bosporus, a twenty-mile-long strait
opening eastward into the Black Sea. To the south and west of
Constantinople stretches the small Sea of Marmara (or Mar-
mora), which in turn connects with the Aegean via a longer strait
known as the Dardanelles. The southern shore of the Dardanelles
forms a part of Turkey, while the European shore consists of a
narrow peninsula extending about forty miles, from Gallipoli, at
the western end of Marmara, to Cape Helles, on the Aegean,
where it ends opposite the Turkish town of Kum Kale.* "The
problem of forcing the Dardanelles—the ancient Hellespont,"
writes one historian, "had engrossed the attention . . . of naval
and military strategists for many centuries before the First World
War." He adds that "the critical area . . . runs from the western
entrance some 13 miles up to the Narrows. The western mouth
of the Dardanelles is only some 4000 yards wide, but as soon as
one has passed the guardian fortresses of Sedd-el-Bahr at the tip
of the Gallipoli Peninsula . . . to the left and Kum Kale, jutting
out on a low promontory from Asia to the right, the channel
widens considerably for about four miles. To the left, the Gallipoli Peninsula rises steadily from Cape Helles, and the western
shore of the Dardanelles becomes tall and uninviting . . . The
Dardanelles then contracts and by the time that the Narrows,

* In fact, the peninsula and the strait run from southwest (on the Aegean)
to northeast (into Marmara). Much of the seaward coast of the peninsula,
where the Allies landed, faces west.

only 1600 yards across, are approached, the Kilid Bahr plateau on the Gallipoli Peninsula rises sharply from the water, while to the right [i.e., on the Asiatic side] the hills behind the town of Chanak are oppressively close."[37]

It requires no expertise to see that this thirteen-mile strip of water presents an awesome obstacle to invasion. The Narrows in particular can be made impassable to ships by artillery fire and mine fields. The mouth, on the Aegean end, being less than three miles wide, should also have been defensible by these means had the Turks early in 1915 taken note of what the British clearly intended. The most promising approach to the Dardanelles would appear to be by way of an amphibious attack which would put a force on the seaward (northern and western) side of the Gallipoli Peninsula. Once safely ashore, this force, under cover of its naval guns and field artillery, might quickly proceed up and across the peninsula, taking the defenses of the Narrows from the rear and opening the Dardanelles to the fleet. After several false starts, this was the strategy the British decided upon. Its originator and tireless champion was of course Winston Churchill, then First Lord of the Admiralty. To an unusual degree, the success of the plan depended upon co-ordination and surprise. If the British to that point had shown little aptitude for either, the Turks at least did not promise to be a very alert or formidable enemy.

Turkey at that time was ruled by a military junta known as the Young Turks, whose leader was Enver Pasha. Thanks to energetic German diplomacy, the country had slid into war on the side of Central Powers. By December, 1914, when Russia's casualties in the west had already exceeded a million, the Turks moved against their old enemy, and in January, in the Caucasus, 100,000 men under Enver himself were narrowly but totally defeated (30,000 froze to death). Enver escaped to fight again; but abortive as it had been, this first Turkish effort so alarmed Grand Duke Nicholas that he appealed to London for help. The result was the Gallipoli campaign, which from the start seems to have been a blighted enterprise. The chief difficulty apparently arose from the diffusion of authority. Since the turn of the century the British army had got round to patterning itself after von Moltke's, incorporating the principle of semiautonomous field commands, or noninterference of the commander in chief in actual operations. At the Cabinet level it was not clear as to who overrode whom, the decisions taken being the outcome of a sort of perpetual combat of personalities, Churchill's usually predominating.

The British War Council of 1914-15 had been created as an improvement upon the larger, slower-moving Cabinet. It was, as one writer remarked, "brilliantly intellectual" but scarcely all of a piece in its views; nor was it as hard-working as it might have been.*[38] It included Churchill, Lloyd George, Lord Kitchener (of Khartoum), Foreign Secretary Sir Edward Grey, Sir Archibald Wolfe Murray (chief of the Imperial General Staff), Prime Minister H. H. Asquith, Arthur Balfour, and Lord Fisher, a seventy-three-year-old admiral who held the post of First Sea Lord. The three most active in the Gallipoli affair were Churchill, Fisher, and Kitchener. At the very first meeting of the Council, on November 25, 1914, Churchill brought up the question of a combined sea and land attack upon the Dardanelles, the issue at that time being the defense of Egypt and the Suez. Later, in January and February of 1915, the issue became to relieve the military pressure on Russia. In the same period Mr. Churchill seems to have veered round to the notion that the Dardanelles might be forced by the navy alone. In whichever direction he swung, he dragged Fisher reluctantly after him, the old admiral evidently succumbing to Churchill's arguments when he heard them in person, only to regret having done so as soon as he had gone off to think matters out for himself. Fisher appears to have favored a large-scale combined operation, involving Greek and Bulgarian, as well as French and English, troops. To weaken the North Sea fleet for a purely naval action which might end with its ships sunk or trapped past the Narrows in the Sea of Marmara, struck him as madness. Even after he had agreed to Churchill's plan for the naval assault, he wrote to him: "You are simply eaten up with the Dardanelles and cannot think of anything else. Damn the Dardanelles! They will be our grave!"[39]

While perhaps preferable to an unsupported naval attack, a

---

* In a memorandum to Asquith, Churchill wrote: "I think the War Council ought to meet daily for a few days each week. No topic can be pursued to any fruitful result at weekly intervals."[38] The same leisureliness in the face of grave and accumulating emergencies was to be shown by many of the top brass at Gallipoli.

Gallipoli landing raised the troublesome question of how many men, if any, could be spared from the European theater just then. Kitchener at first promised to send the 29th Division, withdrawing the offer almost at once. (In the end the 29th was sent.) It was gradually decided that Sir John Maxwell, commanding in Egypt, should furnish some Australians and New Zealanders (Anzacs) from his defense force. The numbers mentioned (30,-000) alarmed him, since he faced a sizable Turkish army in the Sinai Peninsula. (He finally sent the troops requested and more.) How were all these men to be landed and kept supplied on a coast as craggy and nearly beachless as that of the Gallipoli Peninsula? *Could* a landing succeed, on terrain so hostile and defended, as it was likely to be, with artillery and machine guns? The only definite move toward solving this problem appears to have been made by Fisher, who had commissioned some 500-man armored landing craft to be built for use on the Baltic. He vehemently objected to releasing them for service in the Mediterranean. (Some eventually were released.) But for the Gallipoli landings the British mostly used "tows"—strings of ship's boats pulled close inshore by launches and left to row the rest of the distance as best they might. One ship, the old collier *River Clyde*, was made into a kind of LST, with debarking ports cut in her hull.

Even supposing these cumbrous arrangements worked and the bulk of the Allies' forces got ashore, what would they find? Who knew anything about the interior of the peninsula or had accurate estimates of the number and disposition of Turkish forces there? (No one, it turned out; the few available maps and intelligence reports were misleading or plain wrong.) Aerial reconnaissance showed the land to be exceedingly rough and irregular. Most of the western peninsula was in fact a network of natural fortresses—sharp stony ridges dotted with scrub, deep ravines ideal for concealed marches by the flank or for entrapment as the case might be; and commanding eminences such as Achi Baba, from whose summit officers and artillery spotters could keep close track of an invader. Moreover the Turkish army was not the rabble it had been in the days of Baltaji on the Prut, or even as recently as Enver Pasha's disastrous campaign in the Caucasus. German officers—notably General Liman von Sanders at headquarters and Colonel Kannengiesser on the peninsula—had improved discipline and given Turkish operations at least as much orderliness and know-how as those on the other side, if not in some cases more. Certainly the Turks had better arms—more grenades or "bombs" (the British were still in the homemade jam-tin stage), as well as numbers of howitzers, which were far better suited to that hilly country than the flat-trajectory naval guns or the few French 75s which the Allies used. The Turkish army could be maintained, moreover, by land, over relatively short supply lines; and except for a brief period when British submarines penetrated to the Sea of Marmara, their sea routes from the Asiatic mainland remained open as well.

Notwithstanding all these difficulties and uncertainties, the Gallipoli campaign was approved in London, although the exact chain of command and the plan of operations to be followed remained in doubt. As late as mid-February, 1915, the commanders on the spot were still wondering what was expected of them. Maxwell, not yet advised as to how many troops he would have to divert from the defense of Suez, sent a request for information to Vice Admiral S. H. Carden, commanding the fleet in the eastern Mediterranean. Carden replied vaguely that he might be "landing a force of 10,000 men if such a step is found necessary," adding that he imagined these would be opposed by a Turkish army "of about 40,000."[40] Not long afterwards Kitchener told Maxwell that the British would not be attacking in strength but only with a small amphibious force (presumably marines), who would have the job of "taking the forts in reverse"[40]—a phrase whose meaning is unclear, especially since the forces actually landed were hardly sufficient to maintain a beachhead, let alone beleaguer any well-entrenched position. By March 4 Kitchener's plans seemed to envision holding the larger army (30,000-40,000 men) in readiness for an attack on Constantinople, bypassing the Dardanelles and Gallipoli entirely. Inasmuch as the prospects for forcing the Dardanelles by fleet action had by that time become quite poor, this proposal appears to have made no sense at all.*

---

* Gallipoli illustrates a principle which began to be apparent in European wars as early as the Armada. It is that distance lends enchantment to the most crackbrained strategic ideas. Not that the high command or the home

On February 19, long before large-scale landings were ready to be made, the fleet, under Carden, opened fire on the Dardanelles forts. The psychological effect was marvelous. The Allied press responded with great excitement. The Bulgarians wavered toward the Allied side. The Greeks offered to send troop support. There was a sensation in Constantinople and the German High Command was gravely perturbed. None of these results could possibly have been more ill timed. The enthusiasm generated in the Allies by this fake triumph only served to propel them the more inexorably into real reverses; while the Turks and Germans, if they had not already guessed it, now knew exactly what the British were up to. As if to drive the point home, the latter then made a series of commando-style raids aimed at disabling Turkish guns and defense works on the peninsula. The resistance to these quickly became prohibitive; while the attempts of the navy to sweep the mine fields at the Narrows turned out no better—indeed, not as well.

A number of English trawlers, most of them still manned by their civilian crews, had been pressed into service as minesweepers. Once inside the strait at Cape Helles, and particularly as they approached the Narrows, with its cliffs on either shore, these were subjected to heavy howitzer fire which the accompanying British naval vessels seemed unable to silence. (With the help of their German advisers, the Turks quickly became adept at shifting their shore batteries from place to place. They also used smoke pots to decoy fire away from real targets. Moreover, they could lob shells from upland sites difficult for naval guns, with their flatter trajectories, to reach.) What with their own low speeds and the swift current flowing down the strait from Marmara, the trawlers could barely make three or four knots, so that on the inward voyage (when artillery fire was usually hottest) evasive action was not easy to take, and when taken slowed the

---

public is any less well informed about operations in distant theaters. All the necessary facts may be to hand; they simply lack urgency; the imagination has freer play with them. Had Churchill or Kitchener actually gone to Gallipoli at an early stage in the landings, it seems possible the whole campaign might have gone differently, or perhaps simply have been canceled. In the case of Vietnam (see Chapter X) the high command provided against this sort of emergency by a public-relations technique which, while it did not exactly fake success, at least gave a certain gloss to failure.

proceedings even further. Under these conditions it is not surprising that their owner-masters became skittish, sometimes de-
fying orders and making a run for it. The last and most
determined attempt, involving six trawlers and a cruiser, was
turned back when four trawlers and the cruiser were hit by shellfire. The cruiser drifted out of control for some twenty minutes
until her damaged steering gear was put back in commission. In
the end the Kephez mine field at the Narrows was never swept,*
the only British to reach Marmara during the war being a few
intrepid submariners. Some of the first to make the attempt lost
their lives when their craft, meeting the stream of lower-density
fresh water pouring out of Marmara, were forced to the bottom.

It was not until April 25 that the landings on the peninsula began, by which time the Turks should have been far better prepared than they were. The British meanwhile had made a
last-minute effort to centralize at least the military phase of operations. However, instead of appointing General Birdwood, who
was a logical choice (he commanded the Anzacs and had already
drafted a plan of campaign), London gave the post of commander in chief to Sir Ian Hamilton. In a war outstanding for
bad generals, Hamilton was to distinguish himself as one of the
very worst. Probably because his own instructions from London
were so cloudy, his relations with the navy so difficult, and his
subordinates—notably Generals Birdwood, Hunter-Weston, Godley,† and the aged Stopford—were such bumblers themselves,
Hamilton has never quite gotten the attention he deserved. He
was not one to attract it in the first place. He had none of Haig's
natural effrontery or Joffre's implacable ursine air; he was, rather,
a wry, ectomorphic, donnish sort of man, wonderfully young-
looking for his age (he was in his early sixties but in photos of the
time would pass for a trim forty-five) who to the end maintained
a thin good cheer and was reputed to write poetry. (He evidently did not but was clearly of a literary turn, as his battle
diaries later showed.) His officers are said to have reacted vio-

---

* Manned and equipped as they were, it is doubtful whether the trawlers,
even had they reached the Kephez field, could have swept many mines without sinking themselves in the process.

† Known to his men as "make 'em run Alex"—supposedly because Mrs.
Godley, who might have made a fine Nixon Cabinet wife, was overheard at
a review urging him to have his troops go past on the double.

lently to his orders, which were colorful and intricate but often difficult to summarize.

Hamilton's direction of the campaign during the first crucial weeks, from April 25 to August 10, 1915, was a model of mismanagement—one might better say of nonmanagement. Once under way, *everything* was left, à la Moltke, to "run on rails," and as often as not ran off them, a fact which Sir Ian wistfully noted in his journals but seemed unable to do anything about. Not until the last day but one of his last major offensive did he take personal charge, and then with climactically bad results.

Just before Hamilton assumed command, Mr. Churchill in London made yet another strategic *volte-face* ". . . Instead of waiting for a combined operation to be elaborated [he] telegraphed Admiral Carden: 'We suggest for your consideration that a point has now been reached when it is necessary . . . to overwhelm the forts at the Narrows at decisive range by the fire of the largest number of guns . . .' Thus the blunder of February 19-25 was repeated. The attack was made on March 18 and three battleships were lost by running into an unswept minefield."[41]

When the troops finally shipped out of Alexandria for the April 25 landings they did so in the best of spirits, with bands playing and rounds of cheers. At higher echelons these feelings were not shared. Arrangements for supplying an invasion force of this size (about 75,000 men) and for taking care of their wounded had still hardly been made. It was not clear whether Lemnos, a Greek island which the British had summarily occupied and placed under their own military governor, was to become the main base. By the time the landings began, this difficulty had compounded itself. "One of the curses of the present complete lack of organization is that we have *six* bases," an officer wrote, "and no one knows where the ships are."[42] Had it not been for the tardiness of the Turks in strengthening their own forces on the peninsula, the whole adventure might have ended in a repulse at the water's edge. As it was, the losses on some beaches were frightful.

At Sedd-el-Bahr, for instance, just inside the strait near the tip of the peninsula, troops under nominal command of Lieutenant General Sir Aylmer Hunter-Weston were ordered ashore from the *River Clyde* after a stunning naval barrage which was thought to have obliterated the Turkish troops manning the old fort. This last as usual proved to be a miscalculation. For one thing the landing, which involved beaching the *River Clyde* and having additional men towed ashore in ship's boats, was held up by the current, so that the enemy was given time to take stations again after the shelling. The Turkish defense consisted of "a total of three platoons and four old machine-guns." They held their fire to the point that, as the *River Clyde* came in, an officer on board wrote: "6:22 A.M. Ran smoothly ashore without a tremor. No opposition. We shall land unopposed."[43] In a matter of minutes the whole place seemed to blow up. Under the volume of fire produced by the tiny Turkish garrison, some units were stopped dead and the survivors of others left pinned down and helpless. "The scenes . . . have often been described. The shattered cutters, now full only of dead and dying, drifting away from the beach; the floundering screaming troops; the ugly crimson stain which spread rapidly over the placid water; the piles of corpses at the edge of the beach and in front of the barbed wire . . ."[43] Major David French and forty men of the First Battalion, Royal Dublin Fusiliers, managed to get ashore through this holocaust and, with the remnants of other units, took shelter behind a low sand ridge which the defenders had neglected to level. There they remained trapped until nightfall while (as Josiah Wedgwood wrote to Churchill) "the wounded cried out all day—in every boat, lighter, hopper and all along the shore. It was horrible . . ."[43]

The divisional commander responsible, Hunter-Weston, spent the same period only a few minutes' sail away, aboard the *Euryalus* off W beach, apparently unaware of what was taking place at Sedd-el-Bahr. However, Sir Ian Hamilton, Admiral de Robeck, and Commodore Keyes happened by on the battleship *Queen Elizabeth* and were, as one historian puts it, "horrified witnesses of this dreadful scene."[43] The *Queen Elizabeth* delivered an immediate bombardment, without effect. "In Keyes's words, 'that dreadful tat-tat-tat of machine-gun fire burst out afresh.' "[43] The writer goes on to say: "Hamilton was becoming aware of the grave disadvantages of having no direct control over the movements of ships in an amphibious operation . . ." He seems also to have reflected upon whether he should override Hunter-Weston by diverting further troops from Sedd-el-Bahr lest they only add to the confusion and be cut to pieces there too. It was felt, however, that this move by the commander in chief would not be fair play. "When Hamilton suggested that troops destined for V beach [Sedd-el-Bahr] might land at Y beach, Braithwaite [his chief of staff] was doubtful 'as to whether it was sound for G.H.Q. to barge into Hunter-Weston's plans, seeing he was executive commander of this whole southern invasion.'"[44] Sir Ian himself commented later: "It was not for me to force his hand; there is no question of that."[45] All this might have been well enough had Hunter-Weston *had* any plans or known how whatever plans he had had were going. In the end nothing at all was done to clear up the mess. The men simply held out behind their ridge on the beach, and the next day the small Sedd-el-Bahr garrison was overwhelmed, though not without another sanguinary fight. Shortly afterwards Hunter-Weston was promoted from divisional to corps commander.

The battles which followed (in May to mid-August, 1915) were if anything more horrible and less of a success than the landings. They can be roughly grouped into two offensives—the battles of Krithia and the August battles, the latter involving still another landing at Suvla Bay, farther up on the west coast of the peninsula. The battles of Krithia, launched from cramped entrenched positions near the shore with little artillery support beyond what the navy could supply, were aimed at Achi Baba, a mountain which stands a few miles inland from Cape Helles and dominates the region. British losses in the first battle of Krithia were 3000 killed, wounded, and missing out of 14,000 engaged. In the second, which lasted May 6 through May 8, they lost 6000, or 30 percent, for a gain of six hundred yards. "There was no room for optimism as the Allies counted the cost of their defeat in the Second Battle of Krithia. It was no longer a question of when they would occupy Achi Baba but whether they could maintain their precarious foothold on the Peninsula. Apart from eight Territorial battalions and the Indian Brigade, there were no reserves left. The survivors of the landings were now haggard and looked aged. Young eager subalterns had become grim veterans within ten days. 'The beautiful battalions of the 25th April are wasted skeletons now,' Hamilton wrote"[46]—as though of some sad distant event he had been privileged to watch through a telescope.

Third Krithia, fought on June 4, was the best prepared of the three. It was to have been Hunter-Weston's masterpiece and might, in fact, have ended in a great victory had he not, like McClellan at Antietam, broken off the action a moment too soon. The Turks were on the verge of collapse but the British general, concentrating on his intended gain of eight hundred yards, had no inkling of the fact and the one solid opportunity of the campaign was let slip.* Losses: British, 4500; French, 2000; Turks, 9000. Strangely enough, the popularity of the Gallipoli adventure with the home folks was just then at its height. Churchill, in a speech on June 5 to his constituents, declared: "There was never a greater subsidiary operation of war in which a greater harmony of strategic, political and economic advantages has combined, or which stood in truer relation to the main decision."[47] It is no wonder that twenty some-odd years later Sir Winston had difficulty convincing his countrymen that he was the one who might lead them to victory against the Nazis.†

Meanwhile, the troops engaged in this "great subsidiary operation" were making no headway at all. They were held to nearly the same small beachheads they had taken in April, living in trenches stinking of dead—many of whom were only just buried in the walls or underfoot, attracting hordes of corpse flies—or else in airless bunkers dug into the cliffs along the shore. The heat had become intense and hundreds were stricken with the "Galli-

---

* As in Europe, the high command here appeared to have succumbed to a fatalistic acceptance of its own methods, abandoning the Clausewitzian aim of destroying the enemy's army and contenting itself with fighting costly battles for terrain. In R. Blythe's *Akenfield* (Pantheon Books, 1969) a veteran who fought in the ranks at Krithia describes fighting for weeks together to take and then retake the same strip of trench. From the matter-of-fact gruesomeness of his account it is clear he found the whole procedure appalling in part because of its apparent senselessness. It was not, he said, until he reached Gallipoli that he ever thought with longing of the grinding farm life he had left behind in Suffolk.

† Churchill's enthusiasm for Gallipoli died hard. Long after the campaign was an admitted failure and he out of the Cabinet, he and Commodore Keyes continued to plead for one more attempt at forcing the Narrows. The Germans seem to have rated the idea as highly as he did. At the time of Suvla Bay, in August, Tirpitz wrote: "The situation is . . . very critical. Should the Dardanelles fall, the world war has been decided against us."[48]

poli trots." Hospital ships and other transport continued to be scarce. Almost every day rows of sick and wounded lay on the beaches roasting in the sun as they waited to be taken off, and considerably depressing the spirits of those staying behind. There was still a shortage of "bombs," field artillery, and other essentials. And between Second and Third Krithia the naval war was suddenly resumed, this time by the enemy, with great psychological effect.

A German submarine, the U 21, having somehow slipped past Gibraltar, appeared one morning late in May off Anzac beach, where she torpedoed the battleship *Triumph*. Most of the crew was rescued but the ship was lost, pitching forward with a great rumble and diving to the bottom before a vast audience of Allied soldiers and their Turkish enemies (who sent up a cheer). The same day Admiral de Robeck, who had succeeded Carden, decided to withdraw the remaining ships to the Island of Imbros— a move nearly as crushing to those onshore as the loss of the *Triumph* had been. "The air was heavy that evening," Compton Mackenzie wrote, "and what with the wind . . . being in the south, the smoke of every ship was driven down astern which gave the effect of a number of dogs running away with their tails between their legs. The sense of abandonment was acute."[49]

Next day de Robeck sent the old battleship *Majestic* to W beach, off Cape Helles, where she was put behind a screen of smaller craft and fitted out with torpedo nets—all to no purpose. One day later, on May 27 Commander Hersing in the U 21 drew a bead on her—in Hamilton's words, like a hunter "picking a royal stag out of his harem of does."[15] There was a huge explosion and the *Majestic* rolled over and sank. Few lives were lost (she did not sink all the way; she was in shoal water and her crew had evidently been alerted), but the impact on all present was again considerable. Hersing had one more qualified success, on June 3, sinking a decoy ship dummied up to look like the battlecruiser *Tiger*. Fortunately for Allied morale, he then withdrew up the strait to Constantinople, where he remained for the duration.

The early lessons of the campaign seemed in no way to affect Sir Ian Hamilton's later direction of it. He continued to spend much of his time on Lemnos or aboard ship, a spare, clear-eyed sixty-one-year-old, cheering his commanders on and conscientiously letting each go his own gait. Wherever he chanced to be, another part of him, the literary observer, was always active. Of the French advance during the battle for Achi Baba on May 8, he wrote: "No living man has ever seen so strange a vision as this. In its disarray, in its rushing to and fro; in the martial music, shouts and evolutions . . . It seemed, it truly seemed as if the tide of blue grey and scarlet specks was submerging the enemy's strongholds." This happy portent was not to materialize, for while the French were still busy with their "martial music, shouts and evolutions" the Turkish shellfire suddenly burst upon them. "The puppet figures we watched began to waver," Hamilton reported, and "as night slid down into the smoke," the poor puppets were repulsed or lay fallen in heaps.[50]

Such detachment in a commanding general is surely unusual. Since Hamilton was reputed to be brave and had so much at stake himself, it is all the more remarkable that he maintained the distance he did from these almost daily calamities—a practice which may have had less to do with Prussian command theories of the 1870s than with the structure of English society in 1915. Then too, a sensitive commander might be put off his game by coming too close to those "specks" out there on the horizon. But although objectivity is certainly important in modern war, one feels that Sir Ian carried it a shade too far. One can imagine what the effect of some of his reveries might have been had they been read out at the time to the men in the ranks.

For his next attempt to break out of his cul-de-sac on the peninsula, Hamilton developed a most ambitious plan. It called for a three-pronged attack—one in the Cape Helles–Achi Baba sector, one from Anzac beach, further up the west coast, and one from a new jumping-off point still farther up, in the Suvla Bay–Point Nibrunesi area. A considerable force was to be put ashore at this last place, and it was hoped that by acting in concert with the others, this force might drive inland and cut the Turks off. The first attack, near Cape Helles, was to be a feint, tying down Turkish troops, while from Anzac, and especially from Suvla Bay, the Allies got around behind them.

The difficulty with this plan was that it seems to have been hit upon not all at once but piecemeal. As James puts it, more operations simply kept getting "tacked on" until Hamilton at last began to see the outlines of a good strategic combination. However, with his "mania for secrecy" he evidently confided his grand design to no one.[51] The field general who most needed to be informed of it—the aged Sir Frederick Stopford, appointed to lead the landing at Suvla Bay*—was kept wholly in the dark. And when he began to guess what Hamilton had in mind for him, he wrote to him in some dismay, managing to wangle a rewriting of his own orders which limited his responsibility to making good a landing at Suvla Bay. By this act of weakness—as well as in having Stopford as his key subordinate, a misfortune a more energetic commander might have avoided—Hamilton doomed his own offensive.

Even more than Third Krithia, the battles which followed in August resembled Antietam, with Stopford on the left playing the part of Burnside at the bridge, while the troops at Anzac and in the Cape Helles sector sacrificed themselves as uselessly as Sumner's and Hooker's had done at Bloody Lane and in the corn-field. At the time of the landing, the Turkish defense at Suvla consisted of only 1500 men commanded by a nervous German, Major Willmer. Had Stopford's people been alert and capably led, they could probably have gotten ashore in good order and made rapid progress inland. As it was, Stopford had installed himself on the sloop H.M.S. *Jonquil*, which had almost no communication equipment aboard; and on the night of the landing (August 6-7) was fast asleep on deck while the wildest confusion prevailed at lower command levels. (He stayed on the *Jonquil* until the evening of the eighth.) On August 7, with the usual false starts, changes in orders, and uncertainties as to who should be going where, 20,000 men struggled onto the beach where they were "bunched around . . . under a persistent but hardly serious fire. 'I was struck by the restfulness of all around,' an artillery officer wrote in his diary. 'There appeared to be little going on, a good many infantrymen sitting about or having a bathe' . . .†

---

* Stopford's appointment was one of the innumerable military puzzles of the day. He had been right-hand man to a disastrous General Buller in the Boer War, had come home when his chief was relieved, and had lived in retirement since 1909. Stopford himself had never led troops in the field.

† Many writers, including I believe Major Willmer, have commented on this remarkable scene, in which, during a crucial invasion aimed at isolating

The Turks lurked in the scrub and sniped. Here and there a small group of British troops would set off in the general direction of the foothills, falter, and disappear into the scrub. Willmer reported to [General Liman] von Sanders that the British . . . moved 'bolt upright as if on parade,' bunched together, and 'made no use of the available cover.' It was mainly because of this that the British suffered more casualties on August 7th than the total Turk force . . . Attacks were ordered and countermanded at the last moment. It was not until dusk that the British started . . . a belated and hesitant move forward and succeeded in capturing Chocolate Hill and Green Hill just as darkness was falling."[52]

Meanwhile, at Anzac and in the Krithia–Achi Baba sector—the other two principal theaters—savage fights were in progress, their commanders (like Hooker and Sumner in 1862) presumably awaiting good news from their distant left wing. It never came. Throughout August 7 and most of the eighth, Stopford had little to report. Finally at 6:00 P.M. on the eighth Hamilton went ashore at Suvla to look into the situation himself. He was appalled to find that almost none of the surrounding heights, except the ones just mentioned and Scimitar Hill, had been occupied. In particular the commanding ridge of Tepe Tekke remained empty, and being to the north and east was a likely position to be taken up by Turkish reinforcements which were then marching to the relief of Suvla at top speed. Hamilton seems to have assumed they had already gotten there; and in order to mount a proper attack on the (still vacant) position, he took charge personally, pulling back advance units from other strong points in order to regroup them during the night. The consequence was that he gave up valuable ground for the sake of a reorganization which cost hours and if anything increased the confusion it was intended to correct.

Turkish troops under command of Mustafa Kemal Pasha had meanwhile gained the position Hamilton thought they already held. On the night of the eighth Kemal moved his men onto Tepe Tekke and another contingent to a line near Scimitar Hill, one of the positions Hamilton's "reorganization" had apparently left open to him. The outcome the next morning was foreseeable and

---

the main Turkish armies on the peninsula, hundreds of British soldiers were taking time out for a swim, much as if they were on a Boy Scout overnight.

in every sense climactic—for Hamilton, for the Suvla landings, for the whole campaign. As James says: "If [the British] had been on the summit of Tepe Tekke or advancing to a proper plan up the lower foothills, the tumultuous charge planned by Kemal might have resulted in an overwhelming Turk defeat. As it was the charge caught the 32nd Brigade at its most vulnerable, spread out on the steepest part of the hill, tired and bewildered. A party of East Yorkshires which had almost reached the summit before being overwhelmed was annihilated . . . At about 6 A.M. the line broke 'like a crowd streaming away from a football match,' as an officer wrote in his diary."[53]

Sir Ian himself wrote: "My heart has grown tough amidst the struggles of the Peninsula, but the misery of this scene well-nigh broke it."[53] It was the end of his military career. By a margin of only a few hours, the Turks had gained the position and the initiative which he should have held, had crumpled up the entire left wing of his army at Suvla, and by these actions had thwarted the purpose of the actions then being fought, with much valor and pointless loss, by the troops at Anzac and in the Cape Helles sector. Ironically, on the day before Hamilton's last battle,* "unknown to anyone, an officer and a signaller of the 6th East Yorkshire Regiment had climbed almost to the top of Tepe Tekke and found it unoccupied. This momentous report, like so many others, went astray, and Hamilton himself did not learn of it until 1923"[54] —which was rather late, even for that general.

In October Hamilton was relieved by General Sir Charles Monro, an enemy of the Gallipoli adventure and a determined evacuationist who by January of 1916 had skillfully extricated the whole Allied force from the peninsula—this being almost the only successful operation of the campaign. Summarizing the latter, Fuller said: "In all, 410,000 British and 70,000 French soldiers had been landed, of whom 252,000 [52.5 percent] were killed,

---

* It was not quite his last. On August 21-22 he made a desperate effort to recoup the situation by a frontal assault on the positions lately consolidated by the Turks, losing 5000 men out of some 14,000 engaged. The whole action at Suvla Bay—Anzac—Cape Helles involved 50,000 Allied troops, of whom 18,000 were killed, wounded, or missing. It is ironic too that Hamilton's disaster at Suvla resulted from his personal intervention. In November the Allies were hit by still another disaster—a 72-hour blizzard which at Suvla alone caused 5000 cases of frostbite.

wounded, missing, prisoners, died of disease or evacuated sick. The Turkish casualties amounted to 218,000 men of whom 66,000 were killed. The booty left behind was immense. 'It took nearly two years to clean up the ground.' "[55] Today in the forbidding ravines on the peninsula, among the stones and brush, one can still kick up the bones of the men who died there. Next to Haig's disastrous battle at Messines or the interminable struggles for Verdun the following year, Gallipoli perhaps did not amount to much. But for the common soldiers who fought in that distant theater and whose remains, uncommemorated by parks or fields of crosses, lie there yet, it was no less horrible or godforsaken an undertaking. Nor, one imagines, did the survivors of it come away less shaken in certain fundamental beliefs. While it is true that many of the English laboring class—for instance from farm villages such as Akenfield*—went into the service with something like relief, they also appear to have carried with them strongly inculcated and deeply accepted notions about the sanctity of the mother country and the real superiority of their social superiors. Some—though the number was probably overestimated by propagandists at the time—may also have believed in the partisanship of the Lord. Such ideas were among the casualties, and fully as important for the European future as the ghastly losses in men and goods. One has only to read the history of World War I to see the insurgency which has been overtaking us since as quite a logical development.

Gallipoli, like the major campaigns of the war, compares oddly with Wellington's Peninsular Campaign and Waterloo. If one goes by modern standards, which set such store by a university education and proper credentials, Wellington should have had far the worst of it. His officers were not Sandhurst men; many were second sons of titled families whose commissions were bought outright and who learned their profession from their own noncoms, often on the battlefield. At Gallipoli even the numbers engaged were of the same order as those Wellington had handled; but with all the supposed improvements in training and communications which had occurred in the meantime, the results were far less satisfactory. Bad as he was as commander, Hamilton

* Pseudonym for the Suffolk village studied in the book of the same name.

might have been spared much (and his men more) had the field officers to whom he so scrupulously deferred been up to their jobs—had they been, for example, as alert as Wellington's subordinates who on June 16 saw the importance of Quatre Bras and on their own initiative undertook to hold it. It is not only generals of the caliber of the Iron Duke but men such as these who win wars. What had become of them?

In the end victory of sorts came to the Allies, thanks mainly to their advantage in numbers and matériel, but partly also to a British invention, the tank. Although promising, this new weapon was so ineptly used, even in the last great decisive battle (Amiens, 1918, Haig commanding) that it was more psychologically than literally effective.* When tanks were first sent against them *en masse* they seem to have stunned and disheartened the Germans. According to one of his biographers, the Supreme Warlord himself was quite *bouleversé*. ". . . When on the 2nd of September, the English tank-attacks resulted in imminent peril for Germany, the Emperor was so shattered by the news that he fell ill . . . and those around him feared that his excitement and exhaustion might lead to a mental and physical collapse."[56] His less volatile subjects at the fighting front found them almost as upsetting.

"From a mockery the tanks have become a terrible weapon. Armored they come rolling on in long lines, and more than anything else embody for us the horror of war. We do not see the guns that bombard us; the attacking lines of enemy infantry are men like ourselves; but these tanks are machines, their caterpillars run on as endless as the war, they are annihilation, they roll on without feeling into craters and climb up again without stopping . . . invulnerable steel beasts squashing the dead and the wounded—we shrivel up in our thin skin before them, against their colossal weight our arms are sticks of straw, and our hand grenades matches . . ."[57]

In fact, of course, they were highly vulnerable steel beasts, which made four or five miles an hour, provided a poor firing

---

* The plan of the battle was in fact drawn up by General Sir Henry Rawlinson and merely approved by Haig and Foch. At that, it repeated the mistake Haig had made at Cambrai, where the armored attack was too feebly supported—resulting in 45,000 British casualties.

platform and limited visibility to those inside, and were easy targets for the enemy field guns.* At Amiens as much demoralization and probably far more damage were caused by one Whippet tank and a dozen armored cars which broke through the Germans' lines and began shooting them up from behind as the main attack got under way. Even this late in the war, however, the archaic minds in charge of it could not bring themselves to risk a wholly mechanized foray, but tried to combine tanks with cavalry. "As foreseen by the Tank Corps General Staff, this combination proved impossible . . . Because the horsemen moved faster than the Whippets, the latter were left behind during the approach . . . and because the cavalry could not face rifle and machine-gun fire, the Whippets forged ahead during the attack. The result was a continuous shuttle movement in which tanks advanced, cavalry retired, and tanks turned back to bring forward the cavalry . . . Long before dusk [the cavalry] were compelled to retire to water their horses and with them went the Whippets."†[58]

Late in 1918, the whole conflict simply ran down and stopped. It had cost an incredible 8,500,000 lives,‡ brought Tsarist Russia to ruin, begun the undoing of Britain and France's slide into her present insignificance, and in several senses shattered the generation which fought it. As Remarque said, describing himself and his comrades after three years of war: "We are forlorn like children and experienced like old men; we are crude and sorrowful and superficial—I believe we are lost."[59] The same could be said of Scott Fitzgerald's and Evelyn Waugh's world of the twenties, most of whose citizens had never been near Flanders fields. Nor has the psychological climate which sprang up in those days—in the era of Sassoon and Apollinaire and Wilfred Owen—changed greatly since. We too are "crude and sorrowful and superficial" and get small sympathy from our children who are even more

* According to Fuller, tank losses at Amiens and elsewhere regularly ran about 25 percent.[8] Many of these, however, were not total, either for the tank or its crew.

† One wonders if this combination may not have been Haig's idea, a last-minute attempt to vindicate his own views on the value of the horse in modern war.

‡ And an additional 21,000,000 wounded.

so, more forlorn than we and in certain ways cruder and more experienced.

Bad as it was, the settlement of World War I was no more than a confirmation of what everyone already suspected—that their sacrifices had been to no purpose. The men who arranged matters at Versailles—Wilson with his "sermonettes" and his "remarkable capacity for hatred,"[60] the oversupple Lloyd George, the dragon Clemenceau (who reminds one of Clovis I)—appear in varying degrees to have shared the incapacity of the generals and prewar statesmen who had brought them there. It is as though, between them, they had taken Grant's Wilderness Campaign and the Reconstruction as their model.

World War I was decisive not because of what it accomplished, which was little enough, but because it seemed to use up, almost overnight, the last of a moral capital which had taken western man centuries to accumulate. As one writer remarked of the soldiers who fell at Loos: ". . . These men were volunteers. They were the flower of the richest, most powerful nation on earth. Behind them stretched the ordered childhoods of Victorian Britain; decency, regularity, a Christian upbringing, a concept of chivalry; over-riding faith in the inevitable triumph of right over wrong; such notions were imbued in them"[61]—as indeed they were imbued, with characteristic differences, in the French and Germans. As much as it did the lives and property and civil order of the combatants, the war all but wiped out these intangibles. It exacted more devotion and credulity and sheer endurance than was reasonable or decent to expect of men, and did so, moreover, in such bad faith, with such utter indifference to the consequences of its own mismanagement, that more than any event in this century it may be said to have begun the revolutionary collapse of the West. It accomplished what the nineteenth century had barely set out to do; it cut the taproot of idealism, and all that we have seen since was perhaps merely the withering of the tree. Whereas Darwinism had implied the bestiality or further pointlessness of human life, World War I demonstrated it. What had once been no more than a rumor, drifting down from the educated classes, now became the concrete experience of millions.* The result was almost to force

---

* One can say, in the case of mill- or farmhands, it already *was* the concrete experience of millions. For up to World War I, many of the laboring

"ideologies" into being, not only in Russia but in Europe. Men who had never heard of Darwin, who were ignorant even of the rudiments of scientific materialism or who (in the Germany of the thirties) could probably not have absorbed a paragraph of Alfred Rosenberg's "philosophy," were nevertheless quite prepared to accept the ideas underlying Nazism, many of which form the unacknowledged basis of our life today.

It will no doubt sound odd to attribute such vast results to men of the caliber of Joffre and Falkenhayn and General Sir Douglas Haig; but they did their bit, and in view of the numbers they controlled, it was no insubstantial one. As surely as intelligence, stupidity can on occasion move mountains. In this case it was razing one.

PART 3: HITLER AND THE WORLD

Of the Second World War not much need be said except that the Germans had learned the lessons of the First and still lost, while the western allies and Russia had learned little or nothing and still won. It is astonishing, in fact quite unfair, that Germany did lose. She had everything in her favor except brute wealth and numbers, and was strong enough to have offset even that disadvantage had her policies been better worked out and pursued with more tact. It is conceivable that if Bismarck rather than Hitler had ruled the Third Reich, Germany might be the first nation on the Continent today, instead of the divided satellite she is. At the start of World War II she unquestionably had the best army in the world, some of its best (and youngest) generals, an economy superbly organized for war, a thoroughly unified and enthusiastic population, and a backlog of first-rate weapons. Her *Blitzkrieg* had been perfected in Spain and Poland. Her diplomatic *démarches* had kept Europe off balance for nearly a dec-

---

class were almost literally worked to death, it being in part their residual faith and Christian decency which made this sort of exploitation possible. The ghastliness of life in the trenches was still orders of magnitude worse than the worst wage slavery, and for many may have been a sort of apocalypse—the experience by which they were brought finally to see through the whole game. It was this experience which perhaps led (with the help of the Great Depression) to the dissolution of the old class system and to the revolutionary restlessness which has spread through western nations since.

ade, and the morale of the enemies she faced was splendidly low, thanks to the Great Depression in the West and the Moscow Trials and purges in the East. England, as before, was miserably prepared. Our own army was years out of date. The French had holed themselves up in the Maginot Line, largely dispersed their 2500 (excellent) tanks as regimental support weapons, and to no one's surprise were instantly overwhelmed when the German attack began. Their generals were for the most part elderly. Many were veterans of 1914-18 who persisted in the idea of maintaining "the front" weeks after anything resembling a front had ceased to exist. It is usually said that the Depression and the *Front Populaire* had undermined the morale of the French common soldier. A more convincing explanation of the collapse of France may be found in the antiquity of its general staff and the changed nature of war itself. For it is clear that the *Panzer* technique had restored something of the old tempo and fluidity of battle. As when massed knights had ridden out against one another or Hannibal had loosed his elephant corps upon the Romans, combat became volatile once again. The side gaining the psychological upper hand by means of shock might win in minutes. The Germans understood this principle perfectly; the French had apparently dismissed it, along with their notions of *élan*. Defense, they now knew, was supreme. So, like the Carthaginians at Zama, when they found things turning out otherwise—when they saw the enemy who should, by all the rules, have been stopped dead bearing swiftly down upon them—this psychic blow was too much. Added to their faulty tactics and troop dispositions, their wholly inadequate air force, it simply laid them flat.

At this point the Germans all but had the contest won. Their Italian allies did not amount to much but the Japanese were another matter—a power which might, and soon did, draw off a considerable portion of America's strength into a war in the far Pacific. As for the Russians, they seemed to have no notion that the Russo-German peace pact, signed in 1939, was merely the Nazis' way of buying time, of dealing, as Bismarck would have recommended, with their enemies piecemeal. Nor had the Russians profited much by their own disastrous little war against Finland, which had run weeks behind schedule and cost them quite unaccountable casualties. When the Nazi invasion of Russia—called Plan Barbarossa—began in June, 1941, Russian matériel and methods were still sadly behindhand. Their supply lines were thin, their air fields crowded or under construction, the bulk of their tanks and aircraft obsolete, and the disposition of their forces deplorable.

On this last point I was given a curious report by a German friend, an engineer, who at the time Plan Barbarossa went into effect was serving with a mobile reconnaissance unit on the Polish frontier. He told me that in his sector, many miles of which he traversed during the first days' advance, the Russians had only a thin screen of border guards, and behind these, under camouflage netting, enormous amounts of matériel—tanks, field artillery, light armored vehicles—all apparently awaiting the arrival of the army intended to use them.* A few of the tanks, which he looked over during a lull in the advance, were of the latest design—better than the German. Afterwards, on comparing notes with German officers who had been in neighboring sectors on the day the invasion began, he learned that they had found much the same situation in their front. If his and their reports are accurate,† one can only wonder at the line of military reasoning which led the Soviets to make these peculiar arrangements. Possibly the high command or Premier Stalin had reckoned that it was easier to conceal goods than people; with the matériel already in place, it would then be a simple matter to rush in the troops to use it.

---

* On the question of preparedness, tactical as well as material, Alexander Werth reports that Soviet theorists had concluded, from the Spanish War, that tanks should *not* be used in massed formations; that automatic weapons production had been neglected because one Comrade Kulik and certain other commissars doubted their effectiveness (cf. Haig on the machine gun); that still other Soviet military thinkers had dismissed "the *Blitzkrieg* . . . as a lopsided bourgeois theory." Like the French in World War I, the Soviet High Command put its faith in *élan*. The army was simply to fling itself on the invader and rout him. "The question of large forces having to break out of a threatened encirclement was never seriously examined at all."62

As it turned out, the Germans weren't too well prepared either—at least not for the Russian winter—having estimated like Napoleon that the campaign would be over by the time cold weather set in. Their tanks bogged down in the late fall mud and sometimes refused to work at all in the terrible frost which followed. Automatic weapons jammed, men died in hundreds of frostbite, and worst of all, the armies became mired in position warfare, as at Stalingrad, where Hitler, for political reasons, refused to budge.

† I have no reason to suppose they are not and yet I have found nothing quite like them in standard accounts of the war.

The difficulty—if that was indeed the Russians' plan—was that the enemy turned out to be within shorter marching distance than they were of their own heavier weapons. As a soldier's-eye-view of war is necessarily limited, and as Soviet officials have perfected techniques of editing away or burying information which even the Pentagon today can scarcely equal, we will probably never learn just what dispositions had been made on the Russian side by June 22, 1941. The one just described sounds almost too simple-minded to be true; but whatever in fact the arrangements were, they proved disastrously ineffective. During the first weeks—up to the battles around Moscow, from mid-October to December—the Russians sustained fearful losses.*

Then, around Moscow, the tide fell slack and slowly started the other way. It was the Germans whose lines were overextended, who were forced to supply some of their *Panzer* units from the air, whose food and clothing began to be inadequate. Meanwhile, whole new Russian armies were springing up, better weapons were beginning to appear in their ranks; their tactics improved; but most important, a new spirit was taking hold of the nation—one that the Germans themselves had gone to some lengths to inspire. And it is just here, as much as in the sphere of logistics and military strategy, that they made their crucial mistake. It was one which seems to be deep in the grain of modern Germany. The kaiser had personified it with his tough talk—the ferocious fantasies he loved to air in his speeches ("You must know, my men, that you are about to meet a crafty, well-armed, cruel foe. . . . Give no quarter! Take no prisoners!" etc.). Hitler and his people, *arrivistes* to the core, did their predecessors one better. Even at home, they made murder into a heavy industry. Since the Night of the Long Knives in 1934 they had flaunted the brutality of their intentions and, lest anyone doubt them, had backed their rhetoric with quite public action.

It is thus not entirely accurate to say that "these never ending crises generated a violent propaganda against Hitler."[64] It was

---

* For instance, in September the Germans surrounded the armies in the vicinity of Kiev. Of nearly 700,000 Soviet troops, only some 150,000 escaped. On November 6, 1941, Stalin made a speech admitting to losses of 350,000 killed, 378,000 missing, and over a million wounded.[63] In the war as a whole, out of forces totaling about 12.5 million, the Russians are said to have lost an astronomical 7.5 million killed.

not the Jewish-controlled press which aroused sympathy for Loyalist Spain or a fear of Germany in the United States. Hitler, like the kaiser, was his own worst propagandist. The foreign newspapers had only to report what he said and did, and the outlook became plain enough to many readers. While it is possibly true that when Hitler became chancellor "Samuel Untermeyer, a wealthy New York attorney, threw down the challenge," and that in 1937 Bernard Baruch told General George C. Marshall, " 'We are going to lick that fellow . . . He isn't going to get away with it,' "[65] the implied line of reasoning is false. Indeed, it is the line the Germans themselves have consistently used; having by threats and violence stirred up half the world against them, they then maintained that powerful foreign blocs—British traders, international Jewish banking houses, and the like—were conspiring against them. No doubt they were, and with good reason. *Vis-à-vis* the East, the Germans added a refinement, or rather carried over an *idée fixe* from the Middle Ages. They insisted that the Slavs were their biological inferiors, a proper Darwinian prey for such a High Culture as their own. In a certain sense these habits of mind were the essence of the Germans' failure—a type of primal self-indulgence which has gone far toward costing them two wars, if not their national existence. It was this weakness, as much as the difficulties of battle itself, which may have been critical for them in Russia.

Before the war there appears to have been a well-developed Ukrainian separatist movement in the U.S.S.R.; and later one read in the papers of Ukrainian villagers who came out with flowers to greet the German troops. The invaders stamped out such sentiment in short order. By November, with the fall of Moscow seemingly at hand, the country was welded together as it had probably never been. "The Russian people felt the deep *insult* of the German invasion—it was something more deeply *insulting* than anything they had known before. In his sixth of November speech, Stalin had not missed the chance of pointing out the difference between Napoleon and Hitler; Napoleon had come to a sorry end, but at least he had not brought to the invaded countries any *Untermensch* philosophy."[66] Throughout the Russian campaign, the Germans seldom failed to indulge this weakness for the mortal insult.* "In recapturing numerous towns and many hundreds of villages, Russian soldiers got their first-hand experience of the 'New Order.' Everywhere the Germans had destroyed whatever they could; all but three houses had been burned down at Istra, for instance, where they had also blown up the ancient New Jerusalem Monastery . . . Later, in 1942, I explored some of the towns and villages that had been occupied . . . by the Germans—it was always the same grim story."[67]

In his diary entry for May 27, 1942, Count Ciano, Mussolini's foreign minister, wrote: "Sorrentino on his return from Russia gives his impressions and makes forecasts for the future. The first are not pleasant and the second not comforting. The brutality of the Germans, which has now reached the proportions of a continuing crime, stands out from his words so vividly and so movingly as to make one skeptical . . . Massacres of entire populations, raping, killing of children—all this is a matter of daily occurrence.† Against this is the cold Bolshevik decision to resist and fight to the end . . . On the other hand the morale of the Germans is lower than might be imagined."[68] In part this was doubtless due to quite concrete evidence that nobody loved them —that good Germans were as usual surrounded by ferocious foes bent upon their destruction and beginning in fact to accomplish it. In his May 1 and 2 entries Count Ciano says: "Losses in Rus-

* And their casualty rates—in part due to the rising resolve and desperation of the enemy, as well as to his improving methods—went up accordingly. In France, the Germans had lost 156,000 men including 30,000 killed. Alexander Werth gives these cumulative totals (from General Halder's diary) for the period June to November, 1941, in Russia:

To July	31	213,000
Aug.	3	242,000
Sept.	30	551,000
Nov.	13	700,000
Nov.	25	734,000
Nov.	28	743,000

Of these, 200,000 men and 8000 officers were killed. The whole German force numbered about 3,200,000. By December 10, 1941, its losses, exclusive of the sick, were, by another account, 775,078 men, or just under 25 percent.[66]

† How far these events seem from the day when the Prussian soldiers held their fire to salute the brave Gallifet and his troopers at Sedan; or even from the sad, workmanlike *Wehrmacht* men of Remarque's time, who were nauseated by the slaughter of the British at Loos and stopped shooting when the remnants of Haig's force began to retire.

sia are heavy; Ribbentrop says two hundred and seventy thousand dead . . . British aviation is striking hard. Rostock and
Lübeck have been razed to the ground. Cologne has been heavily
hit. The Germans react and strike back at the English cities but
with less violence. Which only partly consoles the German population, accustomed as it has always been to dish it out but never to
take it. Which leads many of them, who have devastated half of
Europe, to weep about 'the brutality of the English, who make
many innocent Prussian families homeless.' The worst of it is that
they really feel this way."[69]

I am aware that this view of the war, even when expressed by
those who fought on the other side, is no longer fashionable. Nor
would I wish to suggest that brutality on the battlefield was in
any way peculiar to the Germans. War *is* brutal. The training for
it systematically undoes what centuries of civilized life have
sought to build up in us; while warfare itself may—as the *Freikorps* movement in Germany clearly showed—deform men morally for life. Incidentally, Robert Graves has reported that in
World War I the British and their colonial troops often murdered prisoners and made "a boast, not a confession" of the
fact.[70] In World War II the Allied bombing of German cities, the
American practice of not taking prisoners during island fighting in
the Pacific, and the Russian excesses committed during the
counterinvasion of Germany, are often mentioned as showing
that where brutality is concerned, we are all pretty much alike.
On the evidence I am not quite convinced that that is so; nor can
one, I think, separate the Germans' domestic from their military
policy and so conclude that the death camps and torture centers
maintained by the SS were a special case, quite apart from the
Wehrmacht, the régime, and the millions who, with apparent
enthusiasm,* supported the whole enterprise. Granted that in
warfare all parties may and usually do commit atrocities, it still
remains true that the Germans pioneered in industrial methods of
extermination. They were the first to build factories for that purpose, to deport the living *en masse* and process them, in certain
installations, not merely into bones and ash but into usable byproducts (soap, leather, reclaimed gold from teeth, etc.). Such

* And no organized resistance except in the *Wehrmacht* itself.

methods certainly rate special mention if only because they contributed materially to the defeat and death of those who invented them.

Perhaps the chief difference between Nazi Germany and its contemporaries lay in the former's thoroughness and want of hypocrisy. The Germans simply took to a logical conclusion what everyone else was doing. Instead of looking the other way, as we did, they faced up to it, systematized their inhumanity, and earned the world's horror and condemnation as a result. The chief result, however, was not moral, it was practical. By the sheer power of the dread they inspired, they drove natural enemies—Russia and the democracies—into a formidable alliance against them; and instead of the single-front war they had wanted, ended up fighting on three.

As the Germans waged it, total war very soon became impossible to win, not only because they would not limit their objectives but even more because they could not keep their mouths shut or restrain themselves from kicking a fallen enemy and so driving him to get up again. If you plan to conquer the world, it is idiotic to announce the fact years in advance. If you mean to defeat just one nation, the politic thing is not to hasten its coalescence against you by gratuitous frightfulness but to practice, where possible, a deceptive lenience and generosity. Much as they seem to pride themselves on their craftiness, the masters of German policy in this century have shown no real gift for stealth and still less for public relations.* The consequence, in Russia in 1941, was to compound the odds against them so rapidly that their first thrusts—which very nearly succeeded—were turned back, and with that, the war was lost. All that followed—Stalingrad, the Normandy invasion, the fall of the Reich itself—was no more than a bloody afterpiece. Hitler has often been blamed for

---

* As an example of the extent to which the policy of frightfulness can misfire, it appears that the German outrages in Poland caused the beginnings of a rift even with their Italian allies. On December 4, 1939, Ciano wrote: "I showed the Duce the report of an Italian . . . the only foreigner permitted to live in Posen . . . With a simplicity which accentuates the horror of the facts, he describes all that the Germans are doing; unmentionable atrocities without reason. The Duce himself was indignant; he advised me to see to it that by indirect channels the American and French newspapers get the contents of the report. The world must know."[71]

interfering with his generals, most notably at Stalingrad. In fact, as the campaign in France showed, he was not lacking in military ability.[72] His deficiency was if anything more deep-seated. He entirely lacked Bismarck's understanding of the principle that in a world of near-equals, unbridled violence and unlimited objectives simply won't do. Particularly if one also telegraphs the punch, such a policy amounts to suicide. The supreme form of bad generalship, one might say, is to have every advantage in one's hands—the world's best army, not a few of its best generals, and enemies, such as Russia and the democracies, whose interests naturally diverge—and then through pure arrogance, through actions which are mere wasteful display or wanton provocation, to blow the whole game. Hitler did so, and those of us, of my generation, who lived through that hideous era, find it amazing that there are schoolchildren today who know scarcely anything about him.

He cost his own people three and a half million lives and his enemies better than twice that number. Compared even to World War I, the indirect costs of this one were past calculating. The inclination to write off Hitler as a gangster and a buffoon, as some did in the thirties, is understandable but still a mistake. It is too easily forgotten that The Leader's speeches, from the first, evoked a vast response. To have heard him—as I did, by short-wave radio, at the time of the Sudeten crisis, in 1938,—addressing the masses of the faithful was an experience hard to describe and impossible to forget. One felt between him and his millions a profound eerie accord; they picked up his animal note and answered it, and it was suddenly as though the Party's Wotan nonsense, the fantasy of a great Return, were coming true. One seemed, for an instant, to be back in the wilderness of ancient Europe, surrounded by strange night cries and movements in the darkness. It was hard to escape the impression that, since Bismarck's time, Germany had somehow become fascinated with this image of herself as The Beast and of the world as her prey, Hitler merely being a purer expression of it than the kaiser had been, and therefore infinitely more dangerous. The sound of his voice and of those massed answering voices had no equal even in the great gatherings in Red Square. Heard from thousands of miles away, by continually fading and crackling wireless, they made the hair stand up on the back of one's neck. Such a man needed no hostile press abroad to rally the world against him. He spoke as clearly to us as to his own, and each responded in his fashion. He was, as William Shirer put it, a kind of genius; but more than that, he was an embodiment. He stood for something which millions apparently felt had to be done, and for a kind of inner destruction which had to be taken to its conclusion. Behind the physical outrages—the systematic murder and torture and debasement of men, Germans included—there lay, as Albert Camus said, a metaphysical one. It was as if the Nazis and their people were possessed by an insane resolve to finish all that World War I had left undone—not merely the conquests but the annihilation of what remained of man's decency and of his hopes for himself. In the practical enterprise they failed; in the metaphysical they may not have done so. Such heroic undertakings should not be let slip from public view, especially in an age which may have been more victimized by them than it knows. As a military statesman, Hitler, like Philip II, was born too soon. Only the Bomb, if either one had got it in time, would have made his policies workable.

CHAPTER X

Johnson vs. the Eastern Intellectuals

The chief thing to be said of the era we have entered since 1945 is that now everyone* has the Bomb and no one's policy is workable. Every move in international affairs, including those of remote "client" nations, carries with it a finite risk not simply of failure but of a general obliteration. As the *ultima ratio* of high policy, the Bomb can cancel history and is the only force since the Black Death which has seemed both able and likely to do so. The reason, as I have been at some pains to suggest, is that in warfare from Crassus' day to our own, essentially nothing has changed but techniques of killing.

Despite two world wars—or possibly just because of them—we try to convince ourselves that in modern nations, democracies in particular, a humane enlightenment is gradually displacing the brutality and passionate shortsightedness of former times. In fact, although often from quite inhuman motives,† governments today *do* take a greater interest than they once did in the welfare of their citizens; their concern for the welfare of the world can still hardly be said to exist. The world, by and large, is the Enemy. Because of the intensity of men's urge to survive and their primitive aversion to the alien or radically unfamiliar, foreign policies

---

* Everyone of consequence, that is.

† Related, for instance, to military efficiency or international competition, as in the case of our own educational reforms stimulated by Sputnik.

are seldom generous or really enlightened but more often of a violent, almost senseless cruelty which, if practiced at home, would precipitate mass uprisings. (Imagine, for example, what the result might have been had President Johnson tried to keep order in the United States by anything approaching the methods he and his generals were using to "pacify" Vietnam in the late 1960s. As it was, the crudely stage-managed Chicago Convention of 1968 produced a tremendous outcry here. A Vietnamese observer, contrasting the Johnson-Daley tactics on that occasion with what was going on in his own country, with the help of half a million Americans, might well have wondered what all the shouting was about.)

It is, perhaps, largely to the instinctive xenophobia of the average man, his tendency to treat nonmembers of his own tribe as nonpeople, that we owe the predicament which in this account I have so often mentioned. The argument in defense of rulers like Mussolini was that "they made the trains run on time"; the real argument in their favor was that while they did unspeakable things, it was all supposedly for the future security and grandeur of the nation. It is *this* argument—really an appeal to tribalism—which gave them the consensus they needed in the first place.

Once he has gotten a secure hold on the machinery of government, a dictator can obviously afford a degree of brutality toward his own people which an elected leader cannot. To suppress dissent—i.e., to jail or murder those few whose thought processes occasionally elude tribal control—he arouses among his own people an internecine savagery which more civilized governments vent chiefly on their neighbors. Democracies, except during periods of extreme national emergency, do not generally permit such license. A leader like Lyndon Johnson must be liberal at home roughly in proportion as he is repressive elsewhere, and soft-spoken in public however coarse and domineering he may be in private. He must persuade The Folks that he loves them and is one of them, a Little Guy tapped by fate for the Big Job and deeply aware of its responsibilities. He must periodically appear in the media, giving an account of the current domestic situation or of the nation's undertakings abroad. If in the latter case he has only failure to report, it is all the more important that the moral aspects of the enterprise be stressed. And the more burdensome a war becomes, the more must he keep the public purse open for welfare projects as well as for the military, even if the popular assent thus bought today mean inflation and bankruptcy tomorrow. It is not an easy role—very far indeed from the straightforward abuse of power enjoyed by rulers such as Philip II.

Another distinguishing feature of modern times, in both democracies and dictatorships, is that the lord who once ruled the realm and led its armies is now split into two persons or several —namely, the head of state or titular commander in chief, and his chiefs of staff who represent the military apparatus he now only indirectly controls. What these two classes have in common is that, like the lords of old, neither is directly concerned with work, which is not, of course, the same as saying that they are lazy. Both may be indefatigable but neither works in the sense in which most of us understand the word. Essentially the politician seeks, by talking and maneuvering, to put himself in the way of profiting from the work of others, skimming off a certain, usually sizable, share of their take in order to pay for enterprises he hopes will cover the nation and himself with glory. The professional military man, while having to do some talking and maneuvering with a view to his further promotion, is basically an administrator and part-time lobbyist. The politician asks to be excused from the ordinary drudgery of life on the promise that if given power he will benefit the realm out of all proportion to whatever he may cost it; the soldier asks to be excused on the promise that he will undertake its defense or aggrandizement whenever commanded to do so. By nature he is perhaps the more simple and earthy, but he too has become subject to a form of Natural Selection* which acts to keep him in some small degree abreast of his times. Of the two, his career is still the more manly, closer to nature. In fact the successful officer can look forward to a nicely variegated life—

---

* Just as democratic leaders are elected or revolutionary ones cast up by a general scramble for power, so the modern knight class is no longer hereditary. In each generation it renews itself by passing through the military university system and on into the world of service politicking and actual war, with the corollary that of course the larger it grows, the more essential war, as its professional *raison d'être*, becomes. Any officer corps, as we are beginning to see, is by definition a lobby. Even Eisenhower, who did much to promote that state of affairs, was alive to its dangers—as his last speech, about the "military-industrial complex," showed.

combat and adventure in his youth, comfort, corporate appointments, and a clubman's life in his declining years.

To these classes should be added a third—that caste of gray eminences* whom science and modern industry have combined to create—men often with one foot still in academia and a grounding in nuclear physics, economics, Sinology, or more exotic disciplines such as general-systems theory or political science. The function of these people, as nearly as an outsider can guess it, is to advise their superiors as to the possible—to calculate the effects of underwater or stratospheric nuclear explosions, to pass on the feasibility of disease-spreading techniques, crop poisoning, genocide via teratogenic or nerve-destroying aerosols, annihilation of cities thousands of miles distant by missile attack, and similar projects. The political scientists presumably offer their opinion as to the "psychology" and other features of nations it is felt desirable to do something about. And these are followed, in the field, by psychological warfare specialists who write the leaflets to be air-dropped on illiterate peasants. Finally, at places like the RAND Corporation, young mathematicians set up complicated war games on computers, in which all sorts of logistical, demographic, economic, and other data are appropriately weighted and stirred together to give predictions as to how this or that move will turn out. (What general-systems theorists do I have never been able to discover.) Below all these is a vast army of specialists—programmers, guidance-systems men, bomb designers, and the like—whom we need not consider here since they have skills but no power.

In America, this complicated apparatus began to grow up first under the stimulus of the Depression (Technocracy, General Hugh Johnson, WPA, etc.) and second in response to the Axis

---

* In fact they are often quite rosy and cheerful eminences. In view of the earnings and privileges many scientists have enjoyed since the coming of the Bomb, these signs of high morale are only to be expected. Nor have they much diminished. A report in the Sunday *New York Times* (September 13, 1970, p. 74) begins: "Despite a seeming disenchantment among the young with the so-called 'military-industrial complex,' the Defense Department is attracting younger and better qualified civilian scientists and engineers than ever before . . . 'We are having no trouble recruiting fine, serious young men who want to contribute to their nation's defense,' said one of the heads of a naval weapons laboratory . . ." which is probably especially true now that funds for nonmilitary research have suffered such a cut.

powers and World War II (OPA, Special Services, AEC, etc.). In the middle 1930s we had an army some twenty times larger than the Union forces at the time of Sumter* but still tiny compared to what it would be in another decade. As the war had the effect of turning Russia and ourselves into major military powers with millions of men more or less permanently under arms; and as a paranoid hostility on both sides, capitalist and Communist, had been inculcated in our respective peoples with great energy (and no great difficulty) since the 1920s, the next phase in world affairs was quite foreseeable. So too was the "equalizing" of strength among the great powers as a result of the spread of nuclear "know-how" and missile capability.† With this development, of course, arrangements for "defense" ceased to have their old meaning and became a sort of suicide pact, involving not only the principals but those second-class powers unfortunate enough to lie in the probable path of fallout. In effect the northern hemisphere now lives under a suspended death sentence; and if the build-up of nuclear arms continues, the survivors of the next world war may amount to no more than a few remote en-

---

* Which Sherman in his memoirs put at 13,000 men.[1] Today (in 1969) we have close to 500,000 men in Vietnam alone, a peacetime draft providing us with large standing forces apart from these, and perhaps the largest arsenal of nuclear and conventional weapons in the world.

† The word should be "pyramiding," not "equalizing." In a recent article in *Science*, Herbert F. York, a physicist and dean of Graduate Studies at the University of California, San Diego, recapitulates testimony he gave before the U.S. Senate Foreign Relations Committee. The essence of his report was that by the mid-sixties the Khrushchev government had perfected, or said it had, an ABM defense system. "As a result we decided to deploy MIRV as the one certain means of assuring penetration of Soviet defenses . . . Using figures generated by the Senate Foreign Relations Committee, we see that the result of the U.S. reaction will be a net increase of around 5000 in the number of warheads aimed at Russia. If every one [of the supposed Soviet ABMs] were effective, they could cope with just 70 of those additional 5000 warheads . . . But that's not the whole story. The Soviets have proceeded with a multiple warhead development of their own." It's behind ours, York says, but will probably catch up. These events transcend the whole problem of bad generalship, even as practiced by Philip II, since they mean that the fate of the world may hang on a few electronic mistakes. A garbled message passing between two top statesmen, a battery of radar scopes incorrectly read, and the deluge could be upon us, à la Dr. Strangelove. But however it happens, whether through error or by intent, a "first strike" which fails to wipe out the enemy will provoke an exchange whose effect could well be to make the northern hemisphere uninhabitable.

claves such as the gentle Tiwi, who have the good luck to live on an island off the southern coast of Australia.

While that outcome might not be altogether bad for the future of mankind (if it is to have any), the astonishing fact is that the behavior of statesmen has in no obvious way been altered by our new prospects. For fear, no doubt, that a sensible discretion might be misunderstood, we in America have become *more* aggressively anticommunist than we were before World War II, and the Communists for their part have become more expansionist and anti-American. It took remarkable courage, if that is the word, to begin setting up missile bases in Cuba directed against the United States, as Khrushchev did in the early sixties. It was equally courageous for the indefatigable John Foster Dulles to have embarked on a policy of "massive retaliation" and "brinkmanship," roughly from 1954 onwards. And for the United States to begin injecting itself into Indochinese affairs at least a year before the French débâcle at Dien Bien Phu was bravery almost to the point of foolhardiness.* It ended by involving us in a war which we could not hope to win; which has made a reconciliation with any of our real enemies next to impossible; and which far from being the superb tactical exercise Westmoreland considered it,† has shown our remarkable lack of military and political inventiveness and so made us not only odious in the eyes of the world but, what is worse, ridiculous. Since 1965 we have increasingly risked a general (nuclear) war—indeed, invited it, by taking up increasingly exposed positions in the Orient—with nothing to show for our daring but a small nation brutally disfigured, a

---

* By one report, the CIA as far back as 1953 showed an active interest in Mr. Ngo Dinh Diem, who was then living in exile. The same report adds: "This new information makes a monkey of the Johnson Administration's claim that we have come to the aid of our allies in Vietnam. In reality we have come to the aid of our . . . puppets." (*New York Times*, February 12, 1968, p. 9.) During the Korean war we naturally had an interest in seeing that the French did not totally collapse, since their presence on the Chinese border tied down some Maoist troops and threatened the Chinese with a two-front war.

† His biographer, E. B. Furgurson, quotes the general as saying he bet the Russians envied the splendid opportunity we had been given in Vietnam for trying out new ideas and perfecting our tactics. There is no question that our experience there has been instructive. Whether any other high command envies it is another matter.

vast tax bill, inflation, disorders and restlessness at home, and an irretrievably damaged "image" almost everywhere.

If the politics of our entry into Vietnam appear unbalanced, what can one say of our military conduct there? Yet the odd thing is that William Westmoreland is not a bad general—at least not in the classic style of Burnside and de Wimpffen. In his first action, in World War II, as a commander of artillery, he proved to be a brisk, resourceful professional. By one account the forced march of Westmoreland's 155s to the Kasserine Pass played a decisive part in bluffing Rommel to a standstill, which in turn led to the Germans' defeat and the fall of Bizerte.[2] With that the Allies were free to turn against Italy. In these actions and later ones, "Westy" seems to have been very much a soldier's soldier. Like Sherman, he made forward reconnaissances in person, often going up with his air spotters to pinpoint a difficult target or to plan his fire tactics from direct observation. He repeatedly exposed himself to danger. Once, in Italy, his jeep struck a mine and had a front wheel blown off. As a commander he was quick to find means of meeting new situations. When his batteries in Africa kicked up enough dust to disclose his position to the enemy, he had the ground around them covered with tarpaulins. When some German bunkers near Bizerte proved impervious to conventional artillery fire (partly because they were beyond the range permitted by the 155s time fuses) he devised a "no-fuse" technique, firing his shells with a maximum-range propellant charge and allowing them to explode by impact. Subsequently he worked out a method of zeroing in quickly on German rocket launchers or *Nebelwerfers*. And recognizing the importance of speed in modern war, he invented "what he called a 'blitz formation' for traveling light in a pursuit situation."[3]

Besides the battle at the Kasserine Pass, he fought in other key engagements, notably the famous Remagen Bridge action on the Rhine. Later he transferred to an airborne unit (he had wanted to be an aviator but failed his Air Force physical) and made numbers of jumps with his men. He appears at all times to have been dedicated to his work, self-possessed, quick-acting, ambitious (but not inclined to pushiness or personal rivalries), attentive to his men's state of mind and their needs, personable to those both above and below him in rank, and altogether the sort of officer who not only should earn quick promotion but had every likelihood of doing so. At forty-two, with the blessing of General Maxwell Taylor, he became the youngest major general in the service. When he was made forty-fifth superintendent at West Point (he was then forty-six), only one officer, Douglas MacArthur, had come to the job at an earlier age.[4]

Whether or not he had studied the lives of commanders like Charles XII, it is clear that "Westy" wanted to be an on-the-spot general rather than one of the back-at-headquarters sort. "A chaplain who served with him . . . recalls that 'he was genuinely interested in his men and would make surprise visits to places where the likes of an officer were never seen . . . He was very much concerned with the attitude of the men . . . He knew everyone by name and catalogued in his mind some personal history about him. It became a familiar occurrence to hear him ask "How's your dad's grocery store coming along, Corporal?" or "Are you going to resume postgraduate work when you're back in civilian life, Sergeant?" He was a meticulous dresser, changed uniforms every day, looked as sharp and smart at night as in the morning. He deplored sloppy dress not so much because of its hygienic or aesthetic aspects as because he reasoned it was a manifestation of an indifferent attitude. He would often say that by his dress you can tell if a man has a positive or negative attitude.'"[*5]

No doubt with a view to maintaining his own positive attitude, the general later, during his junkets around Vietnam, sometimes produced "his stock portfolio of newspaper clippings about the war from his briefcase for review in flight."[7] Another, less sympa-

---

[*] Furgurson, from whose book these excerpts are taken, begins his biography of the general with a description of the round of journeys by jet or helicopter which Westmoreland continually made to his various operational theaters in Vietnam. On one occasion a Huey gunship fired off a rocket by mistake, killing a Vietnamese child and wounding three civilians nearby. "Westmoreland's self-control never wavered."

Elsewhere, Furgurson notes that Westmoreland was "always at school," always discovering new methods—if not as an artillerist dispersing his field guns and tying them into a closely functioning unit by a network of telephone lines (as he did once in Africa), then in the subtler field of human and public relations, in which he seems to have reached near-perfection in Vietnam. Furgurson quotes a friend of the general's as saying, "He was fascinated by how to deal with people."[6]

thetic witness, Lieutenant Colonel William R. Corson (U.S. Marines, ret.), describes in some detail the methods which West-moreland and his staff used to inspire a positive attitude in the visiting dignitaries who, in apparently increasing numbers, began flying into Saigon for a closer look at the war. Corson somewhat archly refers to them as "the birds."

"We may not have learned," he says, "to pacify Vietnam, but the efficiency of [the high command's methods in dealing with visitors] is a wonder to behold . . . Depending on the bird's orientation . . . the first dinner and meeting are scheduled for maximum impact. If the bird is a potential critic or is economy-minded [often, I should imagine, the same thing] the dinner and briefings are used as an initial assault to break down his resist-ance . . . The location of the dinner is determined by the bird's rank . . . When the entourage reaches the briefing room a well-oiled mechanism is brought into play. The various staff officers spring to attention and introductions are made. When the bird is seated . . . the overture begins, with General Westmoreland, Ambassador Bunker, Ambassador Komer or the chief of JUSPAO, Barry Zorthian, providing a 'broad overview.'" Humility at the complexity of the problem is quite understandably a major theme. "The briefers are . . . carefully chosen . . . They must project sincerity, assurance, resoluteness, moral fervor, optimism and confidence. . . . Little is said about how this or that is to be done beyond identifying the 'program,' funded at X number of dollars with Y number of people . . . Because many of the birds are smart and tough* and could possibly see through the fancy footwork, the briefing takes place on the first night. Although it is only 9:00 P.M. in Saigon it is 3:00 A.M. in the bird's physiol-ogy."[8] The exhausted bird, Corson says, takes in very little but is too vain to admit it later or too embarrassed to ask for another such elaborate run-through. The next morning, still exhausted, he is rushed off on a skillfully conducted tour of certain battle areas, after which he flies on home.

* Some of the birds in fact are tough enough to treat the whole outing as they might a vacation in Miami. The late Representative Joe Resnick (D., N.Y.) reportedly "chewed out" a Westmoreland aide for not providing his children with their own helicopter service. "You've nearly ruined my entire trip. Now my daughter won't be able to write an article for *Teen Age America!*"[8]

One class of visitors Corson particularly grew to dislike were the "vultures," visiting scientists anxious to learn how their various projects were working out—electronic tracking gadgets, the smell-o-meter (intended to pick up among other things the characteristic odor of *nuoc-mam* or fish-oil sauce, used by most Vietnamese on both sides), defoliation techniques, the DMZ barrier, or "improved napalm." (The smell-o-meter, I have read, was a failure—too broad-spectrum. Napalm, improved or not, apparently works fine, as does defoliation, which besides affecting the countryside for years and perhaps permanently changing its ecology, may also produce birth deformities and cancer in the human population of heavily sprayed areas.) Corson has an even lower opinion of "think-tank" people who have used the war to float what, in scientific circles, are known as Mickey Mouse research projects. Since 1965 numbers of behavioral scientists have evidently turned up to make on-the-spot studies of available Vietnamese,* using the same cagey-crude methods of questioning which have endeared them to Polynesian islanders, the Navajo, and other indigenous peoples across the world. "Captive subjects for their . . . studies are readily made available by the smiling GVN liaison officer—at a price, of course—in much the same way Central Casting locates 'typical' Indians for a western . . . Some willing Vietnamese have been the subject of so many studies that they are able to prompt their questioners . . . One young student at the university of Saigon has been a 'Vietcong cadre,' a 'peasant farmer,' an 'officer in the ARVN,' an 'RF soldier,' a 'PF soldier,' and a *chieu hoi* in a series of sociological studies."[9]

Colonel Corson reminds us that in February, 1968, shortly after the Tet offensive, "Walt Rostow announced that 'according to captured documents' the Vietcong offensive had failed. Rostow's statement was derived from a 'selective' analysis of captured documents . . . The behavioral scientists that did the analysis . . . for Rostow receive their entire budget from the Department of Defense . . . It is poor business for a non-profit think-tank to come up with an analysis contrary to the interests of their pay-

---

* Corson mentions that these researchers show a strong disinclination to go out into the field, where they might work with the people they most need to know about. Mainly they stay close to Saigon, producing "such 'in depth' studies as the Sexual Repressions of ARVN Widows."[9]

master." He adds that "social and behavioral . . . research, in and about Vietnam, has cost better than $650 million in the past five years"[9]—and that, incidentally, at a time when Lyndon Johnson was announcing to the scientific community in this country that he would like to see a more direct "payoff" from government-supported research in the medical field.*

On the other hand, projects in Vietnam which are not government sponsored and which it is felt may give the war an even seedier "image" than it already has are vigorously, if covertly, discouraged. The Committee of Responsibility, an American group interested in making at least symbolic atonement for the sufferings we have inflicted, has tried to set up a system with private funds by which, for instance, a few of the Vietnamese children whose legs have been shattered by gunfire, or who have been not quite fatally roasted by napalm, can be flown to this country and fitted with prosthetic limbs or patched up by skin grafts. Naturally enough, the group has been ingeniously—at times almost totally—obstructed by the authorities.†[10]

It is of course inevitable, in a guerrilla war fought with modern weapons, that numbers of civilians are going to be caught in the middle. Besides white phosphorus and napalm, the sheer density of fire which we have achieved since World War II makes any attack launched upon irregulars in or near a village likely to wipe out the villagers as well, especially if it involves the "vertical envelopment" technique, calling in bombers or helicopter gunships armed with rockets and cannon. Michael Herr, who spent three months with the marines at Khesanh, describes a variant of this technique in action: "At night you could lie out on . . . sandbags and watch the C-47's mounted with Vulcans doing their work. The C-47 was a standard prop flareship but many of them carried 20 and .762 mm [76.2?] guns in their doors, Mike-

* Which was really, of course, a way of announcing imminent budget cuts, in favor of the more important work then being done overseas. The cuts are still in effect (1970).

† One of the staff of COR told me of a case of a U.S. army doctor in Vietnam who frankly regarded the whole COR program as "Communist" and refused to release a seriously injured child for transport back to the States. The doctor's position was that he would do nothing which might result in publicity adverse to the war effort (and incidentally, to his own career in the service). The child involved was reportedly *in extremis* and likely to die, which from the standpoint of high policy was neither here nor there.

mikes that could fire out three hundred rounds per second [sic], Gatling style. 'A round in every square inch of a football field in less than a minute,' as the handouts said. They used to call it Puff the Magic Dragon, but the Marines . . . named it Spooky."[11] A correspondent for *The New Yorker*, who flew a number of missions in spotter planes in another sector, reports in some detail how a typical aerial search-and-destroy action is apt to go. Through no malign intent on the part of the men—at worst from weariness and a natural aversion to the Vietnamese, friend or enemy, amongst whom they have been cryptically ordered to risk their own lives for weeks or months together—these forays often destroy targets supposed to have been left intact and kill scores of people whom no one can precisely identify as combatants or civilians. The pilots themselves sometimes become haunted by what they are called upon to do, and back at base sing "atrocity" songs which are half satire, half despairing realism, as of men sinking, not without a fight, into the animality officially required of them. One song goes something like this:

> Strafe the town and kill the people
> Drop your napalm in the square
> Get out early in the morning
> Catch them at their Sunday prayer.*

While the majority of U.S. soldiers come to respect the VC as fighters—as in most wars, soldiers salute a brave enemy and have, in the end, more in common with him than with their own military and political brass—the feeling of our troops toward the ARVN seems to be quite unmixed. Another jingle goes:

> Throw candy to the ARVN
> Gather them all around
> And take your twenty mike-mike
> And mow the bastards down!

The feeling is quite natural. The ARVN are after all troops of a puppet régime whose corruption has extended to the wholesale theft of U.S. matériel from the Vietnamese docks or U.S. supply bases (often with some complicity, of course) and the gouging

---

* Which is a considerable distance from the songs (like "Lorena"), or even the jokes, current among our soldiers in the Civil War.

of millions of dollars-for-export from bar-hopping or rent-paying U.S. personnel in Saigon. The stealing of American equipment became so flagrant it was finally reported in our press, while the dollar drain grew to such proportions that in 1968, what with our normal tourist spending abroad and rising imports, we were plunged into an international money crisis.* As the arm of a régime which stands chiefly for the unlimited enrichment of its top officials, the ARVN can hardly be expected to have the highest morale, in particular since the government it represents is not in any sense popular and may one day be abandoned altogether by its foreign sponsors. In that event there is little doubt what would happen; and it is probably this knowledge which makes the South Vietnamese soldier somewhat volatile in combat. In "pacifying" his own people, he and his officers have shown a tendency to looting and out of hand brutality which may be understandable but is hardly good "psychology." In retrospect it is difficult to see why Westmoreland and others ever supposed the strategic-hamlet program and similar reclamation projects might succeed.

Donald Duncan, who served with distinction in the Green Berets into the period overlapping our invasion of Vietnam (in 1965), describes the following action, which involved ARVN troops and a few U.S. "advisers." (The unit has been pinned down by enemy fire from a nearby hamlet; helicopter gunships have silenced most of it, and the allies are now moving in.)

"English and Vietnamese commands mingle with a bugle call, and a ragged line of screaming men are half running toward the trees, shooting wildly. The choppers, rockets unloaded and machine guns empty, turn toward home . . . The tiger-suited line swarms into the treeline . . . Thatched roofs burn on most of the houses . . . The area is an inferno . . . Torn and broken bodies litter the area, their clothes blown off by rocket explosions. A brown leg with a dirty foot lies by a well . . . From a smouldering ruin two soldiers carry a skinny girl of eight or nine, a hand under each arm to keep her frantically flailing feet off the ground;

---

* Financial analysts at the time pointed out that a major factor was the leakage of U.S. dollars from Vietnam into such markets as Hong Kong, where Chinese traders, at a substantial discount rate, were providing dollar exchange to the Red Chinese.

her child voice screams in fear and anger, her matchstick arms try to break free . . . She twists free and scurries on her stem legs . . . toward her baby brother and dead mother. She picks the protesting child from the dirt and blood, and clutches it to her . . . Ignoring the soldiers she walks a short distance and sits down, rocking her little brother and crooning a squeaky song.

"Soldiers ransack the houses that aren't burning, collecting trophies of little value . . . Women, children, and old men dragged from the houses are herded into the center of the village, and as each house yields its last souvenir it is put to the torch . . . An old man dressed in pajama bottoms is dragged forward. An old woman claws at a soldier, a torrent of words pouring from her pink-stained lips . . . A burst from a carbine sits her abruptly in the dust . . . Another woman starts to run back into her burning house and a soldier clubs her with the stock of his carbine; there is a sickening crunch and he kicks her in rage when he finds the wood is broken . . . There is a commotion behind the assembled villagers, who give way as four soldiers drag a young man in black shorts by his feet into the center. His arms are tied behind his back . . . One shoulder is raw as result of the dragging and one leg has been broken below the knee by a bullet.

"The company commander bends over him brandishing his .45 automatic and barking questions. The youth is silent."

The young man is then given the water cure to make him talk. It doesn't work. "One of the soldiers, irritated by the prisoner's stubbornness, gives the broken leg one kick, another. The prisoner—his face twisted . . . with pain, streaming with tears—still refuses to talk."

The natty ARVN executive officer in charge begins to find the delay intolerable. While the villagers continue to look on:

"The little exec whips a knife from his belt and kneels beside the young man, grabbing a handful of hair and yanking up his head. He . . . passes the blade back and forth before the pain-filled eyes. The blade traces a thin line down the bony chest to a point just above the navel. The knife is pressed deep against the bare gut while the question is screeched. Blood around the young man's mouth indicates he has bitten his tongue or through his lip. The question is screeched again—silence. The mustached exec is livid with anger . . . Slowly his weight shifts to his knife arm

. . . the blade disappears into the man as if he were soft butter. A wail of pure agony [bursts from the prisoner] as the blade continues into the ground . . . The senior American NCO turns away . . . 'My God, what's *he* doing?' Mon, the tall Vietnamese platoon leader, straddles the . . . youth and drives a large knife into the bloody gut, extending the opening in one upward slash. The prisoner rises off the ground, rigid and arched from the waist, face distorted, eyes bulging, screaming. Mon's face flashes annoyance and he slams a backhanded fist into the unhuman face, knocking the body flat, and continues his butchering. The body gives a few jerks . . . and is still. Mon shoves his hand [in] and brings out the gall bladder, [holding] his gory trophy overhead for all to see."

The American NCO (apparently Duncan) is staggered, but his lieutenant shuts him up. "Jesus Christ . . . what's wrong with you? We didn't do it, they did. We're not animals, but you have to be practical . . . Hell, man, cheer up; this is a big victory . . . We have a kill ratio of five to one."[12] Within a year or two of this episode American troops were using quite similar "pacification" techniques. Some time, for instance, before the Song My incident became public, I recall reading an account in a popular magazine of an American patrol which raped a woman in a South Vietnamese village and shot up some of the inhabitants, apparently just for the hell of it. War is like that, we say; the brutality threshold goes down; so does it at home. As the German civilians did in the forties, we are becoming inured to our own official violence. Just after the alleged massacre of Vietnamese noncombatants (including children) by our soldiers at Song My, the *Wall Street Journal* made a survey of popular reaction to the incident in this country.* The survey quotes a Chicago lawyer as saying: "Something like this isn't going to change people's views"

* The *Journal* says the survey was "admittedly unscientific." The number interviewed was two hundred men and women "from all walks of life." (*WSJ*, December 1, 1969.)

In a radio editorial delivered January 19, 1970, the manager of station WEEI in Boston reported that a recent Harris Poll showed that a majority of interviewees were for acquittal of the Song My defendants if it could be proved that the massacre had been ordered. From the same or related statistics the editorialist concluded that some 35 percent of the public might be unmoved by the whole affair no matter who had ordered it.

on the war. "Most people interviewed" (the *Journal* adds) "seemed to agree." The translation appears to be: *These things have to be done.*[*] The minority not tough enough to face up to this theorem took the line of denying that it had really been operative. "'I can't believe that a massacre was committed by our boys. It's contrary to everything I've ever learned about America,' says a Lakewood, Ohio, mother of four." One woman felt the press shouldn't carry such stories; "it upsets people." Another refused to think about the war at all: "That's the way I am." A Boston elevator starter was in favor of the implied policy of extermination: "What do they give soldiers bullets for—to put in their pockets?" And finally: "A Cleveland woman says, 'It sounds terrible to say we ought to kill kids but many of our boys being killed over there are just kids too.'" A kid for a kid; it may not make for the best life on earth, or even (in the event of a general war) for any; but it makes a kind of Neanderthal sense. It always has. One must respect it for the ancestral force it is—the tic which our worst statesmen and generals not only share with this lady but owe their own careers to.

Of course civilized habits of mind cannot be stamped out quite as speedily as we would sometimes like. The fact is that even now most of our G.I.s in Vietnam probably do *not* murder the children or rape the women in the villages they pass through. And most army officers, as decent professionals, probably have no wish to see them do so. But just as the enemy has his concept of expediency, which leads him to blackmail villagers into giving him support even though it mean their extermination in a fire fight shortly afterwards, so our people, in a VC-infested area, find themselves obliged to plaster it, the more totally the tougher the resistance they encounter there.

"We never announced a scorched-earth policy; we never an-

---

[*] But not to us, of course; only to the nonpeople of the Other Tribe, which recalls Ciano's remarks in his diary about the savagery of the Germans toward their biological "inferiors" the Slavs, and their remarkable self-pity when it came their turn to be bombed, massacred by invading soldiery, etc. No less indignation would sweep this nation at the prospect of such outrages being committed against us here at home, nor would anyone then stop to think how often (or even whether) we had committed them ourselves. There is, in short, no such thing as thinking in wars; the power of instinct converts thought into something else, mostly the framing of clumsy excuses for doing the unspeakable.

nounced any policy at all, apart from finding and destroying the enemy, and we proceeded in the most obvious way. We used what was at hand, dropping the greatest volume of explosives in the history of warfare over all the terrain within the thirty-mile sector which fanned out from Khesanh. Employing saturation-bombing techniques we delivered more than 110,000 tons of bombs to those hills during the eleven-week containment of Khe-sanh. The smaller foothills were quite literally turned inside out, the steeper of them were made faceless and drawless, and the bigger hills were left with scars and craters of such proportions that an observer from some remote culture might see in them the . . . regularity of religious figures." Elsewhere, Michael Herr speaks of flying over "terrain like moonscapes, cratered and pitted and full of skillful North Vietnamese gunners."[13]

But then expediency creeps closer, involving men in more than long-range mechanical obliteration of the enemy and his coun-tryside. "We interrogate our prisoners in the field" (Jonathan Schell, another correspondent, quotes a G.I. as saying) "and if they don't co-operate that's it . . . Our prisoners are usually peo-ple that we have just picked up in a hamlet that should've been cleared. But there are insufficient facilities for the people in their refugee camps so they come back, and they're automatically considered V.C. Then we give it to them."[14] The line between this approach and plain pillage and massacre is thin, but still a line. He goes on to quote another man: "Those V.C.'s are hard to break . . . One time I seen a real vicious sergeant tie a V.C. up-side down by his feet to the runners of a chopper and drag him three thousand feet in the air* . . . When he came down, hell, he was blabbering. Another time, I seen them get a bunch of V.C.'s in a chopper. They push one out first, and then tell the others that if they don't talk, they'll go out with him. And they talk." The line is now getting thinner. The same man (Schell calls him Sproul, a private from Texas) summarizes the situation this way: "No one has any feelings for the Vietnamese . . . They're lost. The trouble is no one sees the Vietnamese as people. They're not people. Therefore it doesn't matter what you do to them." Later Sproul adds: "Maybe when I go home I'll just crawl

---

* A technique pioneered by the French in the early 1950s.

back inside myself and not say a word . . . Things are so bad nobody would believe it"; and Schell himself goes on to say, "The remark 'They wouldn't believe it back home' was one that I heard almost every day in Quang Ngai, from the many who supported the war as well as from the minority who did not."[*15] The line is almost gone.

Schell's report, like Herr's and innumerable others, describes the incredible systematic devastation of the countryside—in this case in the mountains and on the coastal plain around Quang Ngai, which is on Route 1 several hundred miles north of Saigon. Flying at 1500 feet in Forward Air Control planes on daily missions (in August of 1967), he estimated "that seventy per cent of the villages in the province" had been destroyed. He details with some care how he arrived at this figure and what the ruined villages looked like. Almost the only area intact consisted of a string of settlements "standing in a long belt of few kilometres wide bordering Route 1, a partly paved two-lane road running the full length of the coastal strip."[16] Elsewhere little remained standing and it was seemingly just a question of time before that too would be laid flat. The open country was the same moonscape that Herr saw around Khesanh—shell craters, napalm-blackened fields, mountain sides defoliated, pitted, burned bare. In this sector (probably among many others) leaflets composed by our psychological warfare teams were dropped on the illiterate inhabitants—a system presently superseded by having planes equipped with loudspeakers fly over and address them (no doubt in English), apparently without the slightest effect. Sometimes the surviving villagers were "extracted" for settlement in some government camp while the remains of their dwellings were razed. In other cases they were simply let alone until caught in the crossfire of some passing engagement, or else punished by reprisal bombings for suspected (and probably enforced) collaboration with the VC. Artillery fire was much used around

---

* Earlier in the same article he reports: "In conversations . . . I found very little hatred for the enemy expressed. More often I heard expressions of respect, especially when the enemy was compared to the Vietnamese we were supporting and working with." Small wonder the Thieu-Ky government and the ARVN are a nervous lot. It takes something like a genius for mismanagement to have your allies detest you more than they do the common enemy.

Quang Ngai, sometimes pinpointed as called for from the field, sometimes on an areal or saturation basis. "Just as often," an officer explained, "they'll give us a block five or ten kilometres on a side. At one time or another we've had these blocks just about everywhere in the district." Certain blocks were put as it were on the artillery's open-season list, making them subject to continual h. and i. (harassment and interdiction) fire—a restriction of an earlier policy which had made virtually the whole area a "free-fire zone." In addition, "ground troops could call for artillery fire at any time and these requests were given the highest priority." Further along, Schell tells us: "In . . . three and a half months . . . the batteries at Duc Pho alone had fired 64,044 shells into the populated flatlands" nearby, a figure which he says "does not include shells fired by the Navy from the South China Sea, or shells fired from batteries taken out into the field to supply direct support to operations."[17] It is not surprising that the plan for Pacification and Revolutionary Development for 1967 neglected to include Quang Ngai; it might have been swamped, simply by the homeless; or later still have found no takers at all.*

For besides routine destruction by high explosives, there were the patrols and assault parties which combed the area. "The rule is that you have to send Psy War planes over a village before you hit it," a man told Schell, "unless you get fire, and then you can hit it right away . . . Of course every once in a while the guys on the ground might burn a couple of hootches [huts] that they wasn't supposed to, but that happens everywhere . . . When they've been out in the field awhile, they get a little short-tempered if you know what I mean. You can hardly blame them. This is the toughest war we ever fought . . . You just don't know who's with you and who's against you." The ARVN are more realistic; they know *everyone's* against them. "General Hoang Xuan Lam, the Commander of the I Corps, came down to look at these districts, and when he saw how the place was torn up, he just said, 'Good, good! they are all V.C. Kill them!' "[19]

Quite understandably the same spirit seems to have been de-

---

* One of Schell's interviewees in the field put it this way: "When I got here, some of the villages were wiped out, but quite a lot were still there . . . Then every time I went out there were a few less, and now the whole place is wiped out."[18]

veloping among noncombatants exposed to these methods. ". . . The reprisals against the villages had impelled a number of women, old people and children to take up arms against our troops. Many Vietnamese of the district threw their lives away in desperate impossible attacks on our troops—attacks that were apparently motivated by pure rage. I heard one officer tell wonderingly of two old men who had rushed a tank column, carrying only rifles. 'That's when I stopped worrying about shooting old men,' he added. A G.I. told me he had discovered an old woman trying—and failing—to fire a machine-gun at his unit while two small children attempted to guide the ammunition belt . . . In the mountain valleys, there had been several cases of attacks with bows and arrows."[20] Now there is no line; anyone is the enemy and anything goes. The woman walking toward you with her children may have a grenade under her rags of clothes. Why shouldn't she, given the lunatic destruction she has probably seen, the killing of the few people she knew, the loss of everything that was her world? Why shouldn't you kill her in self-defense—just on the chance that she might get you first? Why not? Play it safe. People at home wouldn't believe . . . But hell, it isn't your show. You didn't *ask* to be here. Fuck it. Shoot.

As for our allies, and the general management of the war behind the lines, a G.I. wrote to a friend in Idaho: "Hello from Vietnam. I'm presently about [deleted] miles from the border between North and South Vietnam . . . I am newly assigned to [a South Vietnamese armored unit] . . . I went on a couple of operations with them last week . . . They moved and shot very well . . . However this excellent state of morale and training of these particular troops is the exception rather than the rule . . . Christ, I've never been so disillusioned with our country after my experiences over here." (Here he describes how newsmen pose shots supposedly taken in action.) "However most of my disillusionment comes from the sorry . . . attitude of the Vietnamese people. Especially the educated leaders of this country are so rotten—dirty no-good thieves. They are Communist-haters but all have fat bank accounts in foreign banks. They deposit every month several times their salary in these bank accounts outside the country. In this one area—where I was adviser to the [deleted] and also adviser in psychological warfare—the U.S. government (through Vietnamese channels) was paying salaries to 338 cadres. The cadres were supposed to be pacifying an area five villages in size. However there were only about 50-60 cadres working in the area. So this meant a group of about three minor government officials (Vietnamese) were stealing $4000 per month. I reported this but nothing was done. I raised so much [flak] about it that they transferred me out to a straight combat unit. At the same time this was going on, the Vietnamese reports were very rosy and you would believe the war was almost won. They said that we distributed some 4 million pills and treated several thousand villagers when we had no medicine at all—it had disappeared before it reached us—more likely sold in the big cities. They said my battalion [250 men] killed or captured 175 Viet Cong. However I have seen only two bodies and about eight prisoners in all of our actions. Even accounting for the ones dragged away after they're dead by the Viet Cong, I think we killed only 21. However we lost 50 of our men killed and 35 wounded and 16 captured. I personally saw and helped carry out 25 of our own dead—but they report we lost about 12. But these false paper reports satisfy Washington. The emphasis is not on what we are accomplishing and what actual progress is being made. Rather if you put down on paper that progress is being made it is sufficient . . . I have been trying to analyze this corrupt and inefficient plan for winning the war . . . I think it boils down to this. We have committed ourselves . . . and will put into this country as much as it takes to win. However the money is given to the Vietnamese officials . . . They are on the gravy train . . . and intend to stay on it . . . The longer the war lasts the more money they can steal . . . The Vietnamese people themselves—the merchants, farmers, etc.—do not appreciate what we are trying to do for them. The restaurants and shops have two prices, one for the Vietnamese and one for the American soldiers . . . A G.I. who spends 60 days living in a foxhole . . . like an animal cannot just refuse to pay . . . The other day a friend of mine, Captain [deleted], was killed in a Viet Cong ambush . . . The Vietnamese soldiers who were with him managed to fight off the Viet Cong. But when his body was returned to our command post, his watch, pistol, rifle, money, etc., were gone. [The missing gear was later found on various of the "Vietnamese allies."]

When I heard this I wanted to go and kill some of them myself. It is so damned rotten and unbelievable . . . I suppose it might seem that I am feeling sorry for myself . . . and I suppose to a certain extent this is the case. But mostly I feel like I need to tell at least one person back there what is really happening over here. Hope I don't make you too angry . . ."[21]

From a historian's standpoint, the significant feature of Vietnam is not that the methods we have used there are immoral; it is that they have not worked. In his Netherlands campaigns, Philip II at least had good generals. His difficulty was that he faced a nation in many ways the equal of his own. Even with all the military aid she has received, the same cannot be said of Vietnam *vis-à-vis* ourselves. What the Vietnamese had—and still have, apparently—was a general neither we nor the French could beat, no matter what the odds. There is a distressing irony in the fact that a collectivist society should have cast up a man of such personal resolve and virtuosity as to make nonsense, not only of the Communist doctrine of supremacy of the group, but of our own idea that we can produce the great individuals, as well as the know-how and the team play, to meet any emergency. The North Vietnamese commander in chief has in effect violated dogma on both sides, and it will be interesting to see what becomes of him if (unlike his political chief) he lives to see the end of the war he has had so large a share in prolonging. In the meantime his career seems assured. No one familiar with his beginnings would have been likely to foresee it.

General Vo Nguyen Giap became a soldier more or less by accident. His father was "a scholar of distinction"[22] who had taken part in an uprising known as the *Révolte des Lettrés* against the French in the 1880s. (The French presence in Indochina dates from 1856.) Giap was born in 1912 and as a schoolboy in the twenties was drawn into the nationalist underground as his father had been. During the same period Ho Chi Minh, after years abroad in which he had been, among other things, an unsuccessful photo retoucher in Paris and an apprentice pastry chef under Escoffier at the Carlton Hotel in London, had emerged as a leader in the same movement. Like almost everything else he did, Ho's decision to become a Communist was essentially practical. If, however, he believed that his program for Vietnam would be supported by the French Left, he badly misread the French character.* The other ally which communism then guaranteed him, Russia, had the advantage of being far away and of sharing a long frontier with Vietnam's traditional enemy, China.

Ho had in addition the personal advantage of being an extremely tough customer who didn't look it. There was nothing of the windbag about him. He avoided der Führer's mistake of parading his intentions and muffled his ferocity, which probably made it all the easier for him to eliminate his nearest rivals, one by one, or later quietly to sign the death warrants of generals who had failed him.† He proved as troublesome an enemy to the foreigners he spent most of his life trying to eject from his country. His mild appearance and gift for silence combined with his will-o'-the-wisp tactics made him something like Marion the Swamp Fox—an opponent you could neither beat nor size up clearly enough to make into an object of public hatred.

"It is difficult for the United States to believably depict a frail

---

* Witness the feeble support given to the Spanish Loyalists by the *Front Populaire*. In the case of Vietnam the old servant-master relationship, with racist undertones, was perhaps of more importance. Colonialism in the old style was far from dead among Europeans. Bernard Fall describes Ho's pathetic efforts to present a petition for "Annamite" independence to the conferees at Versailles in 1919.[23] He had bought a pinstriped suit, derby, and overcoat, secondhand, and spent some weeks being turned away by minor functionaries to whom he doubtless seemed like somebody's Chinese laundryman suddenly turned diplomat—one of those innumerable cranks who gather on the fringes of great events waving placards and plugging strange causes. Little did any of them know the trouble this fragile, shabby little man was one day to cause them.

† For instance, the pre-World War I nationalist leader Phan Boi Chau, whom Ho in 1925 betrayed to French agents in Shanghai, for a price of 100,000 piasters.

Later, during the struggle of the Viet Minh against the French after World War II, Ho sent a General Nguyen Binh into the south to conduct operations. In an ominously succinct note he said: "My dear Binh; The south needs a strategist to lead the Resistance. I am confident that you have the ability and so I have proposed you . . . I hope that you succeed."[24]

Unfortunately, Binh did not. After various reverses he was recalled to North Vietnam, and while en route was betrayed to French troops. During an engagement between Binh's escort party and the latter, a Viet Minh assassin reportedly killed him, the object evidently being to make it appear that the general had died heroically in battle.

seventy-seven-year-old gentleman with a wispy beard and rubber sandals, ruling a country the size of Florida with an army the size of the Swiss militia and a 100-plane airforce, as a 'threat to the freedom of Southeast Asia' and to America's position in the world."[25] Another American in Vietnam asked: "How can you get people to hate a man who looks like a half-starved Santa Claus?" The difficulty was that Santa spoke softly and heaven only knew what he might be carrying in his bag.

During his early years with the movement, Giap seems to have been chiefly a scholar *manqué,* a young man who neglected his history and law to write political pamphlets or organize cadres. And like Ho, he was a deceptively mild-looking man with a lucid gaze and a soft, handsome face. The group which was eventually to dominate the revolutionary movement in Vietnam took shape during a sporting event in 1930. ". . . The original unification meeting of all Communist factions took place at Hong Kong stadium in the middle of the bleacher[s] . . . while a wildly disputed soccer game was in progress and thus blanketed whatever . . . disputes the Vietnamese . . . were thrashing out. Like a floating crap game, the meetings were continued all over town between January 6 and February 3, 1930. But on the later date Ho was able to report that a unified ICP [Indochinese Communist Party] was now in existence."[26]

By the time of the Moscow Trials, the abandonment of the Party's internationalist line, and finally the Russians' brief *rapprochement* with the Nazis, Ho's communism had begun to appear a poor bet. It was, however, the only bet he had;* and as a domestic technique for turning the people against the people, it apparently struck his practical mind as the one most likely to succeed. After World War II, following Lenin's two-stage plan, first of offering land reform so as to win mass support, and later of enforcing collectivization so as to bring the briefly freed peas-

* I.e., as a champion of democracy he would have had no active allies at all, as the Spanish War seemed to have shown. There, although the interests of France, Britain, and the United States clearly lay on the Loyalist side, they allowed Russia to help and did nothing themselves, with the result that the opening battles of World War II were fought exclusively between the U.S.S.R. and the Axis powers. Ho may have guessed that after World War II his chances of obtaining help from the United States or Britain against the French would be nil, no matter what his politics.

antry back under central control, Ho and his lieutenants nearly ruined rural morale and the agriculture of North Vietnam, and with them the Party's prospects.* When it became clear that the land program was a dud, Ho made an example of a high official who had pushed it too hard, and the whole undertaking was in effect suspended.

Giap's hardest years as a novice general were in the early 1950s, fighting against the French under General de Lattre de Tassigny (who fortunately for Giap soon died of cancer). The Viet Minh's important opportunity had come when the Japanese just before the end of World War II turned upon the Vichy French troops in Vietnam and massacred them. Ho's party was quick to fill the vacuum, and when the war ended the French as quickly came back to displace them from it—in part, no doubt, with a view to repairing their own somewhat damaged military "image." Having won some important border actions against them in 1950, Giap made the mistake of fighting three major engagements (the so-called Red Delta battles) which he lost. In these, which cost the Viet Minh over 20,000 casualties, he seems to have learned the methods which he has used with almost unbroken success ever since.

When in November of 1951 Marshal de Lattre de Tassigny (after a visit to the U.S., seeking military aid) made a strike inland at Hoa Binh, on the Black River, Giap did not repeat his earlier blunders. He avoided massing troops where French aircraft could get at them; and rather than attempting to carry Hoa Binh itself, he set out to make it untenable by a well-planned sequence of diversions. "He opened his battle by a series of attacks on the most vulnerable part of the French lines, the Black River. 308 and 312 Divisions launched overpowering attacks on

---

* For one thing, these reforms were much too brutally carried out. Peasants in the hamlets were expected or indeed compelled to denounce the thieving monsters who had been living on their toil—but often there were none, so victims were produced to order. Unlike the south, where large holdings of thousands of acres and absentee ownership were common, North Vietnam was a sort of Oriental New England, with mines and industries and, in the countryside, many family farms amounting to only a few acres. Today, I am told, you can read the state of completion of the land-reform program by looking at the North Vietnamese countryside from the air—the collectives standing out like occasional great rugs in what is still a patchwork of small holdings.

French outposts isolated from their rear support areas by the Black River. Heavy French counterattacks found nothing, because these two divisions had orders to fight only when they enjoyed unquestionable superiority. The weight of the Viet Minh attack shifted to the Hoa Binh basin and to Route 6 in early January, but continuous pressure was maintained along the Black River line . . . The passage of river convoys soon became too hazardous to attempt in the face of Viet Minh rockets and artillery being fired from the water's edge . . ." (Marshal de Lattre died at this stage of operations, to be succeeded by General Raoul Salan.) To any American who has closely studied the sometimes confusing reports of our own military actions in Vietnam, the outcome of this one will be easy to guess. The Viet Minh now set out to cut Route 6, Salan's other main line of supply. "Stubborn French defense made this operation a costly one for the Viet Minh but nonetheless they cut the road so effectively that it took a force of twelve battalions to re-open it. The huge number of French troops required to maintain control of the road had drained off many delta reserves which were being called on to stem the waves of infiltration launched by 316 and 320 Divisions. On February 22, 1952, the humiliating French withdrawal from Hoa Binh began. Persistent attacks by the Viet Minh made the withdrawal a constant running battle. When the final French losses were reckoned up . . . they amounted to several thousand."[27]

Giap now set out to reorganize and improve his supply system, his strategy from here on being to draw the French into the interior by himself making threatening moves westward on Laos. The first results of this plan were not very promising. In Operation Lorraine, General Salan sent a mechanized force into Phu Doan, catching the Viet Minh by surprise and capturing a quantity of arms. On November 14, some two weeks later, this force began to withdraw along Route 2, which runs through the steep-sided valley of Chan Muong. There they "were forced to fight their way back through an ambush of regimental size at a cost of over three hundred casualties. Seven days later this ambush was followed up by an attack on the French rear guard before it had withdrawn across the Clear River."[27] Once more, however, Giap made the costly mistake of attacking a fortified French position, this time at Na San, with his 308th Division (November 23). The assault failed, the division losing 1000 dead and perhaps three to four times that number wounded. It may have been this action which led him to use his exceedingly slow strangulation tactics at Dien Bien Phu.

In May of 1953 General Henri Navarre replaced Salan. "Navarre was looking for ideas and the combination of the marginal success of Na San and the extraordinary eloquence of [Colonel] Berteil in describing the camp in terms of intricate strategic theories, led Navarre into the error of thinking that Na San contained the seed of a new method for defeating the Viet Minh. Navarre was also sufficiently impressed by Berteil to have him re-posted to Saigon as his deputy chief of staff . . . Those who understood the reasons behind Berteil's new appointment began to lay wagers on where the next Na San would be situated."[28]

On June 16, 1953, Navarre called together his field commanders and outlined a many-faceted plan of the kind which American correspondents were to become quite familiar with at the "Five O'clock Follies"* in Saigon a decade and a half later ("a major pacification effort . . . destruction of the Viet Minh in the Southern Highlands . . . prevention of Viet Minh offensives before they were launched . . ." etc., etc.).[29] The "thrust" of Navarre's ideas (to use another now-familiar word) was that the army should set up a "mooring point," or camp, secured by widely ranging mobile defense forces, which could be used as a base in the north from which to attack Giap in the rear in the event that he should again move on Laos. (But what if he didn't, and attacked the camp instead? In fact, as it turned out, he did both.) The "mooring point" concept seems to have originated with General René Cogny and he soon came to regret it. "In November 1953, Colonel Berteil issued Navarre's Operational Directive No. 852 which nominated Cogny as the commander of an operation to re-occupy Dien Bien Phu."[30] Cogny, however, was not in favor of *that* site for a "mooring point" and gave many good reasons for his view, the chief being that the place was too vulnerable (like Sedan, it lay in a basin) and at the same time could not be handily supplied. Nor was it situated so as to present any real threat

* Daily news briefings.

to Viet Minh operations against Laos. However, "despite further letters of protest from Cogny, Navarre felt justified in ordering preparations for Operation Castor, the seizure of the valley by paratroops . . ." Colonel Jean Louis Nicot, the commander of the French air transport, also protested. The flight from Hanoi to Dien Bien Phu was four hundred miles round trip, bad weather would make landings in the valley hazardous, the hills around it would be ideal for enemy antiaircraft batteries (not to mention conventional artillery), French planes were in poor repair. "Navarre did not waver in the face of these objections which, he held, could be overcome with determination."[30] Five days before the operation was set to go (on November 20, 1953), a French official flew in from Paris having just missed being notified by his home government of a change of policy on Laos, one which would have made the Dien Bien Phu operation not even theoretically justified. A second official, Admiral Cabinier, was sent to inform Navarre that Laos was no longer considered worth taking any serious risk for, but he arrived in Saigon on the nineteenth, just after Navarre had left for Hanoi. The operation, in which it appears the general's ego and his career were now deeply involved, began as planned, partly (some have suggested) because he managed not to be in receipt of orders from Paris which would have canceled it.

"It was unfortunate for the French that Navarre did not see the vulnerability of the Viet Minh-held territory close to the [Red River] delta. Giap decided to take a chance on the security of his rear areas in order to force the French out into the more remote areas where they were at a disadvantage."[31] His basic strategy was to begin a number of major diversionary actions at points so far separated that the French troops tied down at any one of them could not easily be moved to the support of others. Moreover, these scattered actions were intended to (and did) lead French intelligence to underestimate the force Giap would eventually be able to throw into the battle around Dien Bien Phu. Finally, they compelled Navarre to reduce the reserves he had planned to use there himself.

Once this plan had been settled on, Giap blew the whistle and the usual hell broke loose. The French commanders obliged him by going, as we have since done, wherever the sound of gunfire called.* In the delta there were ambushes and assassinations of Bao Dai officials. The road between Haiphong and Hanoi was repeatedly cut. Within days (as in the Tet offensive of 1968) the whole countryside seemed to be swarming with Viet Minh. As Bernard Fall put it: ". . . Dien Bien Phu was only a relatively more spectacular part of a drama that was now played throughout Indochina . . . ; General Vo Nguyen Giap's long-promised counter-offensive."[32]

Fall goes on to say that Giap had maintained a corps of four divisions in northern central Vietnam approximately midway between the Red River Delta and Luang Prabang in Laos. "Throughout the rainy season of 1953 (May to October), Giap successfully avoided engaging his main force while Navarre vainly sought to disrupt the Communist timetable or order of battle. In December, Giap was ready. Regiment 101 of the 325th and Regiment 66 of the 304th Infantry Divisions . . . drove across the Annamite mountain chain, sweeping ahead of them-selves French *Groupe Mobile* (GM) Number 2 which had been hurriedly sent out of Hué . . . and whose battered remains now fell back on the Laotian side of the mountains to the unfortified airfield of Seno. Once more Navarre had to disperse . . . his reserves . . . Another fortified airhead was hastily created around Seno and a separate Middle Laos Operational Command (GOML) activated on Christmas Day, 1953; three parachute battalions from the general reserve . . . plus assorted air and supply components were concentrated 400 miles away from the major battlefronts of the Red River Delta and Dien Bien Phu. On December 25, 1953, the Communists reached the Thai border at Thakkek on the Mekong. The overland lifeline to northern Laos was severed and Indochina cut in two."[32]

Fall's account continues, "In the meantime, Regiment 66 of the VPA [Vietnamese People's Army] directly cut across the mountains . . . and one by one crushed the smaller French posts strung out along the road from Viet Nam to Seno. GM 51, sent to the rescue, fell into a severe ambush . . . and its lead battalion was practically annihilated on January 24, 1954, losing all its vehicles."[32]

* Tactics since renamed "search and destroy."

Two paratroop battalions managed to stave off the attack on the airfield at Seno. Bypassing that place, North Vietnamese units continued southward, two hundred miles into Cambodia, "while another pincer from the Annamese coast suddenly attacked the lightly defended posts of the Moï Plateau. In northern Laos the situation had also taken a turn for the worse. The entire 316th Division, after having taken the airhead of Lai Chau 55 miles north of Dien Bien Phu, now again marched upon Luang Prabang in four separated columns, liquidating the small garrisons of Muong Nguoi and Muong Khoua . . . The 2nd Laotian Battalion and the 2nd Battalion, 3rd Regiment, of the French Foreign Legion covered the retreat of the . . . garrisons . . . [and were] nearly wiped out in the process. On February 13, 1954, Navarre airlifted another five battalions, including a parachute battalion, into Luang Prabang . . . Five additional battalions were diverted to Muong Sai . . ."[32]

Navarre's view of these activities seemed to be that the enemy was playing straight into his hands. His New Year's Day message to his troops sounds so familiar that one wonders if "Westy" might not have studied his methods, verbal as well as military. Navarre told his men: "Having lost all hopes of winning a decisive battle in the Red River Delta, the Viet Minh disperses its forces . . . However in that type of warfare we have the advantage of being able to concentrate our forces rapidly at any essential point . . . A campaign begun under such conditions can but turn in our favor . . ."[32]

With the idea of throwing the foe still further off balance, Navarre then launched an amphibious "search and destroy" mission, Operation Atlante, against Tuy Hoa in south-central Vietnam (January 20, 1954).* The mission involved 15,000 troops and was directed against a point "of no military usefulness to anyone . . . After initial success in the landing areas the attack soon bogged down in the jungle-covered hills of the . . . hinterland."[32]

With Operation Atlante well under way, effectively tying down the last of Navarre's surplus forces, and the five-power con-

* Interestingly enough, he did so at a time when he must long since have realized the danger Dien Bien Phu was in. As early as November, French intelligence had intercepted some of Giap's orders which made his intentions for an attack on that fortress plain.

ference on Vietnam due to begin at Geneva in April,* Giap was now in the best position he could have hoped for, and he acted with dispatch to take advantage of it.

"Within a week of the beginning of Operation Atlante Giap called off the attack of the 316th Division upon northern Laos and concentrated the bulk of the 304th, 308th, and 312th Infantry Divisions, and all of the 351st 'Heavy' Division, around Dien Bien Phu. The attack began at 5:30 P.M. on March 13, 1954, by a heavy artillery barrage upon the two major outlying hill positions . . . which were overrun forty-eight hours later after several 'human sea' attacks."[32]

The position of the French defenders was, even before that event, extremely bad. They numbered about 5300 (as against an enemy force ultimately of 40,000), most of whom were lightly armed paratroops. Despite the weeks they had spent at Dien Bien Phu, they had neglected to construct adequate defense works. To withstand artillery bombardment from the surrounding hills they needed cement bunkers, steel supports, and the like which, because of their other more pressing needs, could not be flown in in sufficient quantity. The soil in the region, being light and powdery, was not suitable for trenches; it "lost its cohesion when bombarded so that bunkers collapsed leaving their inmates standing in a heap of fine dust . . ."[33] When the rains began in April the same works turned into vast mud puddles.

To protect their airstrip, the French had split their garrison, roughly a third of their force, or 1400 men, being in a strong point called Isabelle several miles to the south. Isabelle was too far away to give artillery support to Gabrielle and Beatrice—which meant that only about two-thirds of the (already inadequate) French artillery was available to cover these latter. Against the

---

* In the winter of 1953-54 a move was developing to bring the Vietnamese war to a close, since several of the great powers saw in it the possibility of another Korean confrontation. Ho Chi Minh had given the Swedish press, as early as November 29, 1953, an indication of his willingness to negotiate. It was finally agreed that a five-power conference on the matter should meet in April of 1954, and with this Giap was given a deadline. He could risk considerable losses just about that time, on the theory that if he failed to carry Dien Bien Phu, the conference would probably result in a cease-fire anyway and so give him a chance to recoup. On the other hand, if he were to win at that climactic moment, the advantage to Ho at the bargaining table would be immense.

French, Giap concentrated "six regiments of field artillery, which included 105 mm howitzers . . . Cogny allocated approximately one quarter of that strength . . . Strange to relate, this shortage of artillery was not something which had been forced on the garrison commander . . . There were new American weapons still in their crates in Haiphong ample to have trebled the Dien Bien Phu strength. But in the light of the intelligence estimates provided,* the artillery commander, Colonel Piroth, assured his superiors that he would be able to silence any [Viet Minh] artillery . . . within minutes of their opening fire."[34] Worse, his own artillery was not properly dug in or provided with overhead cover, whereas Giap had buried his in the surrounding hillsides in massively protected casemates so that, once in position, even the muzzle of a gun was concealed by a camouflaged cover between firings. Not long after the battle had commenced and the French gunners had discovered how the odds really stood, Colonel Piroth committed suicide.

On March 13 and the night of the fourteenth, Beatrice and Gabrielle were overrun, Giap using "attacks of almost divisional strength against battalion positions."[34] A two-week lull followed, during which the Viet Minh dug a system of concentric trenches around the airfield. (In some places they also dug tunnels almost up to the French position, many of which, in view of the nature of the soil, must have caved in, either burying the sappers alive or suddenly exposing them to short-range fire. North Vietnamese soldiers do not seem easily discouraged by setbacks of this sort, but it is clear that even the victors found Dien Bien Phu a trying engagement. In his later account of it, Giap admitted that Viet Minh morale was badly strained at the time, requiring disciplinary action and political "rebriefing" of some of the men.)

The plan which the North Vietnamese general followed in the remainder of the battle was the same, in miniature, as the one which had led to that action in the first place. By engaging the enemy at one point on the Dien Bien Phu perimeter sufficiently to force him to move in reinforcements, Giap was thereby freed

---

* According to Fall, French intelligence "credited the enemy with an artillery composed of 40 to 60 medium howitzers, capable of firing 25,000 rounds . . . As it turned out [Giap] used an estimated 240 to 300 guns including Soviet heavy rocket launchers, and fired nearly 350,000 rounds."[32]

to attack the fortress in strength wherever else he chose. To achieve this critical advantage, he had simply applied a similar principle on a much grander scale, inducing the French to scatter their army in a dozen theaters across Vietnam and Laos and then suddenly concentrating his own so as to put General Cogny and the tiny Dien Bien Phu garrison at his mercy. No counterattack they might mount could shake his own forces or in any material way alter the outcome; and any last-minute help they might have hoped for was now almost certain to come too late.

In April the French lost the airstrip and were squeezed into a quadrangle roughly a mile square (recalling Sedan: "*Nous sommes dans un pot de chambre . . .*"). All supplies had to be air-dropped to them. And as always—as at Sedan—they fought with the greatest valor. It is natural to ask why, seeing their predicament and the probable political consequences if it were allowed to grow much worse, Navarre did not sacrifice some of his other projects (none of them certainly very promising) and make an attempt, while there was still time, to save Dien Bien Phu. Perhaps by then he had neither the additional air transport nor the mechanized columns needed for such an operation. Or possibly, surveying his other recent undertakings, he had concluded that it was better to write off that one than to risk a multiple disaster by too hastily reducing various other garrisons or strike forces. Understandably he may have lost heart for the "single-battle decision" which had been one of the keystones of his program.

Whatever the reasons, Dien Bien Phu was left to the enemy. By the end of April its survival was a matter of days. On May 8, strong point Isabelle collapsed. The same afternoon, the Geneva conference took up the matter of Indochina. The war, if not the fighting,* was over, or so Giap and his political chief probably supposed. Neither foresaw (or did they? one wonders) that the Eisenhower-Dulles Administration would in 1956 block the national plebiscite promised Vietnam under the Geneva agreement. Did they suspect that within less than a decade, because of the consequences of that maneuver, a new and infinitely more terrible power would be upon them? A French writer remarked in

---

* Which in some places dragged on for months, long after Dien Bien Phu had fallen.

the early 1960s: "The Americans would never have fought as we did. They would have fought a different war. And by crushing the country and the people under a hail of bombs and dollars, they might very well have had more success than we."[35] Despite the best efforts of "Westy" and his successor, General Abrams, it has not quite worked out that way. There is little enough left of Vietnam, North or South, but success—thanks to the incredible, almost unbelievable tenacity of its people—is still far away. And despite the well-thought-out techniques which modern generals have evolved for burying their worst mistakes in Newspeak press reports or simply as "top secret," it is quite clear that in the battles which took place in the Central Highlands late in 1967, and in the Tet offensive which followed, General Giap did it again. At the sound of his guns our forces rushed off into the waste to fight fierce battles for hills which, when finally taken, were found to have nobody on them. There was a report in *The New York Times*, during the "search and destroy" operations at Dak To, that orders had been found there on a dead North Vietnamese officer which plainly showed the strategic intention behind Giap's moves in the Central Highlands. It was, of course, to draw our forces away from the heavily populated areas in preparation for the Tet offensive. The punch was telegraphed but apparently got lost among the other papers at U.S. headquarters.* Even without reading this particular message, however, any general who had campaigned for a while in Vietnam or who had had some briefing on the misfortunes of General Navarre might have guessed what was coming next.

At this time too, many civilian observers thought they detected a parallel between Dien Bien Phu and the ongoing siege of Khesanh. Just as Navarre had convinced himself of the strategic importance of his northern *pot de chambre*, so Westy seems to have felt, with or without the prompting of his President, that Khesanh was somehow vital to our military prospects, a "mooring point" whose loss would threaten all our other gains, whatever those might amount to. The chief difference between the two sieges

* The story ran, as I recall, on the front page of the *Times*, directly below the report of an interview with Westmoreland, in which he took an optimistic view of our situation in general and of the Central Highlands battles in particular. In light of his remarks, many readers, including some at G.H.Q., may have felt it unnecessary to read the second news dispatch.

was that we, who were more numerous and far more lavishly equipped than the French had been, could expect to hold out far longer or even indefinitely. But at that we were very hard-pressed, as the men who fought there can testify; and when relief of the fortress finally came it had, to some of those present, a peculiar air, reminiscent of Nathanael West's description (in *Day of the Locust*) of the battle of Waterloo as it was refought on a Hollywood set (not, incidentally, without real casualties). Nor was the finale at Khesanh bloodless, although it was not exactly a battle either. It should perhaps be classed as a military tableau. The evidence strongly suggests that the real victory, if it can be called that, was Lyndon Johnson's—a back-room diplomatic coup by which he contrived to salvage some remnant of appearances from what was, in fact, the failure of his war and of his presidency.

"The relief of Khesanh began on April 8 [1968, after the Tet offensive]. It was code named Pegasus and . . . included over ten thousand marines and three full battalions of A.R.V.N."[36] Eighteen thousand men of the First Cavalry Division were also involved, and in no time huge quantities of matériel had been sky-lifted in, a new forward operational base set up, and a thousand meter airstrip built. There was little fighting. As Herr puts it: "It was almost as though the war had ended. The day before Pegasus began, President Johnson had announced the suspension of air strikes against the North and put a closing date on his own administration. The Marines' Eleventh Engineers had begun moving down Route 9, deactivating mines and repairing bridges, and they met with no resistance. The shelling of Khesanh had become a matter of a few scattered rounds a day, and it had been more than two weeks now since General Westmoreland [with unusual prescience] had revealed that, in his opinion, the attack on Khesanh would never come. The 304th N.V.A. [North Vietnamese Army] Division had left the area and so had the 325th C. [Vietcong] . . . It seemed that all but a token force of N.V.A. had vanished . . . Pegasus was almost elegant in its tactics and scope. Stendhal would have loved it . . . but it soon came to look more like a spectacle than a military operation. . . . When I told General Tolson I had no real grasp of what the Cav [First Cavalry Division] was doing, he laughed and told me that I was probably brighter . . . than I knew. Pegasus was objectiveless, he said."[36]

It would appear that this rather backhanded triumph—one of the few of any kind we had been able to claim in the war—was novel in being almost the first twentieth-century battle to be fought from a shooting script. Brilliant as it was, it evidently failed in its main purpose. Not long afterwards General Westmoreland anticipated his chief, or more accurately was rewarded by him, in ceasing to command our forces in Vietnam.* As for the fortress itself, Herr continues: "A token American force was kept at Khesanh for the next month, and the Marines went back to patrolling the hills as they had done a year before. A great many people wanted to know how the Khesanh Combat Base could have been the western anchor of our defense one month and a worthless piece of ground the next, and they were simply told that the situation had changed. A lot of people suspected that some kind of secret deal had been made with the North; activity all along the D.M.Z. all but stopped after Khesanh was abandoned. The Mission called it a victory and General Westmoreland said that it had been 'a Dien Bien Phu in reverse.' In early June engineers rolled up the airstrip and transported the salvaged tarmac back to Dong Ha. The bunkers were filled with high explosives and . . . blown up. The sandbagging and wire that remained were left to the jungle . . ."[36]

So much for the "mooring point" in whose defense so much matériel and so many lives were spent. Ralph Ingersoll once described Eisenhower as a "public relations general." But it must be said that Ike and his field commanders won a series of actual victories, and those over an army very nearly as strong as their own. Eisenhower never had what one could call a superb fluency, but under the circumstances he needed none. The facts did not require that he have a special way with them. Our methods, as we continually tell ourselves, have become more "sophisticated" since those days, the question being in what direction the implied improvements have chiefly been made.

From the standpoint of General Giap and Ho Chi Minh, the

---

* Becoming chief of staff, a post, it seems, often reserved for officers of proven incapacity—for instance Hitler's Field Marshal Keitel or Mussolini's Cavallero, of whom Count Ciano had much to say in his diary.

actions just described—the Central Highlands battles, the Tet, and Khesanh—accomplished what they were meant to. They did not end the war; they could not. But the needlessly cruel bombing of the North* was stopped, and remained so for nearly two years. To the common people of South Vietnam—some minimum of whose respect we need—and to the world at large, including most unfortunately our enemies, the Tet offensive made us look ridiculous. Areas we claimed to have freed of VC suddenly

* Lee Lockwood was one of several American correspondents who went to North Vietnam in the winter of 1966-67. In a review of Harrison Salisbury's book *Behind the Lines, Hanoi,* he describes what they both saw there. "We had let ourselves be lulled into believing what we were told: that we were dropping bombs with 'surgical precision' exclusively on targets of 'concrete and steel.' " In fact, he and Salisbury saw quite clear evidence that we were using the antipersonnel area-bombing techniques of World War II, with the added refinement of the so-called cluster bomb unit (CBU).[37] The latter is useless against factories, bridges, etc., but kills people most efficiently, by means of napalm- or phosphorus-covered pellets sprayed over a thousand-yard radius from each of the dozens or hundreds of bombs in the cluster. Of the innumerable places hit with these and high explosives, many seem to have had no military significance, although in some cases the choice of the target may have been dictated not by a policy of frightfulness but simply by faulty intelligence. Salisbury gives an instance in his book—Namdinh, which the Pentagon had described as an important communications center but which seems in fact to have been unimportant small town whose chief installations were a silk mill and a textile factory. It was pounded to pieces. "What earthly meaning could be extracted from this destruction?" Salisbury asked himself. "What military purpose was it serving?" An official in the town said, "The Americans think they can touch our hearts," giving that phrase a somewhat unaccustomed meaning.[38] Lockwood saw a great deal of the same, some of it at first hand. (He was riding by night across the countryside in a jeep when an American plane zipped over the road, laying down a stick of bombs and some tracers on the rice paddies beside a nearby village.) In Antiem, in the delta—a pathetic cluster of perhaps forty huts—he found some ruins which had once been the village school and beside them "a plain stone monument listing the names of the twenty-nine children and one teacher who had died during the raid." As for the CBUs, their "pellets spray out in a symmetrical pattern which one can find perfectly preserved on walls or doors in towns and villages everywhere . . . The only realistic conclusion I could draw at the end of four weeks was that we were indeed bombing civilian targets in North Viet Nam and that the bombing was in large part intentional."[37] From the speech by Senator Javits quoted later on, it appears to have been common knowledge in Washington that Johnson not only endorsed this policy but participated in it to the extent of picking many of the air force's daily targets. It is curious to think that our former President, who was once a schoolteacher himself, may have raised, as it were by his own hand, the monument to the schoolchildren murdered that day in Antiem—a monument as much in our memory as in theirs.

swarmed with them again. Supposedly secure strong points, even close to or in Saigon, were all at once in a state of siege. The reportedly shattered North Vietnamese army reappeared in force at a dozen unexpected places, just as it had done in Navarre's day (and was to do again in Nixon's). And while G.H.Q., from its now embattled premises at Tansonhut Airbase, was announcing that the whole vast uproar had no military significance, the British general who had lately (and actually) pacified Malaya was describing the Tet as an obvious victory and Giap as a tactical genius. (Most of the foreign press concurred.) During the worst days at Khesanh, General René Cogny had words of advice for Westmoreland which were released to the wire services but evoked, so far as I know, no official response. (Giving unheeded advice seems to have been that general's second calling, even after he had left his first one.) Whether intentionally or not, the Tet was also timed to have maximum effect in this country. With the political conventions coming up that summer and Johnson already in trouble over Vietnam, the Tet offensive drove his failure home as perhaps nothing else could have done. Try as they would, our public-relations generals couldn't do anything with that one. In a matter of days the President had lost too much face to be able to run for office again with any hope of winning. The "credibility gap" had ceased to be a phrase; indeed, it had ceased briefly to be a fact. At a stroke, Ho and Giap had got rid of their two chief opponents, the incumbent President of the United States and his commanding general, and were doubtless even then bracing themselves to deal with the next pair to come. One cannot but respect men of such tenacity, resolved like their people to fight on if necessary for the rest of their lives (as Ho in fact did), and skillful enough to stand off an invader unbelievably more powerful and technically *au courant* than themselves. What shall we say—what will history say—of the enemy whom, to put it plainly, they made such fools of?*

---

* It is unnecessary to mention, except in passing, the sequence of events in the spring of 1970 which led up to Nixon's counterinvasion of Cambodia —surely one of the most absurd incidents of the war. The wonder is that another Dien Bien Phu or a second Tet hasn't followed. Perhaps the President foiled General Giap by the same methods he was using to mollify the electorate, qualifying and half-canceling his every move, threatening reescalation in one breath and setting a time limit on our invasion in the next.

This question leads directly to one I raised at the beginning of this book—namely, how much bad generalship may result from the attempt to implement by bloodshed policies which cannot be made to work by any means. Such policies may owe their often remarkable vitality not merely to the temperamental peculiarities of those who invent them but to "errors in belief and outlook ingrained in a whole people" and only too faithfully represented in their first citizens. The judgment of later time may well be that Westmoreland was not an outstandingly bad general.* He simply played a somewhat wooden Duke of Alva to Johnson's Philip II. Instead of conducting mass trials for heresy, as Philip and his general did in the Netherlands, we inundated the heretics of Vietnam, North and South, with napalm and white phosphorus shells and our diabolic CBUs. The slaughter was so to say impersonal and our commanding general at no time showed signs of the unpleasant personal involvement which made Alva a special object of remembrance among those he failed to subdue. Indeed, our man showed no signs at all ("Westmoreland's self-control never wavered . . ."), which does not mean of course that he will not be remembered in much the way Alva still is. That murder and cruelty have become so largely mechanical in no way diminishes the fact of them; on the contrary. Even if one includes the 18,000 whom Alva boasted he had caused to be killed outside of military action, it is doubtful if he cost the Neth-

---

The fact that the move itself, abortive as it was, prejudiced our disarmament talks with Russia, led to a step-up in Russian aid to Egypt, precipitated more student unrest, depressed the stock market, and shook our allies' remaining confidence in us, is a tribute to the power of the idiotic. To begin a campaign by announcing when you plan to end it is also novel. The chief difference between Johnson and Nixon as military thinkers seems to be that the former believed he could win by a straight shoot-out, whereas the latter treats war as if it were a political argument, to be won by taking contradictory positions simultaneously. Whereas Johnson did things and explained them afterwards, Nixon explains them as he does them, which is no help, particularly, one imagines, to his generals.

* He was certainly not an outstandingly good one, a fact which might never have come to light had he not had the bad luck to come up against General Giap. In his speech delivered to the National Press Club in November, 1967, he mentions a "significant" enemy victory at A Shau—significant because it "facilitated his infiltration and gave him control over a piece of real estate in South Vietnam." Some of the trouble may lie here. Giving undue importance to control of pieces of real estate was the downfall of many a World War I general, including Hunter-Weston at Third Krithia.

erlands a tenth as many lives as we have exacted from the Vietnamese. Nor was he, with all his tortures and reprisals, able to inflict as ghastly wounds on as many. Clearly neither Johnson nor Westmoreland was much concerned with the lessons of history. It is understandable that neither may have recalled Philip's difficulties in the Low Countries; but word must surely have reached them about the savage resistance inspired by the Germans' methods of conquest in Russia during World War II, not to mention the failure of the French policy of frightfulness in North Africa, shortly afterwards. Possibly they believed these techniques had merely not been applied thoroughly enough, or by a nation sufficiently powerful and blessed with know-how.

Westmoreland's inadequacy as a commander was not, it seems, simply a matter of repertoire. His professional bag of tricks included many surefire items such as "vertical envelopment" (which, apart from the phrase, was a German invention) and a facility for moving quantities of heavy equipment around rather quickly, sometimes to the right places. Enjoying complete command of the air, with all the advantages that implied in reconnaissance as well as in striking power, and having an immense superiority in ground vehicles, which should have enabled him to concentrate, at least in some areas, more rapidly than the enemy, he should have been able finally to trap and annihilate a sizable force of Vietcong or of the NVA. He appears never to have managed it, even after the Tet offensive, when it was announced that some 50,000 U.S. troops were being deployed in the Saigon area in a great encirclement maneuver. This action, embarrassingly named Operation Surefire or something similar (Can't Fail), did indeed fail, disappearing from the news a few days later, after we learned from a brief communiqué that most of the encircled units had somehow gotten away.* Westy in short was too strong to be beaten—except in the essentially political way that Giap did it—but too lacking in inventiveness or tactical acuity to turn his own overpowering strength to account. Our political management of the war was if possible worse—critically so, as it turned

---

* At this early date, of course, one cannot be absolutely sure on these points. The official histories remain to be written, and much that is now top secret will doubtless be revealed. Still, if Westmoreland *had* won any decisive engagement it seems likely we would have heard about it.

out. Only the crudest precautions were taken to protect the citizens of South Vietnam* from our fearful weapons and our soldiery, or from the armed thieves we recognized as their "elected" government. By allowing the latter to loot the country we had come to save, we—which is to say the Administration and its head-man-on-the-spot, General Westmoreland—all but guaranteed our defeat. For to the average Vietnamese the American presence soon came to mean either random destruction and bloodshed (in battle) or a sort of Mafia rule (in "normal" life) which we not only sanctioned but equipped with most of the tools necessary for its indefinite maintenance. One could hardly have devised a better program for turning once apolitical peasants or townsmen into dedicated partisans and enemies of the régime. Seen in this light the Tet offensive makes splendid sense. It was not so much a battle or a rash of them as a countrywide demonstration. It said in effect what ARVN officers and others in the Thieu-Ky government had long suspected—that now everyone was VC. The Tet showed that Giap's army could infiltrate *any* position, up to U.S. headquarters itself, because his soldiers could find help and shelter anywhere in the land.† Its aim was to make converts of the remaining holdouts and at the same time to reduce our own claims of military and political progress to nonsense. Giap was not equipped to win a victory of the usual sort. His men could not hope to take and hold Hué, for example; nor could they defeat a substantial U.S. force in a stand-up engagement. What they did, and most effectively, was to stage a kind of riot on a national scale. Those who still maintain it was a failure might consider the results: Mr. Johnson was soon gone from office and his general kicked upstairs. Our claims of success in Vietnam today are far more modest than they were in 1967. Peace negotiations, which were beneath Washington's

---

* For instance, by deporting them from their villages and dumping them into shantytowns.

† One can argue that the methods of the VC were no less brutal than our own, and in some cases far more so. The fact is, however, that we are foreigners. For a South Vietnamese the choice has been between a tyranny he knows and one which he does not—between alien misrule here and now as against misrule by his own kind, provided the foreigners and their puppet police state can be got rid of. From his standpoint, the logical choice was obvious—or became so with the help of General Giap.

attention before the Tet, began not long after it. Our withdrawal from the country, even without any clear prospect of a settlement, is now under way. These are not the sequels of a minor reverse.

Fascinated as Westmoreland may always have been by the problem of "how to deal with people," he appears in this case to have been quite unequal to it. Mathematics and related subjects had been his *forte* at West Point, and in that, interestingly enough, he resembled Burnside. ("Burn" too was strongest in math, but not strong as a whole, graduating eighteenth out of a class of 38, or at the 52.6 percent level. In his last two years at the Point, Westmoreland's class standing averaged out at 51.7.[39]) Westmoreland's real bent was apparently for devices, and there seems always to have been something rather mechanical about the man himself. The sort of generalship foreshadowed by Grant and Meade in the Wilderness Campaign perhaps reached a pinnacle in him. He fought literally with bulldozers and with every other machine or technical gimmick afforded him by existing know-how and hired science, only to discover that mountains and palm-thatched huts can be laid flat far more easily than can a brave outraged enemy. Neither the Scouts nor West Point appear to have prepared him for the fact which any second-year student of history—indeed, any thoughtful newspaper reader—knows: that a nation's spirit tends to grow in direct proportion to the brutality of the means used to crush it. The day the two old men went out with rifles to attack our tanks, the bell sounded for "Westy," but so faintly, in the deaths of people so unimportant and far away, he doubtless never heard it. He should have done so, for it sent him home and may soon be ringing for us all.

In fairness, however, one cannot describe Westmoreland's failure as wholly his own. His complicity, great as it was, was that of a dutiful professional commanded to accomplish the impossible, in part by means he should have been forbidden rather than encouraged to use. The crux of our failure was not even Johnson, however well his own rather brutal nature and pliant morality may have suited him to be its first cause. The chief difficulty is that since World War I an anticommunism so intense has been dinned into our people that today it acts to prevent our officials, who are after all answerable to public opinion, from exercising the sort of cold judgment which is essential to the effective conduct of a nation's foreign affairs.

In adopting a stiff fanatical line *vis-à-vis* the Communist powers—the mirror image of theirs toward us—we effectively abandoned the principle of enlightened opportunism which the English, since Elizabeth's time, have used on the whole with great success. It built them an empire which lasted several centuries and enabled them to defend it against a variety of enemies, many as powerful as themselves. Perhaps like the French we are too parochial, too easily victimized by our own *idées fixes*, to do the same. Because any deviation from strict anticommunism is apt to be quickly punished at the polls, our statesmen have been in effect forbidden to use a divide-and-conquer policy —for instance after World War II, when we might have approached Communist China with a view to an entente against Russia, or vice versa. The same horror of the Left which our elected leaders profess today—as often no doubt from political cowardice as from real conviction—has prevented us from encouraging democracy in client nations such as Greece or Iran, or in much of Latin America. Instead, with a cynicism which is not even realistic, we support armed minorities which, while they are corrupt and inefficient and cost us enormous amounts of money, are believed to be a safer investment than some form of truly representative government which might, after all, allow its citizens to vote in undesirable elements. On these grounds the Eisenhower Administration conducted a *Putsch* in Guatemala in 1954, wiping out that country's liberal (but leftish) régime and plunging it into a civil war which has continued, with gradually rising ferocity, ever since.* In the same way, in 1956, Eisenhower and Dulles thought it wise to block the Vietnamese election which would almost certainly have voted in Ho Chi Minh, thereby preparing our own disastrous involvement in that country's affairs less than ten years later.

* The correspondent for the *Manchester Guardian Weekly* (June 24 and August 19, 1954) began his report by saying: "We must call a spade a spade. The Guatemala War was an American intervention." His stories gave a coverage of the event not available in our own press at the time.

A follow-up story, describing the situation today, was written by Henry Giniger ("Guatemala Is a Battleground," *New York Times Magazine*, June 19, 1968).

To repeat, the question is not whether this policy is moral; few policies are. The question is whether it is good sense. Does it work? In the weakest nations—for instance, the Dominican Republic—it does, just barely. But even in the Caribbean we have been losing ground. Had it not been for Cuba's years under our man Batista, the island would very probably not be Communist today. In the same way Vietnam, unless we resign ourselves to a perpetual occupation or destroy the country *in toto,* will almost for a certainty end up in the hands of one of Ho's successors—possibly General Giap—since the name we have made for ourselves, with the help of the thugs we are pleased to call the legitimate government of South Vietnam, all but guarantees disaster in the event of our withdrawal. This time, one imagines, there will be no question of a plebiscite—only a massacre of those South Vietnamese officials not alert enough to have fled with their money, followed by the systematic extirpation of everything else, good or bad, we have tried to accomplish there. As a matter of practical politics we know this to be the situation, and our dilemma is complicated by the fact that any administration which frankly admitted to it would be committing political suicide (or would suppose that it was, which amounts in outcome to the same thing*).

It might be added that from a strictly military standpoint our doctrinaire anticommunism has led us to put ourselves in a series of dangerously exposed positions all across the globe, Greece and Vietnam being the latest examples. When the North Koreans seized and held one of our electronic "spy ships" few in this country seemed to grasp the meaning of that episode. Like the Tet, it appears to have been a demonstration, but of a far more ominous kind, aimed at conveying, at least to our military people, some hint of the trouble America would find itself in should the Communist powers ever agree to gang up on it. There is no question but that, spread out as our forces and our commitments are, such multiple-strike tactics could do us fearful damage. Nor is

---

* By now of course (1970) much of the American business community is against the war in Vietnam, so that almost for the first time in decades, rumors of peace produce an upswing in the stock market. But powerful as it is, business is not the hard-hat vote nor the millions of others who, for better or worse, still believe.

it likely, in the light of our recent performance, that our present allies would be in haste to take sides during the early stages of any such world-wide confrontation. If one develops, it may well find us alone.

The point is, of course, that our pretense of maintaining a "moral" position in international affairs has prevented us from doing efficiently things which are not moral in any case—chiefly keeping ahead of our rivals abroad, in particular the Communists but potentially anyone. This game is usually played without regard to any principle save that of temporary mutual advantage (or as a British prime minister once put it, nations don't have friends, they have interests). When it might have been expedient to do a political *volte-face*—for example in 1956, by befriending the North Vietnamese and permitting Ho to win his election—we could not bring ourselves to try it (possibly even to consider it). In fact such a move might have had excellent results. Vietnam has for centuries lived in fear of the Chinese; nor is that attitude likely to change, given the fact that Vietnam is not only tiny in comparison to China but one of the few Asian nations which (up until recently at least) has been able to produce substantial surpluses of food. A U.S. policy encouraging a Far Eastern Titoism in the person of Ho Chi Minh might have gone far toward giving us a base on the Asian mainland. Some have said that our real object in the Vietnam war was to secure such a foothold; and judging by the way they have handled us, one imagines that the People's Army of Vietnam would have been an excellent ally to have in the event of a war with China. As it is we will probably never have the Vietnamese as allies or their country as a base either.

Indeed, the effect of our policy has consistently been not to split our enemies but to drive them together. On the part of the Vietnamese—ideological claptrap aside—the main reason for the present entente with China is the common threat represented by America. Perhaps the only reason the recent rift between China and Russia did not grow into something far more serious was that the leaders of both countries were too fearful of our military presence in Asia to risk a showdown between themselves. In that rift we were given an opportunity which, by skillful statesmanship, we might have created for ourselves long before. To do so, however, would have meant acknowledging Red China and admitting her into the U.N., an unthinkable move. Instead we continued to back Chiang Kai-shek, a military and political incompetent whose administration became so corrupt that even the Luce publications were finally persuaded to make an exposé of it (mostly the same doings later reported to us from South Vietnam—wholesale thefts of American matériel, sale of it to the enemy etc.). To have dumped Chiang would not have been "moral"; any American official who urged such a policy change would have been depicted as "selling out to the commies." So we saw our man through to the end, and are doing the same with Thieu and Ky. And when, by pure chance, we were offered the opportunity to drive a wedge between the two powers we would least like to see allied against us, we were of course unable to take advantage of it. It is unlikely to come again, or if it does may find us no better prepared. For the moment we are the most powerful of nations; but it is a question how long we will remain so, surrounded as we are by others who outnumber us and may shortly outproduce us as well. To have given those same nations every reason for fearing and wanting to destroy us, for uniting against us in spite of most serious differences among themselves, is a course difficult to find a precedent for except in the brief history of Nazi Germany.

The part played in this infantile drama by Lyndon Johnson was both major and in a sense banal. Given the man and his constituency and the events which preceded both, nothing he did was much of a surprise. Like Philip II he knew the faithful were behind him; he only slightly overestimated their numbers and their patience. And like Philip he was quick to see an opportunity in the situation he had inherited overseas. Whether or not McNamara and others urged the war on him, it is probable that as an ambitious politician and a military ignoramus he may have thought to make easy capital of it. Philip too in his grandeur was confident that the Netherlands, and later England, must bow to him; and even after it became clear that neither was going to do so, he was able to wave the fact away ("Nor is it of very great importance that a running stream should be sometimes intercepted, so long as the fountain from which it flows remains inexhaustible"), going to his grave secure in the affection of his subjects whose future as a great power he had, in fact, all but destroyed. While he lasted, Johnson was no less indefatigable, throwing himself into the prosecution of the war as perhaps few other presidents have done, even including Lincoln, to whom he sometimes compared himself. In a speech delivered on the floor of the United States Senate, February 5, 1968, Senator Jacob Javits said: "Mr. President, I must say parenthetically that I have noted reports alleging that the President has required members of the Joint Chiefs of Staff to sign a paper telling him that they believe that Khesanh can and should be defended. I am not at all sure how this extraordinary procedure can affect the situation on the ground in Vietnam. Nonetheless it seems unlikely that our forces can be defeated, given the skill and valor of our men and their overwhelming firepower."

The senator went on to quote Secretary Rusk's peculiar remark concerning public reactions to the Tet offensive: "Now I have no doubt" (he quotes Rusk as saying) "that there are a few people who are grumpy, because somehow it was not possible to give them complete protection against what has happened in the last few days." (Was the secretary speaking of the mortar and small-arms attacks on our Embassy in Saigon, perhaps? In any case his words have a strange, almost epicene ring. Were some of the courtiers in Philip's entourage "grumpy" at news from the Netherlands of the fall of yet another Spanish-held town or of attacks on the king's officials? Very likely; but it is improbable that Philip's more responsible ministers, however stupid they may have been, expressed themselves in quite this way.)

The senator was also perturbed by certain inconsistencies in the official record: "Last July, General Westmoreland asserted when he appeared on television with the President, and in response to the President's prompting . . . 'The statement that we are in a stalemate is complete fiction. It is completely unrealistic [which turned out to be true enough]. During the past year tremendous progress has been made . . . We have pushed the enemy farther and farther back into the jungle.' "

Yet, the senator continued, "in a guerrilla raid on January 31st the Viet Cong penetrated the U.S. Embassy and pushed to within 300 yards of General Westmoreland's headquarters at Tansonhut Airbase. They knocked Saigon radio off the air, laid siege to the Presidential palace, raised their flag in the Buddhist capital of Hué, and forced a suspension of the Vietnamese constitution. The Viet Cong attacked in 25 of 44 provincial capitals . . . Yet it was just over two months ago in his speech at the National Press Club that General Westmoreland assured us: 'His guerrilla force is declining at a steady rate.'"

The figure, however, who most clearly emerges is not poor Westmoreland—to the end the king's man—but Johnson himself, and the South Vietnamese régime he once saw as his vehicle to glory.

"Let us take a look," the senator continued, "at the Saigon government today, whose highly dubious electoral 'victory' was given such solemn public blessings by the White House, the State Department and our Embassy in Saigon. President Thieu has already suspended the constitution and imposed martial law. In addition . . . there is other recent evidence that it is falling short of the high expectations set for it by administration spokesmen . . . Another signal is the resignation of General Thang, the one conspicuously honest and effective commander in the ARVN."

Javits concludes that the war makes a détente with Russia almost impossible, that it distracts our government from other most pressing problems (e.g., in the Middle East); he then adds: "Generals long ago gave up leading their men into battle. But President Johnson as Commander-in-Chief seems to have a most extraordinary and archaic concept of his role. Quite frankly, his time and energy are too valuable . . . to be used on such tasks as personally selecting each bombing target in North Viet Nam."[4]

Extraordinary and archaic indeed, and quite a waste of his time too, as it turned out. Was it the President's decision to use the cluster bomb on open cities or hamlets like Antiem—the bomb which destroys not factories or rail yards but people, by shooting them full of phosphorus-covered shrapnel? Had all this gruesome effort come down, in the end, to one man's spite toward a weak and distant colonial people who had had the audacity not to knuckle under to him? Was it simply that, having trapped himself in a hopelessly bad gamble, he had become more and more consumed with hatred for those who had caused it to be one— who were about to make him, in his own phrase, "the first president to lose a war"? It is terrible to think that even now, centuries away from our tribal beginnings, in an age better equipped both for progress and for its own annihilation than any our forebears could have imagined, bad generalship of this surpassingly childish and malignant sort is still possible. It is terrible to think, but it is clearly true, and not just of one country.

It is interesting to compare the four principals in the futile struggle I have just described. In America we pride ourselves on our practicality and tend to regard professionalism and the specialist as its supreme manifestations. Both Johnson and Westmoreland were pros; and each in his way has shown a certain distrust of mere intelligence as the faculty of amateurs and sideliners. Johnson, one recalls, had a well-publicized contempt for "eastern intellectuals" and Harvard-educated politicians, and took the hard-lining low-brow's attitude toward science (i.e., that it should pay off fast or stop asking for support—this despite the accumulated evidence of three centuries showing that a *laissez-savoir* policy pays off, in the end, far better).

Westy's position is somewhat different. He rarely deals in "personalities." Addressing the graduating class at West Point the year he left that institution to take command of our forces in Vietnam, he said: "Men welcome leadership. They like action . . . Speculation, knowledge, is not the chief aim of men—it is action . . . All mankind feel themselves weak, beset with infirmities, and surrounded with danger . . . They want above all things a leader with the boldness, decision and energy that, with shame, they do not find in themselves. He then who would command among his fellows must tell them more in energy of will than in power of intellect . . ."[41] He may be said to have adhered to his own precept, almost to a fault.

In contrast to Johnson and Westmoreland, whose antecedents, like themselves, were doers rather than thinkers, both Ho Chi Minh and General Giap were of the mandarin class, thinkers who became doers under pressure of necessity. Ho had received an education in the Chinese classics and while in prison in China wrote a book of verse in the manner of poets of the T'ang dynasty.* Giap received no formal military education at all, but as

* It is hard to imagine Johnson writing verse in any manner; and for that matter, Ho's, at least in translation, seems unlikely to challenge his ancient masters'.

an amateur he seems to have learned his trade well enough. O'Neill, his biographer, summarizes him this way: "Giap of course had shown great skill in coping with the requirements of such a many-sided life, but had he been a member of a society which required him to confine his activities to a more narrow field . . . it is possible his career would have been relatively short-lived . . . I hope the reader's attention will be drawn to the constant interweaving of political and military [elements] in Giap's life, for it is this constant interweaving of two threads, usually separated in Western societies, which has led to his continuing success . . ."[42]

Westmoreland may be compared, in certain ways, to Fighting Joe Hooker. Hooker too was an excellent corps commander and had all kinds of "energy of will"—except at Chancellorsville, where he briefly led an army. Westmoreland's misfortune was perhaps to have been in so many ways a model soldier that his superiors failed to see the one thing he lacked: he was not Big-Time. Given too many-sided an assignment he simply could not get it together. He learned to *talk* as though he had but the reality never shaped up. (Hooker too was a fluent talker, and never more so than just before his greatest defeat.) As a commander Westmoreland was probably as far from the Middle Ages as we have yet come—a specialist, a university-trained man isolated for much of his adult life from the worlds of politics and business, and entirely lacking, it would appear, in the vices and dilettantism of leaders such as Philip VI and Henry of Navarre (whose weakness is said to have been women and who enjoyed the company of Montaigne). It was possibly the very rigor of Westmoreland's training and the tautness of his character which unfitted him for the situation in which he found himself. He had down pat the elements of logistics and tactics which Giap was obliged to learn as he went; but unlike Giap, he never learned the politics which, in Vietnam, form so large a part of the battle. In a war game, fought, say, on conventional terrain in the United States or North Africa, he might have given Giap the worst of it. But the style of fighting in Vietnam was one which the enemy had improvised to fit the odd conditions there, including the great inequality of the forces engaged. Just because Giap came to the job as an intelligent novice with a mind unclouded by the dogmas of his adopted profession, he may have been able to do far better at it than his various well-educated opponents.

If this is the correct interpretation, what are we to make of it? For in a certain sense it puts us back at the beginnings of things— in the era of able untutored individuals like Edward I, who at Falkirk abruptly solved the Problem of the Pike by cutting open the Scotch *schiltrons* with his longbows.* Great nations cannot wait upon such accidents, nor is it fashionable any more to read a man's abilities and his potential except from the credentials he carries (which is why we are all now required to have so many). One cannot recruit a general staff at the last minute or from any walk of life, depending upon one's intuition. The only sensible course is to develop a Method and a System and hope that, in the hands of those who will mostly administer them, they will not freeze hard, becoming a greater liability if possible than no system at all. If Vietnam tells us anything, it is that: that we may already have frozen harder than we know.

In this survey of military malpractice down the ages, we have managed to turn up quite a variety of types. My own favorites are Charles XII, the Fatal Flaw type, and his opponent Peter the Great (the hysteriac). There were, in addition, Crassus, who seems to have misconstrued a knack for making money as an aptitude for anything else he might turn his hand to; Philip VI of France, an ill-educated idiot with some skill at intrigue and none at all in battle; Philip II of Spain, a well-educated idiot who somehow became convinced he had a gift for great strategic combinations and (like his several modern equivalents) remained so in the face of the most alarming evidence to the contrary; Mc-Clellan, the "image" general; Burnside, the Dead Loss; de Wimpffen, the disastrous *deus ex machina;* Haig, the socialite-in-arms; Hamilton, the poetic observer; Cavallero, the ineffable; and of course Westmoreland and Johnson.

Of them all, it is the modern type, the statesmen-generals à la Philip II or the commanders à la Haig, who are the happiest breed of failures—men so absolutely *in,* so securely perched in the topmost branches of a rich society that they can do whole

---

* A solution soon forgotten by his successors and never adopted at all on the Continent.

lifetimes of harm and still neither topple the great tree of state nor themselves be shaken down out of it. Not a few retire with acclaim, making stirring speeches about all the efforts and sacrifices "we" have made, and confident to the end that the courses they chose for their stricken supporters were the right ones. They are the happiest failures, perhaps, but also the most odious. The general who directs vast and unnecessary slaughters from his bombproof, the bloody-minded statesman who orders and meddles in these same events with even less personal risk, arouse a natural wrath in the rest of us, who pay not merely in future security but in present life and assets for their mistakes.

Throughout history, if men have been fortunate enough to survive the wars of their youth, they have lived on, it seems, only to be bereaved and bankrupted by those fought by their sons. That the generals and heads of state who order this incessant business of destruction should themselves have become increasingly shielded from it; that many of them, even now, should continue to be ignorant, inept, and self-righteous in an era in which war is becoming more insanely horrible than it seemed possible, only a few years ago, to make it—are ironies almost beyond human patience. One feels that a day may come when a sudden unanimity of refusal will sweep the world, as in the past whole continents were swept by the unanimity of religious conversion. Should that happy revolution occur, should a kind of global passive resistance at last make war impossible and decently ostracize those who have so often tempted us to wage it—a revolution admittedly not yet in sight—none will have contributed more to it than the heroes of this book, those clumsy, wanton, single-minded men who during the few thousand years of our history have framed the policies and directed the battles which have brought such an extremity of trouble upon the rest of us. To the extent that they just may, one day, outlaw themselves, we should thank God for them. Like Napoleon in Russia, like Westy in Vietnam, like Hitler and his New Order, they have shown us over and over the incredible ease with which prospects once all too attractive can be made embarrassing and finally hideous. If any ever succeed in cutting the deep instinctive roots of war it will be they. *Ave* Caesar assassinated! Hail Charles the Bold, dead at his own last defeat! Three cheers for Philip II who fought and lost, and lived to go on fighting and losing for decades more. Long live Tilly at Breitenfeld and Van Dorn at Pea Ridge! Above all a resounding salute to those saboteurs of the art of war in our own century—Haig and Hamilton and Sir John French, Maurice Gustave Gamelin, General Henri Navarre, Chief of Staff William Westmoreland!

We *need* such men. They are, quite literally, our mortification of the flesh, a Christian penance laid upon us all, not so much for our sins as for our primordial virtues. We may die of them, as many a Coptic hermit probably died of his, but there appears to be no other route to our salvation, at least none we show any signs of taking. So much for what scholars may come to call the social function of bad generalship—or for that matter, of good.

Notes

INTRODUCTION:
THE USES OF THE PAST

1. Mahan, A. T., *The Influence of Sea Power upon History, 1660-1783*, 80-81, 483
2. *Ibid.*, 483
3. *Ibid.*, 501
4. Freeman, D. S., *Lee's Lieutenants*, III, 304
5. *Ibid.*, 588
6. Ciano, G., *The Ciano Diaries*, 484-485
7. Mahan, A. T., 452
8. *Ibid.*, 435
9. Encyclopaedia Britannica, XXVI, 20

CHAPTER I:
CRASSUS—THE NEMESIS OF SUCCESS

1. Tocqueville, A. de, *Democracy in America*, II, 274
2. Mommsen, T. (1), *The History of the Roman Republic*, III, 412
3. Plutarch, *Lives*, 653
4. *Ibid.*, 650
5. Grant, M., *The World of Rome*, 114
6. Mommsen, T. (2), *History of Rome*, 350
7. *Ibid.*
8. Plutarch, 656
9. *Ibid.*, 657
10. *Ibid.*, 658
11. *Ibid.*, 659
12. *Ibid.*, 660
13. *Ibid.*
14. *Ibid.*, 661

15. Mommsen, T. (2), 436
16. Plutarch, 662
17. *Ibid.*, 662
18. Myres, J. L. (in Wells, H. G., *An Outline of History*, I, 508, fn.)
19. Plutarch, 663
20. *Ibid.*, 664
21. *Ginn's Classical Atlas*, 18, A, d
22. Plutarch, 665
23. *Ibid.*, 666
24. Fuller, J. F. C., *A Military History of the Western World*, I, 179
25. Plutarch, 666
26. *Ibid.*
27. *Ibid.*
28. *Ibid.*, 667

CHAPTER II:
MEDIEVAL WARFARE: THE TWI-LIGHT OF COMMON SENSE

1. Fuller, J. F. C., *A Military History of the Western World*, I, 181
2. Gibbon, E., *The Decline and Fall of the Roman Empire*, II, 647
3. *Ibid.*, 648
4. Encyclopaedia Britannica, XXIII, 661
5. Oman, C. W. C., *The Art of War in the Middle Ages*, 17
6. MacMullen, R., *Soldier and Civilian in the Later Roman Empire*, 117

7. Encyclopaedia Britannica, X, 300
8. *Ibid.*, XXI, 378
9. *Ibid.* (cited from Joinville), VII, 542
10. Oman, C. W. C., 17
11. Encyclopaedia Britannica, V, 477, 487
12. Montross, L., *War Through the Ages*, 144
13. *Ibid.*, 185
14. Veblen, T., *The Portable Veblen*, 53ff.
15. Montross, L., 185

CHAPTER III:
THE BRAVE VS. THE EFFECTUAL

1. Oman, C. W. C., *The Art of War in the Middle Ages*, 119
2. *Cambridge Medieval History*, VII, 680-700
3. Oman, C. W. C., 119
4. Encyclopaedia Britannica, VIII, 991
5. Montross, L., *War Through the Ages*, 178ff.
6. Guizot, F., *History of France*, III, 36
7. *Ibid.*, II, 169
8. *Ibid.*, 161ff.
9. *Ibid.*, 195
10. *Ibid.*, 196-197
11. *Ibid.*, 197
12. *Cambridge Medieval History*, VII, 341
13. *Ibid.*, 342-345
14. Guizot, F., II, 214
15. *Ibid.*, 217
16. *Ibid.*, 217
17. Fuller, J. F. C., *A Military History of the Western World*, I, 453
18. Guizot, F., II, 218
19. *Ibid.*
20. Fuller, J. F. C., I, 454
21. *Cambridge Medieval History*, VII, 441
22. *Ibid.*, VII, 441
23. Painter, S., *A History of the Middle Ages*, 133

24. Fuller, J. F. C., I, 460
25. *Ibid.*, 458
26. Buckle, H. T., *History of Civilization in England*, III, 16
27. Guizot, F., II, 242
28. *Ibid.*, 245
29. Blair, C., *European Armour*, *passim*
30. Encyclopaedia Britannica, VII, 389
31. Guizot, F., II, 247
32. *Ibid.*
33. Fuller, J. F. C., I, 465
34. Guizot, F., II, 247
35. Fuller, J. F. C., I, 466
36. *Ibid.*, II, 466
37. Guizot, F., II, 248-249
38. *Ibid.*, II, 249
39. *Ibid.*, II, 219
40. Fuller, J. F. C., I, 468
41. Oman, C. W. C., 130, 139
42. Guizot, F., II, 267-268
43. Oman, C. W. C., 139
44. Encyclopaedia Britannica, XIV, 520
45. Guizot, F., II, 344
46. Fuller, J. F. C., II, 251
47. *Ibid.*, 250
48. *Ibid.*, 265
49. *Ibid.*, 266
50. *Ibid.*, 266-267

CHAPTER IV:
GOODBYE, KNIGHTHOOD; HELLO,
WORLD CONQUEST

1. Trevelyan, G. M., *English Social History*, 159; see also *Paston Letters*, I, 65, 110-111
2. Guizot, F., *History of France*, II, 230ff.
3. Painter, S., *A History of the Middle Ages*, 332
4. Guizot, F., II, 310-311
5. Fuller, J. F. C., *A Military History of the Western World*, I, 420
6. MacKinnon, J., *The History of Edward III*, 533-534
7. Tinbergen, N., *The Study of Instinct*, 177-178

8. MacKinnon, J., 535
9. Encyclopaedia Britannica, XXVI, 591ff.
10. MacKinnon, J., 345
11. Oman, C. W. C., *The Art of War in the Middle Ages*, 62-63
12. MacKinnon, J., 528-529
13. Encyclopaedia Britannica, II, 686
14. Spaulding, O. L., et al., *Warfare*, 451
15. Encyclopaedia Britannica, II, 686
16. Brandi, K., *The Emperor Charles V*, 41
17. Mahan, A. T., *The Influence of Sea Power Upon History, 1660-1783*, 51
18. Encyclopaedia Britannica, XIX, 418
19. *Ibid.*, 419
20. *Ibid.*, XIII, 98
21. Mattingly, G., *The Armada*, 100
22. Fuller, J. F. C., II, 14
23. Mattingly, G., 205
24. *Ibid.*, 204
25. *Ibid.*, 175ff.
26. *Ibid.*, 278
27. *Ibid.*, 310ff., 318ff.
28. Fuller, J. F. C., II, 28
29. *Ibid.*, 24
30. Mattingly, G., 291
31. Fuller, J. F. C., II, 25
32. Mattingly, G., 321
33. Fuller, J. F. C., II, 30
34. Mattingly, G., 333
35. *Ibid.*, 368
36. Fuller, J. F. C., II, 35
37. Mattingly, G., 383

CHAPTER V:
THE TINY LION AND THE
ENORMOUS MOUSE

1. Trevelyan, G. M., *English Social History*, 277; see also Woodward, G. W., *A Short History of Sixteenth-Century England*, 158
2. Encyclopaedia Britannica, III, 40

3. *Ibid.*, XXI, 288
4. Grey, I., *Peter the Great*, 38, 73
5. *Ibid.*, 145
6. Fuller, J. F. C., *A Military History of the Western World*, II, 178
7. Grey, I., 240
8. *Ibid.*, 241ff.
9. Bengtsson, F., *The Sword Does Not Jest*, 298ff.
10. Fuller, J. F. C., II, 173
11. Grey, I., 300
12. Bengtsson, F., 318
13. *Ibid.*, 353
14. *Ibid.*, 369
15. Grey, I., 303
16. Bengtsson, F., 229

CHAPTER VI:
"WHOSE BLOOD HAVE I SHED?"

1. Ludwig, S., *Wilhelm Hohenzollern*, 647
2. Ségur, P.-P. de, *Napoleon's Russian Campaign*, 237-238
3. Encyclopaedia Britannica, XIX, 231
4. Bengtsson, F., *The Sword Does Not Jest*, 383
5. Howarth, D., *Waterloo, Day of Battle*, 52
6. Encyclopaedia Britannica, XIX, 233
7. Ségur, P.-P. de, 264
8. Guizot, F., *History of France*, VII, 251
9. Junot, Mme L., *Memoirs of the Emperor Napoleon*, III, 269, 271
10. Ségur, P.-P. de, 112
11. Fuller, J. F. C., *A Military History of the Western World*, II, 472
12. Sutherland, J. P., *Men of Waterloo*, 82
13. Encyclopaedia Britannica, XXVIII, 375
14. *Ibid.*, IV, 90
15. Sutherland, J., 121ff.
16. Encyclopaedia Britannica, XXVIII, 376

17. Sutherland, J., 123
18. *Ibid.*
19. *Ibid.*, 164
20. *Ibid.*
21. Encyclopaedia Britannica, XXVIII, 378, 379
22. *Ibid.*, 381
23. Guedalla, P., *Wellington*, 277
24. Howarth, D., 143-149
25. Encyclopaedia Britannica, XXVIII, 381
26. *Ibid.*, 381
27. Sutherland, J. P., 183
28. Guedalla, P., 277
29. *Ibid.*, 276
30. Howarth, D., 199
31. Flanner, J., "Letter from Paris"
32. Encyclopaedia Britannica, XXVIII, 381
33. Guedalla, P., 283

CHAPTER VII:
STATE OF THE UNION 1861-62

1. Catton, B., *Mr. Lincoln's Army*, 42
2. *Photographic History of the Civil War*, I, 307
3. *Ibid.*, III, 187
4. *Ibid.*, 157
5. Sherman, W. T., *Memoirs*, II, 390
6. Monaghan, J., *The Civil War on the Western Border*, 207ff., 242; see also Commager, H. S., *The Common Soldier in the Civil War*, II, 326
7. Commager, H. S., I, 317
8. Russell, W. H., *My Diary North and South*, 37
9. *Ibid.*, 165, 167, 164
10. Commager, H. S., I, 337-338
11. *Ibid.*, 264, 270
12. Catton, B., 97
13. *Photographic History of the Civil War*, VI, 134-138
14. *Ibid.*, 177
15. *Ibid.*, 156
16. *Ibid.*, 170

17. *Ibid.*, 168
18. *Ibid.*, 170
19. *Ibid.*, 162
20. Freeman, D. S., *Lee's Lieutenants*, II, 312
21. Rhodes, J. F., *History of the United States*, IV, 192 fn.
22. Russell, W. H., 157
23. *Ibid.*, 250
24. Catton, B., 71

CHAPTER VIII:
FROM THE JAWS OF VICTORY

1. *Memorial Addresses*, 8
2. Woodbury, A., *Ambrose E. Burnside*, 13
3. *Memorial Addresses*, 10
4. *Ibid.*, 13
5. Woodbury, A., 23
6. Burnside, A., *The Burnside Expedition*, 6
7. *Ibid.*, 9-10
8. *Ibid.*
9. Woodbury, A., 23
10. Burnside, A., Appendix
11. *Ibid.*, 1off.
12. *Memorial Addresses*, 13ff.
13. *Ibid.*
14. Woodbury, A., 23ff.
15. Catton, B., *Mr. Lincoln's Army*, 277-278
16. Freeman, D. S., *Lee's Lieutenants*, II, 173
17. Catton, B., 327
18. Williams, T. H., *Lincoln and His Generals*, 170
19. *Ibid.*, 173
20. Freeman, D. S., II, 306
21. *Ibid.*, 307
22. Williams, H. T., 175
23. *Ibid.*, 179
24. *Ibid.*, 180
25. *Ibid.*, 194
26. *Photographic History of the Civil War*, II, 88
27. Freeman, D. S., II, 339ff.
28. *Ibid.*, 344
29. *Ibid.*, 351
30. *Ibid.*, 352-358

31. *Ibid.*
32. *Ibid.*
33. *Ibid.*, 346
34. *Ibid.*, 360
35. *Ibid.*, 329
36. *Photographic History of the Civil War*, II, 94
37. *Ibid.*
38. Freeman, D. S., II, 364
39. *Photographic History of the Civil War*, III, 87-88
40. *Ibid.*, X, 142
41. Freeman, D. S., II, 385
42. *Harper's New Monthly Magazine*, 643
43. Rhodes, J. F., *History of the United States*, IV, 246
44. *Ibid.*, 247-248
45. *Photographic History of the Civil War*, VII, 204
46. Rhodes, J. F., IV, 249
47. Freeman, D. S., III, 365ff.
48. *Photographic History of the Civil War*, X, 144
49. *Ibid.*, III, 66ff.
50. Cadwallader, S., *My Three Years with Grant*, 352
51. *Photographic History of the Civil War*, III, 320
52. Woodbury, A., 28ff.
53. Cadwallader, S., 210ff.
54. *Ibid.*, 212
55. *Photographic History of the Civil War*, I, 348
56. Freeman, D. S., I, 17-18
57. Russell, W. H., *My Diary North and South*, 201, 203
58. Freeman, D. S., III, 45ff.
59. *Ibid.*, 479
60. *Ibid.*, 487
61. *Ibid.*, 488
62. *Ibid.*, 489
63. *Ibid.*, 491
64. *Ibid.*, 492
65. *Ibid.*, 493
66. *Ibid.*, 489 fn.
67. Rhodes, J. F., IV, 490
68. *Ibid.*, 494
69. Freeman, D. S., III, 494
70. *Photographic History of the Civil War*, III, 198

71. Cadwallader, S., 244
72. *Photographic History of the Civil War*, III, 202, 204
73. Freeman, D. S., III, 543
74. Cadwallader, S., 244, 245
75. *Ibid.*, 246
76. Woodbury, A., 30
77. Cadwallader, S., 314
78. Haskell, F. A., *The Battle of Gettysburg*, 131-132
79. *Ibid.*, 6 fn.
80. Catton, B., 229
81. Cadwallader, S., 247ff.
82. Fuller, J. F. C., *A Military History of the Western World*, III, 86 (the subquotation is from Stephen Vincent Benét's *John Brown's Body*)

CHAPTER IX:
THE GERMAN CENTURY

1. *Encyclopaedia Britannica*, XIX, 211ff.
2. *Ibid.*, XVII, 238-239
3. Fuller, J. F. C., *A Military History of the Western World*, III, 100
4. *Encyclopaedia Britannica*, XI, 7
5. Fuller, J. F. C., III, 111
6. *Encyclopaedia Britannica*, XI, 7
7. *Ibid.*, 8
8. *Ibid.*, 10
9. Fuller, J. F. C., III, 115-116
10. *Ibid.*, 119
11. *Ibid.*, 122
12. *Encyclopaedia Britannica*, XXIV, 575
13. Fuller, J. F. C., III, 126
14. *Encyclopaedia Britannica*, XXIV, 576
15. Fuller, J. F. C., III, 126
16. *Encyclopaedia Britannica*, XXIV, 576
17. Fuller, J. F. C., III, 128
18. *Ibid.*, 129
19. *Encyclopaedia Britannica*, XVII, 52
20. Fuller, J. F. C., III, 173
21. Watt, R. M., *The Kings Depart*, 131

22. Drucker, P., *The End of Economic Man*, 203
23. Ludwig, E., *Wilhelm Hohenzollern*, 272
24. Shirer, W., *The Rise and Fall of the Third Reich*, 449
25. Ludwig, E., 253
26. *Ibid.*, 89
27. *Ibid.*, 161
28. *Ibid.*, 178
29. *Ibid.*, 148
30. Moorehead, A., *The Russian Revolution*, 99
31. Fuller, J. F. C., III, 227
32. Remarque, E. M., *All Quiet on the Western Front*, 108ff.
33. Clark, A., *The Donkeys*, 163
34. *Ibid.*, 23
35. *Ibid.*, 39
36. *Ibid.*, 170ff.
37. James, R. R., *Gallipoli*, 1
38. *Ibid.*, 20
39. *Ibid.*, 38
40. *Ibid.*, 42-43
41. Fuller, J. F. C., III, 240
42. James, R. R., 45
43. *Ibid.*, 121-123
44. *Ibid.*, 123
45. Fuller, J. F. C., III, 263
46. James, R. R., 155
47. *Ibid.*, 216
48. Fuller, J. F. C., III, 264
49. James, R. R., 204
50. *Ibid.*, 154
51. *Ibid.*, 250, 247
52. *Ibid.*, 281
53. *Ibid.*, 296-297
54. *Ibid.*, 295
55. Fuller, J. F. C., III, 261
56. Ludwig, E., 477
57. Remarque, E. M., 287
58. Fuller, J. F. C., III, 290
59. Remarque, E. M., 127
60. Watt, R. M., 57
61. Clark, A., 177
62. Werth, A., *Russia at War, 1941-1945*, 133
63. *Ibid.*, 244
64. Fuller, J. F. C., III, 372

65. *Ibid.*, 373
66. Werth, A., 250, 260
67. *Ibid.*, 271
68. Ciano, G., *The Ciano Diaries*, 490
69. *Ibid.*, 479
70. Graves, R., *Good-bye to All That*, 170
71. Ciano, G., 175
72. Fuller, J. F. C., III, 388ff.

CHAPTER X:
JOHNSON VS. THE EASTERN
INTELLECTUALS

1. Sherman, W. T., *Memoirs*, II, 388
2. Furgurson, E. B., *Westmoreland, the Inevitable General*, 125
3. *Ibid.*, 165
4. *Ibid.*, 261
5. *Ibid.*, 97
6. *Ibid.*, 84
7. *Ibid.*, 27
8. Corson, W. R., *The Betrayal*, 247ff.
9. *Ibid.*, 254ff.
10. C.O.R. press release, May 15, 1967
11. Herr, M., "Conclusion at Khesanh," 118ff.
12. Duncan, D., *The New Legions*, 163ff.
13. Herr, M., 118ff.
14. Schell, J., "A Reporter at Large: Quang Ngai and Quang Tin," 60
15. *Ibid.*, 62
16. *Ibid.*, 48-50
17. *Ibid.*, 53
18. *Ibid.*, 60
19. *Ibid.*, 46
20. *Ibid.*, 56
21. *Letters from Vietnam*, 145-150
22. O'Neill, R. J., *General Giap*, 1
23. Fall, B. B. (1), *Last Reflections on a War*, 71
24. O'Neill, R. J., 102
25. Fall, B. B. (1), 60

26. *Ibid.*, 76
27. O'Neill, R. J., 109-110, 114-115
28. *Ibid.*, 123-124
29. *Ibid.*, 124
30. *Ibid.*, 129-130
31. *Ibid.*, 135
32. Fall, B. B. (2), *Viet Nam Witness*, 36ff.
33. O'Neill, R. J., 146
34. *Ibid.*, 145, 152
35. Bodard, L., *The Quicksand War*, 3
36. Herr, M., 123
37. Lockwood, L., 25-26
38. Salisbury, H. E., *Behind the Lines, Hanoi*, 84ff.
39. Furgurson, E. B., 86
40. Javits, J., Congressional Record
41. Furgurson, E. B., 289
42. O'Neill, R. J., x

Bibliography

Abrantès, Duchesse d' (Mme L. Junot), *Memoirs of the Emperor Napoleon*. Washington, M. Walter Dunne, 1901.

Bengtsson, F., *The Sword Does Not Jest*. New York, St. Martin's Press, 1960.

Blair, C., *European Armour*. London, Batsford, 1958.

Blythe, R., *Akenfield*. New York, Pantheon Books, 1969.

Bodard, L., *The Quicksand War*. Boston, Little, Brown, 1963.

Brandi, K., *The Emperor Charles V*. New York, Alfred A. Knopf, 1939.

Buckle, H. T., *History of Civilization in England* (3 vols.). London, Longmans, 1885.

Burnside, A. E., *The Burnside Expedition*. Providence, R.I., N. Bangs Williams, 1882.

Cadwallader, S., *My Three Years with Grant*. New York, Alfred A. Knopf, 1955.

Cambridge Medieval History. Cambridge, England, Cambridge University Press, 1958 (Vol. VII).

Catton, B., *Mr. Lincoln's Army*. New York, Doubleday (Dolphin), 1952.

Ciano, Count Galeazzo, *The Ciano Diaries*. New York, Doubleday, 1945.

Clark, A., *The Donkeys*. New York, William Morrow, 1962.

Commager, H. S., *The Common Soldier in the Civil War* (2 vols.). New York, Grosset & Dunlap, 1952.

Corson, W. R., *The Betrayal*. New York, W. W. Norton, 1968.

Drucker, P., *The End of Economic Man*. New York, John Day, 1939.

Duncan, D., *The New Legions*. New York, Random House, 1967.

Encyclopaedia Britannica, Eleventh Edition, 1911.

Fall, B. B. (1), *Last Reflections on a War*. New York, Doubleday, 1967.

—— (2), *Viet Nam Witness*. New York, Frederick A. Praeger, 1966.

Flanner, J., "Letter from Paris," *New Yorker*, October 18, 1969.

Freeman, D. S., *Lee's Lieutenants* (3 vols.). New York, Charles Scribner's Sons, 1944.

Fuller, J. F. C., *A Military History of the Western World* (3 vols.). New York, Funk & Wagnalls, 1954.

Furgurson, E. B., *Westmoreland, the Inevitable General*. Boston, Little, Brown, 1968.

Gibbon, E., *The Decline and Fall of the Roman Empire* (3 vols.). New York, Modern Library.

Ginn's Classical Atlas. Boston, Ginn and Company, 1886.

Grant, M., *The World of Rome*. New York, World Publishing, 1960.

Graves, R., *Good-bye to All That*. New York, Doubleday (Anchor), 1957.

Grey, I., *Peter the Great*. Philadelphia, J. B. Lippincott, 1960.

Guedalla, P., *Wellington*. New York, Harper & Bros., 1931.

Guizot, F., *History of France*, Robert Black, transl. London, Aldine, 1886.

Harper's New Monthly Magazine, Volume XXXI, June-November, 1865.

Haskell, F. A., *The Battle of Gettysburg*, Bruce Catton, ed. Boston, Houghton Mifflin, 1957.

Heer, F., *The Medieval World*. New York, World Publishing, 1962.

Herr, M., "Conclusion at Khesanh," *Esquire*, October, 1969.

Howarth, D., *Waterloo, Day of Battle*. New York, Atheneum Publishers, 1968.

James, R. R., *Gallipoli*. New York, Crowell Collier and Macmillan, 1965.

Javits, Senator J., Congressional Record, February 5, 1968, Vol. 114, No. 16.

Junot, Mme L., see Abrantès, Duchesse d'.

Letters from Vietnam, Bill Adler, ed. New York, E. P. Dutton, 1967.

Lockwood, L., in *New York Review of Books*, August 3, 1967.

Ludwig, E., *Wilhelm Hohenzollern*. New York, Blue Ribbon Books, 1926.

MacKinnon, J., *The History of Edward III*. London, Longmans Green, 1900.

MacMullen, R., *Soldier and Civilian in the Later Roman Empire*. Cambridge, Mass., Harvard University Press, 1963.

Mahan, A. T., *The Influence of Sea Power upon History, 1660–1783*. Boston, Little, Brown, 1898.

Mattingly, G., *The Armada*. Boston, Houghton Mifflin, 1959.

Memorial Addresses on the Life and Character of A. E. Burnside. Washington, Government Printing Office, 1882.

Mommsen, T. (1), *The History of the Roman Republic* (4 vols.). New York, Everyman's Library, 1930.

—— (2), *History of Rome*. New York, Philosophical Library, 1959.

Monaghan, J., *The Civil War on the Western Border*. Boston, Little, Brown, 1955.

Montross, L., *War Through the Ages*. New York, Harper & Bros., 1944.

Moorehead, A., *The Russian Revolution*. New York, Bantam Books, 1950.

Oman, C. W. C., *The Art of War in the Middle Ages*, J. H. Beeler, ed. Ithaca, N.Y., Cornell University Press (Great Seal Books), 1958.

O'Neill, R. J., *General Giap*. New York, Frederick A. Praeger, 1969.

Painter, S., *A History of the Middle Ages*. New York, Alfred A. Knopf, 1953.

Paston Letters, John Warrington, ed. (2 vols.). London, Everyman's Library, 1924.

Photographic History of the Civil War (10 vols.). New York, Review of Reviews, 1911.

Plutarch, *Lives*, John Dryden, transl. New York, Modern Library, 1932.

Remarque, E. M., *All Quiet on the Western Front*. New York, Grosset & Dunlap, 1929.

Rhodes, J. F., *History of the United States* (8 vols.). New York, Macmillan, 1899.

Russell, W. H., *My Diary North and South*. New York, Harper & Bros., 1954.

Salisbury, H. E., *Behind the Lines, Hanoi*. New York, Bantam Books, 1967.

Schell, J., "A Reporter at Large: Quang Ngai and Quang Tin," *New Yorker*, March 9, 1968.

Ségur, Philippe-Paul de, *Napoleon's Russian Campaign*, J. David Townsend, transl. Boston, Houghton Mifflin, 1958.

Sherman, W. T., *Memoirs* (2 vols.). New York, Appleton, 1875.

Shirer, W., *The Rise and Fall of the Third Reich*. New York, Simon & Schuster, 1960.

Spaulding, O. L., Nickerson, H., and Wright, J. W., *Warfare*. Washington, Infantry Journal, Inc., 1937.

Sutherland, J. P., *Men of Waterloo*. Englewood Cliffs, N.J., Prentice-Hall, 1966.

Tinbergen, N., *The Study of Instinct*. Oxford, England, Clarendon Press, 1951.

Tocqueville, Alexis de, *Democracy in America* (2 vols.). Cambridge, Mass., Sever & Francis, 1863.

Trevelyan, G. M., *English Social History*. New York, Longmans Green, 1942.

Veblen, T., *The Portable Veblen*. New York, Viking Press, 1950.

Watt, R. M., *The Kings Depart*. New York, Simon & Schuster, 1968.

Wells, H. G., *An Outline of History* (2 vols.). New York, Macmillan, 1920.

Werth, A., *Russia at War, 1941-1945*. New York, E. P. Dutton, 1964.
Williams, T. H., *Lincoln and His Generals*. New York, Alfred A. Knopf, 1952.
Winston, R., *Thomas Becket*. New York, Alfred A. Knopf, 1967.
Woodbury, A., *Ambrose E. Burnside*. Providence, R.I., N. Bangs Williams, 1882.
Woodward, G. W., *A Short History of Sixteenth-Century England*. New York, Mentor Books, 1963.

Index

A

ABM, 355n
Abrams, Creighton, 384
"Aces," World War I, 105-6
Aerial spotting, introduced, 204
Agache, Gobin, 84
Agincourt, battle of (1415), 64, 65, 93-94
Albigensians, 139
Alexander the Great, 187
Alexander of Parma, 115, 127-128
   in destruction of Spanish fleet, 132
Alkmaar, siege of (1573), 122
Alligator (Indian), 210, 211
Altranstädt, peace of (1706), 154
Alva, Duke of (Fernando Alvarez de Toledo), as commander, 119-22, 389
Ambush, aristocratic use of, 102
Amiens, battle of (1918), 338
Anderson, Bloody Bill, 214
Anderson, George Thomas, 263
Andersonville (camp), 287

Andromachus, 41
Anjou, Duke of (Louis I), 105
Antietam, battle of (1862), 231, 240-44, 321, 331, 334, 357
Antiem bombing (Vietnam), 387n
Antonine Age, 46
Apollinaire, Guillaume, 339
Apraxin, Feodor, 165n
Archer, James J., 249
Archers
   English, 80
   Mongol, 59
   Parthian, 35
   Roman (Byzantine), 48
Archery, English, 70, 96-97, 112; see also Longbow
Arques, battle of (1589), 113, 115
Ariamnes, 37
Aristocracy
   chivalry among, 104-11
   medieval, 55-59, 63, 68-72, 86-91, 101-6, 122-23
Armed forces, size of U.S., 355n

Armies
  care for wounded in large, 199
  defining characteristics of modern, 45-46
  growth of, 140-41
  unmanageability of large, 180, 206n
  See also Cavalry; Infantry; Weapons
Armor
  of knights, 87n
  tanks, 338-39
Arquebus (weapon), 70
  introduction of, 112, 113
Arrows
  Surena's use of, 38, 39
  wood of English, 83n
Artabazes (King of Armenia), 36, 37
Artevelde, Jacob van, 76-78, 82
Artillery
  development of rifled, 207, 292-94
  field, introduction of, 116-17
  First World War, 316
  medieval, 54n, 70, 112, 116
  Roman, 45
  Second World War, 357
  in Vietnam, 368-69
Arundel, 3rd Earl of (Richard), 85
Aspern, battle of (1809), 206n
Aspern-Essling, battle of (1809), 189n
Asquith, H. H., 323
Ateius, 34
August, Prince, of Prussia, 180
Augustus II (King of Poland), 165
  deposing, 154
  Klissow battle and, 151

Austerlitz, battle of (1805), 184, 201, 206n
Austrian Succession, War of the (1740-48), 140, 141

B

Babington, Anthony, 124
Bacon, Roger, 59, 70n
Balfour, Arthur, 307, 323
Ballista (weapon), 45, 46, 88
Banks, Nathaniel, 207, 280
Bannockburn, battle of (1314), 65
Barbavera (Barbanero), 78-86
Baruch, Bernard, 345
Batista, Fulgencio, 394
Battles, *see specific battles*
Bazaine, Achille, 20, 297-98, 306n
Beaufort, Roger de, 106
Beaumanoir, Sir Robert de, 103
Beauregard, Pierre T., 224, 269-273, 276, 279
Becket, Thomas, 82
Béhuchet, Nicholas, 78-79
Bela IV (King of Hungary), 110
Belisarius, 47
Bemborough, Captain, 103, 104
Benedict XII (Pope), 76
Berteil, Colonel, 377
Big Bethel Church, battle of (1861), 268-69
Bigot, François, 99
Biles, Edwin R., 245
Birdwood, Sir William, 327
Bismarck, Otto von, 230, 279, 311, 314, 341, 342
  characteristics of, 290
  policies of, 294, 310
Blenheim, battle of (1704), 140n
Blood Purge (1934), 313n

Blücher, Gebhard von, at Water-
loo, 191-202
Boisot, Admiral, 121
Bombing in Vietnam, 107, 108n,
367, 387n, 398; see also Ar-
tillery—in Vietnam
Borodino, battle of (1812), 182,
188, 199-200, 206n
Boufflers, Duc Louis de, 140
Bourbaki, Charles, 306
Bourgeoisie, 51-52
Bouvines, battle of (1214), 51
Bowlegs, Billy, 210
Bows
crossbows, 88-89
Parthian, 35-36
wood of English, 83n
See also Arrows; Longbows
Boxer Rebellion (1900), 310n
Brady, Mathew, 204, 206, 284-
285
Bragg, Braxton, 214, 265, 269-70,
281
Bravery, aristocratic, 55-58
Breton War (1351), 82, 103
Bruce, David, 75
Bruce, Robert, 65
Buccelin, Theudebert, 49n
Buckingham, C. P., 246
Buironfosse, battle of (1339), 77
Bull Run, second battle of
(1862), 241
Bülow, Baron Friedrich Wilhelm
von, 196, 198
Bunker, Ellsworth, 359
Burnside, Ambrose, 232-33, 283
at Antietam, 240-44, 321, 334,
357
biography of, 235-37
characteristics of, 196, 205,
207, 258-61, 285, 401
in crater attack, 276-79

at Fredericksburg, 244, 247-
256
in Knoxville attack, 13, 265
in New Bern attack, 237-40
as politician, 13, 279-80
Swinton and, 267-68
Westmoreland compared with,
392
in Wilderness campaign, 261-
266
Butler, Benjamin, 13, 207, 223,
235
campaign of (1864), 270-75
characteristics of, 268-69, 280,
281, 283, 285
removal of, 275-76

C

Cabinier, Georges-Étienne, 378
Caesar, Julius, 33, 60, 179, 225,
230, 402
artillery as used by, 45
Crassus and, 30
Calais, siege of (1346-47), 92,
109
Cambodia, invasion of (1970),
388n-89n
Cambrai, battle of, 338n
Camus, Albert, 350
Canister (weapon), 251n
Cannon, see Artillery
Caprivi, Count Leo von, 313
Caracole attack, 115
Carden, S. H., 325, 326, 328, 332
Carr, Joseph, 212, 213
Carrhae, battle of (53 B.C.), 33-
43
Casero, Colonel, 16
Casilinum, battle of (554), 49n
Cassel, battle of (1328), 74-75
Castle building, 54n

Catapults (weapon), Roman, 45, 46

Catherine (Tsarina of Peter the Great), 175

Cavalry
of Goths and French, 46-48
medieval supremacy of, 54
Mongol, 59-60
Parthian, 35-36, 39-40
See also Archers

Cavallero, Count Ugo, 16

Chancellorsville, battle of (1863), 246, 256n, 262, 267, 400

Channel, Sluys and command of, 78-81

Charlemagne, 50

Charles of Blois, 82

Charles the Bold, 43, 69, 116, 204, 402

Charles V (Emperor), 118, 119, 138

Charles IV (King of France), 52

Charles V (King of France), 97

Charles VI (King of France), 65

Charles VII (King of France), 67n, 98

Charles VIII (King of France), 116

Charles IX (King of France), 126n

Charles XI (King of Sweden), 143

Charles XII (King of Sweden), 142-78, 250, 280, 358
battle cry of, 219
biography of, 143-47, 162-63, 185, 229-30
faithfulness of soldiers to, 148
invades Russia, 155-75, 317
in Klissow battle, 151-54

Napoleon compared with, 182, 189n, 201-2
in Narva battle, 147-51
as politician, 154-55
at Poltava, 168-76, 201

Charles of Valois, 66-67

Château, General, 190n

Chattanooga, battle of (1863), 281

Chiang Kai-shek, 23, 396

Chicago Convention (Democratic party, 1968), 352

Chickamauga, battle of (1863), 214

Childebert, 49

Chivalry, 101-11, 114

Chlodomer, 49

Christianity, chivalry and, 101-2

Churchill, Randolph, 65

Churchill, Sir Winston, 322
Gallipoli campaign and, 322, 323, 328, 329, 331

Ciano, Count Galeazzo, 16, 346, 348n

Cinna, 28, 29

City, "city air makes men free," 71n

Cividale, siege of (1331), 70n

Civil War (U.S., 1861-65), 203-233
army living conditions in, 217-219
army size at start of, 355n
Indians in, 209-15
naval warfare in, 219-23
officers in, 223-32

Clausewitz, Karl von, 163, 180

Clemenceau, Georges, 340

Clement V (Pope), 52

Clisson, Oliver de, 103

Clotaire, 49

Cobb, T. R. R., 251

Cogny, René, 377, 382, 383, 388
Cold Harbor, battle of (1864), 253, 255, 267, 283
Coligny, Gaspard de, 126n
Concentration camps, introduced, 204
Cooke, John R., 251
Cooper, Douglas, 210, 211
Corson, William R., 359-61
Couch, Darius N., 252
Courtrai, battle of (1302), 54-56, 71
Coutras, battle of (1587), 113-115, 137
Crapsey (correspondent), 267, 283
Crassus, Marcus Licinius, 16, 27-43, 168, 309, 401
  biography of, 27-31
  Parthians defeat, 33-42, 57
  Spartacus defeated by, 31-32
Crassus, Publius, 38, 40
Crécy, battle of (1346), 46, 60, 64, 72, 82-97, 100, 194
  battle, 85-92
  flanking attack possible at, 96-97
  forces at, 83, 95, 140n
  lessons of, 51, 92-93
Creutz, General, 170, 171, 173
Crossbows, 87-88
Croy, Duke de, 149, 150
Curtis, S. R., 211-13
Cushman, Pauline, 218n

D

Dak To, battle of (1968), 15, 384
Dana, Charles, 274
Darwin, Charles, 340, 341
Daumier, Honoré, 203

David (King of Scotland), 92
Davis, Jefferson, 269, 272
Deception, Surena's use of, 38
Defoliation, 360
De Gaulle, Charles, 180n, 187n
De Robeck, Sir John, 329, 332
Democracies
  characteristics of modern, 352-354
  de Tocqueville on men in, 27
Derby, Earl of (Henry of Lancaster), 82
Dictatorships, characteristics of, 352-54
Dien Bien Phu, battle of (1953), 41, 356, 377-84, 388n
Diseases in Civil War, 218n
Dixon, George, 220
Dolgoruky, Prince Mikhail, 145
Donelson, battle of Fort (1862), 281
Douay, Félix, 299, 303-4
Downs, battle of the (1639), 120
Draft
  introduced, 204
  peacetime, 355n
Drake, Francis, 126-27
  in destruction of Spanish fleet, 129, 130, 133
Dresden, battle of (1813), 182, 190
Drewry's Bluff, battle of (1864), 274
Drill, Prussian firepower and, 45n-46n
Drinking in combat, 56
Drucker, Peter, 309n
Ducrot, Auguste, 300-5
Dueling, 102n
Du Guesclin, Bertrand, 97, 106
Dulles, John Foster, 356, 393

Duncan, Donald, 363
Du Picq, Ardant, 315
Dyrrhachium, siege of (48 B.C.),
    45

E

Early, Jubal, 224, 250, 262
Edes, Edward, 219
Edward the Black Prince, 85, 90-
    93, 97, 106-7
Edward I (King of England), 19,
    55, 61, 65-69, 72, 80, 401
Edward II (King of England),
    65-66, 73n
Edward III (King of England)
    characteristics of, 60, 64, 66,
        178, 309n
    as commander, 92-96, 108
    at Crécy, see Crécy
    defensive strategy of, 46-47,
        113
    financial difficulties of, 67, 75
    Philip VI compared with, 72-
        73, 76-79
    siege of Calais and, 109-10
    Sluys battle and, 78-82
Eisenhower, Dwight D., 353n,
    386, 393
Eleanor of Aquitaine, 64
Elizabeth I (Queen of England),
    124, 126, 127, 135
Elmira (camp), 287
Emerson, Ralph Waldo, on Na-
    poleon, 183-84, 186
Enver Pasha, 322, 324
Epaminondas, 152
Erlon, Comte d', 193, 194
Esplechin truce (1340), 82
Eugène, Prince, 140
Ewell, Richard, 262

F

Failly, Pierre Louis Charles de,
    299
Falkenhayn, Erich von, 320, 341
Falkirk, battle of (1298), 68, 69,
    80, 96, 401
Fall, Bernard, 379, 380
Farragut, David, 220
Favre, Jules, 279
Feodor (Tsar), 144
Fernel, Jean, 187
Ferrero, Colonel, 243
Feudalism, 50-53, 69-70
    castles and, 54n
Feuerbach, Ludwig, 144n
First World War (1914-18), 24-
    25, 307-41
    commanders of, 319-21
    decisiveness of, 339-41
    Gallipoli campaign in, 319,
        321-38
    killing of prisoners in, 347
    lives lost in, 339
    reasons for, 307-10, 314
    trench warfare in, 316-19
Fisher, Lord, Gallipoli campaign
    and, 323, 324
Fitzgerald, F. Scott, 339
Five Forks, battle of (1865), 284
Foch, Ferdinand, 24, 338n
Fontenoy, battle of (1745), 140
Fort Donelson, battle of (1862),
    281
Francisca (weapon), 49n
Franco-Prussian war (1870),
    291, 294, 298-306
Franklin, William, 250
Franks, 49
Fraustadt, battle of (1706), 156
Frederick, Don, 120, 122

Frederick Augustus (Elector of Saxony), 146-47
Frederick Charles, Prince, 295
Frederick of Hesse, 174n
Frederick II the Great (King of Prussia), 140, 152
Frederick III (King of Prussia), 310, 313
Fredericksburg, battle of (1862), 244, 247-56
Freeman, Douglas S., 14
Frémont, John, 211
French, David, 329
French, Sir John, 280, 403
  in First World War battles, 315, 319, 320, 327
Freud, Sigmund, 183
Frobisher, Sir Martin, 130, 131, 133
Frossard, Charles, 296-97

G

Gabinius, 35
Gallieni, Joseph, 315
Gallifet, Gaston de, 303
Gallipoli campaign (1916), 319, 321-38
Gambetta, Léon, 306
Gamelin, Maurice, 403
Gas masks, development of, 316
Gas warfare, 316
Georgia campaign (1864-65), 213, 263, 266, 268, 284
Gettysburg, battle of (1863), 282
Giap, Vo Nguyen, 391, 394
  against the French, 375-84
  biography of, 372, 374
  characteristics of, 399-401
  early battles of, 375-77

Tet offensive of, 15n, 383-88
Gibbon, Edward, 47, 48
Gneisenau, Count August Neithardt von, 194
Godemar du Fay, Baron, 85
Godfroy of Bouillon, 53
Godley, Sir Alexander, 327
Goldwater, Barry, 257
Goltz, General (Russian general), 157, 158-59, 168
Gordon, George, 262
Goths, 46-52
Gracchus, Gaius, 28
Gracchus, Tiberius, 28
Grant, Colquhoun, 192
Grant, Ulysses S., 215, 224
  Butler's removal and, 275-76
  at Cold Harbor, 253, 255, 267, 283, 284
  as commander, 181, 204, 280-284
  the crater and, 276-79
  drinking habits of, 56
  on McClellan, 227, 228
  Sigel as viewed by, 209
  at Spotsylvania, 262-63
  western campaign of, 280-81
  Wilderness campaign of, 258-265, 280-84, 340, 392
Grasse, Count François de, 13, 23
Graves, Robert, 347
Gregg, Maxcy, 249
Gregory XIII (Pope), 126n-27n
Grey, Sir Edward, 323
Grierson, Sir James, 319-20
Grouchy, Emmanuel de, 181, 194-96, 200, 305
Guerrillas, Parthians as, 35-36
Guibert of Nogent, 70

Guise, Duke of (Henri I de Lorraine), 137
Gustavus Adolphus, 70n, 140, 142, 148, 152n, 176
field artillery used by, 116, 117
Gyllenkrook, General, 164, 166

H

Haarlem, attack on (1572), 121-122
Haig, Sir Douglas, 24, 293-94, 341, 401, 403
in First World War battles, 309, 315, 319-21, 327, 337, 338
Hallart, General, 168-69, 175
Halleck, Henry, 206, 275
Burnside and, 265
characteristics of, 214, 224, 228, 246, 269
Hamilton, Sir Ian, 170-73, 196, 401, 403
at Gallipoli, 327-38
Hampton, Wade, 245
Hancock, Winfield Scott, 259, 261, 262-63, 264, 266
Hannibal, 342
Harding, Warren G., 260
Harold (King of England), 49
Haskell, Frank, 282
Hastings, battle of (1066), 49n
Hattin, battle of (1187), 53n, 105n
Hawkins, John, 125-26
in destruction of Spanish fleet, 130, 133
Heiligerlee, battle of (1568), 119
Henry II (King of England), 64, 82
Henry V (King of England), 65, 93-94

Henry III (King of France), 137
Henry IV (King of France), 70n, 123, 127n, 137, 153, 162, 400
in Coutras battle, 113-15
siege of Rouen and, 115
Henry of Lancaster (Earl of Derby), 82
Herr, Michael, 361, 367, 368, 385-86
Hersing, Otto, 332
Hesse-Darmstadt, Prince, 159
Hickok, Wild Bill, 215
Hill, A. P., 241, 249
Hill, D. H., 14, 15n, 240, 269, 271-73
Hindenburg, Paul von, 24
Hitler, Adolf, 15, 94, 157, 179, 186, 290, 402
halted, 187
policies of, 341-42
purges by, 313n
Russia invaded by, 23, 343-50
in Second World War, 344, 345, 349-50
on Thousand-Year Reich, 311n
Ho Chi Minh, 388, 393, 395
characteristics of, 372-75, 383, 399
Hoa Binh, battle of (1951), 375, 376
Hodgers (Albert Cashier), 218
Hohenlohe, Prince, 302
Hoke, Robert F., 271, 272
Holstein, Baron von, 311
Holtzclaw, James T., 214
Honey Springs, battle of, 215
Hood, John, 263
Hood, Samuel, 13
Hooker, Joseph, 231, 244, 280, 281, 334, 335
at Antietam, 242

Hooker, Joseph (cont'd)
  at Chancellorsville, 246, 256n,
    260-62, 267, 400
  characteristics of, 16, 205, 223,
    281
  Westmoreland compared with,
    400
Howard, Lord Charles, 128, 130-
  133, 135
Hughes, Admiral, 12, 17-20
Huguenot Wars (1562-98), 113
Hundred Years' War (1337-
  1453), 64-67
Hunley, H. B., 220
Hunt, Henry J., 231n
Hunter-Weston, Sir Aylmer, 327-
  331
Hus, Jan, 111-12
Hussite Wars (1419-36), 61, 112
Hyrodes, 37

I

Indians
  in Civil War, 209-16
  extermination of, 215, 216
Infantry
  cavalry displaced by, 54
  creation of English, 76n
  medieval, 67n, 70-72
  modern army as based on, 45
  Scottish, 68
  Swiss, 58n, 68, 72, 96, 116
  See also Archers
Infantry square, 49n
Ingersoll, Ralph, 386
Innocent III (Pope), 51
Intervention, 394
Isabella (Queen of Edward II),
  65, 66, 73n

Italian wars (1494-1529), 116

J

Jackson, Andrew, 211
Jackson, T. J., "Stonewall," 144,
  223, 231, 236
  characteristics of, 226, 229
  at Fredericksburg, 248
James, Frank, 215
James, Jesse, 215
Javits, Jacob, 397-98
Jenghiz Khan, 60
Joffre, Joseph, 315n, 341
  in First World War battles,
    321, 327
John (King of England), 68
John of Austria, Don, 118
John of Bohemia (King), 87-88,
  90
John of Chandos, 111
John of Gaunt, 81
John of Montfort, 82
John II (King of France), 91-93,
  104-5
Johnson, Hugh, 354
Johnson, Lyndon B., 25, 77, 389
  bombing targets and, 387n
  internal policies of, 352
  Khesanh and, 384-85
  as leader, 352-53, 396-99, 401
  policies of, 11, 352, 396-97
  Tet offensive and, 388
Johnston, Joseph E., 263, 285
Jones, William E. "Grumble,"
  245
Joyeuse, Duke of, in Coutras bat-
  tle, 113-14
Junot, Andoche, 186, 186n
Jumper, Johnny, 210
Justin of Nassau, 132
Justinian, 46

K

Kannengiesser, Colonel, 325
Kearny, Philip, 224
Keitel, Wilhelm, 16
Kemal Pasha (Kemal Atatürk),
    Mustafa, 335-36
Kennedy, John F., 162
Keyes, Sir Roger, 329
Khesanh, siege of (1968), 385-
    387, 388, 397
Khrushchev, Nikita S., 355n, 356
King, Martin Luther, Jr., 162
Kitchener, Lord, Gallipoli cam-
    paign and, 323-25
Klissow, battle of (1702), 151-53
Knolles, Robert, 108
Knoxville, battle of (1863), 13,
    265
Komer, Robert W., 359
Koniecpolski, Stanislaw, 152n
Königgrätz, battle of (1866),
    290, 292-94
Krassow, General, 166-68
Kressenbrunn, battle of (1260),
    110
Krithia, battles of (first, second
    and third; 1915), 330-32
Kutuzov, Mikhail, 23, 189n
Ky, Nguyen Cao, 396

L

Laboring class, First World War
    and, 340-41
Lagercrona, Anders, 164-67
Lam, Hoang Xuan, 369
Lane, James H., 249
Laon, charters of, 71n
La Ramée, Pierre de, 126
La Roche, Hugh de, 106

Lattre de Tassigny, Jean de, 375,
    376
Law, E. M., 14
Lawrence massacre (1863), 214
Lebrun, General, 298, 302, 305
Ledlie, James H., 277, 278
Lee, Robert E., 224, 226, 229,
    231-32, 281
    at Antietam, 241-44
    at Fredericksburg, 247, 252
    Grant compared to, 181
    McClellan vs., 230-32
    at Petersburg, 274
    at Spotsylvania, 262-66
    surrender of, 284
    in Wilderness campaign, 264-
        265
Lee, W. H. F., "Rooney," 245
Lefort (friend of Peter the
    Great), 146
Legions, Roman, size of, 36n
Leipzig, battle of (1813), 190,
    206n, 304
Lepanto, battle of (1571), 126n
Leuthen, battle of (1757), 45n-
    46n, 152
Lewenhaupt, Adam Ludvig, 155,
    225
    in invasion of Russia, 161-67,
        170-75
Leyden, siege of (1574), 122
Liddell Hart, Sir Basil, 12
Liebknecht, Karl, 313
Liman von Sanders, Otto, 324-
    325, 335
Limoges, siege of (1371), 106
Lincoln, Abraham, 210
    Burnside and, 244, 255-56, 257
    Butler and, 275
    Curtis and, 213
    Grant and, 284
    McClellan and, 227, 244-45

Lincoln, Abraham (cont'd)
  melancholy of, 206, 222, 285
  organizing war effort, 207, 397
  on Sumner, 223n
Lindemann, Frederick, 107n
Lloyd George, David, 323, 340
Lockwood, Lee, 387n
Longbow (English weapon), 53, 66-68, 70
  decline of, 112
  wood for arrows of, 83n
Longstreet, James, 13-14, 231, 258, 262, 265, 281
Loos, battle of (1915), 24, 320, 321, 340
Louis of Nevers, 73-76, 309n-10n
Louis IX (King of France), 51-52
Louis X (King of France), 52n
Louis Philippe (King of France), 19-20, 204
Lowe (professor), 204
Lubomirski, Hieronymus, 152n
Lucania, battle of (73 B.C.), 31
Luckner, Count Felix von, 105
Lucullus, 32
Ludendorff, Erich, 24
Luis of Requesens, Don, 118
Luxemburg, Rosa, 313
Lyon, Nathaniel, 208-9

M

MacArthur, Douglas, 358
McCarthy, Joseph, 257-58
McClellan, George, 207
  at Antietam, 240-45, 321, 331
  Burnside and, 236-40
  characteristics of, 17, 205n, 224, 226-31, 241, 284, 401
  at Malvern Hill, 14-15, 231-32
  removal of, 244-46

  soldiers under, 179, 275, 284-285, 306
McClernand, John, 207, 280
McCulloch, Ben, 212-13
McDowell, Irwin, 205n
Machiavelli, Niccolò, 118
Machine gun
  development of, 292-93
  First World War, 316
  Haig on, 319
McIntosh, Chilly, 210
McIntosh, Danny, 210
McIntosh, James, 211
Mack, Karl, 189n
McLaws, Lafayette, 13, 231
Mackenzie, Compton, 332
MacMahon, Patrice de, 296-301
McNamara, Robert S., 309, 396
Mafia, 197n, 391
  origin of, 119n
Magruder, John, 14, 269
Mahan, Alfred T., 12
Malines, battle of (1572), 120
Malo-Yaroslavetz, battle of (1812), 182
Malplaquet, battle of (1709), 140
Malvern Hill, battle of (1862), 14-15, 231-32
Marcus Aurelius, 49
Marengo, battle of (1800), 184
Margaret (Duchess of Parma), 119
Marguerite, General, 303
Maria Theresa (Empress), 140-141
Marius, Caius, 28
Marlborough, Duke of, 140, 154, 294
Marne, battle of the (1914), 24, 315-16
Marshal, Colonel, 277

Marshall, George C., 345
Mary (Queen of Scots), 124-25
Mary I (Bloody Mary), 124
Mass deportation of civilians, 204
Matveev, 145
Maximilian (Emperor of Mexico), 292
Maxwell, Sir John, Gallipoli and, 324-25
Mayenne, Duke of, 115, 116
Mazeppa (hetman), 166-67, 175
Meade, George, 224, 227, 261, 264, 276, 392
  as commander, 282-84
  crater and, 277
  in Wilderness campaign, 267
Medina Sidonia, Duke of, in destruction of Spanish fleet, 127-35
Mehemet Pasha (Baltaji), 175
Menshikov, Prince Alexander, 155-56, 189n
  in invasion of Russia, 157, 161, 167, 168, 171, 175
Merovingians, 49n, 50
Merrimac (ship), 221-22
Metellus, Quintus Caecilius, 29
Michel, General, 20, 315n
Mines, introduced, 220
Mirepoix, Prince de, 20
MIRV, 355n
Mitchell, William "Billy," 16
Mitrailleuse, development of, 292-93
Model Parliament, 67
Molay, Jacques de, 109
Moltke, Count Helmuth von (1800-91), 292, 315, 322
  in Franco-Prussian war, 295, 296, 300
Moltke, Count Helmuth von (1848-1916), 310

Monçada, Don Hugo de, 133
Mongols, 56n, 59-61
Monitor (ship), 221, 222
Monro, Sir Charles, 336
Montaigne, 400
Montcalm, Marquis de, 99-100
Montgomery, Sir Bernard, 17
Morley, Sir Robert, 79-80
Mortimer, Roger, 66, 73
Moscow, burning of (1812), 187, 190
Müller, Johann, 128
Mummius, 31
Murray, Sir Archibald W., 323
Muskets
  introduction of, 112, 113
  in U.S. Civil War, 207
  See also Rifles
Mussolini, Benito, 65, 346, 348n, 352

N

Na San, battle of (1952), 377
Naarden affair (1572), 120-21
Napalm, 360
Napoleon I (Emperor of the French), 166, 179-202, 292, 304-5, 317, 345, 402
  characteristics of, 182-91, 229-30, 270
  health of, 182-83, 187, 291
  invades Russia, 15, 157, 187-91
  modern army and, 206-7
  at Waterloo, 182-83, 191-202, 305, 336
Napoleon III (Emperor of the French), 204, 294, 305
  characteristics of, 290-92
Narses, 46-47, 48, 49n

Narva
  first battle of (1700), 147-51
  second battle of (1704), 155
Natalya (mother of Peter the
    Great), 145
National character, 98
Naval warfare
  chivalry in, 105
  in First World War, 332
  French and English, 76-82
  Spanish, 120, 125-37
  in U.S. Civil War, 219-23
Navarre, Henri, 384, 403
  at Dien Bien Phu, 377-84
Nazis
  execution of, 108n
  Mongols compared with, 59,
    60
  resolve of, 350
  in Russia, 121
Nazism, as basis for the present,
    341
Neville's Cross, battle of (1346),
    92
New Bern, battle of (1862), 238-
    240
Ney, Michel, 183
  at Waterloo, 192-94, 198, 200
Nicholas II (Tsar of Russia), 313
Nicot, Jean Louis, 378
Night of the Long Knives
    (1934), 344
Nixon, Richard M., 388, 388n-
    389n
Noise of battle, 64
Normandy, Duke of, 82
North Vietnam, see Vietnam
Northampton, Earl of (Simon de
    Senlis), 85
Nuclear weapons, 350, 351, 355-
    357
Nuremburg trials, 42

O

Odysseus, 35
Ogilvie, General, 156
Opothleyoholo (Indian chief),
    210-11
Ottokar II (King of Bohemia),
    110
Owen, Wilfred, 339

P

Palikao, Comte de, 297, 298-99
Parker, Ely S., 215
Parker, William H., 221, 222
Parma, see Alexander of Parma
Parthians, Crassus defeated by,
    33-42
Patkul, Johann, 144n, 146
Paykul, General, 155
Pea Ridge, battle of (1862), 209,
    211-13
Peninsular Campaign (Welling-
    ton's), 337
Pershing, John J., 24
Pétain, Henri Philippe, 24
Peter the Great (Tsar of Russia),
    23, 142-78, 401
  biography of, 143-47, 185
  in invasion of Russia, 155-75
  in Narva battle, 148-51
  as politician, 155-57
  in Turkish attack, 175-76
Petersburg, siege of (1864), 269-
    276, 316
Petré, Ensign, 167, 201
Pharsalus, battle of (48 B.C.), 45
Philip Augustus (King of
    France), 51
Philip IV (King of France), 19,
    52, 65-67, 71, 72, 75, 109
Philip V (King of France), 52, 70

Philip VI (King of France), 47, 72-77, 138, 400, 401
  at Cassel, 74-75
  as commander, 95
  at Crécy, 51, 85-95
  siege of Calais and, 109-10
  at Sluys, 78-81
Philip II (King of Spain), 139, 350, 353, 401, 402-3
  as commander, 118-20
  as politician, 113, 123-30, 135-138, 396, 397
  as strategist, 113, 122-23, 141, 311, 372, 389
Philip V (King of Spain), 312
Philippa (Queen of Edward III), 81, 97n
Pickett, George, 269, 284
Pike, Albert, 212
Pikes (weapon), 70, 115-16
Pillow, Gideon J., 216-17
Pinkerton, Allan, 230n
Piper, Count, 153, 174-75
Piroth, Colonel, 382
Pleasants, Henry, 276
Pleasonton, Alfred, 245
Plumer, Herbert, 320
Plutarch, Crassus and, 30, 32-33, 35-37, 39, 41
Poitiers, battle of (1356), 64, 91, 92-93
Poltava, battle of (1709), 168-176, 201
Pompey, 60
  Caesar and, 45
  Crassus' jealousy of, 30-33
Pool, Dave, 214
Pope, John, 224, 241
Porter, Fitz John, 224, 244
Porter, Horace, 231n
Posse, General, 153
Price, Sterling, 213, 215

Prim, Juan, 294
Prokop the Great, 61, 112
Prokop the Lesser, 112
Proletarii, Roman, 28
Propaganda, uses of, for "image" of leader, 180
Protestantism, 118-20
Prut, battle of (1711), 175
Psychological shock, Surena's use of, 57
Pultusk, battle of (1703), 153, 155
Punishment
  in battle, 31
  of civilians, 120-21, 122
  of defeated generals, 42-43
  of the mass for the man, 107
Punitz, battle of (1704), 166n

Q

Quantrill, Charles, 214
Quebec, battle of (1759), 98-100
Quiéret, Hugh, 78-81

R

Railroads, U.S. Civil War use of, 208
Ransom, M. W., 271, 272, 276
Raynald de Chatillon, 53, 105
Ravenna, battle of (1512), 116
Rawlinson, Sir Henry, 338n
Realism, nonfunctioning, 49
Reffye, Commandant, 292
Rehnskjold, Count Karl Gustaf, 156, 159, 160, 173, 174-75, 283
  at Poltava, 169-72
Remarque, Erich Maria, 317-18, 339
Reno, Jesse, 240n

Rensel, General, 172
Repnin, Prince, 157, 158-59, 160, 175, 176
Resnick, Joseph Y., 359n
Reynaud, Paul, 291
Reynolds, John F., 250
Reynolds, Mrs., 218n
Revers, Georges, 20
Ribaudequins (weapon), 116-17
Ribbentrop, Joachim von, 347
Rifles
 magazine, 316
 as standard weapon (19th century), 292
 U.S. Civil War use of, 207
 See also Muskets
Robert (King of Naples), 77
Robert of Artois, Count, 43, 54-58, 76, 78
Robertson, B. H., 14
Rodman, Isaac P., 243n
Rodney, George, 13
Roman army, disintegration of, 46
Roman character, destruction of, 28-29
Roman Empire, disintegrating, 27-29, 49-50
Rommel, Erwin, 357
Roos, General, 160, 170-72
Roosevelt, Franklin D., 207
Rosecrans, William S., 214, 235
Rosenberg, Alfred, 341
Roses, Wars of the (1455-84), 64
Ross, John, 209-10, 212
Rostow, Walt, on Tet offensive, 360-61
Rouen, siege of (1589), 115
Round Mounds, battle of (1861), 210
Rusk, Dean, 397

Russell, Bertrand, 180n
Russell, William, 216-17, 227, 228, 269
Russia
 Charles XII's invasion of, 155-175, 317
 Hitler's invasion of, 23-24, 343-350
 Napoleon's invasion of, 15, 157, 187-90
 Russo-Japanese War (1904-05), 315, 316

S

St. Bartholomew, Massacre of (1572), 126
St. Jacob-en-Birs, battle of (1444), 69
St. Martin, Jacques de, 111
St. Simon, Duc de, 312
Saladin, 105n
Salan, Raoul, 376-77
Salisbury, Harrison, 309n, 387n
Samsonov, Alexander, 319
Sanders, Otto, Liman von, 324-325, 335
Santa Cruz, Marquis of, 126n, 128
Sarazin (doctor), 300
Sassoon, Siegfried, 339
Saxe, Marshal (Maurice), 140, 147n
Schell, Jonathan, 367-69
Scheremetyev, General, 148-49, 150, 175, 176
 in invasion of Russia, 155-62
Schiltron (infantry), 68
Schlippenbach, General, 172
Schulenberg, General, 166n, 189n, 219

Scientists, 354
  as "vultures," 360-61
Scipio Africanus, 45, 225
Scott, Winfield, 214, 223
Sea Beggars, 120
Sea warfare, see Naval warfare
Second Bull Run (1862), 241
Second World War, 25, 341-50
  extermination policies in, 346-357
  German offensives in, 341-43
  German losses in, 346n, 349
  Russia invaded in, 23, 343-50
  Russian losses in, 344n, 349
Sedan, battle of (1870), 299-305
Sedd-el-Bahr, landing on, 328-30
Sedgwick, John, 259, 261, 264
Seelye, Sarah (Franklin Thompson), 218
Ségur, Philippe-Paul, 182, 187, 188
Seton, John, 108
Shein (boyar), 146
Sheridan, Philip, 224, 284
Sherman, William T., 95, 208
  characteristics of, 224, 285, 317, 357
  Georgia campaign of, 213, 263, 266, 268, 284
  Grant and, 209, 215, 227, 265, 281
Shiloh, battle of (1862), 280-81
Shirer, William, 350
Sickles, Daniel, 280
Sicre, André, 174n
Siegroth, Colonel, 171, 172
Sigel, Franz, 208-9, 212
Slocum, Henry, 223
Sluys, battle of (1340), 78-82, 91
Smell-o-meter, 360
Smith, William F., "Baldy," 274, 276, 283

Smith-Dorrien, Sir Horace, 320
Social classes
  bourgeoisie, 51
  First World War and laboring, 340-41
  See also Aristocracy
Sofia (half-sister of Peter the Great), 143, 145
Song My massacre (1969), 365-366
Sorrentino, General, 346
South Vietnam, see Vietnam
Spanish Civil War (1936-39), tanks in, 343n
Sparre, General, 170, 171
Spartacan revolt, 31-32
Spartacist uprising (Germany), 312-13
Spartacus
  campaign against, 31-32
  crucifixion of followers of, 42n
Spotsylvania, battle of (1864), 262-66, 317
Sprague, Kate Chase, 206
Stalin, Joseph, 343, 345
Stanislaus (King of Poland), 154, 166
Stanton, Edwin, 222, 241, 246, 275, 282
Steinau, Marshal, 151-53, 155, 189n
Steinmetz, Karl von, 295-97
Stendhal (Henri Beyle), 187n, 317, 385
Stoneman, George, 245
Stopford, Frederick, 327, 334, 335
Stratford, John, 82
Streltsi revolt, 145-46
Stuart, J. E. B., "Jeb," 245
Sturgis, Samuel D., 243

Suffren, Pierre-André, 12-13, 17-21, 158

Sulla, Lucius Cornelius, 28-30

Sumner, Edwin, 223-24, 231, 242-43, 251, 252-53, 334, 335

Surena (Surenas), 57
    Crassus defeated by, 37-41

Suvla Bay, battle of, 333-36

Swinton, William, 267-68, 280

Swiss infantry, 58n, 69, 72, 96, 115-16

T

Taginae, battle of (552 A.D.), 46, 48, 49

Tanks, introduction of, 338-39

Taxation, and war, 67-68, 71

Taylor, Maxwell, 358

Tchitchakov, General, 182

Teias, 48

Templars, 52, 109

Tet offensive (1968), 15n, 77, 384-88, 390, 391, 397
    as failure, 360-61

Teutoburger Wald, battle of (9 A.D.), 41

Thang, General, 398

Theuderich, 49

Thibaut of Champagne, 102

Thielemann, Johann Adolf von, 196

Thieu, Nguyen Van, 396, 398

Thirty, battle of the (1351), 103-4

Thrailkill, John, 214

Thomas, George, 227, 281

Thomas de Marle, 71n

Thurston, C. B., 219

Thyssen, Fritz, 309

Tilly, Count of, 140, 403

Timoshenko, Semyon, 23

Tocqueville, Alexis de, 27

Tolson, General, 385

Tolstoy, Leo, 24

Torpedoes, introduction of, 220

Torstensson, Lennart, 117

Torture, 144n
    of streltsi, 145-46
    in Vietnam, 364-65, 367-68

Totila (Gothic king), 46-52, 58, 92

Tournai, siege of (1340), 82

Tours, battle of (732), 49n

Trench warfare, 316-18
    introduced, 204

Tromp, Martin Harpertzoon, 120, 135

Trous-de-loup, defined, 85-86

Turgeniev, Ivan S., 307

U

Ulm, battle of (1805), 184, 201

United States, Rome compared with, 28-29

Untermeyer, Samuel, 345

Urban VI (Pope), 106

Uxbridge, Earl of, 197

V

Valdez, Don Pedro de, 130

Vallandigham, Clement L., 256-257

Valmy, battle of (1792), 117n

Van Dorn, Earl, 209, 211-12, 213, 229n, 403

Varinius, 31

Varus, Quintilius, 41

Vassoigne, General, 301, 302

Vaudreuil, Marquis de, 98

Veblen, Thorstein, 56n

Venereal diseases in Civil War, 218n
"Vertical envelopment" technique, 361-62
Vicksburg, siege of (1863), 280-281
Victoria (Queen of England), 19-20
Vienne, John de, 109-10
Vietcong, Parthians compared with, 36
Vietnam, 11, 25, 95, 285, 356, 358-59
ARVN troops in, 362-66
atrocities in, 364-72
"birds" visiting, 359-61
bombing of, 107, 107n-108n, 367, 387n, 398
Chicago Convention compared with, 352
destruction of, 368-69
elections in (1956), 393
French battles in, 375-77
leaders of North, 372-75
leaders of South, 370, 391
prospects for peace in, 394-95
U.S. forces in, 355n
"vertical envelopment" technique in, 361-62
villages destroyed in, 368, 369
Villemur, John de, 106
Vinoy, General, 300, 301

W

Wadsworth, General, 224
Wagram, battle of (1809), 188n, 206n, 207
Walker, John G., 231
Wallace, Sir William, 68
Wallenstein, Albrecht von, 140
Warren, Gouverneur K., 264

Washburne, Elihu B., 267
Waterloo, battle of (1815), 181-183, 191-200, 304-5, 337
Watie, Stand, 209-12, 214-15
Waugh, Evelyn, 339
Weapons
ABM, 355n
aerial spotting, 204
archery, English, 70, 96, 112; see also Archers; Longbow
armor, see Armor
arquebus, 70
arrows, see Arrows
artillery, see Artillery
ballista, 45, 46, 88
bows, see Bows
canister, 251n
cannon, see Artillery
catapults, 45, 46
crossbows, 87-88
defoliation, 360
francisca, 49n
gas masks, 316
longbow, see Longbow
machine gun, see Machine gun
MIRV, 355n
mitrailleuse, 292-93
muskets, see Muskets
napalm, 360
nuclear, 350, 351, 355-57
pikes, 70, 115-16
rifles, see Rifles
smell-o-meter, 360
tanks, 338-39
torpedoes, 220
wheel-lock pistols, 112, 113
Wedgwood, Josiah, 329
Wellington, Duke of, 294, 337-38
at Waterloo, 181, 191-200
West, Nathanael, 385
West Point, founding of, 94

Westmoreland, William, 15n, 36, 77, 233, 384, 398, 403
  characteristics of, 357-59
  as commander, 11, 389-93, 399-402
  "energy of will" and, 42
  Khesanh and, 384-86, 388
  Navarre and, 380
  Vietnam as tactical proving ground and, 356
Weyrother, General, 189n
Wheel-lock pistols, introduction of, 112, 113
Whiting, W. H. C., 270-73, 276
Wilderness campaign (1864-65), 258-65, 280-84, 340, 392
Wilhelm I (German Kaiser), 290, 313
Wilhelm II (German Kaiser)
  characteristics of, 309, 310-14, 338
William of Nangis, 105
William of Orange, 120
Willmer, Major, 334, 335
Wilson, Woodrow, 340
Wilson's Creek, battle of (1861), 208

Wimpffen, Emmanuel Félix de, 299, 301-6, 357, 401
Wise, Henry A., 272
Wolfe, James, 98-100
Worden, John L., 222
World War I, see First World War
World War II, see Second World War
Wright, Horatio G., 263, 264, 266

Y

Yakovlev, Colonel, 167
York, Herbert F., 355n
Ypres, battle of (1915), 321

Z

Zannequin, Nicholas, 74
Zieten, Count Hans von, 198-99
Ziska, Jan, 61, 70n, 112, 116-17
Zorthian, Barry, 359
Zotov, Nikita, 143
Zutphen, sack of (1572), 120
Zuyder Zee, battle of (1573), 122